BARRON'S

HOW TO PREPARE FOR THE

COOP/ HSPT/ TACHS

COOPERATIVE ADMISSIONS EXAM/ HIGH SCHOOL PLACEMENT TEST/ TEST FOR ADMISSION INTO CATHOLIC HIGH SCHOOLS

Kathleen Elliott, M.A.
English Teacher
Lexington Catholic High School, Lexington, Kentucky

Carmen Geraci, M.A.
English Department Chairman
Lexington Catholic High School, Lexington, Kentucky

David Ebner, Ph.D.
Former Mathematics Teacher
High School of Fashion Industries, New York, New York
New York University, New York, New York
Touro College, New York, New York

BARRON'S

All inquiries should be addressed to:
Barron's Educational Series, Inc.
250 Wireless Boulevard
Hauppauge, New York 11788
www.barronseduc.com

Library of Congress Catalog Card No. 2004056185

International Standard Book No. 0-7641-2781-0

Library of Congress Cataloging-in-Publication Data

Elliott, Kathleen (Kathleen J.)
    Barron's how to prepare for the COOP/HSPT/TACHS,
Catholic high school entrance examinations / Kathleen Elliott,
Carmen Geraci, David Ebner.
       p. cm.
    Rev. ed. of: How to prepare for the COOP HSPT, Catholic
high school entrance examinations / Jerome Shostak, Max
Peters.
3rd ed.
    Includes index.
    ISBN 0-7641-2781-0 (alk. paper)
    1. Catholic high schools—United States—Entrance examinations—
Study guides—Juvenile literature. [1. Catholic high schools—
Entrance examinations—Study guides.] I. Title: How to prepare
for the COOP/HSPT/TACHS, Catholic high school entrance
examinations. II. Geraci, Carmen. III. Ebner, David, 1942–
IV. Shostak, Jerome. How to prepare for the COOP HSPT TACHS,
Catholic high school entrance examinations. V. Title.

LB3060.24.E44 2005   2004056185
373.126'2—dc22

Contents

4 Verbal Skills 107

5 Language Arts 131

6 Reading Comprehension   163

7 Model Exams   193

Index   428

Introduction

Doing It Right!

Welcome!

As you well know, getting high scores on any modern-day exam, like the Cooperative Admissions Exam (COOP), the High School Placement Test (HSPT), and the Test for Admission to Catholic High School (TACHS), involves preparation. You need to prepare yourself to show mastery of intellectual abilities—like reading comprehension or use of basic mathematic equations. To do this, you need to set aside time to acquire, review, and practice such skills. And, as you probably know by now, knowledge for knowledge's sake has become old fashioned; you must also show off what you know. Therefore, you also need to prepare yourself to show mastery of test-taking skills; you need to show you can do things like pace yourself or know when to guess. In short, exams like the COOP, HSPT, and TACHS simultaneously evaluate your intellectual ability *and* your ability to take standardized exams, and you need to be prepared for both challenges.

Those disciplined enough to set aside time for this kind of preparation are, logically, in the best position to test well on such exams as the COOP, HSPT, and TACHS. However, as well intentioned as your desire might be, time has a way of slipping away. Maybe other activities in your daily life, which are equally important to you, like school or sports or community service, get in the way. Too soon testing day approaches, and you find yourself gripped by feelings of (let's face it) panic. Your pulse races, your hands grow clammy, and your thoughts endlessly cycle through nightmares of self-doubt. Have you studied enough? Are you really ready?

We at Barron's have designed the book you hold in your hands to accommodate all students who find themselves faced with the trial of standardized exams—students who may have studied for months as well as students who have yet to crack a book. If you have had the foresight and the self-discipline to begin preparations for your high school placement exam well in advance, congratulations! Barron's *How to Prepare for the COOP/HSPT/TACHS* is designed to reinforce the skills you already possess with plenty of practice sections and thoroughly explained answer keys. If, conversely, you have purchased this book hoping for last minute tips on acing the exam, rest assured! This book comes to you chock full of study tips, elimination strategies, and information about exam format—information that is sure to help you succeed. Moreover, this book offers numerous and varied practice selections designed to make you comfortable with the testing format, requirements, and pacing.

Now, we know that you want to get right to work. However, we would like to take a minute to thank you for purchasing this book. We strongly believe that our preparation guide to these exams is the best on the market, and we hope that, by the time you finish using this guide, you will feel prepared to succeed when you take the exam. This book offers more information about the exam you are preparing to take, more opportunities for further practice, and more thoroughly researched answer key explanations than our competitors. You have in your hands the best tool for "doing it right."

So let's get started!

Overview of General High School Entrance Exams

The COOP and the HSPT are the main two entrance exams for Catholic high schools. By contrast, the ISEE (Independent Schools Entrance Exam) and the SSAT (Secondary Schools Admissions Test) are the main two entrance exams for other private high schools.

> As of Fall 2004, several dioceses are using the new Test for Admission into Catholic High School (TACHS). We have included specific information about this new exam on the blue pages starting on page 11. Although information on the TACHS exam is limited at this time, using the COOP and HSPT sections of this book in addition to the TACHS section should give TACHS takers a strong basis that they can apply to the exam.

The COOP Versus the HSPT: An Overview

The COOP and the HSPT assess your mastery of essential verbal and analytical skills. You must prove you have a good grounding in vocabulary and an ability to identify main ideas; similarly you must demonstrate prowess in logic and mathematical computation. Regardless of the method used to test or the phrasing of the questions involved, both tests focus on the same skills.

You should be aware, however, that the COOP and the HSPT vary significantly in their organization and in their phrasing of test questions. Make sure to familiarize yourself with the specific information regarding the exam you will take. The following chart gives a quick overview of the two exams.

Comparison of COOP and HSPT*

COOP: approximately 2½ hours given during an approximate 4-hour period

Sequences (see Chapter 3)	20 questions/15 minutes	0.75 min/question
Analogies (see Chapter 3)	20 questions/7 minutes	0.35 min/question
Quantitative Reasoning (see Chapter 3)	20 questions/5 minutes	0.25 min/question
Verbal Reasoning (Words) (see Chapter 4)	20 questions/15 minutes	0.75 min/question
Verbal Reasoning (Context) (see Chapter 4)	10 questions/7 minutes	0.7 min/question
Reading and Language Arts (see Chapters 5 & 6)	40 questions/40 minutes	1 min/question
Mathematics Computation (see Chapter 3)	40 questions/35 minutes	0.9 min/question

HSPT: approximately 2½ hours given in a minimum of a 3½-hour period

Verbal Skills (see Chapter 4)	60 questions/16 minutes	0.27 min/question
Quantitative Skills (see Chapter 3)	52 questions/30 minutes	0.57 min/question
Reading Skills (see Chapter 6)	62 questions/25 minutes	0.40 min/question
Mathematics Skills (see Chapter 3)	64 questions/45 minutes	0.70 min/question
Language Expression Skills (see Chapter 5)	60 questions/25 minutes	0.42 min/question

*For specifics on the TACHS exam, see pages 11–26.

However, you'll want to investigate in much greater detail before you take either exam. This book gives you many details regarding the two tests. First, check out the discussion of the testing formats of the COOP (below) and the HSPT (beginning on page 4) later in this introduction. We give an overview of each exam and discuss the theory on which the exams are based (especially what they test and how they test). Also, don't forget the practice tests (two for the COOP—see page 197—and two for the HSPT—see page 301). Finally, if you have more questions regarding the COOP or the HSPT, you can contact the companies directly yourselves; however, after using this book, we at Barron's feel confident you won't find that necessary.

Cooperative Admissions Examination Office	**HSPT**	**TACHS**
CTB/McGraw-Hill	Scholastic Testing Service	TACHS Examination Office
20 Ryan Ranch Road	480 Meyer Road	P.O. Box 64675
Monterey, CA 93940	Bensenville, IL 60106-1617	Eagan, MN 55164-9522
(800) 538-9547	(800) 642-6STS	(866) 61T-ACHS
www.ctb.com	*www.ststesting.com*	*www.tachsinfo.com*

The COOPerative Admissions Exam

Many diocese require the COOP exam, which is given only **once per year in either October or November**. Exam **applicants must preregister** for the COOP, either through their parochial elementary schools or via applications distributed by parochial high schools. **Applicants** for the COOP **can take the exam only one time. Test takers may list up to three high schools** they hope to attend (identified by the appropriate identification codes and numbers) on their COOP testing application.

The COOP, a **multiple-choice exam,** tests *what you have learned* as well as *how you learn.* The exam consists of **testing sessions that last 2½ hours distributed across a 4-hour testing period. Questions are typically arranged in order of difficulty**, and the **exam does not penalize guessing. You are allowed to write in the test booklet only**.

The COOP tests seven basic academic skills: **Sequences, Analogies, Quantitative Reasoning, Verbal Reasoning (Words), Verbal Reasoning (Context), Reading and Language Arts,** and **Mathematics Computation**. Different sections test different skills, but the exam follows a clear, theoretical logic. For example, the tests on Sequences, Analogies, and Quantitative Reasoning all focus more on judging how well you process new information and detect patterns; by contrast, the Reading and Language Arts and Mathematics sections both focus more on judging how well you remember information learned in school or from other sources. The Verbal Reasoning tests judge your ability to process new information using previously learned techniques, forming a bridge between the two sections.

Visual learners may find the first three tests particularly manageable; these three tests primarily ask you to locate **patterns**. The **Sequences test,** for example, **gives sets of figures, numbers, or letters in a pattern**; you must identify the pattern and be able to supply the next figure, number, or letter that continues that pattern. Similarly, the **Analogies test assesses your ability to locate patterns using pictures**. These questions present you with a question grid that is divided into quadrants and into which are set three pictures; your task is to select the picture that best complements the three originally presented pictures. Finally, like the preceding sections, the **Quantitative Reasoning section** also **asks you to detect patterns**; you may be given series of numbers or figures with shaded areas and asked to locate the pattern within. To find out more specifically how these questions work, check out Chapter 3, which give examples that you can work through.

As we said before, the Verbal Reasoning sections bridge the gap between your ability to reason and to remember formal classroom instruction. The **Verbal Reasoning tests** require you to (1) **identify essential features** of objects, (2) **find logical relationships** between sets of words, or (3) **draw logical conclusions** from facts presented. This section of the exam proves the most flexible. For practice on all the various types of questions that belong in the Verbal Reasoning section, go to Chapter 4.

The **Reading and Language Arts test,** conversely, focuses more than do the previous tests on determining how well your long-term memory functions; this test **gauges your ability to judge good English usage** as you have learned it in school. Here a large vocabulary—as well as an ability to read quickly and for detail—saves the day. This portion of the COOP also tests many skills through coordinated testing exercises. For starters, you will be given various reading passages and asked to identify elements such as the main idea of the passage or the definition of a word based on its usage in the selection. In addition to being asked to show that you understand what you read, you also may be asked, for example, to show your ability to apply the rules of capitalization and punctuation to standard written English. You should be able to read sentences or entire paragraphs and state whether one or none of the statements have a capitalization or punctuation error. The Reading and Language Arts section of the COOP tests your reading comprehension and language usage skills thoroughly. Be sure to practice. We suggest you test yourself on other practice problems in Chapters 5 and 6.

The exam ends with a **Mathematics Computation session.** It **asks you to compute answers to mathematical questions involving mixed numbers, fractions, decimals, percents, and integers**. Try out Chapter 3 for further practice, and remember that like the reading comprehension sections, the mathematics section requires you to utilize information learned in school and other formal educational sources.

The High School Placement Test (HSPT)

The **HSPT** operates according to a very flexible schedule, and its **testing time and location can be set by individual schools and districts** in cooperation with the Scholastic Testing Service; the best way to determine when and where the HSPT will be administered is to **check with your guidance counselor or high school admission's office**. Check for other application requirements that might apply to your situation; **high schools** that use the HSPT **usually consider HSPT test scores as only part of the requirements for admission**. The HSPT may be taken twice—once in the fall and once in the spring.

The HSPT is a **multiple-choice exam** designed to test what you *have learned* as well as *how you learn*. The exam consists of **testing sessions that last 2½ hours distributed across a 3½-hour testing period**. The **exam does not penalize guessing. Test takers are not allowed to write in the test booklet; you will be given scratch paper at the testing site.** The HSPT often includes optional sections; **whether you will have to take any or all of these optional sessions will be determined by your desired school**; at a minimum, **you must take the five required sections of the HSPT**.

The HSPT tests academic skills using five different testing sections: **Verbal Skills, Quantitative Skills, Reading Skills, Mathematics Skills,** and **Language Expression Skills**. The **HSPT alternates between testing your ability to reason out answers and your ability to retain information** learned in your classes. The **Verbal Skills and Reading Skills sections** of the exam, for example, **focus more on your ability to react to stimuli** presented during the exam (word sequences or on-demand reading passages); conversely, the **Quantitative Skills, Mathematics Skills,** and **Language Expression Skills** portions all **focus on judging your mastery of skills** learned in class.

The **Verbal Skills** portion of the HSPT focuses on five specific types of questions: (1) synonyms, (2) antonyms, (3) analogies, (4) logic, and (5) verbal classification; this test **targets your ability to detect patterns and relationships among elements of speech**. While the term "Verbal Classification" sounds tricky, the actual test is not; it merely asks you to figure out which word out of a series of four does or does not belong in a given sequence of words. For practice, see Chapter 4.

The HSPT then shifts to assessing your **Quantitative Skills**. The quantitative section of the exam focuses on your ability to work with **number series, geometric comparison, nongeometric comparison, and number manipulation**. For practice on the kinds of questions you'll encounter, turn to Chapter 3.

The **Reading Comprehensions Skills** part of the HSPT then attempts to judge how well you comprehend what you read and your ability to infer vocabulary meaning. Part A of this section asks you to read and interpret literary passages. While, naturally, you are called upon to use your reading skills, the test **assesses how well you understand what you read**. Part B **tests your knowledge of vocabulary**. For practice, see Chapters 4 and 6.

The HSPT then focuses again on **Mathematics Skills**, in particular **concepts and problem solving**. This portion of the exam **tests your problem-solving abilities and your** ability to use previous **knowledge of mathematic concepts** to solve modern problems. For practice, see Chapter 3.

Finally, the HSPT ends with a test of your **Language Expression Skills**; you will be given questions that **test your understanding of writing mechanics, capitalization, punctuation, usage, spelling, thought expression, and sentence order**. For practice, see Chapter 5.

Countdown

Now, it's time to face facts. You may be frustrated if you plan to pick up enough of the skills necessary to ace an exam like the COOP, the HSPT, or the TACHS on the fly. Mastering these exams most usually comes as the result of hard, consistent work rather than quick attempts to marshal one's wits. Moreover, the usual method of gauging your progress is not available to you in this case; the COOP, the HSPT, and the TACHS do not publish scores achieved on their exams. Therefore, unlike with other standardized tests, you cannot take a practice exam and expect to rank yourself against other entering high school students across the nation. We've said it before, and we'll say it again: your best method for preparing yourself for the COOP, the HSPT, or the TACHS is simply a great deal of basic skills preparation.

Simply put, some skills get better through consistent use. Verbal ability is one such skill. The more you read, the more you encounter verbal skills tested on exams such as the COOP, the HSPT, or the TACHS. Analytical ability is another such skill; making comparisons, detecting contrasts, analyzing theme and main idea patterns are all skills that grow sharper with use and are almost impossible to pick up and drop at need. Absolutely the best way to prepare for an exam— and necessarily reduce test anxiety—is to cultivate an appreciation for all things intellectual.

This isn't as hard as it sounds; after all, you have been preparing for tests like these for the past eight years in class. Besides, cultivating an appreciation for learning outside of class does not have to be tedious. You can find creative and fun ways to incorporate intellectual activity in your life.

First . . . **Read! Read! Read!** Both the COOP and the HSPT, for example, use reading passages ranging from four to six paragraphs long; moreover, both use primarily an informative, newsy writing style. **Select short passages from weekly news magazines or the topical parts of your local newspapers** (e.g., the weekly "science" section or the daily "living and arts" sections), and **accustom yourself to identifying the author's intent in writing, the main points of the passage, and the meaning of unfamiliar vocabulary**. Also **try out the vocabulary-based puzzles** commonly found in local newspapers; games like Scrabble or word jumbles are also great for building familiarity with vocabulary while still having fun. Incorporating clever ways to trick yourself into studying verbal skills, therefore, is a snap—you just have to look for them.

For fun yet useful mathematics skills, **try working through books of logic puzzles, word problems, brain teasers, and number games** either from your local library or local book stores. **Also, check out "Ask Marilyn,"** the column written by Marilyn vos Savant, listed in *The Guinness Book of World Records* Hall of Fame as having the highest IQ. Many newspapers carry her column, which provides free brain teasers and riddles that you can attempt. **The Internet is a good tool, too.** Many companies publish free, on-line IQ assessment tests that are fun to do, quick to assess, and good for limbering up mental muscles.

Probably the second best way to prepare for an exam is to **allow yourself sufficient time** to sit down and **review** useful details such as how the exam is designed and topics covered by the exam. Purchasing a preparation guide is a step in a positive direction. We suggest that you maximize your chance of success by following the suggestions made in the chart entitled **Acing the Exam: Option A**; in this chart, we outline a thorough but comfortably paced course of study.

Now, following Option A requires that you devote a month's preparation to your task. It may be that devoting four weeks of preparation to a project is simply not an affordable luxury for you. Relax. Just because it is difficult to master an exam by cramming does not mean that it cannot be done; just because cramming does not provide you with the long-term results of slower paced studying does not mean that it should not be done. Look at the chart entitled **Acing the Exam: Option B**, in which we offer a more streamlined but more challenging "quick study" program. You will need to have both the time and the drive to really focus your studying energies; you will be working "on deadline." Either Option A or Option B should assist you greatly in your quest for a high exam score.

Regardless of the time you have available for studying, internalize this one bit of advice: **Any study is better than no study at all**.

Acing the Exam: Option A

Four weeks and counting . . .
Re-read the introduction of this book where we discuss the exam for which you are studying (COOP, page 3; HSPT, page 4). These sections will give you a sense of the kinds of questions you face, as well as a sense of the strategy you should use.
Take a practice exam and score yourself.
Identify the subjects and the types of questions that most troubled you; use the answer key explanation section to help you identify these questions.
Study the information regarding the topics that most troubled you.
Be sure to **work through all the practice sessions**.
Read through the answer key explanations; we present them to help you understand the logic behind the questions and their answers.
English Bonus Tip: Work through the word list provided in Chapter 4. The best way to learn new words is to think about them, define them, and use them in sentences.
Ask for help when you need it—if your parents do not know the answer, ask your teacher(s) at school. That's what they're there for! **(Be polite when you ask.)**

Three weeks 'til resolution . . .
Study the chapters that discuss topics that least troubled you.
Be sure to **work through all of the practice sessions**.
Read through the answer key explanations; we present them to help you understand the logic behind the question.
Review your work on the word list from Chapter 4. Skip the ones you know well, and focus on the ones you don't.
Trick yourself into studying—work crossword puzzles, attempt some riddles, take an IQ test on-line, try your hand at logical conundrums. Read! Read! Read!

Two weeks left
Go back and review once more the material that really troubled you.
Retake your first practice exam, focusing on the questions you missed.
Ask for help when you need it—if your parents do not know the answer, ask your teacher(s) at school. Maybe they can hook you up with tutors or suggest useful study tips and mnemonic devices.

One week	**Take a second practice exam** and compare your results. You will likely see improvement, provided you have stuck to your program!
	Review any areas that remain weak.
	Read through the answer key explanations.
Day before – time out!	**Give yourself a break.** Do not study. Do something relaxing, like watching a movie, reading for pleasure, or eating out with friends.
	Get to bed at a reasonable hour; no prep can help if you are exhausted and nervous.

Acing the Exam: Option B

Seven days	**Re-read the introduction of this book where we discuss the exam for which you are studying** (COOP, page 3; HSPT, page 4). These sections will give you a sense of the kinds of questions you face, as well as a sense of the strategy you should use.
	Take a practice exam and score yourself.
	Note particularly troublesome topics.
	Consider talking with your teacher(s) regarding trouble spots; be sure to **make your requests for help in a polite, timely manner**. Teachers are your best resource, but they juggle busy schedules and would probably appreciate advance notice.
Six days	**Identify the types of questions that most troubled you**; use the answer key explanation section to help you identify these questions.
	Study the information regarding the topics that most troubled you.
	Be sure to **work through all of the practice sessions**.
	Read through the answer key explanations; we present them to help you understand the logic behind the question.
Five days	**Study the chapters that discuss topics that least troubled you.**
	Be sure to **work through all of the practice sessions**.
	Read through the answer key explanations.
Four days	**Talk (again) with your teacher(s) at school** if you still need help; they are your most efficient help resource. Perhaps they can suggest study tips or mnemonic devices that can help you. **Again, be polite when asking for help**; after all, you waited this long to start studying, didn't you?
Three days	**Review any stubborn trouble spots**; extra work can't hurt.
	English Bonus Tip: read through the word list in Chapter 4. Skip the words you know, but define and think about the ones you don't. The only way to expand your knowledge of words is to incorporate new words into your working vocabulary. Learn—and use—them.
Two days	**Take a second practice exam** and compare your results. You will likely have improved!
	Read through the answer key explanations.
	Review any areas that remain weak.
Time out!	**Give yourself a break.** Do not study. Do something relaxing, like watching a movie, reading for pleasure, or eating out with friends and family.
	Get to bed at a reasonable hour; no prep can help if you are exhausted and nervous.

Reality Check

No matter your level of test preparation, you run a risk of experiencing test-taking anxieties prior to the exam. We offer in this section a series of anxiety-reducing tips that we hope will help you do your best on the exam. Some of the suggestions require long-term practice before one can see results; however, all are good advice.

Get fit.	People who exercise handle stress better than people who do not. Get in the habit of following a reasonable, sustainable exercise regimen.
Get rest.	Recent studies show that people, especially men, who do not get regular, adequate sleep run a greater risk of developing psychoses than those who do. Your brain and body need sleep; give them adequate rest.
Get packed.	Gather together all items you will need **prior to** testing day so that they are ready to bring **on** testing day. We suggest you bring the following: **admission ticket, three or four No. 2 (or equivalent) lead pencils, an eraser, a pen, and a sweater or light jacket** (in case of a cold room).
Get fed.	Taking tests on an empty stomach—or fueled by the empty carbohydrates in a donut or candy bar—is a sure-fire mistake. Your body needs a constant source of energy—not the roller coaster ride such foods contain. At the very least, drink a big glass of milk.
Get there.	Make sure that you know where your testing site is and how long it takes to get there. Arrive at your testing site a little early—between 8:30 and 8:45 A.M. Late arrivals will not be admitted to the testing site.
Get psyched!	Remind yourself that you are prepared for your exam. Relax. Breathe. Concentrate.
Get focused.	**Follow the directions exactly** as they are asked. **Record your answers clearly** and accurately, filling in the circles on the answer grid completely. **Erase any changes completely** (or else the answering machine may score your erasures as answers). **Pace yourself.** If in doubt, **guess** because there is no penalty!

Conclusion

You have now finished the introductory section of this study guide. You should now have a sense of your task and a sense of how you will master it. Now is the time to begin your study session, probably by taking your first practice exam.

Take a deep breath and plunge in. You'll do fine!

Good luck!

Summary of COOP and HSPT*

	COOP	HSPT
Type of exam	Multiple Choice	Multiple Choice
When should students take the exam?	In the eighth grade	In the eighth grade
Who should apply for the exam?	Students seeking admission to Catholic high schools.	Students seeking admission to Catholic high schools.
Which subjects are tested?	Language, Reading, Mathematics	Language, Reading, Mathematics.
When is the exam given?	Twice in the Fall.	In the Fall and the Spring.
Where may I obtain forms and register for the exam?	From the parochial high school you are interested in attending or from your own parochial school.	From the parochial high school you are interested in attending or from your own parochial school.
Is the exam the same every year?	No, the exam changes to some extent; however, this book can prepare you for the exam.	No, the exam changes to some extent; however, this book can prepare you for the exam.
What purpose(s) other than admission to Catholic high schools does the exam serve?	The test is used for placing students into specific courses and levels.	The test is used for placing students into specific courses and levels. Each test taker is compared to other students taking the exam, both locally and on a national level.
How often may I take the exam?	Only once.	You have two chances to take the test—once in the Fall and a second time in the Spring.
Who develops the exam and where may I obtain further information?	Cooperative Admissions, CTB/McGraw-Hill, 20 Ryan Ranch Road, Monterey, CA 93940; Phone: 800-538-9547; Fax: 800-282-0266; *www.ctb.com*	Scholastic Testing Service, 480 Meyer Road, Bensenville, IL 60106-1617; Phone: 800-642-6STS (6787); Fax: 630-766-8054; *www.ststesting.com*
What is the registration fee?	$30.	The cost is included in the fee the school charges for registration.
Should I guess answers or leave blanks?	Your score is based on the number of correct answers, so there is no penalty for incorrect answers. Guess.	Your score is based on the number of correct answers, so there is no penalty for incorrect answers. Guess.
How can I prepare for the exam?	Review the English and math sections of the book first. Use a timer when you take the practice exams. After checking the answers, go back to the text in this book and review the sections in which you did poorly.	Review the English and math sections of the book first. Use a timer when you take the practice exams. After checking the answers, go back to the text in this book and review the sections in which you did poorly.

*For TACHS exam info, see pages 11–26.

Summary of COOP and HSPT

(continued)	COOP	HSPT
What are the various sections of the exam?	**Sequences**—Spatial relations, patterns, and sequences of numbers, letters, and figures (20 questions, 15 minutes). **Analogies**—Relationships among pictures (20 questions, 7 minutes). **Verbal Reasoning: Words**—Relationships between words and deductive reasoning (20 questions, 15 minutes). **Quantitative Reasoning**—Interpretations of Pictures into Mathematics (20 questions, 5 minutes). **Reading and Language Arts**—Concepts presented in short selections (40 questions, 40 minutes). **Verbal Reasoning**—Context-deduce meaning from contexts (10 questions, 7 minutes). **Mathematics Computation**—General concepts as well as specific skills in algebra, geometry, arithmetic, and probability (40 questions, 35 minutes).	**Verbal Skills**—Antonyms, Synonyms, Analogies, Logic, Verbal Classification. (60 questions, 16 minutes) **Quantitative Skills**—Number Manipulation, Geometric Comparisons, Nongeometric Comparisons, Number Series. (52 questions, 30 minutes) **Reading Skills**—Vocabulary, Comprehension (62 questions 25 minutes). **Mathematics Skills**—Concepts, Problem Solving (64 questions, 45 minutes). **Language Expression Skills**—Punctuation, Capitalization, Usage, Spelling, Composition (60 questions, 25 minutes).
Are there any optional parts on the exam?	No	Yes. Some high schools may ask you to take one additional test in the Catholic Religion, Mechanical Aptitude, or Science; however, any score on this optional part is not included in the total score on the exam.
Is there any passing or failing grade on the exam?	No, each school has its own standards for admission.	No, each school has its own standards for admission.
May I use a calculator?	No.	No.

Introducing the New TACHS

Overview

New to the Catholic high school entrance exam scene is the Test for Admission into Catholic High School. Starting in the Fall of 2004, the TACHS was being used in several dioceses. This new exam tests many of the same academic skills as the COOP and the HSPT. The major areas covered on TACHS are reading, language, mathematics, and general reasoning ability skills.

You will find the review material contained throughout this book to be extremely helpful in preparing to take the TACHS. To assist you further we have included the following overview of the TACHS test. Each section gives a brief description of the types of questions that will be encountered on the exam. Following are some sample questions.

Even though information on this new exam is still emerging, using the COOP and HSPT sections of the book in addition to the TACHS section should give anyone taking the TACHS a strong basis that can be applied to the exam. If you are preparing to take the TACHS, you should read the review chapters in this book before trying the sample questions.

TACHS Mathematics

The level of difficulty of this section is very similar to that of the COOP and the HSPT. The TACHS covers the same skills as the COOP and HSPT but specifically contains general questions, deductive reasoning, reasoning graphs, estimates, and word problems. Read the mathematics review section of this book before tackling the following TACHS sample questions. You should also look at the mathematics portions of the COOP and HSPT sample exams for further review.

TACHS MATHEMATICS SAMPLE QUESTIONS

DIRECTIONS: For questions 1–8, select the best answer for each problem. See answers on page 13.

1. An ocean-going cargo ship has a capacity of 8,000 tons. If it sails from Los Angeles to Hong Kong carrying five-eighths of its capacity and returns carrying three-fifths of its capacity, how many tons did it carry round-trip?

    (A) 6,200   (B) 7,400   (C) 8,300   (D) 9,800

2. If points A (2, 2), B (4, 5), and C (6, 2) represent the vertices of a triangle, determine its area.

    (A) 12   (B) 8   (C) 6   (D) 10

3. What is the difference of the greatest common factor and least common factor of 66 and 33?

    (A) 8   (B) 7   (C) 12   (D) 10

4. On the real number line, if the distance between two numbers is 3.8, which of the following sets correctly represents the two numbers?

    (A) 4.7 and 11.3   (B) 9.6 and 5.8
    (C) 12.4 and 6.5   (D) 9.3 and 3.7

5. Henry receives a salary of $530 per week. José gets 30% more than Henry. If they both receive $70 per week raises, how much will José be earning?

    (A) $650   (B) $458   (C) $759   (D) $568

6. The three digit number $49x$ is divisible by 4 with no remainders. If the sum of the digits is divisible by 5 with no remainders, what is the number?

    (A) 492   (B) 497   (C) 493   (D) 498

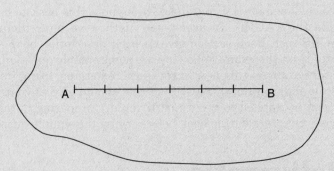

7. On the map, the symbol ⊢—⊣ represents 16 miles. If Jason drives at a speed of 64 miles per hour, how long will it take him to drive from city A to city B?

    (A) 45 minutes   (B) 1 hour, 15 minutes
    (C) 2 hours   (D) 1 hour, 30 minutes

8. Jessica weighs $x + 34$ pounds and Rhonda weighs 12 pounds less. If Jessica gains 5 pounds and Rhonda loses 2 pounds, what is the sum of their new weights?

    (A) $2x + 61$ (B) $2x - 22$ (C) $x + 56$ (D) $3x - 8$

TACHS ESTIMATION SAMPLE QUESTIONS

DIRECTIONS: No written calculations are permitted and an exact answer is not required. For questions 9–10, estimate the answer. See answers on page 16.

9. Estimate the quotient of 652 and 9.

   (A) 15   (B) 65   (C) 110   (D) 145

Attendance at the Olympics

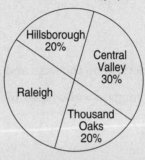

10. Four high schools participated in a local Olympics. The attendees at the Olympics were residents of four local communities: Hillsborough, Central Valley, Thousand Oaks, and Raleigh. If 9,700 people attended, estimate how many were residents of Raleigh?

   (A) 1,000   (B) 2,000   (C) 3,000   (D) 4,000

MATHEMATICS ANSWERS

1.
ANALYSIS
Find five-eighths of 8,000 and three-fifths of 8,000; then add the two figures.

WORK

$$\frac{5}{8} \times \overset{1,000}{\cancel{8,000}} = 5,000$$

$$+ \quad \frac{3}{5} \times \overset{1,600}{\cancel{8,000}} = 4,800$$

$$\overline{\phantom{+ \frac{3}{5} \times 8,000 = }9,800}$$

ANSWER: (D)

2.

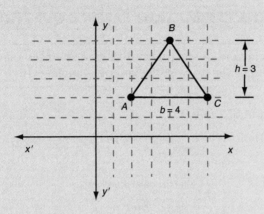

ANALYSIS

Locate the points on a graph and determine the base and height. Then use the formula $A = \frac{1}{2} bh$, where A = area of the triangle, b = the base, and h = the height.

WORK

$$A = \frac{1}{2} bh$$

$b = 4, h = 3$:

$$A = \frac{1}{\cancel{2}}\overset{2}{(\cancel{4})}(3) = 6$$

ANSWER: (C)

3.

ANALYSIS

Find the greatest and the least common factors of 33 and 66 and then subtract.

WORK

$66 = 11 \times 2 \times 3$

$33 = 11 \times 3$

greatest common factor = 11

least common factor = 3

The difference of 11 and 3 is 8.

ANSWER: (A)

4.

ANALYSIS

Subtract each set of numbers in order to find a difference of 3.8.

WORK

$9.6 - 5.8 = 3.8$

ANSWER: (B)

5.
ANALYSIS
José is earning 30% more than Henry or 130% of Henry's wage. Determine José's current wage and then add $70.

WORK

Henry's wage:	$530
José's wage:	130% × $530 or 1.30 × $530 = $689
Jose's wage after a $70 raise:	$689 + $70 = $759

ANSWER: (C)

6.
ANALYSIS
Substitute the possible answers into the given information.

WORK

The three digit number 49x is divisible by 4: $\dfrac{492}{4} = 123$

The sum of the digits is divisible by 5: $\dfrac{4+9+2}{5} = \dfrac{15}{5} = 3$

ANSWER: (A)

7.
ANALYSIS
To determine the number of miles between cities A and B, count the number of symbols and multiply by 16. Then divide the number of miles by 60 miles per hour, the speed of the car.

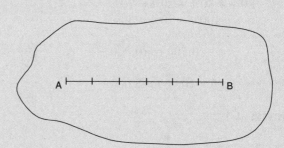

WORK

$$6 \times 16 = 96 \text{ miles}$$

$$\frac{96 \text{ miles}}{64 \text{ miles per hour}} = 1\frac{1}{2} = 1 \text{ hour, 30 minutes}$$

ANSWER: (D)

8.
ANALYSIS
List both current weights. Then list their new weights and add.

WORK

Jessica's current weight:	$x + 34$
Rhonda's current weight:	$(x + 34) - 12 = x + 22$
Jessica's future weight:	$(x + 34) + 5 = x + 39$
Rhonda's future weight:	$(x + 22) - 2 = x + 22$
Total weight:	$2x + 61$

ANSWER: (A)

ESTIMATION ANSWERS

9.
ANALYSIS
Round off 9 to 10 and then divide.

WORK

$$\frac{652}{10} = 65.2 \approx 65$$

ANSWER: (B)

Attendance at the Olympics

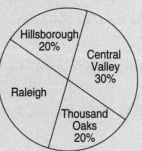

10.
ANALYSIS
Mentally, add up 20%, 30%, and 20% and subtract from 100%. Round off 9,700 to 10,000 and mentally multiply your percent answer by 10,000.

WORK

$$20\% + 30\% + 20\% = 70\%$$
$$100\% - 70\% = 30\%$$

$$9,700 \approx 10,000$$

$$0.30 \times 10,000 = 3,000$$

ANSWER: (C)

TACHS Ability

Students are tested for their overall reasoning ability. Questions call for developing general principles for the information presented and then applying these general principles to specific situations.

TACHS ABILITY SAMPLE QUESTIONS

DIRECTIONS: In questions 1–4, the three first figures are linked in certain ways. Select one of the following five figures so that it corresponds with the first three figures. See answers on page 20.

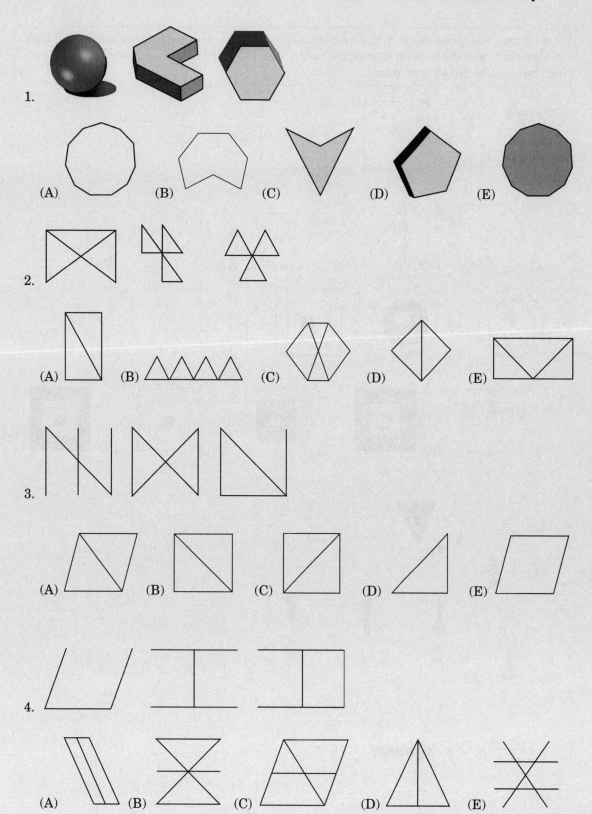

1.

(A)　　(B)　　(C)　　(D)　　(E)

2.

(A)　　(B)　　(C)　　(D)　　(E)

3.

(A)　　(B)　　(C)　　(D)　　(E)

4.

(A)　　(B)　　(C)　　(D)　　(E)

DIRECTIONS: For questions 5–8, the first and second figures are somehow related. Find that relationship, and then, using that relationship, link the third figure with one of the following choices. See answers on page 20.

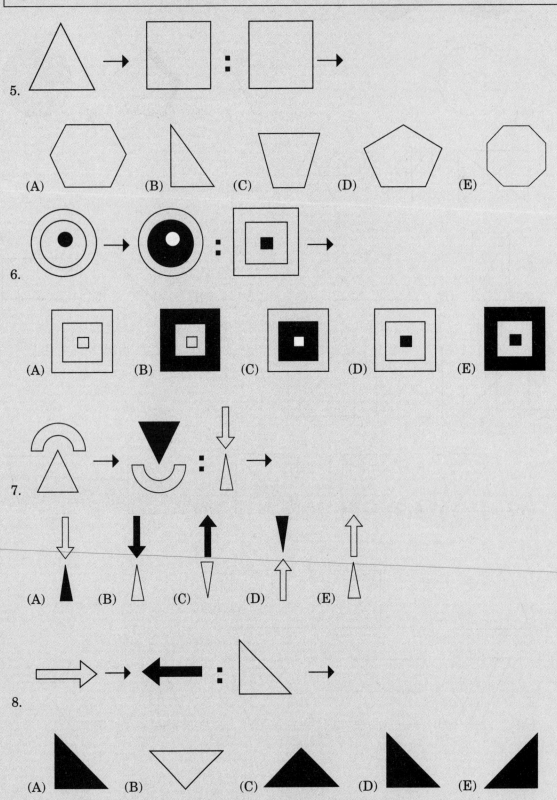

DIRECTIONS: For questions 9–12, the diagrams on the first line indicate how a paper is to be folded and then punched. Select the diagram on the following line that indicates how the paper will appear after it is unfolded. See answers on page 20.

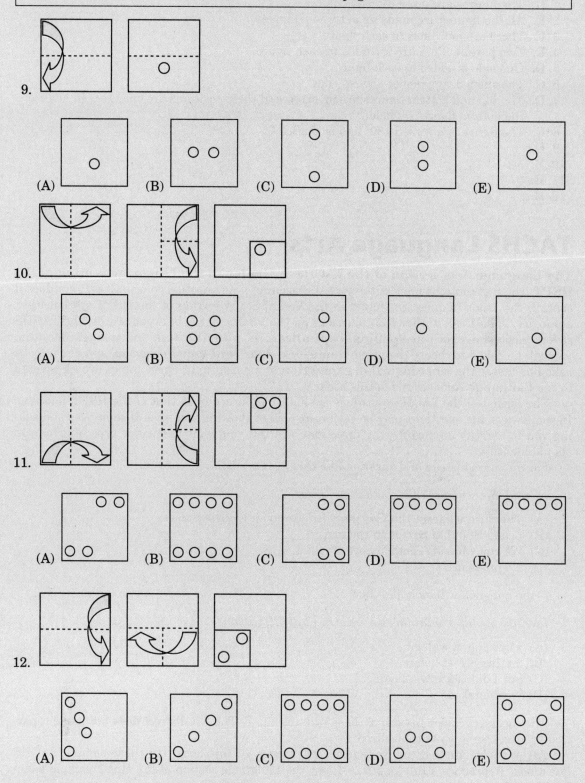

1. **D.** The figures are three-dimensional.
2. **E.** All the figures are made up of three triangles.
3. **E.** There are four lines in each figure.
4. **E.** Two parallel lines are included in each figure.
5. **D.** One side is added to each figure.
6. **C.** The shaded ring moves one ring out.
7. **D.** The top and bottom figures are inverted and their positions are changed. In addition, the bottom figure is shaded.
8. **E.** The figure is reversed 180° and is shaded.
9. **D.**
10. **B.**
11. **B.**
12. **E.**

TACHS Language Arts

The Language Arts section of the TACHS is similar to the Language section of the HSPT. The test contains none of the verbal reasoning-type questions of the COOP, nor does it contain the kinds of questions found in the Verbal Skills section of the HSPT (verbal logic, analogies, opposites). Rather than focusing on the *relationships* between words, the TACHS covers basic skills such as **spelling, capitalization, punctuation**, and **usage**. Moreover, you will be asked to choose the **most concise or clear sentence** in a group, and you may be asked to choose the **most logical organization** of a paragraph. These topics are all covered in the **Language Arts** section of this book.

The format of the TACHS questions is slightly different from that of the HSPT, however. In some ways, the questions may be easier; instead of showing you several sentences and asking you to identify *any* errors, the directions will tell you what particular type of error you should identify.

For instance, instead of a question like this:

Identify the sentence that contains an error.

(A) The Susquehanna Hat Company is located on Floogle Street.
(B) I can't find that Street on the map.
(C) We enjoy having company over to visit.
(D) No mistakes.

—the question will look like this:

*Identify the line containing an error in **capitalization**.*

(A) I have often walked
(B) on this Street before,
(C) but I didn't know its name.
(D) No mistakes.

The incorrect choice in both of these examples is B. The word *street* does not name a particular street, so it is not capitalized.

After you've studied the Language Arts section of this book, try these sample TACHS questions. To practice a full-length test, use the Language section of the HSPT sample exam in this book.

TACHS LANGUAGE ARTS SAMPLE QUESTIONS

DIRECTIONS: Choose the word that is <u>misspelled</u>. See answers on page 22.

1.
(A) adjetive
(B) preposition
(C) adverb
(D) conjunction
(E) No mistakes

2.
(J) fellowship
(K) resolution
(L) different
(M) handle
(N) No mistakes

3.
(A) definate
(B) nickel
(C) origin
(D) stencil
(E) No mistakes

4.
(J) similar
(K) vegetable
(L) collumn
(M) literature
(N) No mistakes

DIRECTIONS: Look for errors in <u>capitalization</u>. See answers on page 22.

5.
(A) The word Wednesday is
(B) named after the chief
(C) Anglo-Saxon god Woden.
(D) No mistakes

6.
(J) The train in
(K) Springfield, New Jersey, runs
(L) right by my Aunt's house.
(M) No mistakes

7.
(A) The house behind
(B) Trinity high school
(C) belongs to Dr. Jenny.
(D) No mistakes

8.
(J) Heather and Teresa
(K) brought a lovely
(L) bouquet of Flowers.
(M) No mistakes

DIRECTIONS: Look for errors in <u>punctuation</u>. See answers on page 22.

9.
(A) I usually prefer English, Irish,
(B) or Welsh poetry, but I also enjoy
(C) the poem *Birches* by Robert Frost.
(D) No mistakes

10.
(J) My uncle Angelo owned
(K) a beauty salon in
(L) Bayside New York.
(M) No mistakes

11.
(A) When you write a sentence,
(B) make sure you don't leave
(C) out essential punctuation
(D) No mistakes

12.
(J) Before we eat
(K) the youngest family member
(L) says grace.
(M) No mistakes

DIRECTIONS: Look for errors in <u>usage and expression</u>. See answers below.

13.
- (A) It's not whether
- (B) you win or loose,
- (C) it's how you play the game.
- (D) No mistakes

14.
- (J) The movie effected me greatly.
- (K) I sat in the theater and cried.
- (L) It was the saddest movie I had ever seen.
- (M) No mistakes

DIRECTIONS: Questions 15 and 16 are based on the following paragraph. See answers below.

---

(1) Early history books are fun to read <u>for the reason that</u> they often contain fantastic stories. (2) For instance, *The Life of St. Columba* includes the very first reference to the Loch Ness monster. (3) It is a fascinating tale. (4) As it is about to devour a swimmer, Columba turns the beast aside with a prayer.

15. Which is the best way to write the underlined part of the first sentence?

- (A) and
- (B) because
- (C) for instance,
- (D) No change

16. Which sentence could be left out of the paragraph?

- (A) 1
- (B) 2
- (C) 3
- (D) No change

LANGUAGE ARTS ANSWERS

1. **A.** The correct spelling is <u>adjective</u>. If you pronounce it correctly (containing the letter *c*), you will have no problem spelling it.
2. **N.** No mistakes.
3. **A.** The correct spelling is <u>definite</u>. Remember that it contains the word *finite*.
4. **L.** The word <u>column</u> contains only one *l*. You might remember this because the words *autumn* and *hymn* contain no double letters, either.
5. **D.** No mistakes.
6. **L.** This is not the **name** of your aunt, so it is not capitalized.
7. **B.** Because it is the name of a specific school, <u>Trinity High School</u> is capitalized.
8. **L.** The word *flowers* is a common noun. Do not capitalize it.
9. **C.** Use quotations marks for a poem: "Birches" by Robert Frost.
10. **L.** Use a comma between the city and state: Bayside, New York.
11. **C.** In this case, we've left out the period.
12. **J.** Use a comma before introductory words, *"Before we eat,"* especially when they can cause confusion such as this. It sounds as if you're going to eat your younger brother!
13. **B.** Check the difference between the words *loose* and *lose*.
14. **J.** The verb form is *affected*.
15. **B.** Using a more concise word is usually more effective. The expression "for the reason that" is a longer way to say "because."
16. **C.** The third sentence is not necessary; the others cannot be removed without making the meaning of the paragraph unclear.

TACHS Reading

Like any other high school entrance exam, the TACHS requires that you demonstrate your ability to understand what you read. You can find examples of the kinds of texts you will be asked to read in this section, but before you check them out, let's quickly review the general types of questions you will find on this exam.

The Reading portion of the TACHS tests your ability to understand what you read, and this section of the TACHS consists of two parts. Part 1 targets your vocabulary skills. You will be given a phrase in which a word has been highlighted, and you will be asked to define words, based on the context in which the word is used. This portion of the exam most commonly asks questions about noun, verb, and modifier usage.

Part 2 targets your reading comprehension skills. You will be given a passage to read and then asked questions that refer to what you have read. The TACHS can use a wide variety of reading passages; it may offer you selections drawn from fiction (such as fables, fairy tales, and poetry) or nonfiction (such as interviews, diaries, biographies, science, and social studies) sources. Although you can be asked questions that merely ask you to remember facts from your reading, you will more often be asked to draw inferences and make generalizations based on what you have read.

Here's some advice. You can count on the fact that reading passages on the TACHS are not designed to be tricky or confusing in any way; you should feel confident that you can understand these passages. Reading carefully and focusing on *identifying the answers to the questions being asked* should allow you to complete this section of the exam with confidence.

That being said, make sure you **read the passage from beginning to end** before even looking at the questions. Reading the selection correctly the first time will save you time re-reading the passage. Often you will be tempted to guess at the answers without reading the passage, but you must answer the questions based on the information given in the passage, not based on information you already have in your brain; after all, research changes facts, and sometimes your memory is faulty. **Read the questions and all of the options** before trying to answer. Finally, **if you have struggled to find the correct answer and simply cannot figure it out, leave the answer blank.**

Now try your hand at some examples modeled on actual samples from the TACHS. If you would like to try more reading questions, check out the reading questions on the model COOP and HSPT exams in this book. In many ways, you may find the reading comprehension section of the TACHS exam to be easier than that on the COOP or HSPT.

TACHS READING SAMPLE QUESTIONS

PART 1

DIRECTIONS: This is a test about words and their meanings. For each question, decide which one of the four answers has most nearly the same meaning as the underlined word(s) above it. See answers on page 26.

1. a thin veneer

   (A) smile
   (B) cloth
   (C) covering
   (D) painting

2. a mature plant

   (J) fully grown
   (K) legal
   (L) manly
   (M) serious

3. a vacant stare

   (A) faraway
   (B) blank
   (C) questioning
   (D) funny

4. a benevolent ruler

   (J) angry
   (K) kindly
   (L) dictatorial
   (M) strict

PART 2

DIRECTIONS: Read the following passage below and then answer the questions. Four answers are given for each question. You are to choose the answer that you think is better than the others. See answers on page 26.

July 30th Monday 1804

Set out this morning early proceeded on to a clear open Prairie on the L.S. on a rise of about 70 feet higher than the bottom which is also a Prairie (both forming Bluffs to the river) of High Grass & Plum bush Grapes &c. and situated above high water, in a small Grove of timber at the foot of the Riseing Ground between those two preraries, and below the Bluffs of the high Prarie we Came too and formed a Camp, intending to waite the return of the Frenchman & Indians. the white horse which we found near the Kanzus river, Died Last night . . .

Jo. & R. Fields did not return this evening, Several men with verry bad *Boils*. Cat fish is cought in any part of the river Turkeys Geese & a Beaver Killed & Cought every thing in prime order men in high Spirits, a fair Still evening Great no. Musquitors this evening.

— taken from *The Journals of Lewis and Clark*

5. Consider the word *cought* as used in the second paragraph; given the context of the sentences, what modern word would modern authors use instead of *cought*?

   (A) coughed
   (B) cowed
   (C) caught
   (D) contained

6. Through which part of the United States were Lewis and Clark most likely traveling when this passage was written?

   (J) Oklahoma and the plains states
   (K) California and the Pacific coast
   (L) Massachusetts and the Atlantic coast
   (M) Florida and the Southern shoreline

The Filipino have a story that they tell their children. The Maker, after creating the world, sat down to admire His work. But after a time, He grew lonely, and He longed for a companion with whom to share the world.

So the Maker resolved to create such a companion.

He mixed ingredients and from them molded the form of Man. He then put the Man into the fire to bake. However, the Maker was impatient to meet Man, and He pulled Man out of the fire before an hour had passed. The Man, to the Maker's disappointment, was pasty white.

The Maker put this first Man aside, and went back to mixing ingredients. He formed a second Man, and put him in the fire to bake. This time, He resolved to be patient, and He went down to the beach to amuse Himself. Two hours passed before the Maker returned to the fire. This time, the Man was dark, nearly burnt.

The Maker put this second Man aside, and once again went back to mixing ingredients. He formed a third Man, and again put him in the fire to bake. This time the Maker hovered nearby, carefully checking on the Man periodically, until finally he pulled this third Man from the fire. To His delight, the Man was perfectly baked to a golden brown.

Delighted, the Maker gave out portions of land to these Men. To the pasty Man He gave the northern regions. To the burnt Man He gave the southern regions. But to the brown man, He gave the Philippine Islands.

7. Which Man did the Maker construct when He felt great impatience?

(A) the golden brown Man
(B) the burnt Man
(C) the pasty Man
(D) none of the above

8. What larger mystery is this story most likely trying to explain?

(J) why people are impatient
(K) why ethnic groups are different from each other
(L) why it's difficult to bake at high altitudes
(M) why the Philippine Islands are so lovely

Consider the lowly potato. Although low- and no-carb advocates, currently decry the tuber, it remains a versatile source of nutrition. Potatoes enhance almost any main dish, whether they be raw, baked, boiled, fried, mashed, scalloped, or whipped. Potatoes are also quite cheap. An average ten-pound bag of white potatoes costs a nominal $1.99. Nevertheless, the potato comes across as bland and unworthy of much attention.

Such was not always the case.

Believe it or not, the potato once struck fear into people's hearts. The plant, native to South America, is related to deadly nightshade. Many people refused to attempt eating the tuber, fearing death by poison. But the brave souls who dared eating the potato found a reliable and efficient source of food that soon found its way to the Europe and the American colonies.

After people became convinced of its edibility, the potato became a favorite food. After Thomas Harriot brought samples to England, the plant grew wildly popular throughout Europe. In fact, 17th century Europeans considered the potato a delicacy, just as we consider imported chocolates or fine wine delicacies; they routinely served potato water (water in which potatoes had been repeatedly boiled) as part of their tea-time delicacies. Farmers began making potatoes a substantial portion of their crops, especially in Ireland, since their popularity ensured a hefty profit.

9. Why did people fear to eat potatoes?

   (A) They were bland.
   (B) They were thought poisonous.
   (C) They were expensive.
   (D) They were difficult to prepare.

10. In the article, the author compares potatoes to

   (J) apples
   (K) carrots
   (L) chocolate
   (M) poison

READING PART 1 ANSWERS

1. **C.** A veneer is an outer layer. The word *covering* is closest to that meaning.
2. **J.** This is the only synonym that makes sense in this context.
3. **B.** *Vacant*, of course, means empty or *blank*.
4. **K.** Remember the root *bene* means *good*.

READING PART 2 ANSWERS

5. **C.** Remove the word *cought* from the sentences and plug in each of the other words one at a time. The only word that makes sense given the context is choice C. (It's interesting to see how the word *caught*—which is pronounced as if it has an *o* in it—actually once was spelled in a way that reflected its sound.)
6. **J.** The passage refers to prairies, bluffs, and the Kanzus (Kansas) River. Of the four regional choices, only the area that includes Oklahoma and the other plains states contains these items. The answer is J.
7. **C.** This myth uses a conceit (or a consistent set of references) that revolves around the art of baking to get its point across. To bake something requires that you mix it and heat it for an exact amount of time. If you are impatient and remove it from the heat too soon, the item will be undercooked; if you are too patient and leave it in too long, you will burn it. Because of his impatience, the Maker removes his creation from the cooking fire too soon and his creation is raw and undercooked. The result is a raw, undercooked, pasty product. Therefore, the answer is C.
8. **K.** Many myths, like the one presented here, try to explain "the way things are." Because of the reference to skin color and geographical region, we can infer that this myth is attempting to explain why people look the way they do. Because most myths especially revere the group creating the myth, it is no surprise that the Filipino Maker favors the golden brown Man, who looks like Filipinos do, rather than the pasty or burnt Men, who represent other ethnicities.
9. **B.** According to the passage, people thought that because potatoes were related to deadly nightshade—which is poisonous—potatoes were, too. It was a case of guilt by association.
10. **L.** The article states that 17th-century folk thought that potatoes were luxuries, just as we, today, think imported chocolates are luxuries.

Mathematics

Introduction

The mathematics review includes the basic skills necessary for the exams.
All the examples are broken down into the following areas:

1. Initial problem
2. Analysis of the problem
3. Work area
4. Answer

The analysis area is probably the most important section because we discuss the general approach to take to solve the problem. The work area shows the "nuts and bolts" operations.

Integers

NATURAL AND WHOLE NUMBERS

The first numbers developed by primitive peoples were the **natural** or **counting numbers**, such as 1, 2, 3, 4, 5, ...

It's usually more useful to describe a collection of similar items by using "set" notation. In the example, the set of natural or counting numbers may be indicated by {1, 2, 3, 4, 5, . . .}.

A zero was later added to introduce the set of **whole numbers**: {0, 1, 2, 3, 4, 5, . . .}.

This set may be represented on the number line:

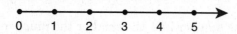

In our number system, the **place** of the digit determines its value. For example, let's take a close look at the following whole number.

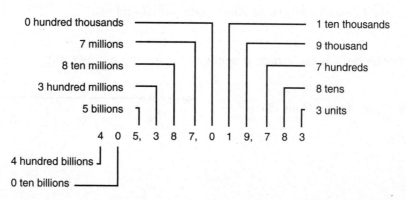

Altogether, the number reads four hundred five billion, three hundred eighty-seven million, nineteen thousand, seven hundred eighty-three.

EXAMPLE 1
Change 456,372 into words.

ANSWER: Four hundred fifty-six thousand, three hundred seventy-two.

EXAMPLE 2
Change "Thirty-six billion, four hundred seventy-nine million, five hundred eighteen thousand, four hundred twenty-six" into numerals.

ANSWER: 36,479,518,426.

PRACTICE (see answers on page 105)
1. What does the digit 4 represent in the number 456,695,098?

    (A) hundreds   (B) thousands   (C) ten thousands   (D) hundred millions

2. Change 304,473 into words.

    (A) thirty thousand, four hundred seventy-three
    (B) three hundred four thousand, four hundred seventy-three
    (C) thirty four thousand, four hundred seventy-three
    (D) three thousand, four hundred seventy-three

3. Change "Eight hundred fifty-three million, four hundred thirty-two thousand, five hundred sixty-four" into numerals.

    (A) 853,432,000   (B) 853,564   (C) 853,432,564   (D) 8,534,325,640

COMPARING INTEGERS

Negative integers (−1, −2, −3, . . .) were added to the whole numbers, so that we arrived at the set of **integers** (. . ., −3, −2, −1, 0, 1, 2, 3, . . .)

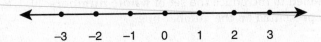

The farther to the left on the number line, the smaller the number. For example, −2 is smaller than 0.

EXAMPLE 1
Using the inequality symbol > (greater than), compare 3 and −8.

ANALYSIS
The integer on the right is the larger. If necessary, draw the number line.

WORK
    3 > −8   (3 is greater than −8)

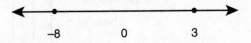

ANSWER: 3 > −8

EXAMPLE 2
Use the inequality symbol < (less than) to compare 6 and 0.

ANALYSIS
The integer on the left is the smaller.

WORK

$0 < 6$ (0 is less than 6)

0   6

ANSWER: $0 < 6$

EXAMPLE 3
Order the numbers 5, –1, and –2, from **smallest to largest.**

ANALYSIS
Draw the number line. The farther to the left, the smaller the number.

WORK

$-2 < -1 < 5$ (–2 is less than –1, which is less than 5)

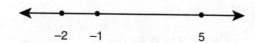

–2   –1   5

ANSWER: $-2 < -1 < 5$

PRACTICE (see answers on page 105)
1. Use the inequality symbol > to compare 2, 0, and –2.

    (A) $-2 > 2 > 0$ (B) $2 > -2 > 0$ (C) $0 > -2 > 2$ (D) $2 > 0 > -2$

2. Use the inequality symbol < to compare –5, 3, and –8.

    (A) $-8 < -5 < 3$ (B) $-8 < 3 < -5$ (C) $0 < -8 < -5$ (D) $-5 < -8 < 0$

3. Order the numbers 6, –2, and 0, from largest to smallest.

    (A) $0 > -2 > 6$ (B) $6 < -2 < 0$ (C) $6 > -2 > 0$ (D) $6 > 0 > -2$

4. Order the numbers –3, 4, and –1, from smallest to largest.

    (A) $-1 < 4 < -3$ (B) $-3 < -1 < 4$ (C) $-1 > 4 > -3$ (D) $4 < -1 < -3$

EXPONENTS

Mathematicians have developed special shorthand notations. One of these very important notations is the exponential notation.

The following products are more conveniently indicated using exponents:

$$6 \cdot 6 = 6^2 \text{(or 36)}$$
$$5 \cdot 5 \cdot 5 = 5^3 \text{(or 125)}$$
$$3 \cdot 3 \cdot 3 \cdot 3 = 3^4 \text{(or 81)}$$
$$a \cdot a = a^2$$
$$b \cdot b \cdot b \cdot b \cdot b = b^5$$

3 is the exponent

Let's get technical: $4^3 = 64$ ←——— The power is 64

4 is the base

EXAMPLE 1

What does $5 \cdot 4^3$ simplify to?

ANALYSIS

Simplify 4^3 and then multiply by 5.

WORK

$$5 \cdot 4^3 = 5 \cdot 4 \cdot 4 \cdot 4 = 5 \cdot 64 = 320$$

ANSWER: 320

EXAMPLE 2

Simplify the following powers and then select the correct answer.

(a) 5^2 (b) 2^5 (c) 2^3

(A) a > b or c > a   (B) c = a or b < c
(C) c > b and a = b   (D) b < a or c < b

ANALYSIS

Simplify each expression and then substitute.

WORK

(a) $5^2 = 5 \cdot 5 = 25$
(b) $2^5 = 2 \cdot 2 \cdot 2 \cdot 2 \cdot 2 = 32$
(c) $2^3 = 2 \cdot 2 \cdot 2 = 8$

(D) b < a   or c < b
32 < 25 or 8 < 32 ✔

ANSWER: (D)

EXAMPLE 3

Simplify $5^2 - 6 \cdot 3^0$.

ANALYSIS

Any base raised to a zero exponent is equal to 1.

WORK

$$5^2 - 6 \cdot 3^0$$
$$5 \cdot 5 - 6 \cdot 1$$
$$25 - 6$$
$$19$$

ANSWER: 19

PRACTICE (see answers on page 105)

1. Simplify $2 \cdot 4^3$

    (A) 128   (B) 64   (C) 156   (D) 32

2. What does $5^2 \cdot 2^4$ simplify to?

    (A) 200   (B) 400   (C) 80   (D) 150

3. Simplify the following powers and then select the best answer.

    (a) 6^2 (b) 3^3 (c) 4^3

    (A) a < c and b > a   (B) c > b or a < b
    (C) a > b and b > c   (D) b > c or c < a

ORDER OF OPERATIONS

Ordinarily, we perform arithmetic operations from **left to right**, with **multiplication and division preceding addition and subtraction.**

If there are parentheses in an expression, the operations inside the parentheses are performed first.

$$(7 + 5) \cdot 3 = (12) \cdot 3 = 36$$
$$480/6 - 3(4 + 6) = 80 - 3(10) = 80 - 30 = 50$$

EXAMPLE
Simplify the expression $3 \cdot 4^2 - 48 \div 6 + 2(9{-}3)$.

ANALYSIS
Simplify the exponential expression as well as the expression in parentheses first. Then multiply and divide, working from left to right. Finally, add or subtract.

WORK

$$3 \cdot 4^2 - 48 \div 6 + 2(9 - 4)$$
$$3 \cdot 16 - (48 \div 6) + 2(5)$$
$$48 - 8 + 10$$
$$40 + 10$$
$$50$$

ANSWER: 50

PRACTICE (see answers on page 105)

1–4. Simplify the expressions.

1. $5^2 - 4 \cdot 3 + 28 \div 4$

    (A) 10   (B) 40   (C) 36   (D) 20

2. $64 - 3^3 + 6 \cdot 2$

    (A) 49   (B) 38   (C) 43   (D) 122

3. $5(-3) + (6{-}1)^2$

    (A) 15   (B) 40   (C) 10   (D) –10

4. $9^1 \cdot (-2)^3$

    (A) –27   (B) 36   (C) –72   (D) 27

ROUNDING OFF INTEGERS

Sometimes we want to get an approximation of a number. In these cases, we don't need an exact answer, so we "round off."

Aunt Rita is the cashier at a local restaurant. At the end of the week, she wants to round off the money in the till to the nearest ten dollars. If $6,384 is in the till, how much is that, **to the nearest $10**?

When we round off to the nearest ten's place, we look at the unit's place first. If the unit's digit is 5 or more, we round the ten's digit up one unit. On the other hand, if the unit's digit is less than 5, we leave the ten's digit alone.

6   3   8   4

↑

Unit's place: 4 < 5

$6,384 rounds off to $6,380

PRACTICE (see answers on page 105)

1. Round off 456 to the nearest ten.

    (A) 450   (B) 400   (C) 500   (D) 460

2. Round off 5,678 to the nearest 100.

    (A) 6,000   (B) 5,600   (C) 5,700   (D) 5,800

3. Find the difference between 153 rounded off to the nearest hundred and 153 rounded off to the nearest ten.

    (A) 50   (B) 40   (C) 60   (D) 47

4. What is the sum of 783 rounded off to the nearest 100 and 437 rounded off to the nearest 10?

    (A) 1,240   (B) 1,140   (C) 2,350   (D) 1,400

PRIME NUMBERS

A prime number is a counting number that can only be divided by 1 and itself without resulting in a remainder. The number 1 is excluded from the set of prime numbers.

The prime numbers less than 20 are 2, 3, 5, 7, 11, 13, 17, and 19.

EXAMPLE 1
Is 48 a prime number?

ANALYSIS
If 48 can be divided by any number other than 1, it is not a prime number.

WORK
48 may be divided by 6: 48/6 = 8.

ANSWER: 48 is not a prime number.

EXAMPLE 2
Which of these numbers is prime?

(A) 17   (B) 18   (C) 22   (D) 35

ANALYSIS
A prime number cannot be divided by any number other than 1 and itself.

WORK
17 can only be divided by 1 and itself.

ANSWER: (A)

PRACTICE (see answers on page 105)

1. What is the next prime number following 28?

    (A) 30   (B) 31   (C) 29   (D) 37

2. List the prime numbers between 12 and 21.

    (A) 13, 15, 17   (B) 13, 17, 19   (C) 13, 17, 19, 21   (D) 13, 15, 17, 19

3. What are the prime numbers greater than 7 but less than or equal to 13?

    (A) 9, 11   (B) 11, 13   (C) 8, 9, 12   (D) 8, 9, 11

FACTORS AND MULTIPLES

Factors are two or more numbers which, when multiplied together, result in another number called a product.

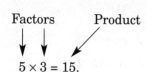

If we multiply 5 times 3, the result is 15: $5 \times 3 = 15$.

Prime factors are prime numbers that, when multiplied together, result in a product.

$$\overset{\text{Factors}}{} \qquad \overset{\text{Prime factors}}{}$$

$$42 = 21 \times 2 = 7 \times 3 \times 2$$

Common factors are numbers that are factors of two or more numbers.

$$\left. \begin{array}{l} 56 = 8 \times \underline{7} \\ 21 = 3 \times \underline{7} \end{array} \right\}$$ The common factor of 56 and 21 is 7.

$$\left. \begin{array}{l} 30 = \underline{5} \times 6 \\ 40 = \underline{5} \times 8 \end{array} \right\}$$ The common factor of 30 and 40 is 5.

The **greatest common factor** of two numbers is the common factor with the largest value.

$$\left. \begin{array}{l} 54 = \underline{18} \times 3 \\ 72 = \underline{18} \times 4 \end{array} \right\}$$ The greatest common factor of 54 and 72 is 18.

A **multiple** of a particular number is the product of that number by other whole numbers.

$0 \times 3 = \textbf{0}$	$4 \times 3 = \textbf{12}$	$7 \times 3 = \textbf{21}$
$1 \times 3 = \textbf{3}$	$5 \times 3 = \textbf{15}$	$8 \times 3 = \textbf{24}$
$2 \times 3 = \textbf{6}$	$6 \times 3 = \textbf{18}$	$9 \times 3 = \textbf{27}$

0, 3, 6, 9, 12, 15, 18, 21, 24, 27, . . . are all multiples of 3.

EXAMPLE
Determine a common factor of 15 and 12.

ANALYSIS
Find the factors of each number and then find the common factor.

WORK
$$15 = \underline{3} \times 5$$
$$12 = \underline{3} \times 4$$

ANSWER: 3

PRACTICE (see answers on page 105)

1. Find a common factor of 15 and 55.

    (A) 11   (B) 3   (C) 15   (D) 5

2. What is the greatest common factor of 48 and 54?

    (A) 8   (B) 3   (C) 6   (D) 9

3. 14, 21, 28, and 35 are all multiples of what number?

    (A) 3   (B) 5   (C) 2   (D) 7

4. What are the prime factors of 30?

    (A) 10, 3   (B) 3, 5, 2   (C) 15, 2   (D) 5, 6

Fractions

numerator

↓

A fraction is a number in the form x/y where y is not 0 or 1 and x and y are whole numbers.

↑

denominator

Definitions	Examples
In a *proper fraction*, the numerator is less than the denominator:	2/5, 4/9, 12/45
In an *improper fraction*, the numerator is equal to or larger than the denominator:	7/4, 8/3, 36/5, 9/9
A *mixed number* is a whole number with a proper fraction remainder:	$8\frac{5}{9}$, $2\frac{3}{4}$, $15\frac{7}{8}$
When we want the *reciprocal* of a fraction, we invert the fraction:	5/3 is the reciprocal of 3/5 1/7 is the reciprocal of 7 (or 7/1)

EXAMPLE

Match the items in the two columns:

A	**B**
1. 4/3	a. Proper fraction
2. $5\frac{2}{7}$	b. Improper fraction
3. 8/9	c. Mixed number

ANSWER: 1b, 2c, 3a

COMPARING AND ORDERING FRACTIONS

If we want to compare fractions, we first have to change all the denominators to the same common denominator.

EXAMPLE

Compare $\frac{2}{3}$, $\frac{1}{2}$, and $\frac{3}{4}$ and then determine which of the following statements are true.

(A) $\frac{2}{3} > \frac{3}{4}$ (B) $\frac{1}{2} < \frac{3}{4}$ (C) $\frac{3}{4} < \frac{2}{3}$ (D) $\frac{2}{3} < \frac{1}{2}$

ANALYSIS

In order to compare, let's change all denominators to the same common denominator, 12.

WORK

$$\frac{2}{3} = \frac{8}{12}$$ With the same denominators, we can now compare fractions.

$$\frac{1}{2} = \frac{6}{12}$$

$$\frac{3}{4} = \frac{9}{12}$$

$$\frac{8}{12} < \frac{9}{12}$$

$$\frac{2}{3} < \frac{3}{4}$$

ANSWER: (B)

REDUCING FRACTIONS

When we reduce a fraction, we keep the numerator and the denominator in the same ratio but with smaller numbers.

EXAMPLE
Reduce 24/32 to its lowest terms.

ANALYSIS
Rewrite the numerator and the denominator as products of factors and then cancel the common factors.

WORK

$$\frac{24}{32} = \frac{\overset{1}{\cancel{8}} \times 3}{\underset{1}{\cancel{8}} \times 4} = \frac{3}{4}$$

ANSWER: $\frac{3}{4}$

PRACTICE (see answers on page 105)

Reduce the following fractions to their lowest terms.

1. 42/49
   (A) 6/7   (B) 5/7   (C) 4/9   (D) 6/9

2. 15/45
   (A) 5/9   (B) 5/15   (C) 1/3   (D) 3/9

3. 40/64
   (A) 1/2   (B) 5/8   (C) 20/32   (D) 7/8

CHANGING IMPROPER FRACTIONS TO WHOLE OR MIXED NUMBERS

EXAMPLE 1

Change 14/7 to a whole number.

(A) 4   (B) 1   (C) $2\frac{1}{2}$ (D) 2

ANALYSIS

When converting improper fractions to whole or mixed numbers, divide the denominator into the numerator.

WORK

$$\frac{14}{7} = 2$$

ANSWER: (D)

EXAMPLE 2

Change 25/6 to a mixed number.

ANALYSIS

Divide 25 by 6.

WORK

$$\frac{25}{6} = 4\frac{1}{6}$$

ANSWER: $4\frac{1}{6}$

PRACTICE (see answers on page 105)

Change the following improper fractions to mixed numbers.

1. 32/7

    (A) $4\frac{4}{7}$ (B) $3\frac{11}{7}$ (C) $5\frac{2}{7}$ (D) $4\frac{3}{7}$

2. 46/9

    (A) 5   (B) $6\frac{1}{9}$ (C) $6\frac{2}{9}$ (D) $5\frac{1}{9}$

3. 54/8

    (A) $6\frac{1}{8}$ (B) $7\frac{5}{8}$ (C) $6\frac{3}{4}$ (D) $6\frac{7}{8}$

CHANGING MIXED NUMBERS TO IMPROPER FRACTIONS

EXAMPLE

Change $3\frac{5}{8}$ to an improper fraction.

ANALYSIS

We want to reverse the previous process, so, in order to change $3\frac{5}{8}$ to an improper fraction, multiply 3 by 8 and add the numerator, 5. Then make this number the numerator and leave 8 the denominator.

WORK

$$3\frac{5}{8} = \frac{3 \cdot 8 + 5}{8} = \frac{29}{8}$$

ANSWER: 29/8

PRACTICE (see answers on page 105)

Change the following mixed numbers to improper fractions.

1. $4\frac{3}{5}$

    (A) 17/5   (B) 23/5   (C) 15/4   (D) 20/3

2. $5\frac{2}{3}$

    (A) 19/3   (B) 17/3   (C) 13/2   (D) 11/3

OPERATIONS WITH FRACTIONS

EXAMPLE 1

Add 2/3 and 5/7.

ANALYSIS

Change both fractions to the common denominator, 21, and then add.

WORK

$$\frac{2}{3} = \frac{14}{21}$$

$$+\frac{5}{7} = \frac{15}{21}$$

$$\overline{\quad\quad\quad\quad}$$

$$\frac{29}{21} = 1\frac{8}{21}$$

ANSWER: $1\frac{8}{21}$

EXAMPLE 2

Simplify:
$$\frac{2 - \frac{2}{5}}{\frac{3}{4} + \frac{4}{5}}$$

ANALYSIS

Simplify the numerator and the denominator and then divide.

WORK

$$1 \quad \frac{5}{5}$$
$$\cancel{2}$$
$$- \frac{2}{5}$$
$$\overline{}$$
$$1\frac{3}{5} = \frac{8}{5}$$

$$\frac{3}{4} = \frac{15}{20}$$
$$+ \frac{4}{5} = \frac{16}{20}$$
$$\overline{}$$
$$\frac{31}{20}$$

$$\frac{8}{5} \div \frac{31}{20} = \frac{8}{\cancel{5}} \times \frac{\overset{4}{\cancel{20}}}{31} = \frac{32}{31} = 1\frac{1}{31}$$

ANSWER: $1\frac{1}{31}$

EXAMPLE 3

Pedro bought a candy bar that weighed $3\frac{3}{4}$ ounces. If he ate 2/3 of the bar, how many ounces did he eat?

ANALYSIS

Change $3\frac{3}{4}$ to an improper fraction and then multiply by 2/3.

WORK

$$3\frac{3}{4} = \frac{15}{4}$$

$$\frac{\overset{5}{\cancel{15}}}{\underset{2}{\cancel{4}}} \times \frac{\overset{1}{\cancel{2}}}{\underset{1}{\cancel{3}}} = \frac{5}{2} = 2\frac{1}{2}$$

ANSWER: $2\frac{1}{2}$ ounces

EXAMPLE 4

Simplify: $\dfrac{4}{5} \div 2\dfrac{2}{5}$

ANALYSIS

Change $2\dfrac{2}{5}$ to an improper fraction and invert. Then multiply $\dfrac{4}{5}$ by the result.

WORK

$$2\dfrac{2}{5} = \dfrac{12}{5}$$

$$\dfrac{4}{5} \div \dfrac{12}{5} = \overset{1}{\cancel{\dfrac{4}{\cancel{5}}}} \times \overset{1}{\cancel{\dfrac{\cancel{5}}{\cancel{12}}}} = \dfrac{1}{3}$$

ANSWER: $\dfrac{1}{3}$

PRACTICE (see answers on page 105)

1. Find $\dfrac{3}{4}$ of $\dfrac{1}{2}$ of 240.

   (A) 80   (B) 60   (C) 110   (D) 90

2. Add $2\dfrac{2}{3}, 3\dfrac{1}{4}$, and $\dfrac{5}{6}$.

   (A) $5\dfrac{1}{2}$ (B) $4\dfrac{3}{4}$ (C) $6\dfrac{3}{4}$ (D) $7\dfrac{2}{3}$

3. A beaker contains $12\dfrac{5}{8}$ ounces of alcohol. If $2\dfrac{3}{4}$ ounces is spilled out, how many ounces remain in the beaker?

   (A) $9\dfrac{7}{8}$ (B) $8\dfrac{5}{8}$ (C) $9\dfrac{5}{6}$ (D) $8\dfrac{1}{2}$

4. Simplify $\dfrac{5}{6} \div 2\dfrac{5}{12}$.

   (A) 12/17   (B) 10/29   (C) 11/19   (D) 9/16

5. Simplify:

$$\dfrac{2 + \dfrac{3}{4}}{1\dfrac{1}{4} - \dfrac{3}{8}}$$

   (A) $2\dfrac{3}{5}$ (B) $3\dfrac{1}{7}$ (C) $3\dfrac{5}{9}$ (D) $4\dfrac{2}{5}$

Decimals

Decimals are another form of fractions. The following list compares decimals with their equivalents in fraction format:

$$0.8 = 8/10$$
$$5.06 = 5 + 0/10 + 6/100$$
$$46.348 = 46 + 3/10 + 4/100 + 8/1,000$$
$$198.7039 = 198 + 7/10 + 0/100 + 3/1,000 + 9/10,000$$

READING DECIMALS

Number	In Words
16. 4	Sixteen and four tenths
234.05	Two hundred thirty-four and five hundredths
6.346	Six and three hundred forty-six thousandths
34.5078	Thirty-four and five thousand seventy-eight ten thousandths

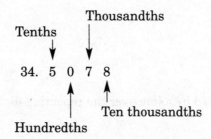

EXAMPLE

What does the digit 4 represent in the number 563.047?

WORK

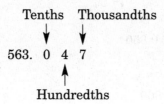

ANSWER: Hundredths

COMPARING DECIMALS AND FRACTIONS

EXAMPLE 1

Change 3/8 to a decimal.

ANALYSIS

Divide 3 by 8.

WORK

$$
8\overline{)3.000} \quad .375
$$

$$
\begin{array}{r}
.375 \\
8\overline{)3.000} \\
-24\text{xx} \\
\hline
60 \\
-56 \\
\hline
40 \\
-40 \\
\hline
\end{array}
$$

ANSWER: 0.375

EXAMPLE 2
Change 0.68 to a fraction.

ANALYSIS
Rewrite 0.68 as a fraction and reduce to lowest terms.

WORK

$$
0.68 = \frac{68}{100} = \frac{17}{25}
$$

ANSWER: 17/25

A repeating decimal is indicated by a line over the repeating digits.
For example,

$$
0.5555\ldots = 0.\overline{5}
$$
$$
3.464646\ldots = 3.\overline{46}
$$

PRACTICE (see answers on page 105)

1. Which decimal is the equivalent of 5/8?

   (A) 0.655   (B) 0.700   (C) 0.625   (D) 0.850

2. Which fraction is the equivalent of 0.78?

   (A) 7/8   (B) 39/50   (C) 7/100   (D) 7/800

3. Which decimal is the equivalent of 2/3?

   (A) 0.6   (B) 0.66   (C) 6.0   (D) 0.666

ROUNDING OFF DECIMALS

EXAMPLE
Round off the product of 3.46 and 2.03 to the nearest tenth.

ANALYSIS
Multiply first. Then look at the hundredth's place. If it's 5 or more, round up. If not, drop all the digits beyond the tenth place.

WORK

$$
\begin{array}{r}
3.46 \\
\times\ 2.03 \\
\hline
1038 \\
6920 \\
\hline
70238
\end{array}
$$

$7.0238 \approx 7.0$

↑

Hundredth's place

ANSWER: 7.0

PRACTICE (see answers on page 105)

1. Round off the sum of 25.06 and 67.43 to the nearest tenth.

   (A) 92.5　(B) 92.4　(C) 92.3　(D) 92.2

2. Round off the product of 8.53 and 0.9 to the nearest hundredth.

   (A) 7.6　(B) 7.681　(C) 7.67　(D) 7.68

OPERATIONS WITH DECIMALS

EXAMPLE 1
Add 4.593, 23.08, and 476.

ANALYSIS
Line up the decimals by adding zeroes as placeholders and then add.

WORK

$$
\begin{array}{r}
4.593 \\
23.080 \\
+\ 476.000 \\
\hline
503.673
\end{array}
$$

ANSWER: 503.673

EXAMPLE 2
Stephanie weighed a beaker filled with liquid. If the beaker and the liquid weighed 15.478 grams and she spilled out 6.9 grams of liquid, how much did the beaker plus the liquid weigh now?

ANALYSIS
Line up the decimals and subtract.

WORK

$$
\begin{array}{r}
15.478 \\
-\ 6.900 \\
\hline
8.578
\end{array}
$$

ANSWER: 8.578

EXAMPLE 3

Multiply 4.56 by 13.7 and round the answer off to the nearest tenth.

ANALYSIS

Add the number of decimal places in both numbers and then use the result to place the decimal in the answer.

WORK

$$
\begin{array}{r}
4.56 \\
\times\, 13.7 \\
\hline
3192 \\
1368 \\
456 \\
\hline
62.472 \approx 62.5
\end{array}
$$

ANSWER: 62.5

EXAMPLE 4

Divide 229.862 by 5.26.

ANALYSIS

$$
\begin{array}{l}
\text{Dividend} \rightarrow\ \dfrac{229.862}{5.26} = \text{Answer} \leftarrow \text{Quotient} \\
\text{Divisor} \rightarrow
\end{array}
$$

Count the number of decimal places in the divisor. Move the decimal place in the dividend the corresponding number of places and then divide.

WORK

$$
\begin{array}{r}
43.7 \\
5_\times 26.\overline{)229_\times 86.2} \\
210\ 4 \\
\hline
1946 \\
1578 \\
\hline
368\ \ 2 \\
368\ \ 2 \\
\hline
\end{array}
$$

$43.7 \times 5.26 = 229.862$ ✔

ANSWER: 43.7

PRACTICE (see answers on page 105)

1. Add 84.29, 234.752, and 45.

    (A) 364.84   (B) 366.839   (C) 364.04   (D) 364.042

2. Jaime packed 12 scales. If each scale weighed 15.73 ounces, what was the total weight of all the scales?

    (A) 188.736 ounces   (B) 188 ounces   (C) 188.76 ounces   (D) 188.754 ounces

3. Multiply 4.58 by 0.7 and round off to the nearest hundredth.

    (A) 3.206   (B) 3.23   (C) 3.208   (D) 3.21

4. Divide 2.0592 by 0.72 and round the answer to the nearest tenth.

    (A) 2.9   (B) 2.86   (C) 2.8   (D) 28.6

SCIENTIFIC NOTATION

Scientific notation is a compact way of writing a number as the product of another number between 1 and 10 and a power of 10.

$$768 = 7.68 \times 100 = 7.68 \times 10^2$$
$$5.04 \times 10^4 = 5.04 \times 10 \times 10 \times 10 \times 10 = 5.04 \times 10,000 = 50,400$$

EXAMPLE
Change 2.35×10^{-2} to its decimal equivalent.

ANALYSIS

$$10^{-1} = \frac{1}{10} \qquad 10^{-2} = \frac{1}{100} \qquad 10^{-3} = \frac{1}{1,000}$$

WORK

$$2.35 \times 10^{-2} = 2.35 \times \frac{1}{100} = \frac{2.35}{100} = 0.0235$$

ANSWER: 0.0235

PRACTICE (see answers on page 105)

1. Change 4.05×10^3 to a whole number.

    (A) 40.5   (B) 405   (C) 4,050   (D) 40,500

2. Change 6941 to scientific notation.

    (A) 69.41×10^4 (B) 6.941×10^2 (C) 69.41×10^3 (D) 6.941×10^3

Percents

Fractions, decimals, and percents are all different methods of indicating a part of a whole unit.

CHANGING FRACTIONS AND WHOLE NUMBERS TO PERCENTS

EXAMPLE 1
Change 4/9 to a two-place percent.

ANALYSIS
Divide 9 into 4.000. Round off to two decimal places. Finally, when changing from a decimal to a percent, multiply by 100 or move the decimal over two places to the right.

WORK

$$.444 \approx 0.44 = 44\%$$

```
       .4 4 4
    9)4.0 0 0
      3 6 x x
        4 0
        3 6
        ────
          4 0
          3 6
          ────
```

ANSWER: 44%

PRACTICE (see answers on page 105)

1. Change 6/7 to a two-place decimal.

   (A) 0.86   (B) 0.87   (C) 87%   (D) 0.89

2. Change 3/11 to a percent. Choose the best answer.

   (A) 28%   (B) 29%   (C) 0.27   (D) 27%

CHANGING PERCENTS TO FRACTIONS

EXAMPLE

Change 45% to a fraction and reduce to lowest terms.

WORK

$$45\% = \frac{45}{100} = \frac{9}{20}$$

ANSWER: 9/20

PRACTICE (see answer on page 105)

1. Change 68% to a fraction and reduce to lowest terms.

   (A) 17/25   (B) 68/100   (C) 4/50   (D) 19/100

CHANGING DECIMALS TO PERCENTS

EXAMPLE

Change 2.33 to a percent.

ANALYSIS

To change from a decimal to a percent, multiply by 100 or move the decimal two places to the right.

WORK

$$2.33 = 233\%$$

ANSWER: 233%

PRACTICE (see answer on page 105)

1. Change 68.5 to a percent.

    (A) 0.685%   (B) 6.85%   (C) 6850%   (D) 68.5%

CHANGING PERCENTS TO DECIMALS

EXAMPLE
Change 7.32% to a decimal.

ANALYSIS
To change from a percent to a decimal, divide by 100 or move the decimal two places to the left.

WORK

7.32% = 0.0732

ANSWER: 0.0732

PRACTICE (see answer on page 105)

1. Change 46.3% to a decimal.

    (A) 463   (B) 4.63   (C) 46.3   (D) 0.463

FINDING A PERCENT OF A NUMBER

EXAMPLE
Find 7% of 430. Round off the answer to the nearest whole number.

ANALYSIS
Change 7% to a decimal and multiply.

WORK

$$7\% = 0.07$$
$$0.07 \times 430 = 30.1$$
$$30.1 \approx 30$$

ANSWER: 30

Certain percentages easily convert to fractions:

$$12\frac{1}{2}\% = \frac{1}{8}$$
$$16\frac{2}{3}\% = \frac{1}{6}$$
$$33\frac{1}{3}\% = \frac{1}{3}$$
$$66\frac{2}{3}\% = \frac{2}{3}$$

APPLICATIONS

EXAMPLE
If there were 300 people at a dinner and nearly 39% ordered fish, approximately how many ordered fish?

    (A) 200   (B) 150   (C) 120   (D) 110

ANALYSIS
Change 39% to a decimal and multiply by 300. Then choose the closest answer.

WORK

$$39\% = 0.39$$
$$0.39 \times 300 = 117$$
$$117 \approx 120$$

ANSWER: (C)

PRACTICE (see answer on page 105)

1. Out of a sample of 450 people, 8% were vegetarians. How many were vegetarians?

    (A) 36   (B) 44   (C) 28   (D) 52

Algebra

Algebra is distinguished from arithmetic in its use of variables.

    A **variable** is any letter or symbol used to represent information and it derives its name from the fact that its value may change or vary.

    A number, on the other hand, is called a **constant** because its value never changes.

    In the algebraic expression $a + 6$, a is the variable and 6 is the constant.

EXAMPLE
Find the value of the expression $a + 6$ when $a = 8$.

ANALYSIS
Substitute 8 for a in the expression $a + 6$.

WORK

$$a = 8: \qquad a + 6$$
$$8 + 6$$
$$14$$

ANSWER: 14

PRACTICE (see answers on page 105)

Find the value of the following expressions when $b = 5$.

1. $4b - 7$

    (A) 10   (B) 12   (C) 13   (D) 15

2. $2b^3 + 8$

   (A) 198   (B) 212   (C) 286   (D) 258

ARITHMETIC OPERATIONS WITH SIGNED NUMBERS

Rules for Addition

i. If the signs of the addends are the same, add the numbers and use that sign.

$$
\begin{array}{r}
(+3) \\
+\,(+4) \\
\hline
+7
\end{array}
\qquad\qquad
\begin{array}{r}
(-2) \\
+\,(-4) \\
\hline
-6
\end{array}
$$

ii. If the signs of the addends are different, subtract and use the sign of the larger.

$$
\begin{array}{r}
+\,(+6) \\
+\,(-3) \\
\hline
+3
\end{array}
\qquad\qquad
\begin{array}{r}
(+2) \\
+\,(-4) \\
\hline
-2
\end{array}
$$

Rules for Subtraction

Change the sign of the subtrahend (the quantity to be subtracted) and use the rules of addition:

$$
\begin{array}{r}
+\ 6 \\
-\ \oplus\ 2 \\
\hline
+\ 4
\end{array}
\qquad
\begin{array}{r}
-\ 7 \\
+ \\
-\ \ominus\ 3 \\
\hline
-\ 4
\end{array}
\qquad
\begin{array}{r}
+\ 3 \\
+ \\
-\ \ominus\ 4 \\
\hline
+\ 7
\end{array}
\qquad
\begin{array}{r}
-\ 2 \\
- \\
-\ \oplus\ 6 \\
\hline
-\ 8
\end{array}
$$

Rules for Multiplication

i. If the signs of the factors are the same, the product is positive.

$$(+3)(+4) = +12 \qquad\qquad (-2)(-9) = +18$$

ii. If the signs of the factors are different, the product is negative.

$$(-4)(+6) = -24 \qquad\qquad (+7)(-3) = -21$$

Rules for Division

i. If the signs of the dividend and divisor are the same, the quotient is positive.

$$\frac{+8}{+2} = +4 \qquad\qquad \frac{-10}{-5} = +2$$

ii. If the signs of the dividend and divisor are different, the quotient is negative.

$$\frac{+6}{-2} = -3 \qquad\qquad \frac{-9}{+3} = -3$$

EXAMPLE 1
The average weight of a student on the soccer team is 159 pounds. Find Ruben's weight if the signed numbers represent pounds above (+) and below (−) the average weight.

Deviation from average weight	+11	−12	+15	−2	+4
Name	Jaime	Ruben	Clotilde	Oscar	Mary

ANALYSIS
Ruben is 12 pounds below the average weight, 159.

WORK

$$\begin{array}{r} +159 \\ -\ 12 \\ \hline 147 \end{array}$$

ANSWER: 147 pounds

EXAMPLE 2
Subtract: $\begin{array}{r}(+34) \\ -(+89) \\ \hline\end{array}$

ANALYSIS
Change the sign of the subtrahend and use the rules of addition.

WORK

$$\left.\begin{array}{r} +\ 34 \\ - \\ -\ \oplus\ 89 \\ \hline -\ 55 \end{array}\right\} +34 - 89 = -55$$

ANSWER: −55

EXAMPLE 3
Multiply: (−3)(+4)(−2)(−4)

ANALYSIS
Multiply the integers, and then count the number of negatives. An odd number of negatives will result in a negative answer, while an even number of negatives will result in a positive answer.

WORK

$$(-3)(+4)(-2)(-4)$$
$$(-12)(+8) = -96$$

ANSWER: −96

EXAMPLE 4
Divide −112 by −8.

ANALYSIS
When the signs of both the dividend and divisor are the same, the quotient is positive.

WORK

$$\frac{-112}{-8} = +14$$

ANSWER: +14

PRACTICE (see answers on page 105)

1. Subtract –47 from +18.

    (A) 65   (B) 29   (C) –65   (D) –29

2. Multiply: (+3)(–2)(–1)(+4).

    (A) –24   (B) –12   (C) +24   (D) +12

3. Divide 1.75 by –0.7.

    (A) 2.5   (B) –2.5   (C) 0.25   (D) –0.25

FORMULAS

A formula links together variables and constants in some sort of relationship. Given certain information, we can go on to find the value of an unknown quantity in the relationship.

In the United States and in English-speaking countries, temperature is generally measured on the Fahrenheit scale. The rest of the world measures heat in Celsius (or Centigrade). The Swedish astronomer Anders Celsius developed the Celsius scale. It actually makes more sense than the Fahrenheit scale because there are 100 degrees between the freezing point of water (measured at standard atmospheric pressure) at 0° Celsius and its boiling point at 100° Celsius. The German physicist Gabriel Fahrenheit devised the Fahrenheit scale in which the freezing point of water (also at standard atmospheric pressure) is 32° Fahrenheit while its boiling point is 212° Fahrenheit.

We frequently want to convert from one scale to another, so we need a convenient formula to help us with the conversion.

EXAMPLE

The formula C = (5/9)(F – 32) shows us the relationship between Celsius and Fahrenheit and allows us to change from one scale to another. Change 113° Fahrenheit to Celsius.

ANALYSIS

Let F = the Fahrenheit temperature.
Let C = the Celsius temperature.
We'll use the formula and simply substitute 113 for F.

WORK

	C = (5/9)(F – 32)
F = 113:	C = (5/9)(113 – 32)
	C = (5/9)(81)
	C = 45

ANSWER: 45° Celsius

PRACTICE (see answer on page 105)

1. Use the formula C = (5/9)(F − 32) to change 140° Fahrenheit to Celsius.

   (A) 36°C   (B) 60°C   (C) 45°C   (D) 81°C

EQUATIONS

EXAMPLE

Find the value of x in the equation $5x + 12 = 47$.

ANALYSIS

Subtract 12 from both sides of the equation and then divide by 5.

WORK

$$5x + 12 = 47$$
$$-12 = -12$$
$$5x = 35$$

$$\frac{5x}{5} = \frac{35}{5}$$

$$x = 7$$

ANSWER: 7

PRACTICE (see answer on page 105)

1. Find the value of x in the equation $3x − 8 = 19$.

   (A) 8   (B) 9   (C) 6   (D) 7

SIMPLIFYING EXPONENTIAL EXPRESSIONS

Occasionally we can simplify exponential expressions. For example, $3^4 \cdot 3^6 =$
$(3 \cdot 3 \cdot 3 \cdot 3)(3 \cdot 3 \cdot 3 \cdot 3 \cdot 3 \cdot 3) = 3 \cdot 3 \cdot 3 \cdot 3 \cdot 3 \cdot 3 \cdot 3 \cdot 3 \cdot 3 \cdot 3 = 3^{10}$

We can see if we multiply powers with the same base, we simply add the exponents.
What happens when we divide powers with the same base?

$$\frac{7^8}{7^5} = \frac{\overset{1}{7} \cdot \overset{1}{7} \cdot \overset{1}{7} \cdot \overset{1}{\cancel{7}} \cdot \overset{1}{\cancel{7}} \cdot \overset{1}{\cancel{7}} \cdot \overset{1}{\cancel{7}} \cdot \overset{1}{\cancel{7}}}{\underset{1}{\cancel{7}} \cdot \underset{1}{\cancel{7}} \cdot \underset{1}{\cancel{7}} \cdot \underset{1}{\cancel{7}} \cdot \underset{1}{\cancel{7}}} = 7^3$$

If we divide powers with the same base, we subtract exponents.
Let's see what happens when we divide a power by itself.

$$\frac{4^{35}}{4^{35}} = 4^{35-35} = 4^0$$

Any time a number is divided by itself, the quotient is 1, so

$$\frac{4^{35}}{4^{35}} = \boxed{4^0 = 1}$$

A base raised to a zero exponent simplifies to 1.

EXAMPLE
Find the value of $\dfrac{8^7 \cdot 6^9 \cdot 5^0}{8^5 \cdot 6^8}$

ANALYSIS
$5^0 = 1$. Whenever we divide powers with the same base, we subtract exponents.

WORK

$$\frac{8^7 \cdot 6^9 \cdot 5^0}{8^5 \cdot 6^8} = \frac{\overset{8^2 \cdot 6^1 \cdot 1}{\cancel{8^7} \cdot \cancel{6^9} \cdot \cancel{5^0}}}{\underset{1 \cdot 1}{\cancel{8^5} \cdot \cancel{6^8}}} = 8^2 \cdot 6^1 = 64 \cdot 6 = 384$$

PRACTICE (see answer on page 105)

1. Simplify the following expression.

$$\frac{9^4 \cdot 6^3}{9^3 \cdot 6}$$

(A) 54   (B) 486   (C) 1,816   (D) 324

ROOTS AND RADICALS

Let's find the square root of 25.

$$\sqrt{25} = 5$$

or

The index is 2. ──→ ←── The radical is $\sqrt{25}$.

$$\sqrt[2]{25} = 5$$

The radicand is 25.   The radical sign is $\sqrt{}$.

When no index appears, 2 is understood to be the index.

There are actually two square roots of 25:

$(+5)(+5) = 25$

$(-5)(-5) = 25$

We indicate a positive and a negative square root in the following manner:

$$\pm\sqrt{25} = \pm 5$$

When we want the **positive square root** of a number, we call it the **principal square root**:

$$\sqrt{25} = +5$$

The negative square root is indicated by placing a negative sign in front of the radical:

$$-\sqrt{25} = -5$$

SIMPLIFYING RADICALS

EXAMPLE 1
Simplify $\sqrt{b^8}$.

ANALYSIS
We want to find a particular monomial which, when multiplied by itself, results in b^8.

WORK
$$\sqrt{b^8} = b^4$$
$$b^4 \cdot b^4 = b^8$$

ANSWER: b^4

EXAMPLE 2
Simplify $\sqrt{50}$.

ANALYSIS
Try to write 50 as the product of a square and another number and then simplify the result.

WORK
$$\sqrt{50} = \sqrt{25 \cdot 2} = \sqrt{25} \cdot \sqrt{2} = 5\sqrt{2}$$

PRACTICE (see answers on page 105)

1. Simplify $\sqrt{c^{12}}$.
   (A) c^3 (B) c^6 (C) c^4 (D) $6c^2$

2. Simplify $\sqrt{98}$.
   (A) $6\sqrt{3}$ (B) $5\sqrt{3}$ (C) $4\sqrt{5}$ (D) $7\sqrt{2}$

OPERATIONS WITH RADICALS

We can perform the basic arithmetic operations of addition, subtraction, multiplication, and division on radicals.

$$13\sqrt{7} - 4\sqrt{7} = 9\sqrt{7}$$
$$12\sqrt{6} - 17\sqrt{6} = -5\sqrt{6}$$
$$5\sqrt{b} \cdot 3\sqrt{c} = 15\sqrt{bc}$$

PRACTICE (see answers on page 105)
Simplify the following radical expressions.

1. $5\sqrt{7} - 2\sqrt{7} + 6\sqrt{7}$
   (A) $11\sqrt{7}$ (B) $10\sqrt{7}$ (C) $13\sqrt{7}$ (D) $9\sqrt{7}$

2. $8\sqrt{2} \cdot 3\sqrt{2}$

(A) $24\sqrt{2}$ (B) $48\sqrt{2}$ (C) 48   (D) 4

INEQUALITIES

The following examples illustrate the inequality symbols:

Illustration	Translation
$6 > 3$	6 is greater than 3
$9 < 12$	9 is less than 12
$-3 \geq -4$	−3 is greater than or equal to −4
$0 \leq 0$	0 is less than or equal to 0

PRACTICE (see answer on page 105)

1. Which of the following statements is true?

(A) $4 < -5$ and $9 > 3$
(B) $7 \geq -2$ and $6 < -5$
(C) $12 \leq 19$ or $-5 > 0$
(D) $-9 > -8$ or $7 < 0$

OPERATIONS WITH MONOMIALS AND POLYNOMIALS

EXAMPLE 1

Simplify $+4t - 5t + 9t - 3t$.

ANALYSIS

Perform the additions and subtractions separately and then combine terms.

WORK

$$+4t + 9t = +13t$$
$$-5t - 3t = -8t$$
$$+13t - 8t = +5t$$

ANSWER: $+5t$

EXAMPLE 2

Subtract $2a - 4$ from $-3b - 6$.

ANALYSIS

Change the signs of the subtrahend and then add.

WORK

$-3b$	-6	(minuend)
$-$	$+$	
$-\oplus 2a$	$\ominus 4$	(subtrahend)
$-5a$	-2	(difference)

ANSWER: $-5a - 2$

EXAMPLE 3
Find the product of $4t^5$ and $-6t^3$.

ANALYSIS
Multiply the coefficients and add the exponents.

WORK
$$(4t^5) \cdot (-6t^3) = (4)(-6)(t^5)(t^3) = -24t^8$$

ANSWER: $-24t^8$

EXAMPLE 4
Find the quotient of $24g^7 - 18g^5$ and $-6g^4$.

ANALYSIS
Divide the coefficients and subtract the exponents.

WORK
$$\frac{24g^7 - 18g^5}{-6g^4} = \frac{24g^7}{-6g^4} - \frac{18g^5}{-6g^4} = -4g^3 + 3g$$

ANSWER: $-4g^3 + 3g$

PRACTICE (see answers on page 105)

1. Simplify: $-3g - 4h + 8g - 3h$

   (A) $4g + 7h$ (B) $-5g - 11h$ (C) $5g - 7h$ (D) $11g + 7h$

2. Subtract $8t - 4z$ from $-5t - 8z$.

   (A) $-13t - 4z$ (B) $13t + 4z$ (C) $-3t - 4z$ (D) $3t - 12z$

3. Find the product of $5a^3$ and $4a^7$.

   (A) $20a^{21}$ (B) $15a^{10}$ (C) $20a^{10}$ (D) $35a^{21}$

4. Find the quotient of $18r^6 - 12r^7$ and $-6r^5$.

   (A) $3r - 2r^2$ (B) $-3r - 2$ (C) $3r - 2r^2$ (D) $-3r + 2r^2$

ABSOLUTE VALUE

The absolute value of a number, x, is defined as
$$|x| = \sqrt{x^2}$$

For example,
$$|-3| = \sqrt{(-3)^2} = \sqrt{9} = 3$$

$$|4| = \sqrt{4^2} = \sqrt{16} = 4$$

More practically, the absolute value of any number is its distance from the origin (disregard direction).

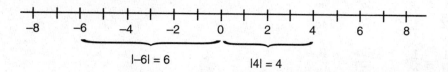

$$|-6| = 6 \qquad |4| = 4$$

EXAMPLE
Simplify $5|-6|$

ANALYSIS
Remove the absolute value sign and multiply by 5.

WORK

$$5|-6| = 5\,(6) = 30$$

ANSWER: 30

PRACTICE (see answers on page 105)

Simplify the following expressions:

1. $6|-4| + 4\,|7|$

   (A) –24   (B) +4   (C) 52   (D) –4

2. $7\,|7| - 3\,|-2|$

   (A) 55   (B) 45   (C) 27   (D) 43

RATIOS AND PROPORTIONS

The odds of a new business remaining open more than a year are 1 out of 3. What does this mean?

It means that only 1/3 of all new enterprises will remain in business longer than a year, while 2/3 will close within the year.

1/3 is a ratio that also may be expressed as 1:3.

The ratio $a{:}b$ may be expressed as the fraction a/b.

The ratio 9:27 may be reduced:

$$\frac{9}{27} = \frac{1}{3}$$

If two ratios are equal, we have a proportion:

$$\frac{a}{b} = \frac{c}{d} \quad \text{or} \quad a{:}b = c{:}d$$

$a, b, c,$ and d are called the first, second, third, and fourth terms, respectively.

The two outer terms are called the extremes, while the two inner terms are called the means.

Means
$$a : b = c : d$$
Extremes

EXAMPLE 1

Do these ratios form a proportion?

$$\frac{4}{12} \overset{?}{=} \frac{5}{15} \qquad \frac{3a^2}{7a} \overset{?}{=} \frac{6a}{14a^2}$$

$$\frac{1}{3} = \frac{1}{3} \qquad \frac{3a}{7} = \frac{3}{7a}$$

Yes!   No

In a proportion, the product of the means equals the product of the extremes. In the proportion $a : b = c : d$, $bc = ad$

EXAMPLE 2

Find the fourth term in the proportion $2{:}7 = 12{:}x$.

ANALYSIS

The product of the means equals the product of the extremes.

WORK

$$2 : 7 = 12 : x$$
$$2x = 84$$
$$x = 42$$

ANSWER: 42

PRACTICE (see answer on page 105)

1. Find the fourth term in the proportion $7 : 9 = 21 : x$.

   (A) 21   (B) 18   (C) 27   (D) 36

CONSECUTIVE INTEGERS

Consecutive integers are integers that follow one another:

   1, 2, 3, . . .
   22, 23, 24, . . .
   75, 76, 77, . . .
   −4, −3, −2, . . .

If we let x represent an integer, $x + 1$ represents the next consecutive integer, $x + 2$ the integer after that, and so forth:

   $x, x + 1, x + 2, \ldots$

Consecutive even integers are even integers that follow one another:

   2, 4, 6, . . .
   18, 20, 22, . . .
   62, 64, 66, . . .
   −8, −6, −4, . . .

We have to add 2 to the first even integer to get to the next consecutive even integer.

$$8$$
$$8 + 2 = 10$$
$$10 + 2 = 12$$

If n represents the first even integer, $n + 2$ represents the next consecutive even integer, $n + 4$ the even integer after that, and so forth:

$$n, n + 2, n + 4, \ldots$$

If $n + 1$ represents the first even integer, $(n + 1) + 2$ and $(n + 2) + 4$ represent the next two consecutive even integers.

$$(n + 1), (n + 1) + 2, (n + 1) + 4, \ldots$$

Consecutive odd integers are odd integers that follow one another:

$$5, 7, 9, \ldots$$
$$13, 15, 17, \ldots$$
$$79, 81, 83, \ldots$$
$$-11, -9, -7, \ldots$$

Just as with even integers, we have to add 2 to the first odd integer in order to get to the next consecutive odd integer.

$$5$$
$$5 + 2 = 7$$
$$7 + 2 = 9$$

If $x - 4$ represents the first odd integer, $(x - 4) + 2$ represents the next consecutive odd integer, $(x - 4) + 4$ represents the odd integer after that, and so forth.

$$(x - 4), (x - 4) + 2, (x - 4) + 4, \ldots$$

EXAMPLE 1

Find two consecutive integers whose sum is 71.

ANALYSIS

Let x = the first integer, and let $x + 1$ = the next consecutive integer. The sum is 71.

WORK

$$x + (x + 1) = 71$$
$$x + x + 1 = 71$$
$$2x + 1 = 71$$

Subtract 1: $\qquad\qquad 2x = 70$

Divide by 2: $\qquad\qquad x = 35$

$$x + 1 = 36$$
$$35 + 36 = 71 \ ✔$$

ANSWER: 35, 36

EXAMPLE 2

Find two consecutive even integers whose sum is 86.

ANALYSIS

Let x = the first even integer, and let $x + 2$ = the next consecutive even integer. The sum is 86.

WORK

$$x + (x + 2) = 86$$
$$2x + 2 = 86$$

Subtract 2: $\qquad\qquad 2x = 84$
Divide by 2: $\qquad\qquad\;\; x = 42$
$$x + 2 = 44$$
$$x + (x + 2) = 86$$
$$42 + 44 = 86 \;\checkmark$$

ANSWER: 42, 44

PRACTICE (see answers on page 105)

1. Find the largest of three consecutive integers whose sum is 231.

    (A) 79   (B) 83   (C) 80   (D) 78

2. What is the smaller of two consecutive even integers that add up to 70?

    (A) 32   (B) 36   (C) 34   (D) 38

3. Find the second of three consecutive odd integers whose sum is 141.

    (A) 45   (B) 47   (C) 51   (D) 49

Plane Geometry

POINTS

Points have no specific size or shape. Points are usually named with capital letters and are used to position objects and lines.

LINES

Lines, like points, have no specific width but they extend infinitely in opposite directions.

Line $\overleftrightarrow{AB}$ or $\overleftrightarrow{BA}$

Intersecting Lines

Lines $\overleftrightarrow{RS}$ and $\overleftrightarrow{TU}$ intersect at point V. Both lines are in the same plane.

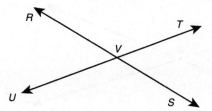

Line Segments

Line segments, unlike lines, have a definite length and may be measured.

Line segment AB or $\overline{AB}$.

Rays

Rays are parts of lines that extend from one endpoint indefinitely in one direction.

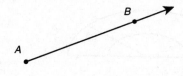

Ray AB or $\overrightarrow{AB}$

PLANES

Planes are composed of an infinite set of points on a flat surface. Planes extend infinitely in all directions. The picture below is only a section of the entire plane.

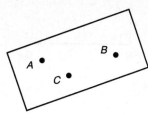

Plane ABC is indicated by three points on the plane. The three points are not located on the same line.

ANGLES

If two rays meet at a point, they form an **angle** at the point of intersection, called the vertex.

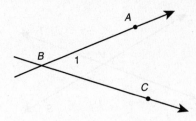

The angle thus formed may be designated in a number of different ways:

    i. ∠*ABC*
   ii. ∠*CBA*
  iii. ∠1

PRACTICE (see answer on page 105)

  1. What is another name for ∠*DEF*?

    (A) ∠*D*   (B) ∠*DFE*   (C) ∠*E*   (D) ∠*FDE*

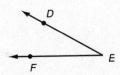

A protractor is used to measure the number of degrees in an angle. In the figure below, for example, the protractor measures an angle of 29°.

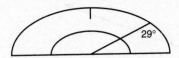

Right Angles

Right angles measure 90°. In this case, *AB* is perpendicular to *BC*. Symbolically, $AB \perp BC$.

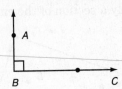

Acute Angles

Acute angles measure less than 90°.

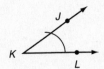

Obtuse Angles

Obtuse angles measure more than 90° but less than 180°.

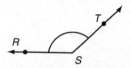

Straight Angles

Straight angles measure 180°. The two adjoining sides, *IH* and *IJ*, extend in opposite directions and form a straight line.

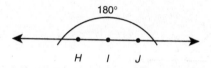

Reflex Angles

Reflex angles measure more than 180° but less than 360°.

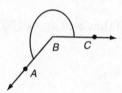

PRACTICE (see answers on page 105)

1. What is another name for ∠1?

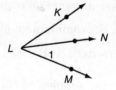

    (A) ∠*L*   (B) ∠*NLM*   (C) ∠*KLN*   (D) ∠*NLK*

2. What sort of angle is illustrated on the right?

    (A) right   (B) acute   (C) obtuse   (D) reflex

Complementary Angles

Two angles are **complementary** if their sum is 90°.
In the diagram at the right, m∠*a* + m∠*b* = 90°.

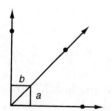

EXAMPLE

Find the complement of 24°.

ANALYSIS

Complementary angles add up to 90°.

WORK

90 − 24 = 66

ANSWER: 66°

Supplementary Angles

Supplementary angles are two angles that add up to 180°.

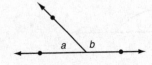

$$m\angle a + m\angle b = 180°$$

EXAMPLE

Find the supplement of 47°.

ANALYSIS

Supplementary angles are two angles that add up to 180°.

WORK

180 − 47 = 133

ANSWER: 133°

PRACTICE (see answers on page 105)

1. What is the complement of $(3x)°$?

   (A) $(180 − 3x)°$ (B) $(90 − 3x)°$ (C) $5x°$ (D) $(100 − 3x)°$

2. What is the supplement of $(9b)°$?

   (A) $(100 + 9b)°$ (B) $(180 − 9b)°$ (C) $(90 − 9b)°$ (D) $(100 − 9b)°$

Adjacent Angles

If two angles share a common side as well as a common vertex, they are known as **adjacent angles**.

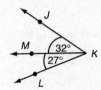

Angle *JKM* and angle *MKL* are adjacent angles because they share common side, *KM*, and a common vertex, *K*.

EXAMPLE
Add the two adjacent angles.

WORK

$$
\begin{array}{r}
32° \\
+\ 27° \\
\hline
59°
\end{array}
$$

ANSWER: 59°

PRACTICE (see answer on page 105)

1. Find the measure of ∠*a*.

(A) 101°   (B) 47°   (C) 106°   (D) 53°

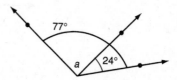

Vertical Angles

If two straight lines intersect, they form four angles. As we can clearly see, there are a number of adjacent angles:

∠1 and ∠3 are adjacent angles
∠3 and ∠4 are adjacent angles
∠2 and ∠4 are adjacent angles
∠1 and ∠2 are adjacent angles

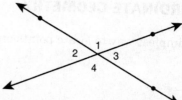

We also have two sets of angles that are opposite each other, called **vertical angles**, and their measures are equal:

$$m\angle 1 = m\angle 4 \quad \text{and} \quad m\angle 2 = m\angle 3$$

If the measures of two angles are equal, the angles are called congruent.

EXAMPLE
Find the value of *x*.

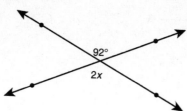

ANALYSIS
Since the angles represented by 2*x* and 92° are vertical angles, their measures are equal.

WORK

$$
\begin{array}{r}
2x = 92 \\
x = 46
\end{array}
$$

ANSWER: 46°

PERPENDICULAR LINES

Perpendicular lines intersect in the same plane and form right angles (90°).

$AB \perp CD$

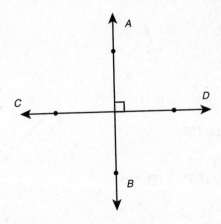

COORDINATE GEOMETRY

The simplest way to locate points on a plane (flat surface) is to use a graph.

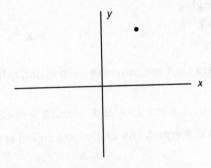

The horizontal axis is called the *x*-axis or abscissa.

_____ x

The vertical axis is called the *y*-axis or ordinate.

|
| y
|
|
|
|
|

The point of intersection of the two major axes is called the **origin**.

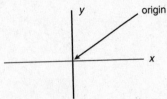

The integers on the major axes locate points on the plane.
   For example, the ordered pair (4,3) is located 4 units to the right and 3 units above the origin.

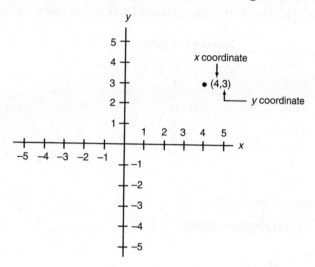

The first digit of the ordered pair indicates a move to the right (+) or left (−) and the second digit indicates a move up (+) or down (−).

PRACTICE (see answers on page 106)

1. Name the coordinates of point A.

    (A) (−2, 2)
    (B) (−2, 3)
    (C) (2, −2)
    (D) (2, 2)

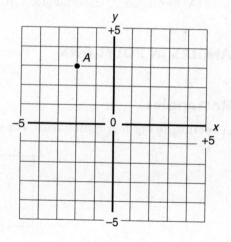

2. Which of the following points lies below the line $y = 1$ and to the right of the line $x = 0$?

    (A) D   (B) B   (C) C   (D) A

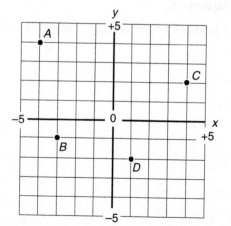

Polygons

A **polygon** is a plane (flat) figure totally enclosed by three or more straight lines.

Name of polygon	Number of sides
Triangle	3
Quadrilateral	4
Pentagon	5
Hexagon	6
Heptagon	7
Octagon	8
Nonagon	9
Decagon	10

PRACTICE (see answers on page 106)

What do we call the following plane figures?

1. A six-sided figure

   (A) octagon   (B) pentagon   (C) hexagon   (D) decagon

2. An eight-sided figure

   (A) heptagon   (B) triangle   (C) nonagon   (D) octagon

ANGLES IN POLYGONS

Rectangles

A **rectangle** has four right angles. The sum of the measures of the angles of a rectangle is 360°.

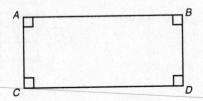

Squares

A **square** has four right angles. The sum of the measures of the angles of a square is 360°.

Parallelograms

The sum of the measures of the angles of a **parallelogram** is 360°. Opposite angles are congruent: $\angle A \cong \angle C$, $\angle B \cong \angle D$. Two successive angles are supplementary:

$$m\angle A + m\angle B = 180°$$
$$m\angle C + m\angle D = 180°$$

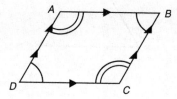

PRACTICE (see answers on page 106)

1. What is the sum of the angles in a rectangle?

    (A) 180°   (B) 360°   (C) 270°   (D) 90°

2. In parallelogram *ABCD*, if the measure of angle *A* is 123°, find the measure of angle *B*.

    (A) 123°   (B) 246°   (C) 57°   (D) 114°

Triangles

Sum of the Angles in a Triangle

The measure of angle *A* + the measure of angle *B* + the measure of angle *C* = 180°.

$$m\angle A + m\angle B + m\angle C = 180°$$

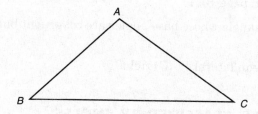

Isosceles Triangle

In an **isosceles triangle**, the base angles are congruent.

$$\angle B \cong \angle C$$

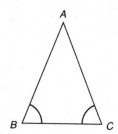

Equilateral Triangle
In an **equilateral triangle**, all the angles are congruent.

$$\angle A \cong \angle B \cong \angle C$$

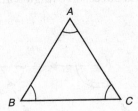

Right Triangle
In a **right triangle**, one angle is a right angle:

$$m\angle C = 90°$$

The other two angles are complementary:

$$m\angle A + m\angle B = 90°$$

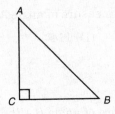

PRACTICE (see answer on page 106)

1. Select the type of triangle whose base angles are congruent but whose vertex angle is different.

    (A) isosceles   (B) equilateral   (C) right

TYPES OF TRIANGLES, CLASSIFIED BY ANGLES

Acute

Three acute angles

Right

One 90° angle

Obtuse

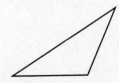

One obtuse angle

Equiangular

Three angles of equal measure

PRACTICE (see answer on page 106)

1. What do we call a triangle with three equal angles?

(A) right triangle (B) obtuse triangle
(C) isosceles triangle (D) equiangular triangle

TYPES OF TRIANGLES, CLASSIFIED BY SIDES

Isosceles

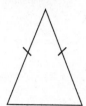

Two sides of equal length

Equilateral

Three sides of equal length

Scalene

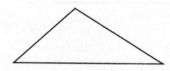

No sides of equal length

PERIMETERS

By definition, the **perimeter** (P) of a polygon is equal to the sum of its sides.

Rectangles

The perimeter of a rectangle is equal to the sum of its sides.

$$P = b + b + h + h = 2b + 2h$$

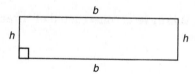

PRACTICE (see answer on page 106)

1. If the perimeter of a rectangle is 42″ and is width is 6″, find its length.

(A) 8″ (B) 12″ (C) 14″ (D) 15″

Squares

The perimeter of a **square** is equal to the sum of its sides.

$$P = s + s + s + s = 4s$$

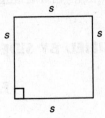

Triangles

The perimeter of a **triangle** is equal to the sum of its sides.

$$P = a + b + c$$

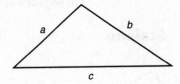

Isosceles Triangles

In an **isosceles triangle**, two of the sides are equal.

$$P = a + a + b = 2a + b$$

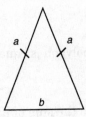

Equilateral Triangles

By definition, an **equilateral triangle** is constructed of three equal sides and the perimeter is the sum of those three sides.

$$P = s + s + s = 3s$$

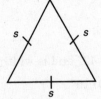

PRACTICE (see answers on page 106)

1. If the each of the congruent sides of an isosceles triangle is 11″ and the base is 4.6″, find the perimeter of the triangle.

   (A) 13.8″   (B) 37.6″   (C) 20.2″   (D) 26.6″

2. If the perimeter of an isosceles triangle is 45.9″ and one of the congruent sides is 8.6″, find the base of the triangle.

   (A) 37.3   (B) 28.7   (C) 35.6   (D) 27.4

3. Find one side of an equilateral triangle if its perimeter is 8.

   (A) 2 2/3   (B) 3 1/3   (C) 2.5   (D) 2.45

AREAS OF POLYGONS

Rectangles

The area (inside space of a rectangle, A, is determined by multiplying its base, b, by its height, h.

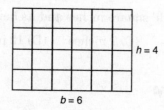

In the diagram, the base is 6, while the height is 4.

$A = bh$
$A = 6 \cdot 4 = 24$

Squares

All the sides of a square are equal, so, to find the area of a square, we multiply side, s, by side, s.
   On the right, both sides are 5.

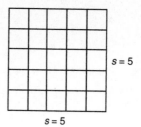

$A = s \cdot s = s^2$
$A = 5 \cdot 5 = 25$

Parallelograms

Area = Base × Height

$A = bh$
$A = 5 \cdot 4 = 20$

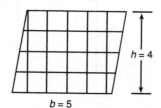

Triangles

$$\text{Area} = \left(\frac{1}{2}\right)\text{Base }(b) \times \text{Height }(h)$$

$$A = \left(\frac{1}{2}\right)bh$$

$$A = \left(\frac{1}{2}\right)(8 \times 4) = \left(\frac{1}{2}\right)32$$

$$A = 16$$

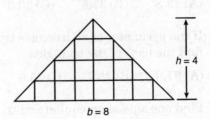

PRACTICE (see answers on page 106)

1. The area of a rectangle is 54. If its length is 12, find its width.

   (A) 3   (B) 4   (C) $4\frac{1}{2}$ (D) $5\frac{1}{2}$

2. If the base of a parallelogram is 24.3 and its height is 8, find the area.

   (A) 194.4   (B) 188.6   (C) 203.8   (D) 200.6

3. If the area of a triangle is 36 square inches and its height is 8 inches, find its base.

   (A) 8 inches   (B) 9 inches   (C) 7 inches   (D) 12 inches

PYTHAGOREAN THEOREM

The ancient Greek mathematician Pythagoras determined a relationship among the sides of a right triangle. He showed that if you erect squares on the sides of a right triangle, the sum of the areas of the two squares on the legs of the right triangle equals the area of the square erected on the hypotenuse of the right triangle.

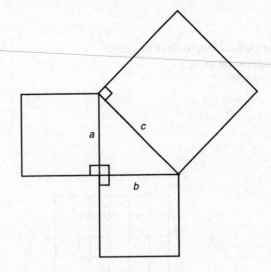

Pythagorean Theorem
$a^2 + b^2 = c^2$, where a and b are the legs, and c is the hypotenuse of the right triangle.

EXAMPLE
Find the hypotenuse of a right triangle whose two legs are 5 and 12.

ANALYSIS
Use the Pythagorean Theorem.

WORK
$a = 5, b = 12$:

$$a^2 + b^2 = c^2$$
$$5^2 + 12^2 = c^2$$
$$25 + 144 = c^2$$
$$169 = c^2$$

Take the square root of 169:

$$13 = c$$

ANSWER: 13

PRACTICE (see answer on page 106)

1. Find the hypotenuse of a right triangle if its two legs are 6 and 8.

    (A) 5   (B) 12   (C) 9   (D) 10

Circles

RADIUS AND DIAMETER

This is circle O, with center O. AB is the diameter and AO and BO are the two radii. As you can see, the diameter, AB, is twice the size of the radius, AO.

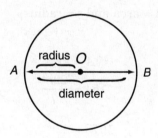

CIRCUMFERENCE

The **circumference** is the length of the line that demarcates the circle. The circumference, C, is equal to the product of 2, π, and the radius, r:

$$C = 2\pi r$$

EXAMPLE
Find the circumference of a circle whose diameter is 6. Round the answer to the nearest tenth.

ANALYSIS
Use the formula $C = 2\pi r$, where C = circumference and $\pi = 3.14$.

The radius is $\dfrac{1}{2}$ the length of the diameter.

WORK

$$r = \frac{1}{2} \cdot d = \frac{1}{2} \cdot 6 = 3$$

$$C = 2\pi r$$

$\pi = 3.14, r = 3:\quad C = 2 \times 3.14 \times 3 = 18.84 \approx 18.8$

ANSWER: 18.8

PRACTICE (see answer on page 106)

1. If the circumference of a circle is 31.4, find its radius. Use the formula $C = 2\pi r$, where C = circumference, $\pi = 3.14$, and r = radius.

    (A) 4   (B) 5   (C) 6   (D) 9

AREA

$A = \pi r^2$, where $\pi = 3.14$ and r = the radius.
In this case, $r = 3$, so

$$A = \pi r^2$$

$$A = (3.14)(3)^2 = 3.14\,(9)$$

$$A = 28.26$$

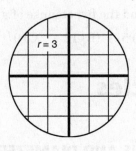

EXAMPLE

If the area of a circle is 154 square inches, find its radius. Let $\pi = 22/7$.

ANALYSIS

Use the formula $A = \pi r^2$, where A = area and r = radius.

WORK

$$A = \pi r^2$$

$A = 154, \pi = 22/7:\qquad\qquad 154 = \dfrac{22r^2}{7}$

Multiply by 7: $1078 = 22r^2$
Divide by 22: $49 = r^2$
Find the square root of 49: $r = \pm\, 7$

ANSWER: 7

PRACTICE (see answers on page 106)

1. Find the area of a circle whose radius is 8. Use the formula $A = \pi r^2$, where A = area, $\pi = 3.14$, and r = radius. Round the answer to the nearest tenth.

    (A) 199.9   (B) 200   (C) 201.0   (D) 200.9

2. If the area of a circle is 12.56, find its radius. Use the formula $A = \pi r^2$, where A = area, $\pi = 3.14$, and r = radius.

    (A) 3   (B) 4   (C) 5   (D) 2

CENTRAL ANGLES

A **central angle** of a circle has its vertex at the center of the circle.

EXAMPLE
If two central angles of a triangle are 40° and 80°, find the measure of the third central angle.

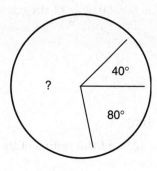

ANALYSIS
All of the central angles add up to 360°, so add up the two given angles and subtract the result from 360°.

WORK
$$x + 40 + 80 = 360$$
$$x + 120 = 360$$
Subtract 120: $$x = 240$$

ANSWER: 240°

PRACTICE (see answer on page 106)

1. If three central angles measure 65°, 87°, and 112°, respectively, find the measure of the fourth central angle.

    (A) 96°   (B) 104°   (C) 118°   (D) 76°

SECTORS

A **sector** of a circle is an area of the circle determined by the intersection of two radii and the circumference of the circle.

EXAMPLE
If the radius of the circle at the right is 4 and the central angle is 60°, find the area of the shaded sector. To simplify matters, let π = 3.

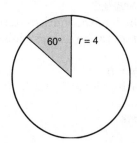

ANALYSIS
Find the area of the circle. Then determine the fraction of the entire circle the sector occupies.

WORK

Let A = area of the circle, r = radius.

$$A = \pi r^2$$

$\pi = 3, r = 4$: $\quad A = (3)(4)^2$

$$A = 3(16) = 48$$

There are 360° in the circle. 60° is 60/360 or $\dfrac{1}{6}$ of the circle.

$$\frac{1}{6} \times 48 = 8$$

ANSWER: 8

PRACTICE (see answer on page 106)

1. If a central angle measures 45° and the radius of its circle is 2, find the area of its sector. Let $\pi = 3$.

   (A) 2   (B) 1.5   (C) 3   (D) 2.5

Volumes

A great deal of present-day two- and three-dimensional geometry still depends upon the propositions developed by the Greek mathematician, Euclid. His most significant contribution to geometry is contained in his 13 books of the *Elements*. Next to the Bible, the *Elements* is probably the most widely distributed and studied book in the world. The first four books cover plane geometry. The fifth and sixth include the theory of proportions and similarity, while books seven through nine discuss number theory—prime numbers, divisibility of integers, and so on. The last four books discuss solid geometry, and it is precisely in this area that we are going to discuss the formulas originally developed by Euclid, who lived from 306 to 283 B.C.E.

RECTANGULAR SOLIDS

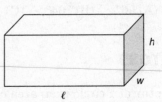

Volume = Length × Width × Height

$$V \ = \ l \ \cdot \ w \ \cdot \ h$$

EXAMPLE

If the length, width, and height of a box are respectively 8″, 7″, and 4.6″, find its volume, correct to the nearest cubic inch.

ANALYSIS

Multiply length, width, and height and then round off, correct to the nearest cubic inch.

WORK

$$V = l \cdot w \cdot h$$

$l = 8, w = 7, h = 4.6$: $\quad V = (8)(7)(4.6) = 257.6 \approx 258$

ANSWER: 258 cubic inches

PRACTICE (see answers on page 106)

1. Find the volume of a rectangular solid whose length is 6″, width is 8″, and height is 7″.

   (A) 56 cu in   (B) 336 cu in   (C) 288 cu in   (D) 294 cu in

2. We want to construct a box in the shape of a rectangular solid. If its volume is supposed to be 144 cubic inches, its length is 8″ and its width is 3″, find its height.

   (A) 4″   (B) 6″   (C) 9″   (D) 8″

CUBES

A **cube** is a rectangular solid whose sides are equal. If we label each edge e, then the volume, V, is equal to $e \cdot e \cdot e$, or $V = e^3$.

EXAMPLE
Find the volume of a cube whose edge is 2.4 meters.

ANALYSIS
Just use the formula $V = e^3$ and substitute for e.

WORK
$$V = e^3$$
$e = 2.4$: $V = (2.4)^3 = (2.4)(2.4)(2.4) = 13.824$

ANSWER: 13.824 cubic meters

PRACTICE (see answers on page 106)

1. Find the volume of a cube whose edge is 7 inches.

   (A) 49 in.^{3} (B) 343 in.^{3} (C) 98 in.^{3} (D) 2,401 in.^{3}

2. If the volume of a cube is 216 cubic inches, find one edge.

   (A) 6″   (B) 8″   (C) 4″   (D) 12″

RIGHT CIRCULAR CYLINDERS

Volume = Area of base · Height
Volume = π · Square of the radius · Height
   $V = \pi r^2 h$

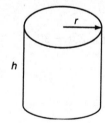

EXAMPLE
Find the volume of a cylinder whose diameter is 8 feet and whose height is 5 feet. Let $\pi = 3$.

ANALYSIS
To find the radius, take half of the diameter. Then just substitute the values into the formula.

WORK

$d = 8$:

$$r = \frac{1}{2}(d) = \frac{1}{2}(8) = 4$$

$$V = \pi r^2 h$$

$\pi = 3, r = 4, h = 5$:

$$V = (3)(4)^2(5)$$
$$V = 3\,(16)(5)$$
$$V = 240$$

ANSWER: 240 ft^3

PRACTICE (see answers on page 106)

1. Find the volume of a cylinder whose radius is 2 in. and whose height is 6 in. Use the formula $V = \pi r^2 h$, where V = volume, $\pi = 3$, r = radius, and h = height.

    (A) 72 in.^{3} (B) 36 in.^{3} (C) 48 in.^{3} (D) 40 in.^{3}

CONES

Volume = $\frac{1}{3}$ · Area of the base · Height

Volume = $\frac{1}{3}$ · π · Square of the radius · Height

$$V = \frac{1}{3}\pi r^2 h$$

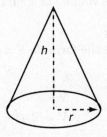

EXAMPLE

Find the height of a cone when its radius is 2 millimeters and its volume is 20 cubic millimeters. Let $\pi = 3$.

ANALYSIS

Substitute the given values into the formula.

WORK

$$V = \frac{1}{3}\pi r^2 h$$

$V = 20, \pi = 3, r = 2$:

$$20 = \frac{1}{3} \cdot 3\,(2)^2 h$$

$$20 = 4h$$

$$5 = h$$

ANSWER: 5 millimeters

PRACTICE (see answer on page 106)

1. Find the volume of a cone whose radius is 1″ and whose height is 6″. Use the formula $V = \frac{1}{3}\pi r^2 h$, where V = volume, $\pi = 3$, r = radius, and h = height.

    (A) 12 in.^{3} (B) 8 in.^{3} (C) 6 in.^{3} (D) 14 in.^{3}

SPHERES

Volume = $\frac{4}{3} \cdot \pi \cdot$ Cube of the radius

$$V = \frac{4}{3}\pi r^3$$

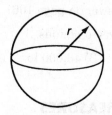

EXAMPLE

Find the radius of a sphere whose volume is 56 cubic inches. Let $\pi = 3$.

WORK

$$V = \frac{4}{3}\pi r^3$$

$V = 256, \pi = 3$:
$$256 = \frac{4}{3}(3)r^3$$

$$256 = 4r^3$$

Divide by 4: $64 = r^3$

Find the cube root of 64: $r = \pm 4$

ANSWER: 4 inches

PRACTICE (see answer on page 106)

1. Find the volume of a sphere whose radius is 2″. Use the formula $V = \frac{4}{3}\pi r^3$, where V = volume, $\pi = 3$, and r = radius.

(A) 32 in.^{3} (B) 48 in.^{3} (C) 28 in.^{3} (D) 16 in.^{3}

Measurements

U.S. WEIGHT MEASURES

1 pound = 16 ounces
1 ton = 2,000 pounds

EXAMPLE

Change 128,000 ounces to tons.

ANALYSIS

There are 32,000 ounces in one ton. Divide 128,000 ounces by 32,000.

WORK

1 ton = 2,000 pounds = 16 ounces × 2,000 pounds = 32,000 ounces

$$\frac{128,000 \text{ ounces}}{32,000 \text{ ounces}} = 4 \text{ tons}$$

ANSWER: 4 tons

PRACTICE (see answer on page 106)

1. Change 46 tons to pounds.

    (A) 4,600 lb   (B) 46,000 lb   (C) 92,000 lb   (D) 9,200 lb

U.S. LENGTH MEASURES

The ancient Romans needed a uniform standard for measuring length. They decided to use the length of the foot of a soldier as this standard measure, the *foot*.

The Romans divided the foot into 12 sections, or *inches*. For longer distances, a mile was the distance marched by 1,000 steps of a Roman soldier, or 5,280 feet.

The natives accepted these measurements during the Roman occupation of Britain. In the twelfth century, the king's arm was accepted as a standard measure for a *yard*, or three feet.

> 1 foot = 12 inches
> 1 yard = 3 feet
> 1 yard = 3 feet × 12 inches (per foot) = 36 inches
> 1 mile = 5,280 feet

EXAMPLE

Jesse can run 44,880 feet per hour. In terms of miles, what is his speed?

ANALYSIS

To change 44,880 feet to miles, divide by 5,280.

WORK

$$
\begin{array}{r}
8.5 \\
5{,}280\overline{)44{,}880.0} \\
42{,}240 \text{x} \\
\hline
2\,6400 \\
2\,6400 \\
\hline
\end{array}
$$

ANSWER: 8.5 miles

PRACTICE (see answers on page 106)

1. How many feet are there in 4 miles?

    (A) 23,760 ft   (B) 21,120 ft   (C) 22,500 ft   (D) 20,000 ft

2. Change 216 inches to feet.

    (A) 12 ft   (B) 4 ft   (C) 21 ft   (D) 18 ft

3. How many feet are there in 13 yards?

    (A) 52 ft   (B) 65 ft   (C) 78 ft   (D) 39 ft

U.S. LIQUID MEASURES

    1 quart = 2 pints
    1 gallon = 4 quarts

EXAMPLE
How many pints are there in 16 gallons?

ANALYSIS
Change gallons to quarts, then to pints.

WORK
    16 gallons = 16 × 4 quarts (per gallon) = 64 quarts
    64 quarts = 64 × 2 pints (per quart) = 128 pints

ANSWER: 128 pints

PRACTICE (see answers on page 106)

1.   How many quarts are there in 9 gallons?

    (A) 27 qt   (B) 36 qt   (C) 4 qt   (D) 45 qt

2.   Change 24 pints to quarts.

    (A) 8 qt   (B) 48 qt   (C) 12 qt   (D) 6 qt

METRIC LENGTH MEASURES

During the French Revolution, in the last decade of the 18th century, French scientists developed a standard unit of measurement, the **meter**. The meter is one ten-millionth of the distance between the North Pole and the Equator.

  The system was so rational that most other countries—except for the United States and Great Britain—adopted it.

    1 meter = 100 centimeters
    1 kilometer = 1,000 meters

METRIC WEIGHT MEASURES

    1 kilogram = 1,000 grams

CHANGING METRIC MEASURES AND U.S. MEASURES

    1 meter = 39.37 inches
    1 kilometer = 0.62 mile
    1 kilogram = 2.2 pounds
      1 liter = 1.06 quarts
      1 mile = 1.61 kilometers
    1 pound = 0.45 kilograms

EXAMPLE

Change 13 kilometers to miles.

ANALYSIS

One kilometer equals 0.62 mile, so just multiply 13 by 0.62.

WORK

$$\begin{array}{r} 0.62 \\ \times\ 13 \\ \hline 186 \\ 62 \\ \hline 8.06 \end{array}$$

ANSWER: 8.06 miles

PRACTICE (see answers on page 106)

1. Change 12 miles to kilometers and round off to the nearest tenth of a kilometer.

    (A) 7.4 kilometers   (B) 472.8 kilometers
      (C) 19.3 kilometers   (D) 19.32 kilometers

2. How many pounds are the equivalent of 15.4 kilograms? Round off to the nearest whole pound.

    (A) 34 lb   (B) 31lb   (C) 16 lb   (D) 45 lb

Graphs and Tables

LINE GRAPHS

The average monthly prices for a gallon of regular gasoline are listed below.

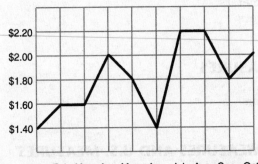

EXAMPLE

What is the difference in the average price per gallon of gasoline between the months of May and June?

ANALYSIS

Each horizontal line represents $0.20. Subtract the June price from the May price.

WORK

May price – June price:

$1.80 – $1.40 = $0.40

ANSWER: $0.40

PRACTICE (see answer on page 106)

1. Find the average price per gallon of gasoline for the months of February, March, and April and round off to the nearest cent.

    (A) $1.68   (B) $1.73   (C) $1.62   (D) $1.55

CIRCLE GRAPHS

The **circle graph** below indicates how an average resident of Middletown spends her time in a 24-hour day.

EXAMPLE

Using the information in the chart, how much time is spent sleeping?

    (A) 7 hours, 12 minutes
    (B) 7 hours, 14 minutes
    (C) 7 hours, 34 minutes
    (D) 7 hours, 46 minutes

ANALYSIS

Multiply 24 hours by 30% and then change the decimal part of the answer to minutes.

WORK

$$0.30 \times 24 = 7.2 \text{ hours}$$
60 minutes = 1 hour: $0.2 \times 60 = 12 \text{ minutes}$
$$7.2 \text{ hours} = 7 \text{ hours, 12 minutes}$$

ANSWER: 7 hours, 12 minutes

PRACTICE (see answer on page 106)

1. Use the circle graph and determine, out of a 24-hour day, how much time the average resident of Middletown spends working.

    (A) 7 hours, 12 minutes   (B) 8 hours, 24 minutes
      (C) 4 hours, 18 minutes   (D) 9 hours, 8 minutes

BAR GRAPHS

A bar graph is simply another useful method of pictorially displaying some information.

EXAMPLE
Using the information in the bar graph below, determine how much sales tax a person would save if she purchased a television set costing $450 in the State of New York rather than in the State of California.

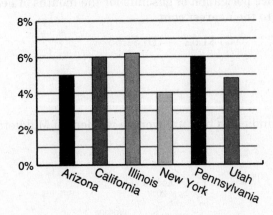

ANALYSIS
The state income tax in New York is 4% while it is 6% in California, resulting in a difference of 2%. Multiply $450 by 2% to find the difference in sales tax.

WORK
Change 2% to 0.02: $0.02 \times \$450 = \$9$

ANSWER: $9

PRACTICE (see answer on page 106)

1. Review the graph below and then indicate approximately how many more people reside in Columbus than in Las Vegas.

Population of Cities

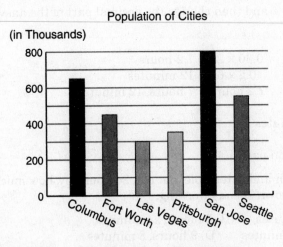

(A) 300,000   (B) 250,000   (C) 400,000   (D) 350,000

TABLES

Banks usually change their interest rates monthly. The following table lists the **simple annual interest rates** offered by the indicated banks.

Bank	Annual Interest Rate
Homeland	3.0%
Nautica	2.0%
Bennington	1.0%
Kendale	3.0%

EXAMPLE

Using the table above, determine the interest earned on a deposit of $5,000 at the Kendale Bank for one month.

ANALYSIS

If we only want to determine the interest for one month, just divide the given simple annual interest rate by 12.

WORK

$$\text{Kendale Bank's interest rate for one month} = 0.03/12 \qquad = 0.0025$$
$$\text{Actual interest for one month} = 0.0025 \times \$5,000 = \$12.50$$

ANSWER: $12.50

PRACTICE (see answer on page 106)

1. Use the table to determine how much more interest could be earned for the year on a deposit of $8,000 at the Nautica Bank rather than at the Bennington Bank.

(A) $80.00   (B) $88.00   (C) $64.00   (D) $48.00

Word Problems

WAGE PROBLEMS

EXAMPLE 1

Kendra is a programmer. She earns $26.50 per hour. How much does she earn in 16 hours?

ANALYSIS

Just multiply the wages per hour by the number of hours worked.

WORK

$$16 \times \$26.50 = \$424$$

ANSWER: $424

EXAMPLE 2

Julio earns $12.54 per hour while Shanequa earns $13.04 per hour. In 12 hours, how much more than Julio does Shanequa earn?

ANALYSIS

Multiply the wages per hour by the number of hours worked by each person. Then subtract Julio's total wages from Shanequa's total wages.

WORK

Shanequa's wages:	$12 \times \$13.04 = \$ 156.48$
Julio's wages:	$- 12 \times \$12.54 = 150.48$
	$\$6.00$

ANSWER: $6

EXAMPLE 3

Mildred earned $22.88 per hour and got paid $1\frac{1}{2}$ times that amount for overtime. If she worked 44 hours last week and any hours over 40 are considered overtime, how much did she get paid?

ANALYSIS

Multiply 40 hours by the amount she normally gets paid per hour, $22.88. She worked 4 hours overtime, so, for overtime pay, multiply 4 by $1\frac{1}{2}$ by $22.88. Then add the two results together.

WORK

Regular pay:	$40 \text{ hours} \times \$22.88 = \$915.20$
Overtime pay:	$+ 4 \text{ hours} \times 1\frac{1}{2} \times \$22.88 = 137.28$
	$\$1,052.48$

ANSWER: $1,052.48

PRACTICE (see answers on page 106)

1. Murray makes $12.74 per hour. How much does he earn in 38 hours?

   (A) $104.12   (B) $484.12   (C) $456   (D) $144.40

2. Hilda earns $14.36 per hour, while her friend, Janice, gets paid $13.37 per hour. If they both work 39 hours, how much more money does Hilda earn?

   (A) $38.61   (B) $560.04   (C) $521.43   (D) $49.30

3. Jules gets paid $12.48 per hour, for his first 40 hours of work per week. He gets paid $15.75 per hour for overtime, which is considered over 40 hours per week. How much does Jules make when he works 47 hours for the week?

   (A) $499.20   (B) $740.25   (C) $586.56   (D) $609.45

INVESTMENT PROBLEMS

EXAMPLE

Malcolm has $10,000 to invest. If he invests some money at 4% per year simple interest and the rest at 3% per year simple interest and he derives an income of $385 for the year, how much should he invest at 4%?

ANALYSIS

Let x = the amount invested at 4%, and let $10,000 - x$ = the amount invested at 3%.

Investment	Percent Interest	Principal ($)	Interest = Percent × Principal ($)
Investment 1	4%	x	4%(x)
Investment 2	3%	$10,000 - x$	3%($10,000 - x$)

WORK

The interest from the two investments adds up to $385.

$$4\%(x) + 3\%(10,000 - x) = 385$$

Change to decimals:

$$0.04(x) + 0.03(10,000 - x) = 385$$

Multiply by 100:

$$4x + 3(10,000 - x) = 38,500$$
$$4x + 30,000 - 3x = 38,500$$
$$x + 30,000 = 38,500$$

Subtract 30,000:

$$x = 8,500$$

CHECK

$$0.04(x) + .03(10,000 - x) = 385$$

$x = 8,500$:

$$4(8,500) + 0.03(10,000 - 8,500) = 385$$
$$340 + 0.03(1,500) = 385$$
$$340 + 45 = 385$$
$$385 = 385 \ ✔$$

ANSWER: $8,500

PRACTICE (see answer on page 106)

1. Mrs. Jackson has $7,000 to invest. If she invests part at 6% simple annual interest and part at 8% simple annual interest, she will get an annual return of $520. How much should she invest at 8%?

   (A) $2,500   (B) $3,000   (C) $5,000   (D) $2,000

MIXTURE PROBLEMS

EXAMPLE 1

A grocer mixes 12 pounds of Brazilian coffee at $3.84 per pound with 20 pounds of Venezuelan coffee at $5.12 per pound. How much should he sell one pound of the new mixture for?

ANALYSIS

Let x = the price of the new mixture.

Type	Price Per Pound (P)	Number of Pounds (N)	Total Price = PN
Brazilian	$3.84	12	$12(3.84)
Venezuelan	$5.12	20	$20(5.12)
Mixture	x	32	$32x$

WORK

Add the total prices of the two coffees and set that sum equal to the total price of the mixture.

$$12(3.84) + 20(5.12) = 32x$$
$$46.08 + 102.40 = 32x$$

Multiply by 100:
$$4608 + 10240 = 3{,}200x$$
$$14848 = 3{,}200x$$
$$4.64 = x$$
$$x = \$4.64$$

ANSWER: $4.64

EXAMPLE 2

An adult ticket to a movie is $7.50, while a child's ticket is $3.60. If a total of 280 people were admitted, and the receipts amounted to $1476, how many children's tickets were sold?

ANALYSIS

Let x = the number of adult tickets sold, and let $280 - x$ = the number of children's tickets sold.

Type of ticket	Price per ticket (P)	Number of tickets (N)	Total = PN
Adult	$7.50	x	$7.50x$
Child	$3.60	$280 - x$	$3.60(280 - x)$

WORK

Set the sum of the totals equal to $1,476.

$$7.50x + 3.60(280 - x) = 1{,}476$$

Multiply by 100:
$$750x + 360(280 - x) = 147{,}600$$
$$750x + 100{,}800 - 360x = 147{,}600$$
$$390x + 100{,}800 = 147{,}600$$

Subtract 100,800:
$$390x = 4{,}688$$

Divide by 390:
$$x = 120 \text{ (adult tickets)}$$
$$280 - x = 160 \text{ (children's tickets)}$$

CHECK

$$7.50x + 3.60(280 - x) = 1{,}476$$
$x = 120, 280 - x = 160$:
$$7.50(120) + 3.60(160) = 1{,}476$$
$$900 + 576 = 1{,}476$$
$$1{,}476 = 1{,}476 ✔$$

ANSWER: 160

PRACTICE (see answers on page 106)

1. A grocer mixes 10 pounds of Brazilian coffee at $4.20 per pound with 20 pounds of Venezuelan coffee at $7.20 per pound. How much is one pound of the new mixture?

   (A) $5.40   (B) $6.20   (C) $5.80   (D) $7.10

2. A total of 210 tickets were sold at the junior prom. Members of the Student Organization paid $5 while nonmembers paid $11. If the total receipts amounted to $1,830, how many tickets were sold to Student Organization members?

   (A) 80   (B) 200   (C) 130   (D) 90

AGE PROBLEMS

EXAMPLE

Jack is twice as old as Lillian. Six years ago Jack was five times as old as Lillian was then. How old is Lillian now?

ANALYSIS

Let x = Lillian's age now.
Let $2x$ = Jack's age now.
Let $x - 6$ = Lillian's age 6 years ago.
Let $2x - 6$ = Jack's age 6 years ago.

WORK

Six years ago Jack was five times as old as Lillian was then.

$$2x - 6 = 5(x - 6)$$
$$2x - 6 = 5x - 30$$

Add 6: $2x = 5x - 24$
Subtract $5x$: $-3x = -24$
Divide by -3: $x = 8$
                    $2x = 16$

ANSWER: 8 years old

PRACTICE (see answers on page 106)

1. Jenny is now 18 and Carmen is 12. How many years ago was Jenny twice as old as Carmen?

   (A) 3 years ago   (B) 8 years ago   (C) 6 years ago   (D) 4 years ago

2. A father is now 28 years older than his son. Ten years ago the father was 15 times as old as his son. How old is the father now?

   (A) 40 years old   (B) 28 years old   (C) 36 years old   (D) 42 years old

DISCOUNTS AND PRICE INCREASES

EXAMPLE

If the city of Pottersvillle has 8,000 residents now and is projected to lose 8% of its population next year and another 5% the following year, what will be its population at the end of two years?

ANALYSIS

If Pottersville will lose 8% of its population, it will retain 92%, so take 92% of 8,000. Then, if loses another 5% of its population, it will retain 95%, so take 95% of the 92% of 8,000.

WORK

$0.92 \times 8,000 = 7,360$
$0.95 \times 7,360 = 6,992$

ANSWER: 6,992

PRACTICE (see answer on page 106)

1. The price on a $200 suit was increased by 25%. The merchant was unable to sell the suit, so it was then discounted by 12%. What was the final selling price?

   (A) $225   (B) $220   (C) $240   (D) $210

PERCENTAGE PROBLEMS

EXAMPLE 1
If a suit is reduced by $40 and this represents 25% discount, what was the original price of the suit?

ANALYSIS
Let x = the original price, and set $40 equal to 25% of the original price, x.

WORK
$$40 = 0.25x$$
Multiply by 100: $$100 < 40 = 0.25x >$$
$$4,000 = 25x$$
Divide by 25: $$160 = x$$
$$x = 160$$

ANSWER: $160

EXAMPLE 2
What percent of 50 is 90?

ANALYSIS
Let x = the unknown percent. "Of" indicates multiplication, so we have to multiply 50 by a percent in order to arrive at 90.

WORK
$$x \cdot 50 = 90$$
Divide by 50: $$x = 90/50 = 1.8 = 180\%$$
$$x = 1.80$$
Change to percent: $$x = 180\%$$

ANSWER: 180%

EXAMPLE 3
Tiesha works on a base salary of $400 per week plus an 8% commission on sales. If she sold $2,400 worth of items last week, how much was her total salary?

ANALYSIS
Find 8% of $2,400, and add to her base salary of $400.

WORK
$$0.08 \times \$2,400 = \$192$$
$$+ \ 400$$
$$\overline{\$592}$$

ANSWER: $592

PRACTICE (see answers on page 106)

1. An auto dealer increases the price of a used car 15%. If the new price is $6,900, what was the original price of the car?

   (A) $5,000   (B) $6,200   (C) $5,900   (D) $6,000

2. Fifty is what percent of 20?

   (A) 250%   (B) 40%   (C) 25%   (D) 400%

3. Maria is a salesperson. She works on a base salary of $400 per week plus an 8% commission. If she sold $7,000 worth of pharmaceuticals last week, what was her salary?

   (A) $780   (B) $960   (C) $840   (D) $984

DISTANCE PROBLEMS

EXAMPLE

Glen drove a distance of 182 miles in $3\frac{1}{2}$ hours. What was his average rate of speed?

ANALYSIS

Use the distance formula $d = rt$, where d = distance, r = rate, and t = time.

WORK

$$d = rt$$

$d = 182, t = 3\frac{1}{2}$: $\qquad 182 = r\left(3\frac{1}{2}\right)$

$$182 = \frac{7}{2}r$$

Multiply by $\frac{2}{7}$: $\qquad \frac{2}{7} < 182 = \frac{7}{2}r >$

$$r = 52$$

ANSWER: 52 mph

PRACTICE (see answer on page 106)

1. Aristide is a train engineer. If the distance between two cities is 350.4 miles, and he wants to make the trip in six hours, what should his average rate of speed be?

   (A) 58.4 mph   (B) 62.6 mph   (C) 87.6 mph   (D) 43.8 mph

Statistics

Whenever we're presented with a lot of data, we usually have to sort it out. Statistics helps us make sense of the loads of data we're constantly receiving.

THE MEAN OR AVERAGE

We are often interested in a typical product, consumer, voter, or the like. When we talk about "typical," we are looking for something representative of an entire group. We are talking about some sort of central tendency.

We can measure central tendency in three ways:

1. The mean or average
2. The mode
3. The median

The mean or average is simply the sum of the various pieces of data divided by the number of data. In mathematical notation, the arithmetic mean is indicated by $\bar{x}$, read "x bar."

$$\bar{x} = \frac{\sum_{i=1}^{n} x_i}{n} = \frac{x_1 + x_2 + x_3 + \ldots + x_n}{n}$$

where n = the number of pieces of data, x_1 through x_n.

EXAMPLE

Julio is on the track team. He recorded the miles he ran each day for the past week: 5.9, 6, 3.7, 6.2, 4.5, 6.1, 3.8. To the nearest tenth of a mile, what was the mean number of miles he ran a day?

ANALYSIS

Add up all the miles and divide by 7, the number of days Julio ran.

WORK

$$\bar{x} = \frac{5.9 + 6 + 3.7 + 6.2 + 4.5 + 6.1 + 3.8}{7} = \frac{36.2}{7} = 5.17\ldots \approx 5.2$$

ANSWER: 5.2

PRACTICE (see answer on page 106)

The Basic Cookware Company has a quality control program. On a weekly basis, inspectors check damages in their manufactured dishes. During the first 6 weeks of the program, inspectors found the following numbers of dishes damaged, by week: 23, 18, 34, 27, 26, 19.

1. For seven weeks, if management wants to hold the mean number of damaged dishes per week to 24, what is the maximum allowable number of damaged dishes during the seventh week?

(A) 21   (B) 24   (C) 18   (D) 25

THE MEDIAN

Sometimes we're not interested in determining the mean. We want to find the middle number. The **median** is the middle number in an ordered set of data.

EXAMPLE 1

Over the past week, Jose has slept the following numbers of hours per night: 9, 8, 9, 7, 6.5, 7.4, 6.3. Find the median.

ANALYSIS

In order to determine the median, list the numbers from smallest to largest and then select the middle number.

WORK

Median: 6.3, 6.5, 7, 7.4, 8, 9, 9

$\uparrow$

Middle number

ANSWER: 7.4

EXAMPLE 2

Find the median of the following numbers: 34, 56, 9, 67, 25, 49.

ANALYSIS

In this case, we have an even amount of numbers, so we'll first arrange the numbers in ascending order and then we'll add the two middle numbers and divide by 2.

WORK

$$9 + 25 + \frac{34 + 49}{2} + 56 + 67$$

$$\frac{34 + 49}{2} = \frac{83}{2} = 41.5$$

ANSWER: 41.5

PRACTICE (see answer on page 106)

1. Students in the physics class received the following grades on their last exam: 80, 75, 65, 92, 56, 79, 48, 58, 92, 85, 76, 68. Find the median.

    (A) 76   (B) 74.5   (C) 75.5   (D) 74

THE MODE

The mode is the easiest measure in statistics. It's simply the number that occurs most frequently in a given set of data.

EXAMPLE

Mr. Vargas, the owner of Vargas' Shoe Store, has recorded the daily sales of shoes in his store for the past 12 days: 23, 18, 19, 12, 18, 16, 22, 12, 19, 15, 23, 19. Find the mode and the median and compare the two.

ANALYSIS

List the numbers in ascending order. Find the number occurring most often as well as the middle number.

Work
Mode: 12, 12, 15, 16, 18, 18, **19, 19, 19**, 22, 23, 23

Nineteen occurs most often, so it's the mode.

Median: 12, 12, 15, 16, 18, **18, 19**, 19, 19, 22, 23, 23

$$\frac{18 + 19}{2} = \frac{37}{2} = 18.5$$

ANSWER: The mode is 19; the median 18.5.

PRACTICE (see answer on page 106)

1. Mr. Hiarnachy, the owner of Howie's Shoes, has recorded the daily sales of shoes for the past 12 days: 35, 19, 23, 32, 19, 28, 35, 31, 23, 18, 17, 19. Find the mode.

    (A) 35   (B) 23   (C) 22   (D) 19

PROBABILITY

Probability means the likelihood of a particular event occurring. Probability is a number between and including 0 and 1. A probability of 0 means that the event will absolutely not occur. A probability of 1 means that the event is certain to occur.

Probability is expressed as a percent or a ratio.

$$P(\text{event}) = 25\% \text{ or } 1{:}4$$

EXAMPLE

A jar contains 6 blue marbles, 7 red marbles, and 2 white marbles. Without looking, find P(blue).

ANALYSIS

The probability of selecting a blue marble, P(b), is equal to the number of blue marbles, B, out of the total number of marbles, T.

WORK

$$P(\text{b}) = \frac{B}{T}$$

$B = 6, T = 15$: $P(\text{b}) = \frac{6}{15} = \frac{2}{5}$

ANSWER: $\frac{2}{5}$

PRACTICE (see answer on page 106)

1. Out of a deck of 52 cards, what is the probability of selecting a king?

    (A) 1/13   (B) 1/4   (C) 2/13   (D) 3/52

Sequences

In a sequence, we have to determine the pattern.

REPEATED PATTERNS IN SEQUENCES

Some patterns reappear in the sequences.

EXAMPLE 1
Find the missing term in the sequence 3, 7, 11, __, 19, 23, ...

ANALYSIS
The terms are increasing by 4.

WORK
Add 4 to 11: 11 + 4 = 15

ANSWER: 15

EXAMPLE 2
Review the sequence: 5, 8, 11, 11, 14, 17, 17, 20, 23, 23, . . . and find the next number.

ANALYSIS
The sequence is divided into groups of three. Within each group, 3 is added to the first and second terms to arrive at the second and third members of the group, respectively. The next group begins with the third member of the previous group, and the pattern is repeated.

WORK

    5, 8, 11   11, 14, 17   17, 20, 23   23, **26**

ANSWER: 26

EXAMPLE 3
Review the sequence: VI, 3, IX, 5, _, 7, XV, 9, XVIII, 11, . . . , and find the missing number.

ANALYSIS
The Roman numbers are increasing by 3 while the Arabic numbers are increasing by 2.

WORK
$$IX + III = XII$$

ANSWER: XII

EXAMPLE 4
Review the sequence: 32, 33.5, 35, 36.5, 38, 39.5, . . . , and find the next number.

ANALYSIS
The sequence is increasing by 1.5.

WORK
$$39.5 + 1.5 = 41$$

ANSWER: 41

EXAMPLE 5
Review the sequence: 86, 15, 81, 15, 76, 15, 71, 15, _, 15, 61, 15, ... What number should fill in the blank space?

ANALYSIS
The number 15 repeats alternately and the rest of the sequence reduces by 5.

WORK

```
        15,    15,    15,    15,    15,    15,
   86, ^  81, ^  76, ^  71, ^   _,  ^  61,   . . .
```

$$71 - 5 = 66$$

ANSWER: 66

EXAMPLE 6
Find the next two terms in the following sequence:

13, 15, 18, 23, 25, 28, 33, . . .

ANALYSIS
In this sequence, the differences between the terms are increasing in a repeating pattern.

WORK

Sequence:	13		15		18		23		25		28		33		**35**		**38**
Differences:		◄+2►		◄+3►		◄+5►		◄+2►		◄+3►		◄+5►		◄+2►		◄+3►		◄+5►

The numbers in the sequence are increasing in the pattern 2, 3, 5.

ANSWER: 35, 38

PRACTICE (see answers on page 106)

1. Find the missing term in the sequence 8, 13, 18, 23, __, 33, ...

   (A) 25   (B) 27   (C) 26   (D) 28

2. Review the sequence 12, 15, 18, 18, 21, 24, 24, __, 30, ... What number should fill in the blank ?

   (A) 27   (B) 25   (C) 26   (D) 24

3. Look at the sequence III, 1, V, 5, VII, 9, IX, 13, ... What number should come next?

   (A) 17   (B) XI   (C) XII   (D) 15

4. Find the missing term in the sequence 33, $31\frac{1}{2}$, 30, $28\frac{1}{2}$, 27, __, 24, $22\frac{1}{2}$.

   (A) 24   (B) $24\frac{1}{2}$ (C) $25\frac{1}{2}$ (D) 25

5. Review the sequence 15, 7, 13, 7, 11, 7, 9, 7, . . . , and find the next term.

   (A) 8   (B) 7   (C) 5   (D) 9

6. Look at the sequence 14, 15, 17, 18, 20, 21, 23, __, 26, . . . , and determine the missing number.

   (A) 23   (B) 24   (C) 25   (D) 22

SQUARES IN SEQUENCES

Some sequences include squares of numbers. Occasionally, constants are imbedded in these sequences.

EXAMPLE 1
Find the next term in the sequence 4, 9, 16, 10, 9, 16, 25, 10, ...

ANALYSIS
There is a constant imbedded in a sequence of increasing squares.

				Constant				Constant	
				↓				↓	
Sequence:	4	9	16	10	9	6	25	10	<u>16</u>
Without 10:	4	9	16		9	16	25		<u>16</u>
Power:	2^2	3^2	4^2		3^2	4^2	5^2		4^2

ANSWER: 16

EXAMPLE 2
Find the next term in the sequence 6, 36, 5, 25, 4, 16, ...

ANALYSIS
The sequence is in decreasing order of integers and their squares.

WORK

Sequence:	6	36	5	25	4	16	$\underline{3}$
Power:	6^1	6^2	5^1	5^2	4^1	4^2	$\underline{3^1}$

The next number in the sequence is 3 or 3^1.

ANSWER: 3

PRACTICE (see answers on page 106)

Find the next term in each of the following sequences:

1. 1, 8, 27, 64, 125, . . .

  (A) 250   (B) 180   (C) 216   (D) 256

2. 4, 8, 9, 27, 16, 64, . . .

  (A) 25   (B) 125   (C) 128   (D) 192

ALPHABETICAL SEQUENCES

An alphabetical sequence follows certain patterns, as does a numerical sequence.

EXAMPLE 1

Find the next letter in the sequence A, C, E, G, I, ...

ANALYSIS

Let's insert more spaces between the letters. Then we'll attempt to determine some sort of pattern.

WORK

Sequence:	A	▼	C	▼	E	▼	G	▼	I	▼	$\underline{K}$
Missing letters:		B		D		F		H		J	

The sequence is in ascending alphabetical order, with one letter between each term in the original sequence.

ANSWER: K

EXAMPLE 2

Find the next term in the sequence X, U, R, O, L, ...

ANALYSIS

Leave some space between the letters and then determine which letters are missing.

WORK

Sequence:	X	▼	U	▼	R	▼	O	▼	L	▼	I
Missing letters:		W, V		T, S		Q, P		N, M		K, J	

This sequence is in descending alphabetical order, with two letters between each term in the original sequence.

ANSWER: I

EXAMPLE 3
Find the next term in the sequence D, F, I, M, R, ...

ANALYSIS
The sequence is in increasing alphabetical order. Just determine the number of missing letters in the given sequence.

WORK

Sequence:	D ▼	F ▼	I ▼	M ▼	R ▼	X
Missing letters:	E	G, H	J, K, L	N, O, P, Q	S, T, U, V, W	
Number of missing letters:	1	2	3	4	5	

The number of missing letters in this sequence is increasing in the pattern 1, 2, 3, 4, 5, ...

ANSWER: X

EXAMPLE 4
Find the next letter in the sequence P, P, R, S, P, P, T, U, P, P, V, ...

ANALYSIS
Here, there's no obvious relationship between individual letters in the sequence. Therefore, let's try another approach. Let's try dividing the sequence into groups of two.

WORK

PP reappears: PP RS PP TU PP VW

R, S, T, U are in alphabetical order, with PP in between.

ANSWER: VW

PRACTICE (see answers on page 106)

In the following sequences, determine the next letter.

1. J, M, P, S, V, . . .

   (A) Z   (B) Y   (C) W   (D) X

2. X, T, P, L, H, . . .

   (A) F   (B) G   (C) D   (D) E

3. B, D, G, K, P, . . .

   (A) V   (B) U   (C) T   (D) W

LETTER/NUMBER SEQUENCES

A3   C6   E9   G12   ?

In this sequence, we have a combination of letters and numbers. The sequence for the letters is independent of the sequence for numbers, so we have to determine each sequence independently.

It is often useful to convert alphabetical letters to their numerical order so that we can spot the pattern. When we take this approach, we should list the letters of the alphabet prior to determining a pattern:

A B C D E F G H I J K L M N O P Q R S T U V W X Y Z
1 2 3 4 5 6 7 8 9 10 11 12 13 14 15 16 17 18 19 20 21 22 23 24 25 26

EXAMPLE
Find the next term in the sequence B_9, E^{10}, H_{12}, K^{13}, N_{15}, Q^{16}, __.

ANALYSIS
The subscripts and superscripts alternate. The pattern for subscripts and superscripts is +1, +2.

$$16 + 2 = 18$$

Change the letters to numerical order to determine a pattern.

WORK
Alphabetical sequence: B   E   H   K   N   Q   __
Order of letter in alphabet: 2   5   8   11   14   17

The letters are increasing by 3.

$$17 + 3 = 20 \ (T)$$

ANSWER: T^{18}

PRACTICE (see answer on page 106)

1. Find the next term in the sequence D_1, H^4, L_7, P^{10}, __, ...

    (A) S_{12} (B) T^{13} (C) S^{12} (D) T_{13}

Analogies

An **analogy** is a pattern between a several objects.

For example, in the following picture, let's first try to determine what the arch really is. It appears to be a hole in the wall, so let's find the analogy between a mouse and a hole in the wall and a woman and one of the choices offered:

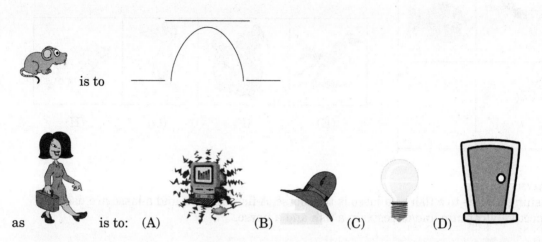

The key to the analogy is the relationship between the mouse and the hole in the wall. One obvious interpretation is that the mouse is going home after a hard day's work chasing that piece of cheese. If we accept that interpretation, the woman is also going home, but she's entering through a door, choice (D).

EXAMPLE 1

Here's another analogy problem. In this case, select the picture at the right that will fill the empty box so that the two lower pictures are related to each other in the same manner as the two upper pictures.

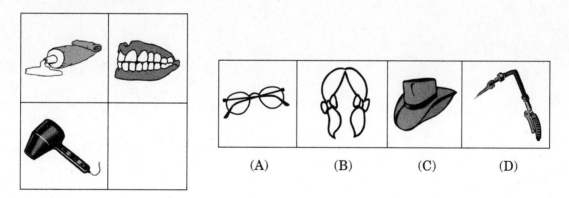

ANALYSIS

We brush our teeth with toothpaste, and we use a hair dryer on our hair, so (B), hair, is the correct answer.

ANSWER: (B)

EXAMPLE 2

This last example should "lock in" analogies. Once again, select the picture at the right that will fill the empty box so that the two lower pictures are related to each other in the same manner as the two upper pictures.

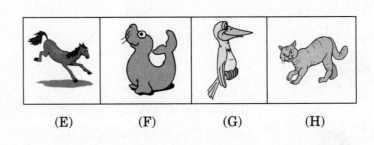

(E)   (F)   (G)   (H)

ANALYSIS

A fishing hook is to a fish as a lasso is to a horse. A fishing hook and a lasso are used to, respectively, capture and/or restrain a fish and a horse.

ANSWER: (E)

Answers to Mathematics Review Exercises

For detailed explanations on how to arrive at these answers, please refer back to the review section for each topic.

Natural and Whole Numbers, p. 27
1. D   2. B   3. C

Comparing Integers, p. 28
1. D   2. A   3. D   4. B

Exponents, p. 29
1. A   2. B   3. B

Order of Operations, p. 31
1. D   2. A   3. C   4. C

Rounding Off Integers, p. 32
1. D   2. C   3. A   4. A

Prime Numbers, p. 32
1. C   2. B   3. B

Factors and Multiples, p. 33
1. D   2. C   3. D   4. B

Reducing Fractions, p. 36
1. A   2. C   3. B

Changing Improper Fractions to Whole or Mixed Numbers, p. 37
1. A   2. D   3. C

Changing Mixed Numbers to Improper Fractions, p. 38
1. B   2. A

Operations with Fractions, p. 38
1. D   2. C   3. A
4. B   5. B

Comparing Decimals and Fractions, p. 41
1. C   2. B   3. D

Rounding Off Decimals, p. 42
1. A   2. D

Operations with Decimals, p. 43
1. D   2. C   3. D   4. A

Scientific Notation, p. 45
1. C   2. D

Changing Fractions and Whole Numbers to Percents, p. 45
1. A   2. D

Changing Percents to Fractions, p. 46
1. A

Changing Decimals to Percents, p. 46
1. C

Changing Percents to Decimals, p. 47
1. D

Applications, p. 48
1. A

Algebra, p. 48
1. C   2. D

Arithmetic Operations with Signed Numbers, p. 49
1. A   2. C   3. B

Formulas, p. 51
1. B

Equations, p. 52
1. B

Simplifying Exponential Expressions, p. 52
1. D

Simplifying Radicals, p. 54
1. B   2. D

Operations with Radicals, p. 54
1. D   2. C

Inequalities, p. 55
1. C

Operations with Monomials and Polynomials, p. 55
1. C   2. A   3. C   4. D

Absolute Value, p. 56
1. C   2. D

Ratios and Proportions, p. 57
1. C

Consecutive Integers, p. 58
1. D   2. C   3. B

Angles, p. 62
1. C

Reflex Angles, p. 63
1. B   2. B

Complementary and Supplementary Angles, p. 63
1. B   2. B

Adjacent Angles, p. 64
1. D

Verbal Skills

The HSPT and COOP test verbal skills in different ways. It used to be said that the HSPT focused a bit more on *what* you know, whereas the COOP tested *how* you know something. Changes in the tests have blurred these differences, so a solid knowledge base *and* strong thinking skills are necessary to do well on both tests. When possible, we will identify which facts or skills are emphasized on which test, but it would be a good idea to study all the material listed here. In fact, it would help you to take all four practice tests in this book. The more practice you get, the better you'll do on any test.

Vocabulary

A strong vocabulary is an essential skill not only for the HSPT but also for many of the other standardized tests (SAT, ACT, GRE, LMNOP, etc.) you will take in your academic career. In fact, some sections of these exams have been accused of being nothing more than complicated vocabulary tests. This is not entirely true, of course, but, obviously, the richer your vocabulary is, the easier it is to solve that portion of the test.

Preparing for the vocabulary section may take the most effort, but the rewards will be great—not only in improving your exam score but also in improving your studies in all other subjects in school. Moreover, a well-spoken person will win great respect in life.

The best way to strengthen your vocabulary is to READ. Wow, how old-fashioned! Read what you enjoy. Some students love reading the sports section of the newspaper every day, and that's a great start. Branch out and read some sports magazines. Maybe you enjoy reading the comics section of the paper. You would enjoy checking out some of the many fascinating books on the history of comics.

Many middle school students are proud that they read adult best-sellers. However, you should probably know that many of these books are actually written **below** your reading level! So if you like Stephen King, you should try Edgar Allen Poe, a horror writer with an incredibly large vocabulary. Remember how much fun the Hardy Boys and Nancy Drew were to read? Agatha Christie mysteries and the Sherlock Holmes stories by Sir Arthur Conan Doyle are just as much fun.

To learn the most vocabulary from these books, you'll have to make yourself a promise to look up unfamiliar words in the dictionary. Any kind will do, but the best dictionary for you will have pronunciations and word histories (etymologies).

Oh, it's really a pain to have to get the dictionary off the shelf and then to open it up to find the word. It's so much easier just to skip learning it.

The solution is simple: have a dictionary on your desk in front of you whenever you read or do homework. Furthermore, have it open **already**. This simple arrangement will improve your vocabulary immensely. It's not difficult just to flip a few pages and learn the word, its spelling, its pronunciation, its history (which can help you remember it and learn its root), and its various forms.

This brings us to one of the most interesting books of all: the dictionary itself. Don't laugh! Just skipping around in the dictionary is a fascinating way to learn, for every word contains a story. For instance, the adjective *maudlin* means excessively sentimental or (to use a more casual term) weepy. *Maudlin* is an alternate version of *Magdalene*. Mary Magdalene was frequently portrayed in art as crying, so something causing this weepy reaction is considered maudlin.

The dictionary is one book that is not going to come out on video and DVD, so don't wait for the movie. Stop being so slothful / indolent / lazy / idle / lethargic; use the dictionary!

VOCABULARY MEMORY AIDS

Reading about a word is one thing; remembering the information is another. One of the best ways to study and remember vocabulary words is to use flash cards. Have a stack of cards handy and write down any word that is new to you. These are so easy to carry around with you anywhere, and you can study them whenever you have a few minutes to spare—in the car, before class, after lunch, or in study hall.

To make the words even easier to remember, add some detail to your cards. Write the word on one side and the definition on the other side, of course. Then add a ridiculous picture to help you remember it. We're visual people, so don't be afraid to draw a crazy picture; the more outlandish it is, the better you'll remember it.

Finally, write a sentence about the picture. A student once learned the word *sputum* by writing the definition (saliva and mucous spit out of the mouth) on the back of the card and adding a simple picture of a stick person vomiting up some large antacid tablets. The sentence he wrote was "The boy spewed Tums in his sputum." It was disgusting, to be sure, but he never forgot the word.

Try some of these yourself. Draw pictures and compose sentences using the following words.

> *travesty*—a grotesque, mocking, or inferior imitation
> *duplicitous*—deceitful; double-dealing
> *panegyric*—a speech of high praise
> *penultimate*—next to last
> *spurious*—not genuine; not authentic

COMPUTERS

If you use a computer and log onto the Internet, you have access to a myriad (many thousands) of reading sources. The next time you're on-line, turn off your Instant Mail program, get out of the chat rooms, and read an article about something that interests you. If you have trouble getting started, go to a trivia site and get some ideas.

You can also painlessly improve your vocabulary by registering for one of the many organizations that will e-mail you a new word every day. Most of these include sentences, word histories, and interesting information about vocabulary. If you check your e-mail every day, learn the new word, and use it several times that very day, the word will become part of your vocabulary.

Several sites also contain word games, such as vocabulary hangman. Do a web search for *SAT* or *ACT* and *hangman* or *vocabulary*, and you'll get many responses. Challenge the machine, and you will emerge victorious!

CROSSWORD PUZZLES

Speaking of word games, another fun way to learn vocabulary is to work crossword puzzles. These are especially helpful in preparing for vocabulary exams because they are filled with tricks in which a word can be used as different parts of speech. For instance, a crossword clue might simply read *test*. You have to read this two ways; it's either a noun (*a test*) or a verb (*to test*). You can fight the good fight, jump the high jump, and land on the land. Some words are pronounced differently and have different definitions. Is *desert* the hot, dry area (DEsert) or is it the verb meaning to leave or abandon (deSERT)? Both entrance exams contain words like this to test the flexibility of your thinking.

Be aware that if you play the crossword puzzle in the newspaper every day, the editors publish easy clues and puzzles on Monday. Then the puzzles get harder and harder every day. Don't try working your first puzzle on a Friday! By the way, some people think that using a dictionary while you work the crossword puzzle is cheating. We disagree; we call it **learning**.

Word Histories

Knowing the roots of words is another great aid in figuring out definitions. You'll learn a lot of these in the dictionary, but we'll go over some common ones.

For instance, the root *mor* (or *mort* or *mors*) means *death*. Got it? So if you're reading about some characters named Mordred, Morgan, Voldemort, and Professor Moriarty, and they live in a place called Mordor, you're pretty safe in assuming that these people are **bad** news. Are your parents upset when they make their mortgage payments? Of course they are, because these house payments are named after a "death pledge." Dead bodies are kept in a mortuary. A mortician prepares a body for a funeral. Something immortal cannot die.

Let's try a few more. Take a few minutes to memorize these.

> *sub*—under
> *super*—over
> *medi*—middle
> *extra*—beyond
>
> *sol*—sun
> *luna*—moon
> *terra*—earth (Latin)
> *geo*—earth, ground (Greek)
> *mar*—sea

PRACTICE
Define the following words.

1. sublunary—
2. Mediterranean—
3. subterranean—
4. extraterrestrial—
5. submarine—

ANALYSIS
1. sublunary—under the moon. This refers to earthly things, perhaps worldly or mundane.
2. Mediterranean—middle of the earth. The people who named the Mediterranean Sea obviously thought they were the center of everything!

3. subterranean—under the earth. Your underground hideout is subterranean, Batman.
4. extraterrestrial—beyond earth. UFOs are often thought to originate beyond the limits of earth.
5. Well, how easy can these get? A submarine travels under the sea.

Eating

If you've ever studied dinosaurs, you're familiar with the root *vor*, meaning *eat*. Since *carne* means meat, a *carnivore* is a meat-eater. An *herbivore* is a plant-eater. If *omni* means all or everything, what is an *omnivore*?

Well, people are omnivores. We eat pretty much everything, alas. Something with a huge appetite is *voracious*.

Breathing

Something else we do is breathe. The root *anima* means breath or spirit or soul. An *animal*, of course, is a living, breathing creature. Someone *animated* is full of life. Animated cartoons move as if alive. Something *inanimate* is lifeless.

Spir also means breath or soul. Your spirit lives. To *inspire* literally means to breath into, but we use it in its metaphorical sense, to arouse an animated or exalting influence.

Cant means to sing. We get the word *chant* from this root, as well as *cantor*, the leader of singing, and *incantation*, the chanting of spells.

Dic or *dict* means to speak. When you *dictate*, you speak aloud. When you *contradict*, you speak against. Your *diction* is your choice of words. Need we mention the word *dictionary*?

Locut or *loqu* also means to speak or talk. Someone who talks a lot is *loquacious*.

Sleeping

Somnus was the Roman god of sleep, so we have the words *somnolent* (sleepy, drowsy, or causing sleep), *somnambulist* (a sleepwalker), and *insomnia* (an inability to sleep.)

Before you fall asleep, try to memorize these roots. Then practice.

PRACTICE
Bene means good or well.
Vale means goodbye or farewell.

1. What is a *benediction*?
2. What is a *valediction*?
3. What is a *carnival*?

ANALYSIS
1. A *benediction* is a blessing (good speech, good words).
2. A *valediction* is a farewell speech. (A valedictorian delivers one.)
3. A *carnival* is a farewell to meat! You would have a carnival right before Lent.

Studying the following lists of roots, prefixes, and suffixes can help you break down many words into understandable sections. For the following roots, can you name some words that use these as prefixes? For instance, for the root *uni,* you could write the word *unicycle,* the one-wheeled vehicle.

Counting

semi/hemi/demi—half
mono—one
uni—one
duo—two
bi—two
tri—three
quad/quat—four
qunit—five
pent—five
sext—six
sept—seven (September used to be the seventh month.)
oct—eight (October used to be the eighth month.)
nov—nine (You get the picture.)
dec—ten
cent—hundred
mill—thousand
poly—many
proto—first

Okay, if the Latin root *ped* or *pod* means foot (think *pedal* or *pedestrian*), you should know the following words:

biped
quadruped
tripod
centipede

Note: The Greek root *ped* or *pedia* means child. So a *pediatrician* is a children's doctor; a *podiatrist* is a foot doctor.

Fear

The root *phobia* means fear or dislike. These are interesting to a lot of people. Surely you've heard of many of these phobias:

acrophobia—fear of heights
brontophobia—fear of thunder
pedophobia—fear of children
philophobia—fear of love
phonophobia—fear of sound
photophobia—fear of light
pyrophobia—fear of fire
somniphobia—fear of sleep
sophophobia- fear of learning
triskaidekaphobia—fear of the number 13

. . . and the most ironically named one of all:

sesquipedalophobia—the fear of long words!

Study

The root *logos* literally means word, so a *monologue* is a speech for one person. Another form of this root is *ology*, which means the science or study of something.

archaeology—study of ancient history
biology—study of life
cosmology—study of the universe
etymology—study of word origins
genealogy—study of family origins

geology—study of the earth
graphology—study of handwriting
psychology—study of the mind
seismology—study of earthquakes
sociology—study of society

Opposites

Take a look at these opposites. You've probably heard most of these; now you know how they work in words.

cide—kill
viv—live, alive   If you are full of life, you are *vivacious*.

micro—small   A *microscope* is an instrument you use to see small things.
macro—large

hyper—over, above
hypo—under, beneath

endo—within
exo—out of, outside

inter—between
intra—within

homo—alike
hetero—different

belli—war
pace—peace

pre—before
post—after

pro—forward
retro—backward

The following prefixes contain negative and positive feelings. There seem to be more negative roots. Hmmm . . .

Negative
a/an—not or without
a/ab—away or from
anti—against, opposite
contra—against
dis—apart, away
dys—bad, ill
mal—bad, ill
mis—hate

in/im—not
non—not
un—not
e/ex—out
ob/op—against

Positive
bene—good
eu—good
philo—love
con/col/com/cor/co—together, with
syn/sym—together, with
pro—forward

PRACTICE
Learn the following roots:

auto—self
sophos—wisdom
biblio—book
bio—life
anthropos—people
morph—form
graph—write, draw
potens/potent—power

Now identify the following words. If you can't define them, divide them into their component roots. For instance, for the first one, simply write out *biblio* and *phile*. Does that help you define the word?

1. bibliophile
2. misanthrope
3. philosopher
4. anthropomorphic
5. autograph
6. autobiography
   (You might have to go back earlier in the chapter for the next two.)
7. postmortem
8. omnipotent

ANALYSIS
1. *biblio + phile* = book lover
2. *mis + anthrope* = one who hates people
3. *philo + sopher* = lover of wisdom
4. *anthropo + morphic* = in the shape of man
5. *auto + graph* = self-write, your signature
6. *auto + bio + graphy* = your self-written story of your life
7. *post + mortem* = after death
8. *omni + potent* = all powerful

Family Roots

pater—father
mater—mother
frat—brother
sor—sister
gen—birth (*Progeny* means children or offspring.)

Senses and Such

vis / vid—see
tact / tangi—touch
audi—hear
son—sound
patho / pathy—feelings, suffering
corp—body
man—hand

Location

ad—to
ante—before
circum—around
con / com—together, with
de—from, down
in / il / im—in, into, on
inter—between
intro—within
peri—around, about
re—again, back
se—apart
tele—distant
trans—across, beyond
super—over, above

PRACTICE

If the root *port* means to carry, what do the following words mean?

1. transport
2. teleport
3. import
4. report
5. deport

ANALYSIS

1. transport—to carry across
2. teleport—to carry a long distance
3. import—to carry in
4. report—to carry back
5. deport—to carry away from

More Movement

tors / tort—twist
flect / flex—bend
fract / frag—break
rupt—break, burst
prehend / prehens—seize, grasp
ject—throw
vers / vert—turn
cur / curr / curs—run
grad— step

Faith

deo / theo—god
cred—believe
fid—faith, trust, loyalty

Did you know that Jupiter (deo-pater) is the father god?

Now you know why dogs are named Fido.

Authority

archy—rule
vict / vinc—conquer
cracy—government
mand—order, command

Conclusion (to close with)

Try combining and recombining these roots. You'll make up some new words and stumble onto some real ones you may not have heard yet!

Word List

This list of commonly tested words will get you started. We've supplied some of the definitions; be sure to read your dictionary and write your flashcards.

abet—to aid
abjure—to renounce, to give something up
abstemious—
accede—to agree to
acquiesce—
acrid—
adamant—hard, stubborn
affable—
agile—nimble, quick
alleviate—to make easier
aloof—
ambiguous—
ameliorate—to make easier
antediluvian—
antithesis—the opposite
apex—
apocryphal—doubtful in authenticity
ardor—passion
assuage—to make easier

astute—
autocrat—
avuncular—
bellicose—warlike
benefactor—
benighted—
benign—good
blatant—
blithe—happy
boon—a gift
breach—(n) a break, (v) to break
cacophony—
candid—
capitulate—
chaff—
circumlocution—talking in a roundabout way
cogent—
colloquial—
concur—to agree
console—to comfort
copious—
corporeal—
counterfeit—
credulous—
defer—
deplete—
deter—
dexterous—
dilemma—
diminutive—small
discreet—
discrete—
divulge—to tell
dormant—
dross—
edible—
egress—an exit
elegy—
engender—to bring forth
enmity—
equivocate—to lie by using ambiguous language
evoke—
extinct—
facile—
fallacy—
feign—to pretend
frugal—
fulsome—
garrulous—
gregarious—
guile—
gullible—
hamper— to hinder; to get in the way of; to interfere with
haughty—

heinous—
hew—
ignoble—
immaculate—
impair—
impede—
inane—
incite—
incredulous—
indelible—
indolent—
innocuous—harmless
intrepid—
ire—anger
jocular—
jubilant—
laudable—
lax—loose; not strict
lexicon—a dictionary
lithe—
lucid—
malcontent—
meander—
mendicant—a beggar
mettle—
mimic—
mollify—
morose—
mundane—ordinary
nadir—
noisome—having an offensive odor
obdurate—
oblique—
obstreperous—
odious—
opulent—
ostracize—to exclude
palpable—
panegyric—
paragon—
paramount—
pathos—
perfidious—
peripatetic—walking
pernicious—extremely harmful
petty—
pied—
pique—anger
plea—
potent—powerful
precocious—
prim—
protean—
prudent—

pugnacious—
query—
rapacious—
raze—to tear down
redoubtable—intimidating
regicide—
repugnant—offensive
ruminate—to turn over in your mind (literally, to chew cud)
sage—wise
sanguine—
serendipity—
shrewd—
smite—to strike, to hit
solace—
soporific—something that puts you to sleep
squalid—
stealthy—
submerge—
subtle—
taciturn—
tenacious—persistent, stubborn
torpid—
transient—
travail—hard work
trepidation—
truculent—
ubiquitous—
unctuous—
usurp—
valor—courage
veneer—
veracity—truthfulness
verbose—
vex—irritate, annoy
visage—
vivify—
wan—pale
wane—to decrease in size (along with *wax*, often used when describing the moon)
wax—to increase in size
zealot—
zenith—
zephyr —

Lists

On the HSPT and COOP, you will be shown a list of words and asked which word does not belong. These are not too difficult if you get a lot of simple, concrete nouns. For instance, which of the following words does not belong with the others?

(A) apple
(B) orange
(C) corn
(D) pear

The words are related to try to confuse you. You can *eat* all of these, and they all grow on *plants*, but apples, oranges, and pears are fruits that grow on trees. The odd one out is C, corn, a vegetable that grows on a stalk.

Oh, if life were always so easy . . . . It gets trickier. Sometimes you will be given three specific nouns and a general one (or vice-versa). For instance, which of the following words does not belong?

(A) novel
(B) book
(C) autobiography
(D) science fiction

Hmmm. You can read all of these, but A, C, and D are specific *kinds* of books, so the answer is B, book. Try another one:

(A) study guide
(B) test preparation
(C) learning aid
(D) *Barron's How to Prepare for the HSPT/COOP/TACHS*

This time it's the opposite. We have three general descriptions of a book and one specific one. The correct answer is D (of course).

Often you'll find lists of other parts of speech, such as adjectives and verbs.

(A) handsome
(B) comely
(C) unsightly
(D) alluring

Perhaps you don't know that *alluring* means attractive. You probably do know that *handsome* and *comely* are positive descriptions. *Unsightly* is negative, so it does not belong. Here's a trickier one:

(A) obvious
(B) obscure
(C) apparent
(D) clear

The choice that doesn't belong is B. The test makers tried to trick you by using opposite words that use the same prefix (*obvious* and *obscure*). However, if you **ask yourself what the words have in common**, you'll probably realize that *obvious* means clear and apparent, so B does not belong.

Let's try a list of verbs:

(A) receive
(B) refuse
(C) accept
(D) obtain

If you have trouble with this one, try picturing yourself performing these verbs. When you *receive*, *accept*, or *obtain* something, you are **getting** an object—you're opening your hands and taking it. When you *refuse* something, you are holding up your hands and **not** taking it. The answer is B, refuse.

This brings us to the most insidious (treacherous) trick of all: homographs, words that are spelled the same but have different definitions. What part of speech are the following two words?

(A) refuse
(B) object

Well, they seem like negative-sounding verbs: to reFUSE and to obJECT. However, look at the next two choices:

(A) refuse
(B) object
(C) scraps
(D) garbage

C **might** still be a verb, but it is a different form than the others (I object, I refuse, I scraps . . . . Naahh.) *Garbage*, however, is definitely a noun. In fact, pronounced a different way, they are all nouns: REFuse, OBject, scraps, and garbage. The word *object* is the only one that does not necessarily mean trash, so the answer is B.

Lesson: Read ALL of the choices.

PRACTICE
Choose the word that does *not* belong.

1. (A) jovial
   (B) content
   (C) melancholy
   (D) mirthful

2. (A) stroke
   (B) massage
   (C) swim
   (D) dive

3. (A) woodpecker
   (B) beak
   (C) puffin
   (D) bluejay

ANALYSIS
1. **C.** *Melancholy* is the only sad word; the others describe happiness.
2. **B.** This one contains a trick. If you look at the first two words, *stroke* and *massage* seem to be synonyms. However, *swim* and *dive* are associated with water activity. *Stroke* can also be in that category, but *massage* cannot.
3. **B.** The other choices are birds. This choice is a specific **part** of birds.

Synonyms and Antonyms—HSPT

Some HSPT questions will ask you to identify words that have similar meanings (synonyms). Other questions will ask you to identify words that have opposite meanings (antonyms).

Since you are acquiring a large, huge, voluminous, immense, massive, tremendous, enormous, capacious, colossal vocabulary, this will be easy, simple, and facile. Here's a sample question:

Similar most nearly means _____.

Without looking at the answers, how would you fill in the blank? Perhaps you'd use the word *alike*. Now look at the four choices that the test gives you.

(A) alike
(B) merry
(C) identical
(D) different

Ah, your choice is there, so you can be confident that the correct answer is *alike*. Something similar is not really identical; that choice is put there to lead you astray. Guessing ahead of time can sometimes help you to avoid confusion.

Try a harder one:

Dissident most nearly means _____.

(A) loyal
(B) weak
(C) feeble
(D) rebellious

Let's say that you don't know what the word *dissident* means, so you can't guess ahead of time. Look at the choices. Are any of them similar?

Yes, *weak* and *feeble* are synonyms. Well, you know you can't mark **both** B and C as correct answers, so those two are out. You're left with *loyal* and *rebellious*, words with opposite meanings. You can guess at this point, but give it just a bit more thought. Does the word *dissident* give you any kind of a feeling, positive or negative? Well, it's got the prefix *dis*; that doesn't sound very positive. *Rebellious* is our choice then, and it's correct.

Antonym questions involve the same process as we've already practiced. However, when you see the word, think of its **opposite**. It's easy to forget this when you're in a hurry, so take the time to register in your mind that you are looking for the choice that does **not** mean the same.

Similar means the opposite of _____.

Similar means *alike*, and the opposite of *alike* is *different*. What are our choices?

(A) alike
(B) merry
(C) identical
(D) different

There it is.

The same guessing and elimination strategies that you practiced for synonyms hold true for antonyms. Try it and see.

Dissident means the opposite of _____.

(A) loyal
(B) weak
(C) feeble
(D) rebellious

PRACTICE

1. *Diminutive* most nearly means _____.

(A) faded
(B) small
(C) dark
(D) dull

2. *Perilous* means the opposite of _____.

(A) safe
(B) dangerous
(C) precarious
(D) risky

ANALYSIS

1. (B) *Diminutive* means small. It does not mean dim.
2. (A) *Peril* means danger, so the only choice that is the opposite of dangerous is safe.

Some synonym questions will give you some context—but not much. In the Reading Vocabulary section of the HSPT, you will be given a phrase that contains an underlined word. For example, the question will look like this:

To <u>circumvent</u> the truth

(A) get around
(B) air out
(C) reveal
(D) speak

If you're familiar with the word, treat it as you would any other synonym question. The context can *sometimes* help you eliminate choices. Choice B, for instance, is awkward if you replace it for the underlined word. Do you ever "air out" the truth? You can eliminate that choice. You can also use the context phrase to check you answer in this way.

If you know that the prefix *circum-* means around (as in the word *circumference*), then you know that the answer is A.

Analogies—HSPT

How can you do well on analogies? Of course, the best way is to **know** all of the words! Analogies seem difficult at first, but they are actually the easiest type of question to figure out.

Analogies are sometimes written like this:

A : B :: C : D

What it means is this: A is to B as C is to D. Or, A relates to B in the same way that C relates to D.

Okay, now that you know that, you can forget it. The best way to learn analogies is to make your **own** sentence that includes the first pair of words. Try to make the sentence short, and try to use the word *means* or *is*, if possible. The relationship you're trying to build between these words should be clear and obvious.

For instance, let's say you get the following sentence.

Food is to pantry as clothes is to _____.

The sentence you create might be *Food goes into a pantry.* Then, use the next word in your sentence: *Clothes go into a _____.*

You may not even have to look at the choices. Fill in the logical word, *closet*. Then look at the choices to see if the word *closet* is there. If so, you've got the answer. If not, you'll need to create another sentence. Yours might not have been specific enough.

Oh, don't go crazy. You can overthink analogies and make them too complicated. *Food is edible and is kept cool and dark in a pantry; clothes are edible and they are kept cool and dark in a . . . .* No, this is **too** specific.

PRACTICE
Create sentences for the following pairs of words. Try to make the sentence as simple and logical as possible.

1. piece, puzzle
2. grass, green
3. caterpillar, butterfly
4. practice, succeed

ANALYSIS
1. A piece is part of a puzzle.
2. Grass is green.
3. A caterpillar becomes a butterfly.
4. If you practice, you will succeed.

Here's a **trick** from the last section that you can use if you're stumped by an analogy. Look at the choices. Are any of them synonyms? If so, they can't **both** be correct, so you can eliminate them! So even without looking at the analogy, can you eliminate any of the following choices? (Remember to look for **synonyms**.)

(A) error
(B) guilt
(C) mistake
(D) innocence

An *error* and a *mistake* are the same, aren't they? We can eliminate A and C as choices, as they can't both be the correct answer. This leaves us with *guilt* and *innocence*. We've just doubled our chances of getting the right answer.

Note: If you see two **opposite** choices (such as *guilt* and *innocence*), one of these is very often the correct answer.

Still completely stumped by an analogy? This shouldn't happen too often, since you now know so many vocabulary words and several tricks for solving the questions. However, as a final attempt, you can work backwards. You can make sentences with the answer words. If any of those make a very strong, logical connection, that *could* be the right answer!

[Unknown word] is to [another unknown word] as core is to _____.

(A) apple
(B) tree
(C) squirrel
(D) leaves

The answer is A. The other relationships with *core* make no sense.

PRACTICE

1. Freedom is to independence as purity is to _____.

    (A) error
    (B) guilt
    (C) mistake
    (D) innocence

2. Trust is to doubt as confess is to _____.

    (A) own
    (B) deny
    (C) admit
    (D) deter

3. Empathy is to feeling as comprehension is to _____.

    (A) understanding
    (B) ignorance
    (C) malevolence
    (D) enmity

ANALYSIS

1. **D.** Freedom is a part of independence. Purity is a part of innocence.
2. **B.** *Trust* is used as a verb here. If you trust something, you **don't** *doubt* it. If you confess something, you **don't** *deny* it.
3. **A.** Empathy is feeling. Comprehension is understanding.

Verbal Reasoning (Analogies)—COOP

Another type of verbal logic question will ask you to identify relationships among words. It's actually an analogy taken a step further; instead of two words, you have to relate three words.

For instance, what is the relationship between these words?

    horse   cow   pig

Again, making a sentence will help you. *A horse, a cow, and a pig are all farm animals.* Next, the test will ask you to choose a fourth word that belongs in that group.

    (A) chicken
    (B) goat
    (C) barn
    (D) corn

A chicken is a farm animal. Yes. *A goat is a farm animal.* Hmmm, yes again. *A barn is a farm animal.* No, it's not. *Corn is a farm animal.* No.

So we've got **two** possible answers. Can we go back and make our sentence more specific? *A horse, a cow, and a pig are all four-legged farm animals* or *A horse, a cow, and a pig are all farm mammals.* The answer is B. A goat has four legs; a goat is a mammal.

PRACTICE

Choose the word that is most like the underlined words.

1. Mars   Venus   Jupiter

    (A) moon
    (B) Neptune
    (C) comet
    (D) asteroid

2. monotonous   uniform   unvarying

    (F) alone
    (G) unchanging
    (H) variegated
    (J) incongruous

ANALYSIS

1. **B.** *Mars, Venus,* and *Jupiter* are planets. The *moon* is not a planet. *Neptune* is.
2. **G.** Something *monotonous* is *uniform* and *unvarying*—and *unchanging*. Because of the prefixes *mono* and *uni*, you might be tricked into thinking that the answer is F, *alone.* Make sure you take **all** of the words into account: *unvarying* does not mean *single* or *alone.* Do you know what *incongruous* means? The prefix *in* means *not*, and *con* means *with* or *together*, so you can already figure out that *not together* isn't a synonym for *uniform* or *unvarying*. (By the way, *incongruous* means *out of place* or *inconsistent. Variegated* means *varied in appearance* or *multicolored*.)

Easy enough, eh? You shouldn't have any trouble with these if you've been practicing making sentences, so it would be a good idea to review the last section on analogies and do the exercises.

The COOP isn't willing to leave this alone, however. You'll find additional questions that essentially double this exercise. So now that you've seen analogies and three-part analogies, get ready for double three-part analogies! The problems look like this:

walk	jog	sprint
hour	minute	_____

The words in the top row have a particular relationship, and you are to figure that out and apply it to the bottom row. Let's break it down. Start with the top row only: *walk, jog,* and *sprint.* These are all ways of traveling distance on foot. Furthermore, they increase in speed or intensity. So make a sentence and a mental picture of these words:

*Walk*ing is slower than *jog*ging, which is slower than *sprint*ing.

Now fill in the blank for the related sequence in the bottom row.

hour	minute	_____

Okay, we'll give you four choices: *race, day, second,* or *clock.*

Did you guess the word *second*? That's correct. The relationship is not exactly the same as the first example, but it is similar enough that you can infer the answer.

Here's another type of relationship. The following words are the top row:

mammal	feline	tiger

Try to make a sentence using the words. Sometimes it might be easier to use the words in reverse order:

A *tiger* is a type of *feline*, which is a type of *mammal.*

Now try the bottom row. Using the same kind of sentence, choose the missing word.

vegetable	melon	_____

(A) fruit
(B) seeds
(C) cantaloupe
(D) vine

The answer is C. A cantaloupe is a type of melon, which is a type of vegetable.

PRACTICE

The words in the top row are related. The words in the bottom row are related in a similar way. Choose the word that completes the sequence in the bottom row.

1.

violin	cello	guitar
guppy	minnow	_____

(A) sardine
(B) dolphin
(C) whale
(D) fish

2. pamphlet   magazine   book

    hut   _____   mansion

    (F) wood
    (G) skyscraper
    (H) cottage
    (J) room

ANSWERS

1. **A.** The words in the top row are all types of stringed instruments. The words in the bottom row are all types of fish. Choice D, *fish*, is too general; choices B and C are water animals, but they are not fish.

2. **H.** The fact that a pamphlet, magazine, and book are all types of reading material is not specific enough in this case, so you'll have to try another sentence. A pamphlet is smaller than a magazine, which is smaller than a book. A hut is smaller than a *cottage*, which is smaller than a mansion. The other choices are related to housing, but they do not fit the intermediate size that belongs in the sequence.

More Verbal Reasoning—COOP

On the COOP, you will be given a word and asked to choose a word that is a **necessary part** of that word. This sounds a bit complicated, but it isn't really. For example, you will be given a word such as this:

<u>fortress</u>

When you look at the choices, ask yourself, "Does a fortress HAVE to have ____?" Let's try it.

    (A) stone
    (B) roof
    (C) moat
    (D) walls

Does a fortress HAVE to have stone? No, a fortress can be made of wood or mud. *Does it HAVE to have a roof?* No, many do not. *Does it HAVE to have a moat?* It's true that many fortresses were surrounded by moats and ditches, but that isn't a necessary part of it. *Does a fortress HAVE to have walls?* Yes, in order to provide protection, a fortress has walls of some sort. The answer is D.

Another way to approach this is to picture the first word and then read each of the following choices. Take that choice *out* of your picture and see if anything is left.

<u>flower</u>

    (F) stem
    (G) leaves
    (H) petals
    (J) soil

Picture a *flower*. Take away the *stem*. Is it still a flower? Yes, it is. It could be a corsage or a boutonniere. Take away the *leaves*. Is it still a flower? Yes, the leaves are often removed by florists, and what's left is still a flower. Take away the *petals*. Is it still a flower? No, what you have now is a plant. Take away the *soil*. Is it still a flower? Yes, it's still a flower. Put it in a vase with some water. The answer is H.

PRACTICE
Find the word that names a necessary part of the *underlined* word. (Remember to try asking yourself the question *"Does it have to have . . .?"*)

<u>bird</u>

(A) feathers
(B) flight
(C) wings
(D) song

ANALYSIS
Does a bird HAVE to have feathers? Well, it could be a baby bird; it's still a bird. Does a bird HAVE to have flight? No, it could be a penguin or an ostrich. Does a bird HAVE to have wings? Yes, that makes it a bird. Does it HAVE to sing? No, it's still a bird when it's quiet. The answer is C.

Verbal Logic—HSPT

The logic questions on the HSPT can give you a headache. You don't have a lot of time, and they're throwing trivial information at you about a bunch of people you don't know.

Picture it. You've got seconds to absorb this information:

Sierra owns more troll dolls than Aspen. Sierra owns fewer troll dolls than Bismarck. Bismarck owns more troll dolls than Aspen. If the first two statements are true, the third statement is _____.

(A) true
(B) false
(C) uncertain

You will fail the exam if you scream, "Who cares?" So pretend that you care deeply. Sadly, you don't have much time to spend with Sierra and friends.

Fortunately, we have a quick way for you to figure out this problem/dilemma/quandary/puzzle/enigma. Developed by our cave ancestors, it's called *drawing a diagram.*

You don't have to use fancy pictures; letters work best. As soon as you read the first sentence (Sierra owns more troll dolls than Aspen.), write the letter S in the margin—right there in the test booklet. **Below** it, write the letter A, since Sierra owns more troll dolls than Aspen. It will look like this:

S *Sierra owns more troll dolls than Aspen.* Sierra owns fewer troll dolls than
A Bismarck. Bismarck owns more troll dolls than Aspen. If the first two statements are true, the third statement is _____.

The next sentence tells us that Sierra owns fewer troll dolls than Bismarck. Since Bismarck has more, place the letter B <u>above</u> the S.

B
S Sierra owns more troll dolls than Aspen. *Sierra owns fewer troll dolls than*
A *Bismarck.* Bismarck owns more troll dolls than Aspen. If the first two statements are true, the third statement is _____.

Now stop drawing, and look at the third sentence: *Bismarck owns more troll dolls than Aspen.* A glance at our diagram shows us that this is **true**. He/she/it does. Congratulations to all.

Sometimes you can't draw a clear diagram. Try this one:

Palestrina is taller than Monteverdi. Palestrina is taller than Josquin. Monteverdi is taller than Josquin. If the first two statements are true, the third statement is
_____.

The first sentence is easy enough to draw. *Palestrina is taller than Monteverdi.*

P
M

The next sentence doesn't help us much, though. *Palestrina is taller than Josquin.* Where do we put poor Josquin? He goes under Palestrina, but we are given no relation to Monteverdi. They're both shorter than Palestrina, so the best we can do is this:

P
M J

Therefore, the third sentence—*Monteverdi is taller than Josquin*—cannot be proven. The answer is C, uncertain.

You may encounter another type of logic question on the HSPT. Rather than greater or less-than relationships, it may be a connection among parts and a whole. For instance,

No sixth graders take Geography. Beowulf takes Geography during first period. Beowulf is in the sixth grade. If the first two statements are true, the third statement is _____.

(A) true
(B) false
(C) uncertain

This type of question may be easy enough that you don't need a diagram. If you do, though, it might look like this:

The rectangle is Geography class. The circle is the sixth grade. It is outside of the Geography class, since no sixth graders are scheduled there. The B is our friend Beowulf, who is in the Geography class. Obviously, he is NOT in the sixth grade. The third statement is false, B.

Verbal Logic—COOP

The Verbal Reasoning in Context section of the COOP tests how well you can make inferences given a certain amount of data. You will be given two or three sentences. Based on the information in these sentences, you are to choose a true statement that follows. This is an interesting little challenge; the choices will all be related, but only one can be true. This one is a fact, while the others are simply assumptions.

Read the first three sentences. Then look at each choice, and ask yourself if it MUST be true. Is it NECESSARILY true? Let's try a few.

Izzy likes to draw with crayons. She has a box containing many colors of crayons. The picture she drew for me is all blue.

(A) I asked Izzy for an all-blue picture.
(B) Izzy was feeling sad that day.
(C) I have a blue picture.
(D) Izzy doesn't like me.

Okay, here's what we know: Izzy has a lot of crayons, but she gave me a picture that was all blue.

Let's go through the choices. *I asked Izzy for an all-blue picture.* This could be true, but our information does not make it necessarily true. *Izzy was feeling sad that day.* We are given no information about whether she was happy or sad, so that is merely an assumption. *I have a blue picture.* This is definitely true. *Izzy doesn't like me.* This is a silly conclusion; does our information make that necessary? No, it does not. Only one choice is obvious: C.

The lesson here is that you should not be afraid to pick the obvious choice. Only one is based on facts. For the rest, you'll be jumping to conclusions.

Try another one:

Mrs. Drake teaches history. She also has a degree in English. She will be teaching at another school next year.

(F) Mrs. Drake is taking a job teaching English.
(G) Mrs. Drake is unhappy teaching history.
(H) Mrs. Drake is still a teacher.
(J) Mrs. Drake is being transferred.

Mrs. Drake is taking a job teaching English. We know she has a degree in English, but we are never told she is going to teach it. *Mrs. Drake is unhappy teaching history.* We are never told this, either. It's an unfounded guess. *Mrs. Drake is still a teacher.* We are indeed told this. She will be teaching at another school. *Mrs. Drake is being transferred.* Again, this is not necessarily true. She could be moving for other reasons; she could have gone to another school by choice, for instance. The answer is obviously H.

When I was in elementary school, I used to get a new lunch box every year. It made going to school more fun. Now I eat in the school cafeteria.

(A) School is no longer fun.
(B) Cafeteria food is delicious.
(C) Our school does not allow students to bring lunch.
(D) I don't bring my lunch to school.

School is no longer fun. This is not necessarily logical. Perhaps now that you're older, you don't need a lunchbox to make school fun. *Cafeteria food is delicious.* Again, this does not necessarily follow. Maybe it's good on some days, and maybe it's not on others. *Our school does not allow students to bring lunch.* We were never given this information. *I don't bring my lunch to school.* Well, it's not a very interesting answer, but it's the only one we know for certain. The answer is D.

It doesn't take a Sherlock Holmes to see that these are not difficult problems to solve—as long as you stick to the original facts.

Language Arts

Introduction

Both the HSPT and the COOP require you to demonstrate your knowledge of English punctuation, usage, and composition. The HSPT contains an entire section devoted to these skills, while the COOP now integrates the Language Arts questions into the Reading Comprehension section.

The types of questions INCLUDE the following:

HSPT	COOP
Identify errors in usage, capitalization, and punctuation	Identify errors in usage, capitalization, and punctuation
Combine sentences	Combine sentences
Choose the clearest sentence	Choose the clearest sentence
Choose the correct word in a sentence	Choose the correct word in a sentence
Choose the sentence that does not belong	Choose the sentence that does not belong
Choose the sentence that fits a topic or paragraph	Choose the sentence that fits a topic or paragraph
Place a sentence logically in a paragraph	Place a sentence logically in a paragraph
Identify spelling errors	No corresponding section on spelling
Choose an appropriate topic for a paragraph	No corresponding section

As you can see, recent changes to the tests have resulted in more overlap between them than ever before. Therefore, a general review of grammar and composition will help you with both tests. Furthermore, having a command of what makes a good composition, including grammar, usage, and mechanics, is a tremendous tool for identifying the correct answers.

You should flag any answer choice that contains an error of any kind. If the directions ask you to identify errors, you have found the correct response. In all other cases, that answer can be eliminated. For instance, one section of the test asks you to choose a sentence that best completes a paragraph. In that case, you can eliminate a sentence that contains a comma error.

Study the following review **in order**; read through all of it, even if you think you already know some sections. You don't need to memorize every label, but you will need to understand a concept in order to master a later one. Relax. Take the time to learn each section thoroughly. Don't try to tackle all of this in one sitting. **Take a break to let each skill sink in, and then go back over it again before moving on.** Brain research shows that this rest and repetition technique is a great way to learn and retain information.

Sentences: Subjects and Predicates

A **sentence** contains two essential elements.

1. It names something (the subject).
2. That something performs an action (the predicate).

| A sentence | states a complete thought. |
| Subject | Predicate |

| The predicate | contains a verb. |
| Subject | Predicate |

| The reader | is waking up right about now. |
| Subject | Predicate |

But that's not all! The predicate (besides describing a physical action) can also identify a state of being. That is, it can describe or rename the subject using verbs such as *am, is, are, was, were, be, being,* or *been.*

| This sentence | is simple. |
| Subject | Predicate |

| The subject | is always a noun. |
| Subject | Predicate |

| The reader | was so excited by the grammar chapter. |
| Subject | Predicate |

One of the most powerful techniques you can use in Language Arts is to **identify the simple subject and the simple predicate of a sentence.** You can tame the most complicated grammatical construction with this strategy, so let's review. The simple predicate is the **verb,** the action or state of being in the sentence; the **subject** is the actor—the person, place, or thing (noun) performing that action. Can you underline the simple subject and the simple verb in the following sentence?

For example, the stalwart student, forced to endure the longest, most tedious, most tortured sentence in the most obscure, archaic, dust-covered book, finds both a simple subject, which will always be a noun, and a simple predicate, which will always be a verb.

This sentence can be broken down to this: **<u>Student</u> <u>finds</u>.**

That's it. The actor of the sentence is the **student.** The student <u>finds</u> stuff.

In present-day English, we like the subject to appear first, followed by the verb. However, this is not always the case. Read the following sentences; in each, the subject is in bold print and the verb is underlined.

The **dog** <u>chased</u> her tail.
(This is a standard S-V construction: **dog** <u>chased</u>.)

<u>Am</u> **I** calm and confident?
<u>Did</u> **you** <u>remember</u> to bring a pencil?
(Questions mix the usual order: **I** <u>am</u>, **you** <u>did remember</u>.)

On the very top of the hill <u>stands</u> my **house**.
(The subject is delayed for effect: **house** <u>stands</u>.)

There <u>was</u> a young **man** from Peru.
(**Man** <u>was</u>. *There* is not a noun; it tells where the man was.)

COMPOUND SUBJECTS AND PREDICATES

A sentence can contain more than one subject and verb. They should **not** be separated by commas unless they are part of a series.

My **aunt** and my **uncle** <u>are visiting</u> us.   (Compound subject)
They <u>write</u> and <u>edit</u> books for a living.   (Compound verb)
Mia, Isabella, and **Josie** <u>are</u> my cousins. (Notice that no comma appears after *Josie*.)

COMPOUND SENTENCES

A **compound sentence** combines two complete sentences (**subject** and <u>verb</u> + **subject** and <u>verb</u>) with a comma and a conjunction (a connecting word such as *and, or, but, for, nor, so,* and *yet*).

My **cousins** <u>are visiting</u> , *and* **they** <u>brought</u> their parents with them.

My **aunt** <u>is</u> a friendly woman, *but* my **uncle** only <u>talks</u> to dogs.

SUBJECT-VERB AGREEMENT

Now that you can identify subject and verb, you have the skill to answer a common test question: checking subject-verb agreement. The subject and verb of a sentence should agree in number (singular, plural) and person (first, second, or third person). This sounds more complicated than it is. The easiest way to approach this type of question is to **isolate the subject and verb** as we did earlier; then hear if it makes sense. The trick here, of course, is that the subject and verb may be separated in the sentence, so it is important to identify these two elements correctly, even if you must mark them on the exam. Cross out or bracket any phrases that separate the subject and verb; they are there to confuse you.

PRACTICE
Are the following sentences written correctly?

1. Many questions on the test asks you to identify errors in subject-verb agreement.
2. Is the following sentences written correctly?
3. June and July goes by so quickly.

ANALYSIS
1. In this sentence, the verb is *asks*. What asks? The test does not ask. The **questions ask**. If you marked it, the sentence would look like this:

   Many **questions** [on the test] <u>asks</u> you to identify errors in subject-verb agreement. (Questions asks? This sentence is incorrect. **Questions** <u>ask</u>.)

2. In this example, the subject is in the middle of the sentence.

> <u>Is</u> the following **sentences** <u>written</u> correctly?
> (Incorrect. **Sentences** <u>are written</u>.)

3. In the third example, the subject is plural.

> **June** and **July** <u>goes</u> by so quickly. (Incorrect. **June** and **July** <u>go</u>. **They** <u>go</u>.)

MORE PRACTICE

Are the following sentences written correctly?

1. Both of the exams require you to demonstrate your verbal skills.
2. Each of the exams require you to demonstrate your verbal skills.
3. One of the exams requires more memorization.

ANALYSIS

Ignore the prepositional phrase *of the exams*, and identify the subject and verb.

1. **Both** [of the exams] <u>require</u>.   Correct. *Both* is plural. (Two require.)
2. **Each** [of the exams] <u>require</u>.   Incorrect. *Each* is singular.
   It should read **Each** <u>requires</u>. (Each one requires.)
3. **One** [of the exams] <u>requires</u>.   Correct. One <u>requires</u>.

SENTENCE FRAGMENTS

Remember, a sentence **must** have a subject and a verb. (This is called a clause.)

> **Santa** <u>is</u> a Claus.   A **sentence** <u>is</u> a clause.

Note: Commands have only a verb because the understood subject is *You*.

> Remember that.
> [**You**] <u>remember</u> that.

We often speak in fragments, but formal writing on the exams should consist of complete sentences.

> No one may write in fragments. Except for me.
>   (*Except for me* is a fragment.)

If you have trouble identifying fragments, try placing the words *I heard that...* or *Is it true that ... ?* in front of the passage. This often makes the fragment more obvious.

> I heard that except for me.
> Is it true that except for me?   (These make even less sense.)

A sentence must also make complete sense standing alone. (This is called an *independent* clause.) So be on the lookout for subordinating conjunctions such as *because, since, even though, if, unless,* and *while*. These are called subordinating because they must depend on a complete sentence to make sense.

Because I would not stop for the bus.

This contains a noun and a verb, but it is a *dependent* clause. It cannot stand alone because of the word *because*. Try the test.

I heard that because I would not stop for the bus.
Is it true that because I would not stop for the bus?

This is obviously a fragment. It needs to depend on a sentence to make sense.

Because I would not stop for the bus, **it**   <u>stopped</u> for me.
                                 subject   *verb*

Note: This "I heard that" test only works with a traditional subject-verb sentence. You'll have to add the implied subject in a command.

Keep off the grass.
I heard that keep off the grass. Confusing—add the subject.
I heard that [you] keep off the grass. [Ah. Yes.]

You'll also have to rearrange questions.

<u>Are</u> **you** ready?
I heard that are you ready. Confusing—rearrange the subject and verb.
I heard that **you** <u>are</u> ready. [Yes, it's a complete sentence.]

PRACTICE
Are the following examples written in complete sentences?
1. He has trouble with fragments. Even though he is an excellent reader.
2. Fragment or not a fragment?

ANALYSIS
1. I heard that he has trouble with fragments. (This sounds fine.)
   I heard that even though he is an excellent reader. (Fragment. Incorrect.)
2. Fragment. (Some of these are just easy.)

REVIEW
Okay, let's see if you can identify these sentence errors before we move on.

Repetition, and reinforcement is important in the learning process. Because we retain more when we practice. We should also give the material time to sink in while we rest. Don't this make grammar seem like a sport? Take a break after this exercise.

CORRECTIONS
Repetit<u>on and</u> reinforcement **are** important in the learning pr<u>ocess because</u> we retain more when we practice. We should also give the material time to sink in while we rest. **Doesn't** this make grammar seem like a sport? Take a break after this exercise.

Parts of Speech

Grammarians generally agree on eight parts of speech: **nouns, verbs, prepositions, pronouns, adjectives, adverbs, conjunctions,** and **interjections**. You can't always tell what part of speech a word is—it depends on its context in the sentence, so now you'll have to read the test sentences carefully in their entirety.

We **are trying** to win. (*Are trying* is the verb.)
Trying is better than quitting. (*Trying* is a noun in this example.)
I found it to be a **trying** lesson. (Here it is an adjective.)

The tests will sometimes try to confuse you by playing with the different parts of speech. For instance, can you make sense of the following sentence?

Time flies like an arrow; fruit flies like a banana.

Think about this for a few seconds. Without looking at the answer, can you reword or rewrite the sentence so that the meaning is clearer?

ANSWER
Time <u>flies</u> like an arrow; fruit **flies** <u>like</u> a banana.
  S   V   S   V

Time takes flight as an arrow does, but the insects around fruit enjoy a banana.

NOUNS

A **noun**, as you know, is a person, place, thing, or idea. You've seen that it can act as the subject of a sentence, but it can also be an object or a complement. For instance, a **direct object** receives the action done by the subject.

The **dog** <u>chased</u> her *tail*.   What did the dog chase? Her tail.
subject   verb   object

A noun complement (also called a subjective complement or a predicate noun) renames the subject.

That **dog** <u>is</u> a poodle.   (*Poodle* is a noun telling what kind of dog it is.)
Her **name** <u>is</u> Sophie.   (*Sophie* identifies the subject.)

PRACTICE
1. Finding this subject requires more thinking. (Identify the subject.)
2. Finding this object requires more thinking. (Identify the object.)
3. Actually, these *-ing* nouns are called gerunds. (Identify the noun complement.)

ANALYSIS
1. Even though we usually think of the word *find* as a verb, some *-ing* forms may act as nouns. The subject is *Finding*.

   Finding this subject <u>requires</u> more thinking.

2. Ask yourself: Finding requires what? The direct object is *thinking*, another *-ing* noun.
3. Actually, these *-ing* **nouns** <u>are called</u> gerunds. (The word *gerunds* is the predicate noun because it identifies the subject.)

VERBS

You should also be able to identify the correct forms and tenses of **verbs**. You don't need to be able to label them (past participle, future perfect, etc.), but you should be able to tell if they are correct or incorrect by the sound of the sentence. Again, read the entire sentence to make sure the verb makes sense in context.

PRACTICE

Correct the following sentences:
1. I take the test yesterday.
2. I had took the last doughnut.
3. I brung my lunch to school.

ANALYSIS

1. The tense here is obviously wrong. I <u>took</u> the test yesterday. *Yesterday* is a key word.
2. The correct form is *I had taken*.
3. Brung? I <u>brought</u> my lunch to school.

PREPOSITIONS

A **preposition** is a word that connects a noun to a sentence, usually indicating a relationship in space or time. You probably learned the following mnemonic device (memory aid), in which you can fill a preposition in the blank.

> The mouse ran ___ the house. [in, on, through, around, under, over, to, from, behind, etc.]
> The mouse ran ____ vacation. [during, before, after, etc.]

However, remember that some prepositions don't fit this formula; **the word *of* is a very common preposition**, along with *with*, *for*, *due to*, *except*, *instead of*, etc. You probably will not be asked to identify prepositions on the exams, but **you will need to understand how they work** in order to identify other sentence errors.

Prepositional phrases consist of the prepositions and the nouns they connect to the sentence. For instance, in the following sentence, we'll put brackets around the prepositional phrases.

> The nouns in brackets are the **objects** of the prepositions.

> The **nouns** [in **brackets**] <u>are</u> the **objects**   [of the **prepositions**].
>   *subject*   *prep.*   *o.p.*   *verb*   *complement*   *prep.*   *o.p. (object of the preposition)*

The basic sentence simply states that ***nouns <u>are</u>*** objects. The prepositional phrases simply add more information.

PRACTICE

In the following sentence, put brackets around the prepositional phrases (the prepositions and the nouns they connect).

1. Some of the stories in the Bible speak to me on a personal level.

ANALYSIS

1. **Some** [of the stories] [in the Bible] <u>speak</u> [to me] [on a personal level]. Again, this will help you with subject-verb agreement. For instance, the verb *speaks* would be incorrect in the above sentence.

REVIEW
REVIEW
Identify the nouns, verbs, and prepositional phrases in the following. Some are used correctly, while others are not.

1. The number of push-ups increases in gym class yesterday.
2. In the opinion of many doctors, walking is an effective exercise for most people.
3. After exercise, you should rest and recuperate.
4. Rest before the next section.

CORRECTIONS
1. The **number** [of push-ups] __increased__ [in gym class] yesterday.
       subject   *verb—past tense because it took place yesterday*

2. [In the opinion] [of many doctors,] **walking** is an effective **exercise** [for most people].
                                      subject *verb*   *noun complement*

3. [After exercise], **you** should rest and recuperate.
                      subject   *verb*

4. Rest [before the next section].
   verb *(The subject **You** is understood in commands.)*

PRONOUNS

Pronouns are words that take the place of nouns. The nouns they replace are called the **antecedents**. For instance, without pronouns, we would write this way:

> Colonel Mustard calmly picked up the piece of paper and put the piece of paper in Colonel Mustard's pocket. Mr. Green saw Colonel Mustard.

Pronouns can simplify the sentence.

> Colonel Mustard calmly picked up the piece of paper and put **it** in **his** pocket. Mr. Green saw **him**.

It is the pronoun replacing the antecedent *piece of paper. His* and *him* replace the antecedent *Colonel Mustard.*

Pronoun-Antecedent Agreement

Pronoun agreement is a problem for many writers, and it's a tricky construction to identify. Make sure that a pronoun agrees in number with the noun that it replaces. For instance, in the previous example, it would make no sense to write this:

> Colonel Mustard calmly picked up a piece of paper and put it in **their** pocket.

PRACTICE
1. Is the following sentence written correctly? If not, correct it.

> The reader is often confused when they encounter disagreement of this sort.

ANALYSIS

1. If we mark the pronoun and its antecedent, it looks like this:

> The <u>reader</u> is often confused when <u>they</u> encounter disagreement of this sort.

We can see that this is incorrect. *Reader* is singular and *they* is plural. We can rewrite the sentence a couple of ways.

> The <u>reader</u> is often confused when <u>he or she</u> encounters disagreement of this sort.
> <u>Readers</u> are often confused when <u>they</u> encounter disagreement of this sort.

Pronoun Case

Pronoun case is just a fancy way of saying that you should be able to tell whether a pronoun is a **subject** (doing an action) or an **object** (receiving an action). The following chart can help:

Subjects		Objects	
(They ACT. They DO things!)		(They RECEIVE action. They just take it.)	
I	am talking	to	me.
He	is talking	to	him.
She	is talking	to	her.
They	are talking	to	them.
We	are talking	to	us.
Who	is talking	to	whom.

The object forms in this chart are actually objects of prepositions. However, this pattern is easy to remember; study these sentences, and you should have no trouble with *who* and *whom*. (Owls are supposed to be so smart, but they say "To-who" when they should say "To-whom." An owl has never successfully passed the HSPT/COOP.)

Note: On the exams, don't let added words trick you. For example:

> She and me deduced the answers to the COOP questions.

Take out one of the pronouns and see if it still makes sense.

> **She** deduced the answers. Okay.
> **Me** deduced the answers. Is Tarzan speaking? Incorrect.
> **She** <u>and I</u> deduced the answers. Correct. They are both SUBJECT pronouns.

PRACTICE

Correct the following sentences. Why should they be changed?

1. Him and her passed the test.
2. Whomever will help us?
3. These questions don't bother you and I.

ANALYSIS

1. *Him* and *her* are objects. (He talks to him. She talks to her.)
   Correction: **He** and **she** passed the test.
2. We know that *whom* is an object. (Who talks to whom.)
   Correction: **Whoever** will help us.

3. These questions don't bother **you**.   (This sounds fine.)
    These questions don't bother **I**.   (Incorrect. *I* is a subject.)
        Correction: These questions don't bother **me**.
    (That's better. The word *me* is an object.
        So: These questions don't bother **you** and **me**.)

Possessive Pronouns

Now we're moving into another problem area. Most student writers have difficulty with the words *it's* and *its*. Here is a way to remember the correct usage. The possessive pronouns that end with the letter *s* are *his*, *hers*, *theirs*, *yours*, and *its*. They do **not** use apostrophes. We do not write *her's*, *hi's*, *their's*, and *your's*, so we do not use *it's*.

> **Remember**: *It's* **always** stands for a contraction: *it is* or *it has*.

> Likewise, *you're* stands for *you are*. The possessive pronoun is *Your*.

> > Your hat belongs to you. You're so attractive in it.

> The contraction *they're* stands for *they are*. The possessive pronoun is *their*.

> > Their shoes have three-inch platforms. They're stuck in the 1970s.

> The contraction *who's* stands for *who is*. *Whose* is possessive.

> > Whose weasels are those? Who's writing these things, anyway?

> Whenever you see the words *it's*, *you're*, *they're*, or *who's,* mentally fill in the words *it is, you are, they are,* or *who is*. Make this a habit.

PRACTICE
Are these sentences correct or incorrect?

1. It's a beautiful day in the neighborhood.
2. You're so confident that its scary.
3. The test contains its share of sentences such as this one.

ANALYSIS
1. Fill in the contraction. It is a beautiful day. Correct.
2. *You are so confident* is correct, but *its scary* should be a contraction: *it's (it is) scary*. Incorrect.
3. If the test were a person, you could say *The test contains his share* or *The test contains her share*. It requires a possessive pronoun. The word *its* is correct.

ADJECTIVES AND ADVERBS

Adjectives describe (modify) nouns.

> The <u>precarious</u> bridge could not hold us. (*Precarious* describes the noun *bridge*.)

Adverbs describe other parts of speech: verbs, adjectives, and other adverbs.

> The bridge was swinging <u>precariously</u>. (*Precariously* describes how the bridge <u>was</u> <u>swinging</u>.)

Note: Adverbs often end with **-ly**—but not always.

Two common adverbs are *very* and *not*.

> I <u>do</u> **not** <u>run</u> **very** well after a big lunch.

The adverb *not* describes the verb *do run*. The adverb *very* describes the adjective *well*.

Note the usage:

> You write **good**.
> (*Good* is always an adjective. It only describes nouns. Incorrect.)
> You write **well**.
> (*Well* is used as an adverb describing *write*. Correct.)

However, *well* is used as an adjective when describing health.

> You look **well**. I don't feel **well**. Correct.

Comparisons

> He is the best of the pair. (Incorrect—*best* is an adjective used with more than two items.)
> He is the better of the pair. (Correct.)

> If you can run a mile in six minutes, you are a **good** runner.
> If you beat your friend in a race, you are the **better** runner of the two of you.
> If you outrun more than one friend, you are the **best** runner in the race.

When comparing with adjectives of one syllable, *-er* and *-est* endings are usually standard:

> big, bigger, biggest   fast, faster, fastest

With adjectives of three or more syllables, it is more common to use the adverbs *more* / *most* and *less* / *least*.

> more confident, most confident   less difficult, least difficult

With adjectives of two syllables, the practice varies; however, the use of *more*, *most*, *less*, and *least* is more common.

> handsomer *or* more handsome   commonest *or* most common

Note: When comparing **adverbs**, we generally use the words *more*, *most*, *less*, and *least*.

> more quickly   most likely   less elegantly   least willingly

PRACTICE
Are the following sentences correct*ly* written?

1. The friendly giant protected the village.
2. Tweedle-Dee was the fattest of the duo.
3. The air is more drier in the desert than in the tropics.

ANALYSIS

1. Even though it ends with *-ly*, *friendly* describes the noun *giant*, so it is an adjective. Correct.
2. *Fattest* is an adjective used with more than two items. Incorrect. Change it to this: Tweedle-Dee was the *fatter* of the duo. Correct.
3. This sentence uses two comparative words in succession. Incorrect. Remove the word *more*. The air is drier . . . .

REVIEW

Correct the following errors in pronoun use, adjectives, and adverbs.

> My cousin and me disagree on an important issue. Whom is the better superhero—Batman or Superman? She likes Superman because he is invincible. I like Batman because he definite is not. He is the most human of the two. A reader is always unsure of the outcome when they read a Batman comic. A story is more exciting when its more suspensfuler.

CORRECTIONS

> My cousin and **I** disagree on an important issue. **Who** is the better superhero—Batman or Superman? She likes Superman because he is invincible. I like Batman because he **definitely** is not. He is the **more** human of the two. **Readers are** always unsure of the outcome when **they** read a Batman comic. A story is more exciting when **it's** [it is] **more suspenseful**.

CONJUNCTIONS

Conjunctions are connecting words. **Coordinating conjunctions** connect equal parts of a sentence. The acronym FANBOYS can help you remember these: *for, and, nor, but, or, yet,* and *so*. When two sentences (independent clauses) are joined, they use one of these coordinating conjunctions **and a comma**.

> **You** <u>remember</u> this rule **, but**   **we** <u>will repeat</u> it anyway.
> *subject*   *verb*   *,conjunction* *subject*   *verb*

> **You** just <u>read</u> this rule **, yet**   **we**   <u>repeat</u> it again.
> *subject*   *verb*   *,conjunction* *subject* *verb*

Certain conjunctions are used in pairs. Check these **correlative conjunctions** to make sure one of them is not left out of a sentence.

Either _____ or _____	You're either with us or against us.
Neither _____ nor _____	That's neither here nor there.
Whether _____ or _____	I can't tell whether you're happy or sad.
Both _____ and _____	Both Mutt and Jeff arrived early.

We discussed **subordinating conjunctions** (*because, since, even though, if, unless, while,* etc.) under the section entitled "Sentence Fragments" on page 134.

INTERJECTIONS

Easy! **Interjections** are words that express strong feeling. They usually use an exclamation point, but they can be punctuated with a comma.

Oh! I knew this one!   Oh, I understand.

PRACTICE
1. Neither the wind or the rain bothered the mail carrier.
2. Swimming! I'd love to learn how to swim, but I'm afraid of deep water.

ANALYSIS
1. *Neither* should be paired with the word *nor*. Incorrect.
2. Correct. Not only is the interjection appropriate, but the comma and conjunction join two independent clauses.

OTHER MODIFIERS

Dangling and Misplaced Modifiers

A **dangling modifier** is a word, phrase, or clause that is meant to describe a word in a sentence, but that word is missing.

While eating, the radio plays soft music. (Can a radio eat?)
While we're eating, the radio plays soft music. (Better.)

A **misplaced modifier** is placed awkwardly in a sentence so that it seems to describe something else.

Placed in an awkward position, the reader cannot understand the modifier.
  (Why? Is the reader hanging from the ceiling?)
Placed in an awkward position, the modifier confuses the reader.
  (Oh, now I get it.)

PRACTICE
Are the following sentences clear?

1. The teacher brought in paper for his students with narrow lines.
2. The fruit was finally served by the waiter, wrapped in pancakes.

ANALYSIS
1. We hope that the writer means *paper with narrow lines*. The prepositional phrases are confusing. Incorrect.
2. Uh . . . . The waiter finally served the fruit, wrapped in pancakes.

Conjunctive Adverbs

Words such as *however, thus, moreover,* and *furthermore* are useful in transitions, but it is important to remember that these function as adverbs. They **cannot** connect two sentences into one. You **must** use a period or a semicolon before these transitions.
  Consider the use of *however (thus, moreover,* etc.) here:

This is a good transitional word, however it is not a coordinating conjunction. Incorrect.
This is a good transitional word. However, it is not a coordinating conjunction. Correct

Conjunctive adverbs *can* also be used as interrupters.

It is , nevertheless, a good transitional word. It is not , however, one of the FANBOYS.

Note: Interrupters, separated by commas, can be lifted out of a sentence without changing its meaning.

> Interrupters[, moreover,] can be lifted out of a sentence without changing its meaning.
>
> Interrupters can be lifted out of a sentence without changing its meaning.

Double Negatives

Double negatives may be proper in other languages, but they are incorrect usage in English.

> I don't use no double negatives.   (You just did: *not* and *no*.)

Beware of words such as *hardly, barely,* or *scarcely*. They are considered negative.

> I can't hardly wait. Incorrect. (I can <u>not hardly</u> wait?)
> I can hardly wait. Correct

PRACTICE
1. I like old movies, for instance, *The Wizard of Oz* is one of my favorites.
2. I'm not afraid of nobody.

ANALYSIS
1. The expression *for instance* cannot connect sentences. Use a period or semicolon to end the sentence before it.

> I like old movies. For instance, *The Wizard of Oz* is one of my favorites.

2. Nowhere, nohow. Not correct. (I'm not afraid of *anybody*. Correct.)

REVIEW
Correct the following errors with conjunctions, dangling and misplaced modifiers, conjunctive adverbs, and double negatives.

1. The Wicked Witch doesn't have no power in Munchkinland, however, she threatens Dorothy during the journey.
2. Neither the Tin Man or the Straw Man is affected by the poppies.
3. Because they are not mammals, the poppies' scent cannot harm them.

CORRECTIONS
1. The Wicked Witch doesn't have **any** power in Munchkinland. However, she threatens Dorothy during the journey.
2. Neither the Tin Man **nor** the Straw Man is affected by the poppies.
3. Because they are not mammals, they cannot be harmed by the poppies' scent. Or—The poppies' scent cannot harm them because they are not mammals. [Make it clear that you are saying that the Tin and Straw men are not mammals.] We are mammals, so let's rest a bit here before we move on.

Parallelism

In clear composition, each item in a series should be written using the same grammatical structure. Now that we've reviewed some grammar, you should be able to spot errors of inconsistency.

Grandmother lives **over the river, through the woods,** and **extravagantly.**
                          prep. phrase   prep. phrase   adverb

This is a fun sentence (if that's your idea of fun), but you won't see one like it on the test unless it's an error. It uses two prepositional phrases and an adverb in a series. Detecting errors in parallelism is often on the exams.

PRACTICE

Are the following sentences written correctly, using parallelism?

1. I like walking with the clouds, skipping with the trees, and to run with the badgers.
2. Get fit, get rest, get packed, and you should feed yourself.

ANALYSIS

1. Again, you can simplify the sentence by marking out extraneous phrases.

   I like <u>walking</u> [with the clouds], <u>skipping</u> [with the trees], and to run [with the badgers].

   Incorrect. *Walking, skipping,* and *to run* are not parallel. I like <u>walking</u>, <u>skipping</u>, and <u>running</u>.
2. The repeating verb *get* sets up a pattern, so it is jarring to break the rhythm.

   <u>Get</u> fit, <u>get</u> rest, <u>get</u> packed, and <u>get</u> fed.

   Note: Parallelism is important enough that you should read this section again. Try writing a few parallel sentences of your own. Then get some rest before we go on to a new topic. (We'll let you choose your own resting places from now on.)

Sentence Completions

Many of the sentence completion (fill in the correct word) questions on the HSPT and COOP involve transition words. The trick here is to make sure you know which words indicate a relationship of **agreement** and which words indicate **disagreement**. You already know the difference between the words *and* and *but; and* indicates an agreement or expansion, while *but* signals a disagreement or contrast.

Agreement	Disagreement
and	but
therefore	however
because	nevertheless
furthermore	conversely
for instance	although
for example	though
moreover	while

PRACTICE
Fill in words that correctly complete the sentences.

1. I would go to the movies, _____ I have to work tonight.
2. I have to work _____ I'm saving for college.

ANALYSIS
1. The beginning of the sentence, *I* <u>would</u> *go*, signals that a contrast will follow. The word *but* fits well. The word *however* can't work here because it would have to start a new sentence.

> I would go to the movies<u>, but</u> I have to work tonight.
> [I would go to the movies<u>. However</u>, I have to work tonight.]

2. The word *because* indicates a logical relationship between the two clauses.

> I have to work <u>because</u> I'm saving for college.

Composition

COHERENCE AND DEVELOPMENT

Both exams test elements of good composition. For instance, you will be shown a paragraph and asked whether the sentences all fit the topic. You may also be asked to place a sentence logically in a paragraph. Let's prepare with an exercise that combines these tasks.

PRACTICE
Rearrange the following mixed-up sentences to create a coherent paragraph. One of these sentences, however, will **not** belong! Mark that one out.

(A) The sentences that follow present support for this topic sentence, using examples and explanations of the examples.

(B) Most paragraphs begin with a topic sentence, identifying the point for the reader.

(C) The paragraph may close with a sentence that restates the topic sentence or sums up the main point.

(D) A paragraph is indented five spaces on a word processor.

(E) These sentences can further unify the paragraph by using related ideas, grammatical structures, and words.

ANALYSIS
How did you decide on the correct order? You looked for clues to show **logical development** in the paragraph.

1. **B.** Most paragraphs **begin** with a topic sentence . . . .
   The word *begin* tells us that this is chronologically the beginning of the paragraph.
2. **A.** The sentences that follow it present support for **this** topic sentence . . . .
   The words *following it* tell us that something has come before. The words *this topic sentence* shows that it refers to sentence B.

3. **E. These** sentences can **further** unify the paragraph . . . .
   The word *further* tells us that this sentence belongs later in the paragraph.
   The adjective *these* shows that it refers back to the sentences introduced in sentence A.
4. **C.** The paragraph may **close** with a sentence that restates the topic sentence or sums up the main point.
   This is logically and chronologically the last sentence.

D. A paragraph is indented five spaces . . . .
   This may be true, but it does not fit the overall point of the paragraph.

By the way, what is the overall point of the paragraph? The COOP will specifically ask you to identify the topic sentence of a paragraph.

PRACTICE

Which of the following is the topic sentence of the paragraph you just unscrambled? Read it again, in order, and ask yourself what the main point is.

(A) The word *paragraph* derives from the Greek word *paragraphos*.
(B) A paragraph is unified by a single point.
(C) A paragraph should open with an interesting sentence.
(D) Paragraphs are the building blocks of a clear essay.

ANALYSIS

(A) This is interesting, perhaps, but it has nothing to do with the other sentences. Incorrect.
(B) The other sentences do all focus on unity. This is a good possibility.
(C) This is good advice, but the overall paragraph does not deal with the opening sentence alone. Incorrect.
(D) Yes, they are, but the sentences do not really discuss essays. Incorrect.
   The answer is B. All of the sentences point to this main point of unity.

SENTENCE COMBINING AND CLEAR WRITING

The COOP will also ask you to combine sentences. The HSPT will show you several sentences and ask you to choose which one is most clearly written.

PRACTICE

Choose the single sentence that most clearly combines the pair of sentences.

1. Good writing is vigorous. Good writing is concise.

   (A) Concise writing is vigorous.
   (B) Vigorous writing is concise.
   (C) Good writing is both vigorous and concise.
   (D) Writing is good when it is vigorous, and it is also good when it is concise.
   (E) Writing, vigorous and concise, is good.

2. My brother is Joseph. He is too young to drive. He rides a bike.

   (A) My brother Joseph is too young to ride a bike, so he drives.
   (B) Because my brother Joseph is too young to drive, he rides a bike.
   (C) My brother Joseph, he's too young to drive, so he rides a bike.
   (D) Joseph, my brother, is too young to drive.
   (E) Brother Joseph, too young, drives a bike.

ANALYSIS:

1. **C.** *Good writing is both vigorous and concise.* The word *both* binds the two adjectives. A and B do not mean the same thing as the original sentences. D is neither vigorous nor concise. If we take out the adjective phrase between the commas in E, we get the sentence *Writing is good.* This is not the message of the original sentences.

2. **B.** *Because my brother Joseph is too young to drive, he rides a bike.* This sentence uses an appositive (*my brother Joseph*) and a dependent clause (*Because he is too young*) to combine these sentences. A and D are grammatically correct, but they do not relate the same information as the original sentences. C uses a comma splice to connect a fragment, and E is just stupid. You get choices like this sometimes.

GUESSING

What if you're stumped or can't choose between a couple of choices? When guessing the most clearly written sentence out of a group of choices, **choose the shortest sentence or the next-to-shortest sentence.** This is certainly not always the correct response, but because good writing is concise it's a more likely choice than a longer, wordier sentence. Check the shortest sentence to make sure it's not *too* short; it may be short because it's eliminating necessary material.

Also, a choice containing an active verb is more likely to be the clearest sentence rather than ones written with passive construction or forms of the verbs *have* or *to be*. The subject of a strong sentence should ACT rather than receive action.

> I wrote an active sentence. (The subject *I* acts!)
> A passive sentence was written by me.
> (The subject *sentence* receives the action.)

Punctuation, Capitalization, Usage, and Spelling

Punctuation, capitalization, usage, and spelling are specifically tested on the HSPT; the COOP does not include specific questions on spelling, but you are expected to know the other skills. Furthermore, remember that identifying grammar errors can help you make a choice among the possible answers. Some questions will ask you to identify an error. Other questions will ask you to choose the best sentence (as we did in the last exercise), so you can eliminate choices that contain grammatical errors. Eliminating choices increases your odds of finding the correct answer.

PUNCTUATION

Early writing did not use punctuation all of the writing ran together like this it must have been difficult to tell when a sentence stopped and a new thought began eventually pauses had to be marked. This helped readers and speakers immensely. Later, when books were printed, publishers began developing logical rules for punctuation.

Periods

Periods are easy. Use a period at the end of a sentence (unless it's a question or an exclamation). Also use a period for abbreviations.

> Dr. Smith is engaged to Ms. Mendez.

Question Marks

We use a **question mark** after a direct question.

> Are you serious?

We do not use it after an indirect question.

> He asked if I was being serious.
> I wonder why he asked me that.

Exclamation Points

Exclamation points are not used often. They should be reserved for instances of strong emotion.

> Help me! I've fallen, and I can't get up!

Commas

Many students use **commas** randomly, but the rules for commas do make sense, and they are well worth learning. Because most punctuation errors involve commas, we'll spend more time looking at these. Strap yourself in! Concentrate!

1. Use a comma to separate **two independent clauses** connected by a conjunction (*and, but, or, nor, for, so, yet*).

    A **clause** is a group of words with a subject and a verb. An *independent* clause makes sense standing alone; it's a sentence.

    > **Murray** <u>plays</u> a red guitar , and **Jeff** <u>plays</u> a purple accordion.
    >   *subject*   *verb*   *subject verb*

Think of the comma as a point of balance; it **must** have a subject and verb on both sides of it.

Warning! Many people do this:

> Murray plays a red guitar , Jeff plays a purple accordion.

The comma is not a strong enough pause to separate two sentences. This is called a **comma splice**. It is the ultimate error in comma usage. Use a period or a conjunction instead.

> Murray plays a red guitar . Jeff plays a purple accordion.
> Murray plays a red guitar , **and** Jeff plays a purple accordion.

Better yet, if the sentences are closely related, use a semicolon.

> Murray plays a red guitar; Jeff plays a purple accordion.

If you substitute semicolons for comma splices, you will be using a sophisticated style of punctuation. Everyone will assume you are a grammatical genius. **A semicolon is like a period; it ends sentences.** However, it's not as strong as a period, so it shows that the sentences are related.

2. Do not use a comma before a conjunction joining two verbs.

> Nate visited Russia, and bought a fur hat.   Incorrect.
> Nate <u>visited</u> Russia *and* <u>bought</u> a fur hat.   Correct.
>   (no comma)

Remember that you must have a subject and verb on both sides of the comma.

> **Jack**   fell down the hill **,** *and* **he**   <u>broke</u> his crown.
> *subject*   *verb*   **,**   *subject*   *verb*
>
> **Jack**   <u>fell</u> down the hill *and* <u>broke</u> his crown.
> *subject*   *verb*   *verb*

However, use commas in a **series** of verbs:

> Nate <u>visited</u> Russia **,** <u>bought</u> a fur hat **,** <u>and pretended</u> to be a Wookie.

3. Use commas to separate items in a series of three or more.

> I brought sandwiches, salad**,** and cake to the picnic.

4. Separate two or more adjectives before a noun.

> Matt's filthy **,** dilapidated bicycle broke down.

Remember this test! In a series, use a comma if the word *and* makes sense in its place.

> Matt's filthy *and* dilapidated bicycle broke down.

PRACTICE
Are the following sentences punctuated correctly?

1. The ice, cream truck drove through our neighborhood yesterday.
2. Should I punt, or pass?
3. Semicolons are tricky devices; you should not overuse them.

ANALYSIS
1. With these adjectives, you cannot replace the comma with the word *and*. The ice *and* cream truck drove through our neighborhood yesterday. Incorrect.
2. If we identified the subjects and verbs we would have

> <u>Should</u> **I** <u>punt</u> **,** or <u>pass</u>?
> We do not have a balance on either side of the comma. Incorrect.
> <u>Should</u> **I** <u>punt</u> or <u>pass</u>? Correct.
> <u>Should</u> **I** <u>punt</u>, or <u>should</u> **I** <u>pass</u>? Correct.

3. If you used a comma instead of a semicolon, you would have a comma splice. A period or semicolon both work here. Correct.

5. In the following examples, commas isolate sections of a sentence that can be **left out.** Try removing these sections to see if the sentences still make sense.

5a. Use commas to set off nonessential phrases and clauses.

> What is nonessential? If the sentence doesn't need it to express its meaning, it's nonessential. It's usually just **descriptive**.

Morgan, who has red hair, is in our class.

The phrase *who has red hair* is *not essential,* so we put commas around it. We could take out the section within the commas and it conveys the same message.

Morgan[, who has red hair,] is in our class.
Morgan is in our class.

However, what if we said this?

Morgan is the only person in our class who has red hair.

We don't use a comma in this case; the phrase *who has red hair* is *essential.* If we took it out, the sentence would **not** mean the same thing!

Morgan is the only person in our class[, who has red hair].
Morgan is the only person in our class. Incorrect.

5b. Use commas to separate adjectives that follow a noun.

Mr. Villanueva, tall, dark, and handsome, was born in Florida.

You can take out *tall, dark, and handsome,* and the sentence still makes sense.

Mr. Villanueva[, tall, dark, and handsome,] was born in Florida.
Mr. Villanueva was born in Florida.

5c. Use commas to set off parenthetical phrases (phrases that interrupt a sentence).

Aubrey can, of course, stand on one hand.
By the way, you're soaking in it.
You are, in my opinion, an infectious, beef-witted clotpole.

5d. Use commas to set off an appositive. An appositive renames a noun.

Ernie, an excellent student, always attended class.
Ernie always attended class.

However, if we **need** to know the information for the sentence to make sense, don't use a comma. These are called **restrictive phrases or clauses**. This is often the case with proper appositives.

The novelist Nathaniel Hawthorne is Brandon's favorite author. Correct.

We lose the meaning if we write:

The novelist, Nathaniel Hawthorne, is Brandon's favorite author.
The novelist[, Nathaniel Hawthorne,] is Brandon's favorite author.
The novelist is Brandon's favorite author.   Incorrect. *Which novelist?*

Compare this to the reverse order:

Nathaniel Hawthorne, a novelist, is Brandon's favorite author. Correct.

In this case, *a novelist* is not necessary, so we can separate it with commas.

> Nathaniel Hawthorne [, a novelist,] is Brandon's favorite author.
> Nathaniel Hawthorne is Brandon's favorite author.

PRACTICE
1. Poe's poem, "The Raven," is my favorite.
2. Our test, which falls on a Monday, will not be difficult.
3. I can't stand work, that is scheduled on Mondays.

ANALYSIS
1. Try taking out the words between the commas. Does it still have enough information to make sense?

    > Poe's poem is my favorite.

    Which poem? The title is essential, so we can't separate it with commas. Incorrect.

    > Poe's poem "The Raven" is my favorite. This is correct.

2. Taking out the words between the commas does not affect the meaning. Correct.
3. *I can't stand work.* This is not necessarily true. The speaker is saying that working on Mondays is disagreeable. That part of the sentence is essential, so it should not be set off by a comma. Incorrect.

6. Use commas to set off nouns of direct address.

    > Allison, I just don't know.
    > I just don't know, Allison.

    (I am speaking to Allison; I am not saying that I have never met Allison.)

    > Honestly, Allison, I just don't know what has become of Sarah.

7. Use a comma after introductory words and mild interjections.

    > Why, I do declare!
    > Yes, we have no bananas.
    > Well, I've never seen anything like it!
    > Wow, I do love these comma rules.

8. Use a comma after most introductory clauses and phrases.

    Introductory adverbial clauses:

    > While Santa Claus slept, C.J. left presents under the tree.
    > (This clause acts as an adverb, telling us when C.J. left the presents.)

    More than one introductory prepositional phrase:

    > To the students in the far corner, this information will be useless.

Participial phrases (basically, *-ing* or *-ed* phrases):

> Frothing like a rabid hippopotamus, I opened my grammar book.

9. Use a comma to separate the year when you write a particular date.

> July 4, 1776, is considered our first Independence Day.

10. Use commas after a name with a title such as Jr. or M.D.

> Raymond J. Johnson, Jr. Julie Beth Drake, Ph.D.
> Bugs Bunny, Esq. Rev. Arthur Fiddle, D.D.

11. Use commas when you write addresses.

> Every year in Louisville, Kentucky, we attend the Kentucky Derby.
> I lived in an old house at 1985 East 124th Place, Cleveland, Ohio 44106.

12. Use commas to introduce a quote with words such as *says, writes, comments,* and *adds.*

> Dickens **writes** , "Scrooge was better than his word."

Do **not** use commas with connecting words such as *that* or *as.*

> Dickens writes **that** "Scrooge was better than his word."

PRACTICE
1. For most of the students the homework was not difficult.
2. Oh, now the rules get complicated.
3. The author said that, "I never intended to write a fairy tale."

ANALYSIS
1. A comma after the second prepositional phrase makes the sentence clearer.

> For most of the students, the homework was not difficult.

2. *Oh* is used as a mild interjection and uses only a comma. Correct.
3. Do not use a comma after a connecting word such as *that.* Incorrect. You may correct this sentence a couple of ways:

> The author said, "I never intended to write a fairy tale."
> The author said that he "never intended to write a fairy tale."

Colon

The **colon** introduces a list, an example, an explanation, or a quote. If the colon could talk, it would say, "And here they are!" or "And here it is!"

> I brought the necessary supplies: bread, peanut butter, and a butter knife.
> The author expressed strong disagreement: "I never intended to write a fairy tale."

Note: A colon is **not** used after a verb.

> The necessary supplies were: bread, peanut butter, and a butter knife.
> Incorrect. The colon is unnecessary. Take it out and see.

Apostrophes

You already know how an apostrophe is used in contractions.

it's = it is   can't = cannot
you've = you have   we'll = we will

It gets more complicated when an apostrophe is used for possessives.
Any noun that **does not end with the letter s** uses *'s* to form a possessive. It does not matter whether the noun is singular or plural

This man's army   The horse's hooves
The men's locker room   The children's room

Plural nouns that **do** end in *s* form the possessive by simply adding an apostrophe.

The ladies' invitations   The twins' books
The horses' stables

Here's where it gets tricky. With singular nouns that end with the sound of *s* or *z*, a single apostrophe usually forms the possessive. This is often the case with ancient or biblical names.

Moses' importance   Jesus' miracles

However, if the possessive of a single syllable word ending in *s* is pronounced with an extra syllable, many people use *'s*. Either form is acceptable.

Charles's report   OR   Charles' report
the class's valedictorian   OR   the class' valedictorian

Quotation Marks

1. Use quotation marks for direct quotations.

    She said, "I can't forget to put a comma after the word *said*."
    She added that she would "never forget" to omit the comma in a construction such as this.

    Note: In American usage, commas and periods always go *inside* the quotation marks at the end of a quote. This is a common error, so be aware of it.

    "Oh, Todd! You're such an genius," she laughed.

2. Though it seems difficult for many students to remember, you should make sure that the titles of poems and short stories are enclosed in quotation marks.

    "Miniver Cheevy"   "The Tell-Tale Heart"

    Note: If the poem is book-length, however, the title will be underlined or italicized, just like a book.

    I shelved my copy of Homer's *Iliad* next to the *Odyssey*.

More Parallelism

Punctuation also requires a certain degree of parallelism. Make sure that parenthetical, additional, or nonessential material is set off from a sentence with consistent marks of punctuation. That is to say, if you see a comma at the beginning of a sentence interrupter, then you should make sure that interrupter ends with a comma, as well.

A sentence interrupter, like this one, is set off by commas.

It can also be set off—in some cases—with dashes.

Sometimes these are called (obviously enough) parenthetical words or phrases.

It would be incorrect, not to mention bizarre—to mix the punctuation.
Note that the above uses a comma paired with a dash. Incorrect.

PRACTICE
1. "I feel I'm forgetting something, she remarked.
2. I really enjoyed Lowry's novel "The Giver."
3. I have mastered three marks of punctuation: colons, apostrophes, and quotation marks.

ANALYSIS
1. Incorrect. You have forgotten something (and here it is): the closing quotation mark.

   "I feel I'm forgetting something," she remarked.

2. Incorrect. Novel titles are not enclosed by quotation marks. They are underlined or italicized. *The Giver* is a novel.
3. Correct. You have mastered them (and here they are): colons, apostrophes, and quotation marks.

CAPITALIZATION

You probably already know the rules of capitalization from everyday use. Here's a quick refresher list to reinforce your knowledge.

1. Capitalize the first letter of the first word of a sentence. That's easy enough. However, make sure you also capitalize the first letter of the first word of a sentence when it is part of a quote.

   He said, "**The** above example is obvious, isn't it?"
   "It is," she replied. "However, it needs to be said."
   "This sentence," he added, "**is** different because the sentence is interrupted."

2. Capitalize proper nouns: the names of particular people, places, organizations, languages, religions, nationalities, products, etc. Also capitalize adjective forms of these words.

   The Missouri River is the longest river in the United States.
   Notice that *river* is not capitalized when used in general.

Mexico	Mexican	New Yorker
Greenbriar Drive	Department of Education	Red Rose Tea
John Adams	CIA	Oxford University

3. Capitalize specific regions, but do not capitalize directions.

   I live in the Deep South.   We pray for peace in the Middle East.
   Georgia is located south of Tennessee. The sun rises in the east and sets in the west.

4. Capitalize titles and words used as parts of people's names. Do NOT capitalize them in other cases.

   My family physician is Dr. Zaius.   Have you met Aunt Pina?
   He is a good doctor.   She is my favorite aunt.

5. Capitalize the days of the week and months of the year.

   My father was born on a Friday in September.

6. Capitalize the pronoun *I*. You're important.

   My mother and I bought him a camera for his birthday.

7. When writing the title of a work, capitalize the first word, important words, and the last word. Do not capitalize articles, short prepositions, and conjunctions unless they are the first or last words.

   Book: *A Tale of Two Cities*   Movie: *Raiders of the Lost Ark*
   Poem: "The Clod and the Pebble"   Play: *A Raisin in the Sun*
   Short Story: "A Rose for Emily"   Painting: *Still Life with Fruit*

   Note: Also remember when to use quotation marks and when to italicize (or underline).

8. Capitalize holidays, historical documents, and historical events.

   On Independence Day, we celebrate the signing of the Declaration of Independence, which led to the Revolutionary War.

9. Important religious terms are capitalized (deities, sacred books, religious groups).

   Roman Catholic   God (He, His, Him)   Old Testament   Judaism
   Bible   Koran   The Book of Job Jesuits

USAGE

We've already covered some common usage errors, such as *it's* and *you're* (contractions) versus *its* and *your* (possessives) and the difference between *well* and *good*.

   It's a good thing **you're** doing **well** in your studies, for knowledge is **its** own reward.
   (It is)   (you are)

accept/except

Check these carefully; they are commonly misused.

   Don't **accept** credit cards **except** from people you know.

affect/effect

These are so often misused that you should always check them.

> *Affect* is a verb.   Soft drinks **affect** my system.
> *Effect* is a noun.   They produce a jittery **effect**.

Note: What makes this pair difficult is that the word *effect* can sometimes be used as a verb meaning to cause or to bring about. We wish this weren't the case, but there it is. If you can substitute the words *cause* or *bring about* in its place, *effect* is correct.

> The politician thought he could **effect** change.
> The politician thought he could **bring about** change. Correct.

a lot

This is another common error. *A lot* is two words.

all right

All right is two words.

among/between

Use *between* when you are talking about two people or items; use *among* with larger numbers.

> The thirty students argued **among** themselves, but we had no problems **between** the two of us.

farther, further

Farther deals with distance. *Further* deals with degree.

> The waterfall is **farther** downstream.
> Let's discuss this **further**.

fewer, less

Use *fewer* with countable items. *Less* is for noncountable items.

> If I use **fewer** ice cubes, I'll have **less** work.

have, of

These are confused because they sound similar when spoken in sentences. This is a common error on the tests. Remember that *have* is a verb, and *of* is a preposition.

> I could of sworn this was right.
>   Incorrect. The word *of* does not connect a noun to the sentence.
> I could have sworn this was right.
>   Correct. *Could have sworn* is the complete verb.

lay/lie, set/sit

We **lay** or **set** something down. (Test: You can replace these with the word ***put***.) We *ourselves* **lie** or **sit**.

> I am so tired that I have to **set** down my backpack and **sit**.
> Then I **lay** my head on my pillow and **lie** down.

loose/lose

Why is this so difficult? *Lose* is a verb meaning to be without something. *Loose* is an adjective meaning not tight or bound.

> I **lose** pages when writing on **loose**-leaf paper.

> **Problem:** *Loose* is also an old-fashioned verb meaning to loosen or to release something. This sounds too archaic for common use. Save it for poetic writing.

> He **loosed** a barrage of insults.

myself, yourself, himself, herself, ourselves

These words are called intensifiers. They cannot be used alone as a subject or object.

> I **myself** don't make such errors. Correct.
> Sandy, Ursola, and **myself** worked all day. Incorrect.
> Sandy, Ursola, and **I** worked all day. Correct.

there, their, they're

They're (They are) so unsure of **their** destination that they don't go **there** without a map.

that/which

We use the word *that* to connect essential information to a sentence. Remember, too, that we do not use commas when the information is essential.

> The sentence **that** explains this usage contains essential information.

> We use the word *which* for nonessential information, and we separate it with commas.

> This sentence, **which** is a lovely sentence, contains nonessential information.

For more review of this, see Rule 5 under Commas on pages 150–152.

to, two, too

You know the difference. You've known for years. *To* is usually a preposition, *two* is a number, and *too* means *also* or *excessive*. Check these when you see them.

> **To** me, **two** is **too** many.

unique

When something is unique, it is one of a kind. Therefore, you cannot say something is **very** unique or **more** or **less** unique or **most** unique. It can **only** be unique. This is a common error, but now you know not to make it! (Does this make you unique?)

Other Confused Words

In general, beware of similar-sounding words. Other confused pairs include the following:

advice/advise	coarse/course	principal/principle
already/all ready	counsel/council	quiet/quite
cite/site/sight	desert/dessert	stationary/stationery
capital/capitol	forth/fourth	than/then
		weather/whether

Look these up in a dictionary and read the **entire** definition. The act of looking them up will impress them more strongly on your memory.

SPELLING

Spelling? We don't need to know spelling; we've got spell-check, wright?

No, not wright. Nor is it rite. Or write. You see the problems with depending on a program to do our work for us; it doesn't come out quite . . . well, right.

English spelling seems a mess, but there's usually a logical explanation for why a word is spelled a certain way. People throughout history have been trying to organize this huge language that derives from many, many sources. For instance, speakers of Old English didn't write much, so when early Christian writers tried to transcribe these English words into their Roman alphabet, they did their best to write what they heard phonetically. So most of the words that give us trouble today were indeed spelled phonetically at one time. The word *night* was pronounced the way it is spelled—sort of like "nikt." The word *eye* sounded something like "ehyeh." Silent *e* was not always so quiet!

Similarly, many good spellers simultaneously have two pronunciations of a word going on in their heads. We say "vejtabul," but when we write, we silently say to ourselves "ve-ge-table," like the furniture we eat on in the dining room. We say "byootiful," but we hear "B-E-A-yoo-tiful" as we write it down. We hear "WED-nes-day," "calen-DAR," "bEEn," "a-GAIN," "temp-er-a-ture," and, of course, "gramm-AR." When you learn a word, try this double pronunciation technique, and see if it works for you. If you mistakenly pronounce the wrong version in public, just explain to people that you speak fluent Middle English. Then ask them how many early languages they know!

You can also use memory aids (often called mnemonic devices). Which is the correct spelling, *tomorrow* or *tommorow*? One way to recall this is to remember that *Tom* is in *tomorrow*: **Tom borrowed** my **barrow** until **tomorrow**. Some problem spelling words include the following:

*ac*quire	eighth	mortgage
antique	entrepreneur	necessary
arctic	exercise	nuclear
athletic	February	parallel
bachelor	forehead	parliament
calen*dar*	four, fourteen, forty	popular
column	friend	prejudice
comput*er*	humorous	psychological
conque*ror*	library	receipt
definite	mischievous	villain

What are your personal problem words? Make a list and study them. Create your own mnemonics if that helps you.

Spelling Rules

The history of English is long, complicated, and interesting. Learning the many sources (especially Latin, German, French, and Greek) and the roots, prefixes, and suffixes that make up the language will help your vocabulary and spelling. Having a language with so many sources, though, means that the rules of spelling will have many exceptions.

1. For instance, here's one we've all heard:

    I before E, except after C, or when sounded like "ay" as in *neighbor* and *weigh*.

    This rule often works, but it also has many exceptions. Some words we've adopted from French and German, for instance, don't follow this. You'll just have to learn the exceptions. Here are some of them, Einstein:

    E before I: **Neither** the **sovereign sheik** nor the **counterfeit foreigner** (nor the **feisty heifer**) could **seize** the **heights** of such **weird sleight** of hand without **forfeiting either** work or **leisure** time. **Their heirs** cannot drink **caffeine** without **protein**.
    I-E after C: That **ancient species** of **omniscient financiers** has no **sufficient conscience** when it comes to **science** in **society**.

    Note: Part of the rhyme holds true, though. Words with the "ay" sound will always be spelled E-I after the letter C.

PRACTICE
Here's a problem word. Write the word *receive* ten times right now. As you do so, enunciate it clearly and forcefully at the same time. RECEIVE. Go ahead. Write it in the margins. Re CE ive. You'll now remember how to spell one of the most widely misspelled words.

2. Let's look at a rule with no exceptions. When you add a prefix to a word, just add it. You won't have to drop any letters from the root word.

PRACTICE
Which of these spellings is correct?

1. mispell or misspell
2. extrordinary or extraordinary
3. unatural or unnatural

ANALYSIS
1. The prefix *mis-* is added to *spell* to make *mis-spell*. It looks odd, but it's correct.
2. *Extra-ordinary*.
3. The prefix *un-* is added to *natural*, making two *ns*: *un-natural*. You'll never have to wonder about this again.

3. When you add a **consonant suffix** (a suffix that begins with a consonant, such as *-less,* *-ful,* or *-ment*) to a word, just add it, unless the root ends with the letter *y.* In that case, change the *y* to *i* and then add the suffix.

harm	pity	neighbor	care
harm**less**	piti**less**	neighbor**ly**	care**ful**
harm**ful**	piti**ful**	neighbor**hood**	care**less**

4. When you add a consonant suffix (*-less, -ful, -ment,* etc.) to a word ending with silent *e,* just add it. (See Rule 3.) When you add a vowel suffix (*-ed, -ing, -er, -al,* etc.) to a word ending with silent *e,* you *usually* drop the silent *e.* The new vowel replaces it.

care	store	captive	love
car**ing**	stor**ing**	captiv**ity**	lov**ing**
car**ed**	stor**age**	captiv**ate**	lov**able** (but *loveable* is also accepted)

5. When do you double letters when adding a suffix? When you add a **vowel suffix** to a word (*-ed, -ing, -er, -al,* etc.), check to see whether the root word ends with a single vowel-consonant combination. Also note which syllable is stressed. Double the root's final consonant if the final syllable is stressed (or is only one syllable).

con**trol**	**big**	oc**cur**	re**fer**
controlling	bigger	occurred	referring
controlled	biggest	occurrence	referral

This is a tough rule. Congratulations if you got it before three readings.

PRACTICE

Which of the following sentences contain misspelled words?

1. The English language contains over fourty sounds.
2. The Roman alphabet, developed for the Latin language, consists of 26 letters.
3. Still, it has proved usful to us until the Internet made it difficult 4 u.

ANALYSIS

1. *Forty* is a problem word for many people because it is spelled differently than *four* or *fourteen.*
2. The word *develop* ends with a single vowel-consonant combination, but it is **not** stressed on the final syllable. Therefore, the final *p* is not doubled (*developed*).
3. The word *use* does not drop the silent *e* when adding a consonant suffix (*useful*). Also, *4 u* is e-mail spelling, and we've had enuf. lol.

Guessing

If you're faced with a question that you simply cannot figure out, skip it and come back to it. When you do, an error might look more obvious the second time. If you still don't know the answer, eliminate the choices you know are wrong; your odds of choosing the correct response will increase. Remember, there are no penalties for guessing incorrectly, so you should always guess.

Conclusion

Even if some of the material you've just studied might seem new, realize that you've really been using it every day as you speak, read, and write. Don't be too concerned about fancy grammatical labels; use your common sense—and your ears. You instinctively know what sounds correct or incorrect. After a thorough review of this section, you should be able to trust yourself.

Reading Comprehension

Introduction

Both the HSPT and the COOP require you to demonstrate your ability to understand what you read. You can find examples of the kinds of texts you will be asked to read and interpret in this section as well as in the practice exams listed in the Appendix. However, the following chart outlines the kind of reading passages you will be asked to read, the number of questions you will be asked to answer, as well as the time period during which you must record those answers.

	HSPT	COOP
Number of passages	6 (somewhat short)	4 (somewhat long)
Length of passages	Slightly less than ½ page of regular book	Slightly more than ½ page of regular book
Number of questions	5–8 questions/passage	4 questions/passage
Questions per minute	60 questions/25 minutes	40 questions/40 minutes
Projected rate of answering	½ minute/question	1 minute/question

You can count on the fact that reading passages on the HSPT/COOP are not designed to be tricky or confusing in any way; students preparing to enter high school should feel confident that they can understand these passages. Reading carefully and focusing on *identifying the answers to the questions being asked* should allow you to complete this section of either exam with confidence.

Make sure you **read the passage from beginning to end** before even looking at the questions. Reading correctly the first time saves you time reading the passage again. Often you will be tempted to guess at the answers without reading the passage, but you must answer the questions based on the information given in the passage, not based on information you already have in your brain. **Read the questions and all the answers** before trying to answer. Finally, **if in doubt, guess**. Neither the HSPT nor the COOP penalizes as much for incorrect answers as they do for skipping questions altogether.

Making yourself aware of the types of reading comprehension questions the HSPT and COOP exams typically use is also a good idea. The HSPT and the COOP both use identifiable phrases and strategies that give clues as to the type of question you are answering. You can read some examples of the methods authors use to call your attention to the type of questions they are asking in the following chart.

Main-idea questions (finding the main idea)	Typically asks you to **find the main point** of the passage Typically phrased in one of the following ways: • The passage deals mainly with . . . • The main idea of this selection may be expressed as . . . • The title that best expresses the ideas of this passage is . . . • The writer's main purpose is apparently . . . • The best name for this story is . . . • The best title for this passage is . . .
Word-in-context questions (figuring out meaning from context clues)	Typically wants you to **figure out meaning of words** from the context of other words in the sentence Typically calls your attention to definitions and word context: • The word ____, as underlined and used in this passage, most nearly means . . . • Which of the following gives an example of . . . • Which of the following definitions most closely fits . . . • Which of the following is an example of ____ . . .
Fact questions (distinguishing fact from opinion)	Typically asks you to **identify facts** in the reading passage Typically phrased in a very direct, straightforward manner: • When did the action described in this passage take place? • Why did (so-and-so) do (such-and-such)? • What is the setting of this reading passage? • What did the protagonist of this passage *not* do? • All but which of the following facts are true?
Inference questions (drawing conclusions)	Typically asks you to **infer information from facts** given in the reading passage Typically uses words that imply judgment or possibility: • Why do you think that . . . • What is most likely . . . • Comparing the two paragraphs in this reading passage, we can say that . . . • The author implies that . . . • Based on the information in this passage, the reader can infer that . . . • Which of the following is most likely true . . .

Each of the upcoming sections in this chapter, therefore, offers (1) discussion of the four types of reading comprehension questions; (2) discussion of useful strategy for answering each type of question; and (3) some opportunities to practice the skill under discussion. We strongly recommend that you work your way through all of the review material before attempting the practice tests included in this book.

Main-Idea Questions: Finding the Main Point of a Passage

STRATEGY

Finding the main point of a reading selection takes some practice, but you can rely on certain hints to help you. After all, authors *want* you to be able to identify their main point. To help you, they either begin or end their passages with a topic sentence that not only introduces their topic but also *summarizes* their main point in writing that passage.

PRACTICE

Read the following selection and answer the questions that follow.

> *Shrek,* the popular children's movie about an unlikely hero (Shrek the ogre) and an equally unlikely heroine (the lovely Princess Fiona), turns the traditional concept of the fairy tale on its head. Traditional fairy tales present the reader with a passive, innocent, and weak heroine who requires rescuing by her <u>stalwart</u> hero. By contrast, *Shrek* offers a heroine who burps, eats like a horse, and, thanks to her knowledge of martial arts, actually saves her own rescuer at one point. One can only attribute this change in acceptable "heroine" characteristics to social changes affecting women in the U.S. since the 1950s.

The writer's main purpose in writing this passage is _____.

(A) to make the point that *Shrek* was a box office hit
(B) to make the point that traditional fairy tales have a passive heroine and a brave hero
(C) to make the point that changes in social expectations for women have redefined the roles fairy tale heroines can play
(D) to make the point that modern heroines are disgusting creatures who teach modern readers bad behavior

ANALYSIS

How did you do? The correct answer is C. Let's analyze the various answers.

Choice A argues that *Shrek* was a box office hit. While this claim is true, the reading passage does not discuss box office returns at all. The only mention this reading passage makes of *Shrek*'s popularity is one brief descriptive word in the first sentence. One reference is not enough to apply to the whole passage. Therefore the correct answer is not A.

Choice B states that traditional fairy tales typically have a passive heroine and a strong hero; this is true. However, this comment comes as part of a chain of logical statements leading to a larger point. Remember that authors typically put their topic sentence at the beginning or end of reading passages; in this case, the author has put the topic sentence at the end of this passage.

Choice D emphasizes the reader's possible judgmental reaction to Princess Fiona's love of burping and violence. While one might be disgusted at these personal characteristics, nothing about the passage *necessarily* criticizes her actions. The final sentence, crucial to understanding the purpose of the passage, does not pass judgment on the "new heroine," but only makes a guess as to the *inspiration* on which the character is based.

Choice C is the correct answer. This passage argues that fairy tales have changed over time to accommodate the tastes of modern audiences, no more and no less.

Word-in-Context Questions: Determining Hidden Meanings Through Detective Work

STRATEGY

The word-in-context question asks you to select definitions of words based on the context of the rest of the sentence. Having a big vocabulary helps, but logic and patience do too. After you read the passage, find the word you are being asked to define. Often this word will be brought to your attention in some way (for example, italicized, bolded, or underlined); look for context clues in the surrounding words to help you. Look in particular for **synonyms, a definition, or an example**.

PRACTICE

*The term **stalwart** can be defined as* _____.

(A) handsome
(B) foolish
(C) rash
(D) brave

ANALYSIS

The correct answer is D. Did you get it? Let's analyze your options.

Choice A refers to a trait most fairy tale heroes have. However, nothing about the sentence indicates that this hero is necessarily handsome; also, if the reader knows that ogres are ugly, smelly, and misshapen, then one can infer that Shrek (referred to in the first sentence as both a hero and an ogre) is definitely not handsome by human standards.

Choices B and C might be acceptable possibilities, since many fairy tale heroes must perform foolish and dangerous deeds to prove their bravery. However, you should consider two points when selecting your answer. First, the passage is setting up a contrast of the hero-heroine relationship in the traditional fairy tale. The wording of the sentence implies that the hero and the heroine are opposite in personality; typically one does not use the word *foolish* as an antonym for *weak*. Second, your job is to select the **most appropriate** answer, not just an **acceptable** answer. You should force yourself to read and consider all of the possible answers rather than selecting the first possible answer that comes your way.

Choice D is the correct answer. The passage is setting up a contrast of the hero-heroine relationship in traditional fairy tales. The wording of the sentence implies that the hero and the heroine are opposite in personality; therefore, if the heroine is weak, then the hero must be something opposite, like strong or brave. A check in the dictionary proves that one definition for *stalwart* is indeed brave.

Fact Questions: Deceptively Simple

STRATEGY

These fact questions seem the easiest to handle, yet they often prove difficult. After all, you are only being asked to pinpoint fact-based statements and use this information in your answers. Too often, however, test takers skim these questions too quickly, hoping to make up time lost on other portions of the exam, and miss obvious answers. Often, too, authors use synonyms in their writing, turning the fact question into a kind of word-in-context question. What's the bottom line? Don't rush, and pay attention to the actual question being asked of you.

PRACTICE

Shrek rejects which traditional elements?

(A) a weak heroine and her stalwart hero
(B) an unlikely hero and heroine
(C) a heroine who burps and knows martial arts
(D) a passive heroine and an innocent hero

ANALYSIS

This one should have been a piece of cake. The correct answer is A.

This question asks you to use backwards logic to get the answer. The passage describes details about *Shrek* that obviously do not fit with traditional fairy tales (burping, etc.); however, the question asks you to identify the elements of traditional fairy tales rather than restate the details that defy tradition. Choices B, C, and D all mention notable words and phrases from the reading passage and hope to catch you incorrectly associating these facts with the purpose of the question. Only choice A relates a description of traditional fairy tale elements.

While this sample question limits itself to questioning factual descriptions in this passage, not all fact questions are set up this way. Often factual questions can include data about science or mathematical topics; equally often, factual questions can require you to **use** the data discussed in the passages, for example, actually reading a series of historical dates and figuring out what century must be involved or subtracting one figure from another to get a difference.

Inference Questions: Drawing Logical Conclusions from Written Statements

STRATEGY
Inference questions are by definition trickier and wider ranging than main-idea questions. Inference questions can ask you to detect a hidden meaning in the passage or use the information you read to infer logical conclusions. Moreover, the question can require you to apply the logic of one passage to another, related situation.

The best way to approach an inference question is to make sure you understand the author's *purpose* in writing. Don't allow yourself simply to restate information given in the passage; inference questions ask you to *go beyond* the superficial meaning of the sentences you read.

PRACTICE
The author implies that _____.

(A) s/he likes fairy tales the way they used to be
(B) s/he thinks the reader will like movies similar to *Shrek*
(C) s/he thinks the movie *Shrek* is about an unlikely hero and an equally unlikely heroine
(D) s/he approves of the change in traditional fairy tales

ANALYSIS
The correct answer is D. Ready for the breakdown?

Choice C can be eliminated more quickly than any of the others. Choice C merely restates a factual statement in the passage; since inference questions ask you to draw inferences, a simple restatement of fact is a direct warning. Choice B, on the other hand, is a bit more compelling, since it clearly involves making an inference—that of deciding whether someone will like a movie based on her reaction to a similar one. Unfortunately, choice B demands that you make assumptions that are simply not supported by the question. At no point, for example, does the author imply that s/he has a clue as to the reader's taste in movies, nor does s/he try to match the reader's taste to other movies similar to *Shrek*.

Choice A is the most troubling answer on the list. Authors, unless they are writing editorials or critical reviews, usually strive to be unbiased in their writing; unbiased writing is respected in our culture. Choices A and D require the reader to attempt to figure out the author's approval or disapproval of a topic about which the author is trying to discuss in a disinterested manner. Nevertheless, the author has left clues about her/his opinion on the "new" fairy tale. Words such as *passive* and *weak* have negative connotations, and the author associates them with the traditional heroine; moreover, the author seems to approve of Fiona's martial arts skills ("thanks to her knowledge"). Together these details seem to suggest that the author approves of the changes in fairy tale lore; hence, the best answer for this inference question is D.

Practice Sessions

We hope that this extended discussion of the types of questions you will find on the HSPT and COOP exams was useful to you. However, practice makes perfect, and in this section, we offer you more opportunities to practice.

MAIN-IDEA QUESTIONS

Everyone nowadays feels the pressure to recycle certain products. Communities expend monies to provide recycling bins and other means by which to turn used products back into usable ones. Ad campaigns, from billboards to mail to backs of milk cartons, encourage and even threaten us to recycle. Yet recent scientific investigations present us with startling news: often we pay more to recycle a product than to destroy it and simply make a new one.

1. *The writer's main purpose is apparently _____.*

   (A) to shame people into recycling if they are not already doing so
   (B) to present a point of view opposite from the popular one
   (C) to offer new options for dealing with waste
   (D) to scoff at new scientific theories

Video games have changed substantially since people first conceived them. Gamers today probably do not even remember Pong, a simple hand-eye challenge in which players tried to keep a moving "ball" from bouncing out of bounds—essentially a game of Ping Pong against the computer. Pong, as well as its successors Centipede and PacMan, with their humble graphics and simple sound effects, seem horribly out of date compared to slick modern games such as Civilization, SimCity, and the notorious Grand Theft Auto series.

And yet gamers might notice a disturbing trend—a rejection of actual gaming in favor of glorified fantasy role playing. Today's video games function more like personalized movies. More often than not, players act out variations on preprogrammed scenarios that grant the player an illusion of creativity and personalized entertainment but downplay the dexterity and skill required of the old games.

2. *The writer's main purpose is apparently _____.*

   (A) to give an overview of how video games have changed over the years
   (B) to make the case that video games are unhealthy for gamers
   (C) to make the case that Grand Theft Auto is a particularly bad game, full of flaws
   (D) to assess which games are good and which are bad

Ever notice that kids' movies share a common theme? Consider, for example, the writing of Roald Dahl. The protagonist of his stories is typically a smart, good-looking kid, who nevertheless suffers great abuse at the hands of the adults surrounding him/her. In *Matilda*, for example, Matilda lives with a despicable father who constantly tells her that she is stupid and denies her access to intellectual activities. Although Matilda manages to escape her family's poisonous grasp, she does so only to fall victim to a second, equally evil force: a stupid, power hungry, bureaucrat. Throughout the course of the book, Matilda encounters only one decent adult, Ms. Honey, who has her own difficulties to overcome in the adult world.

Similarly, in *Charlie and the Chocolate Factory*, protagonist Charlie begins the movie in a run down and dejected state due to his long-term exposure to poverty and malnutrition that the adults in his life cannot combat. Charlie wins a once-in-a-million chance to tour a magical chocolate factory, only to meet example after example of despicable adults in the process of recreating themselves through bad parenting of their offspring.

Yet while the children in these movies begin their stories in a powerless state, they end their stories greatly empowered and usually well insulated from harmful adults. The protagonist learns to adapt to his or her situation, maturing until he or she understands his or her place in society. He or she then fights back, willfully yet appropriately, until he or she shapes his/her initially sour situation into a more acceptable one. Matilda, for example, ultimately stands up to Principal Trunchbull and selects for herself the mother of her dreams, represented by Ms. Honey. Similarly, Charlie, through his personal integrity, eventually inherits a surrogate father and a golden kingdom bursting with chocolate and financial security. Essentially, then, these stories warn the reader about possible treachery represented by adults and teach the reader how to find one's place in society through personal endeavor.

3. *The main idea of this selection may be expressed as _____.*

   (A) kids' movies are simplistic stories with no deeper meaning other than plot-based amusement
   (B) kids movies show adults depicted in ridiculous, demeaning situations
   (C) kids movies show kids how to mature in a confusing, adult-ruled world
   (D) kids movies cost a great deal to produce, especially *Charlie and the Chocolate Factory*

ANSWERS:

1. **B.** This reading selection does not deal with offering new ways to recycle; therefore, rule out choice C. Nor does the article state an opinion on new scientific theories; therefore, you can rule out choice D, since scoffing implies stating an opinion. This passage does seem (superficially) to encourage recycling, so you need to compare choices A and B to find the best answer. The passage begins by stating that society encourages people to recycle. But the passage ends by saying that new scientific evidence states recycling may cause more damage than we originally thought. Since you begin with one idea only to end with its exact opposite, look for an option that shows change. The only option that does so is choice B.

2. **A.** The reading does not try to evaluate any type of game, whether that be in terms of programmer skill, gaming skill, or moral correctness. Therefore, you can rule out choices B, C, and D. Only choice A fits the intent of the passage: to give readers a general sense of how video games have changed over time.

3. **C.** The reading discusses kids' movies and the benefit the author sees in them. Nowhere does the article mention the cost of producing movies, so rule out choice D. While the article briefly cites how adults are depicted in the movies—and while these depictions are not positive ones—this is not the focus of the passage. Rule out choice B. Break down the reading and check:

   Paragraph One: Kids movies show kids in bad situations ruled by mean adults.

   Paragraph Three: Kids nevertheless deal maturely with their bad luck, and they turn their negative situations into positive ones, gaining personal responsibility, power, and ultimately money.

   The piece clearly moves from one point of view to another: from showing kids faced with adversity to showing kids triumphing over their situations. You can rule out, therefore, choice A, since the author's message is an optimistic, uplifting one. The correct answer is C.

WORD-IN-CONTEXT QUESTIONS

The word "jazz" is another one of those words that have experienced significant change over time. Originally, people used the word "jazz" to refer to activities that took place in the naughtier sections of exciting but dangerous towns like St. Louis and New Orleans, places that prided themselves on their ability to provide immoral yet fun things to do. Later, however, the word came to apply to one activity in particular: the hot music that sprang up from these areas. Musicians like Charlie Parker, Louis Armstrong, and Miles Davis owed their fame (and their livelihood) to jazz. Still later, the word came to be used in such phrases as "All that jazz," meaning "stuff."

4. *Which of the following definitions most closely fits the word "jazz"?*

   (A) The article does not state
   (B) music
   (C) drugs
   (D) violence

> Mark Twain, author of such texts as *The Adventures of Tom Sawyer, Life on the Mississippi,* and *The Adventures of Huckleberry Finn,* is himself one of literature's best known creations. The man behind the myth, Samuel Clemens, created an alter ego, Mark Twain, as a way of bridging the gap between two very different personalities. On the one hand, Clemens prided himself on his ability to fulfill the role of Southern Gentleman: the well-mannered, chivalrous, wealthy, and charitable slave-owner. Yet, simultaneously, Clemens prided himself on his ability to adopt Yankee behaviors: the educated, principled, industrious abolitionist.
>
> As a result, Twain/Clemens's views strike the reader as both witty and amusing— and often <u>contradictory</u>. Consider, for example, the tone of *The Adventures of Tom Sawyer* with that of *The Adventures of Huckleberry Finn,* written 20 years later. *Tom Sawyer* has a light-hearted tone and focuses on telling an adventure story that honors the glory of the Old South—the South the way Clemens remembers it in the good ol' days. By contrast, *Huck Finn* tells a much darker tale about two people who cannot find peace anywhere in the South due to racial tensions—the New South following the Civil War. Caught somewhere between Clemens and Twain, these literary works grow out of a greatly troubled and inconsistent mind.

5. *The word* contradictory, *as underlined and used in this passage, most nearly means* _____.

   (A) insane
   (B) hateful
   (C) confusing
   (D) evil

> You may never have heard of the delightfully noisy little insect known as the cicada before, but if you live in the eastern part of the United States, you are certainly about to. Cicadas live in various parts of the United States year round, but every 17 years, they come out in <u>droves</u> in places like Virginia and Kentucky. The little, red-eyed, singing bugs burrow up out of the ground and spread out in plague-like quantities until you can't walk for crunching them to death with every step. The little guys, however, do no real harm to plant life or anything else; they really only become problematic due to their great numbers. However, like most things Mother Nature sends our way, the cicadas provide a benefit to humanity—they make quite tasty snacking, as the recipes for Cicada Dumplings attest.

6. *Which of the following gives an example of a definition of the word* droves?

   (A) a word that refers to dogs
   (B) a word that means the past tense of *drives*
   (C) another word for a large collection of trees
   (D) a word that indicates a large number of things

ANSWERS

4. **B.** The whole paragraph is written to tell you what *jazz* means, but it does not obviously state the meaning of the word until late in the paragraph; therefore, rule out choice A. The paragraph refers to "naughtier" topics in reference to "jazz," and although drugs and violence, choices C and D, respectively, are naughty, indeed illegal topics, the article is not referring to them. The final sentences of the passage specifically define the word "jazz" as having something to do with music; your only correct answer is B.

5. **C.** Twain is described in the paragraph as being two sided—on the one hand trying to be a Southerner (and all the things that go along with being a Southerner) and on the other hand trying to be a Northerner (the complete opposite of being a Southerner). Therefore, you are looking for a word that accommodates a person trying to be two conflicting things at once. This is a confusing task; and the word *confusing* is your best choice. The correct answer is C.

6. **D.** You can rule out choice A right off the bat; it is present as an option merely to confuse you into thinking a connection exists between the word *droves* and *Rover*. Ignore it. Choices B and C are more enticing, but they are also wrong. The correlation between *droves* and *drives* is false; the word actually being defined by choice C is *groves*. Ignore these, too. Choice D is the correct answer. Even if you don't know the word *droves*, the piece contains many context clues to help you out—several times the author makes references to quantities of things—phrases like "plague-like quantities" and "great numbers," and the description of someone unable to walk around without stepping on cicadas—a description that implies a *lot* of cicadas. Therefore, you must select choice D as the best answer.

FACT QUESTIONS

Author Stephen King loves to play inside jokes on his readers. From his first short stories to his latest work, his made-for-TV adaptation of his own novel *The Shining,* this generalization rings true. Take, for example, King's early novel *Christine,* a story about a haunted car who gives her owner popularity and long life in return for souls. The car, a vehicle of death, possesses a radio that only plays the music of dead musicians (like Buddy Holly or the Big Bopper) or musicians whose names mention death (like the Grateful Dead). Later in his miniseries adaptation of *The Shining,* King provides a ghostly band playing mood music for a bunch of revelers; the bandleader is none other than Gage, the little boy killed by a truck in King's *Pet Sematary,* now grown up and evil. These are grisly jokes, indeed, yet amusing for the avid King reader to discover.

7. *Which of the following bands does the car's radio play?*

(A) Madonna
(B) Buddy Holly
(C) The Gyoto Monks
(D) Rage Against the Machine

Recent events in outer space popularized shirts sporting the phrase, "My other car is on Mars." The quip attempted to remind people that NASA has finally enjoyed a success in its many attempts at space explorations. After recent fiascos and disasters that claimed the lives of the astronauts aboard exploding rockets, a success is undeniably welcome.

The car to which the t-shirt slogan refers is actually a 400-pound, solar-powered robot, packed with sensors and cameras that allow viewers on earth a rare glimpse at the red planet. So far the rover has managed to send to earth quite a few photos, including one depicting the Granicus Valles systems, rock formations formed by constant wind patterns. Soon to come will be long-distance testing of soil and rocks in the hopes of sighting evidence of useful and informative minerals on Mars, like iron. The success of the mission thus far has thrilled the scientific community—and President Bush, who now calls for a manned mission to Mars.

8. *To what does the slogan on the t-shirt refer?*

(A) the wearer's other car, which is in the shop in Memphis
(B) the wearer's feet; the reference is ironic
(C) the wearer's pet project, the 400-pound rover now deployed on Mars
(D) the wearer's candy-apple blue BMW

The art of Shaolin has, as have many other forms of martial arts, suffered at the hands of Americans. You may not know Shaolin by its name, but you have seen it played out, provided you have watched movies such as *Crouching Tiger, Hidden Dragon*. Shaolin ranks among the most dangerous and demanding of the martial arts, but few in America are aware of this fact, blinded as they are by their interest in flashier martial arts forms, like Tae Kwon Do or Karate. Only three Masters of Shaolin remain alive in the world today; this fact is true only partly because of the great dedication and patience becoming a master requires. It is true in large part because of the simple lack of interest (and attention span) of possible Shaolin apprentices.

9. *How many Masters of Shaolin remain alive today?*

  (A) one
  (B) two
  (C) three
  (D) none

ANSWERS

7. **B.** This question is designed to be a "no-brainer." You check over the reading one last time and notice that nowhere are Madonna, The Gyoto Monks, or Rage Against the Machine mentioned. Your only real option is choice B, Buddy Holly.

8. **C.** Again, for fact questions, you are simply regurgitating a fact you remember from the reading passage. Here, three of the answers are silly. The only one with any basis in fact is choice C, which refers to the Mars rover, the subject of discussion in the reading passage.

9. **C.** Careful reading of the passage tells you that only three masters remain alive today.

INFERENCE QUESTIONS

I really enjoy the new mystery fiction written by Jonathan Gash. His main character, an odd but captivating antiques dealer, captures the reader with a combination of humor and bravery. The plots are exciting yet believable, things I respect about a good book. I hear that the author will be in town next week for a book signing.

10. *What do you think that the author will do next?*

  (A) Go to the library and check out more Jonathan Gash books.
  (B) Go to the used book store and get rid of all his or her Jonathan Gash books.
  (C) Go to the author's books signing next week.
  (D) Go to bed.

One of America's favorite old books remains a favorite today. Although the language is, to put it mildly, rough, and some of the plot elements morally questionable, people find a great deal in J. D. Salinger's *The Catcher in the Rye* to justify the book's existence. The book brings up a serious and important issue—the need for the young to come to terms with the lack of morality in the world that surrounds us.

Readers remain gripped by the existentialist dilemma faced by main character Holden Caulfield. Holden sees those around him losing their integrity as they become older, a process he calls "becoming phony." Holden's fear of becoming phony as he matures into adulthood symbolizes our own as we face what we might call the next evolutionary step in Salinger's projection. We live in an age in which marketing executives pedal thong underwear and tight, saucy t-shirts to 10-year-old girls, and young kids everywhere increasingly think high fashion consists of prison-garb-inspired clothing that falls well past the hips. Salinger's concept of phoniness seems to have been superceded with one of moral emptiness. As Yeats once put it, "the center cannot hold . . . mere anarchy is loosed upon the world."

11. *Based on the information in this passage, the reader can infer that* _____.

    (A) the author agrees with J. D. Salinger's worldview

    (B) the author disagrees with J. D. Salinger's worldview

    (C) the author remains neutral regarding J. D. Salinger's worldview

    (D) We cannot answer the question based on the details disclosed in the passage.

> School administrations face increasingly tough decisions. Recently, southern schools find it difficult to raise money for needed services; in order to locate that funding, schools have turned to fund-raising in the form of vending machines on school property to get cash.
>
> Students, those with tight schedules that allow for few leisurely meals as well as those who just like junk food—have responded with delight, pouring money hourly into drink and food machines. Teachers have responded with less enthusiasm; while they appreciate the funds generated by student spending, teachers pay a definite cost: shortened attention spans and "juiced up" students too addled with sugar to focus on lessons.
>
> Parents seem to be caught in the middle. On the one hand, they don't like the sinking grades and spiking behavior reports their students receive; on the other, they don't like removing the "free will" represented by allowing maturing students opportunities to manage their money, nutrition, and time.

12. *What subject might the author discuss next?*

    (A) Interviews with local mall merchants regarding how vending machines paid for new football uniforms when they were kids

    (B) An alternative plan, generated by students, that the author wants to put before the audience

    (C) SPCA spokespeople weighing in on the debate

    (D) The article will end here.

ANSWERS

10. **C.** While the author of this passage clearly states that he or she likes Jonathan Gash books very much, certain actions presented to you as options simply are not implied by this passion. He or she may certainly go to the library and get more books (choice A) or go to bed (choice D), but nowhere in the selection are you given any reason to think he or she might do so at this particular time. You know that choice B is very unlikely, since the author loves Gash's work so much that he or she would be unlikely to get rid of it. The passage does mention the upcoming book signing; most likely, therefore, given the author's love of Gash, he or she will make definite plans to attend the signing.

11. **A.** The author seems to take a side in this passage; therefore, you can rule out choices C and D, which state either that you can't tell what the author's point of view is (D) or that the author is neutral (C). Since the author does not use words that imply disagreement with Salinger, you can rule out choice B. The best answer is A, supported by the fact that the author even brings in an outside author (Yeats) in support of Salinger's point.

12. **B.** The article seems to present a problem and be all set for discussing it thoroughly. Since only the problem has been discussed, with no mention of possible solutions, it seems very unlikely that the article will end here. Therefore, rule out choice D. Interviews with people seem like a good idea, but why would the author of this piece choose to interview an adult about how vending machines helped his or her school decades before? This choice is simply not the best answer. Rule out choice A. The SPCA is a popular group whose purpose is to protect animals; why they would get to voice an opinion is unclear. Rule out choice C. The best thing, given these options, would be to hear proposed solutions to the problem; choice B offers exactly this logical path.

MORE PRACTICE SESSIONS: A MIXED BAG (see answers on page 183)

Using the theory that practice makes perfect, we offer you now even more opportunities to practice. This section offers several reading passages and questions related to each, much like the last section did. However, we model this series of practice questions on the type of questions (and the format followed) on the actual COOP/HSPT. We suggest you work through these texts and questions; we also suggest you practice identifying the kind of question you are being asked to answer. Therefore, each passage lists reading selections, questions, as well a space in which to write your guess as to the category of question you are answering (see page 164). Check your answers at the end. Good luck!

People seem to be the products of their society, upon reflection. U.S. citizens, for example, demand variety and speed above most things; modern marketing strategies seem to focus particularly on getting exactly what one wants with the least degree of inconvenience. It seems unthinkable that something as simple as a postcard can travel from Kentucky to Louisiana within eight hours, a farther distance and a quicker time period than a person could travel less than fifty years ago.

The desire for speed applies to most areas of modern life, including areas of medical treatments. Modern patients seem increasingly interested in quick-fix answers to long-term health problems. Various cities, Lexington, New Orleans, and Atlanta included, have poured vast quantities of money into the prescription drug business, predicting that quick treatments would increase in popularity over time; they were right.

Surprisingly, however, modern studies show that new drugs, ranging from allergy medications to anti-depressants to new treatments for cancer, seem to be increasingly ineffective. Recent clinical studies of patients suffering from depression, for example, studied the effect of new drug therapy. Doctors prescribed actual drugs for some patients, while prescribing <u>placebos</u> for others. Interestingly, patients on placebo-regimens enjoyed improvement at the same rate as patients on real-drug-regimens. Optimists point to these results as proof of the power of positive thinking; critics point to these results as justification for their skepticism.

1. *The best title for this passage would be _____.*

   This question is a/an _____ question.

   (A) Doctor Knows Best
   (B) Placebos: The Miracle Drug
   (C) Go Ask Alice
   (D) Quick Fix Solutions: Not Always What the Doctor Ordered

2. *The author's use of the word* placebo *implies that the word can be defined as _____.*

   This question is a/an _____ question.

   (A) a miracle drug
   (B) a chemical compound that does not actually contain medicine
   (C) a diet aid
   (D) a new treatment for cancer

3. *One city that has poured a great deal of money into drug research is _____.*

   This question is a/an _____ question.

   (A) Louisville
   (B) Lexington
   (C) Savannah
   (D) Shreveport

4. *Which of the following statements is implied by the passage?*

   This question is a/an _____ question.

   (A) People who crave speed and convenience are most likely to be depressed as well.
   (B) Positive attitudes necessarily aid in recuperation.
   (C) Travel has become faster and more common over time.
   (D) Cities like Lexington have actually lost significant amounts of money invested in drug research.

   > Impressionism, an art form favored by artists such as Camille Pissarro, Pierre Auguste Renoir, and Mary Cassat, allowed artists a new form of self-expression. Based on the idea that art did not have to be limited to mirror images of real life or to boring pictures of stately historical buildings, Impressionism allowed the imagination more influence. Consequently, Impressionism created enemies for itself almost immediately; indeed Impressionism got its name from a sarcastic comment made by French art critic Louis Leroy about how amateurish he considered the artistic style.
   >
   > Two very different painters, Claude Monet and Edgar Degas, in particular favored Impressionism. Claude Monet (1840–1926) found great inspiration in nature, and he consistently uses nature in his work. He frequently depicted the interplay of light and shadow in gardens (usually his own). Before his death, Monet managed to complete perhaps his most famous piece, an enormous work of water lilies. Because of his use of nature, some argue, Monet's style is characterized by an ability to express the movement and the joy of life in still life format.
   >
   > Edgar Degas (1834–1917), by contrast, preferred even more immediate—yet more fleeting—subjects: the swirling mass of humanity surrounding him. He drew inspiration from Japanese art forms and incorporated brilliant hues into his paintings of racetracks, dancers, and café frequenters. His interest in Japanese art also encouraged him to experiment with innovative, asymmetrical angles of observation. Degas' work especially <u>encapsulates</u> a distinctive, sympathetic interest the struggles and defeats of women; perhaps the work that best shows Degas' sympathy for women is his work entitled, *In a Café (The Absinthe Drinker)*.

5. *Which artist discussed in the passage died just before the end of World War I?*

   This question is a/an _____ question.

   (A) Mary Cassat
   (B) Claude Monet
   (C) August Renoir
   (D) Edgar Degas

6. *The author implies that _____.*

   This question is a/an _____ question.

   (A) art created prior to Impressionism was far more realist and conservative
   (B) art created after Impressionism was far more realist and conservative
   (C) without the use of Japanese art forms, Impressionism would not have been created
   (D) Monet only created one piece of art during his career

7. *The use of the word* encapsulates, *as used in this passage, is most likely defined by which of the following?*

   This question is a/an _____ question.

   (A) denies
   (B) leaves behind
   (C) obscures
   (D) shows

8. *This passage's main purpose is most likely _____.*

   This question is a/an _____ question.

   (A) to convince the reader that Impressionist art is somewhat lacking in value
   (B) to introduce some basic principles of Impressionism, as well as some famous examples of Impressionist art and artists, to the reader
   (C) to make the point that Impressionist art is better than modern art
   (D) to encourage the reader to investigate Japanese art forms

   Ryan and Sue, aged 30, found themselves in the same boat as so many other parents have done: tearing out their hair trying to maintain discipline over their three kids. Ryan and Sue's kids behaved relatively well when at home, closely monitored by their parents. However, whenever Ryan and Sue tried to hire a babysitter to watch the kids so that they might have a little time away from home all to themselves, their kids acted so badly that they found it difficult to find anyone willing to babysit.

   No amount of threatening, punishment, screaming, or cajoling seemed to work against Ryan and Sue's kids. Finally, instead of relying on traditional methods, Ryan and Sue sat down to figure out a logical, innovative method for dealing with <u>insubordinate</u> behavior.

   Ryan and Sue devised the following plan. First, they called a family meeting. They sat the kids down at their places around the kitchen table. In the center of the table, Ryan and Sue placed the kids' allowance for the week. All the crisp, green bills made quite a pretty picture against the wood grain of the table.

   Ryan and Sue then informed their kids that they were going out to dinner that evening and that Kelly, a local neighbor, would be coming to babysit. Ryan and Sue told the kids that they would leave the weekly allowance on the table, without any explanation to Kelly. However, should Kelly report a single act of disobedience taking place that evening, Ryan and Sue promised to add the weekly allowance to the fee already being paid to Kelly. Should the kids behave, they would be allowed to retrieve their allowance the following morning.

   When Ryan and Sue returned from dinner, they were pleased to have a glowing report of the kids' behavior.

9. *The word **insubordinate** as it is used in the passage most closely means _____.*

   This question is a/an _____ question.

   (A) aggressive
   (B) passive
   (C) unruly
   (D) ridiculous

10. *The main point of this passage is _____.*

    This question is a/an _____ question.

    (A) good babysitters are hard to find
    (B) older parents come up with wiser solutions than younger parents do
    (C) threats are the best means by which to discipline kids
    (D) the best means by which to discipline kids is to find appropriate motivation, in particular something the kids like that they don't want taken away

11. *How many kids do Ryan and Kelly have?*

    This question is a/an _____ question.

    (A) none
    (B) one
    (C) two
    (D) three

12. *The event that would most likely take place next would be _____.*

    This question is a/an _____ question.

    (A) Ryan and Sue's kids collecting their allowance
    (B) Ryan and Sue's babysitter collecting the kids' allowance
    (C) Ryan and Sue going out to dinner again the next evening
    (D) Ryan and Sue giving their babysitter a raise

    According to the latest statistics, the average American lives in a dirty, cluttered, disorganized mess. To combat the mess, 10 million of us tune in weekly to shows like "Clean Sweep," "Clean House," and "Mission: Organization," shows devoted to the purpose of cleaning up after ourselves. Furthermore, we spent $4.36 billion last year on home-storage products, an increase of 10% since 1998. Luckily, if we can't figure out how to use these products on our own, we can call in the cleaning cavalry. Professional organizers, people whom you can pay to come organize your bedroom closets, will come and help out, charging—and getting—from $50 to $200 an hour for their services.

    Why the sudden interest in housecleaning? The answers are plentiful. Statistically speaking, the average American spends 12 weeks per year searching for misplaced stuff; simply put, we want those 12 weeks back. Interior designers point out that people simply like the look of a clean, uncluttered house; check out any *House Beautiful*-type magazine, and you'll notice that the best looking houses are also the least filled with traditional bulky furniture and blocky TVs, favoring instead streamlined futons, wood floors, and flatscreen TVs. Psychologists say that people look at organizing their homes as a way of grabbing control of an uncontrollable world: We can't control the state of the union, but we sure can control the state of our sock drawer.

    Whatever the cause, Americans are finally coming clean about an embarrassing fact: We simply don't know how to keep track of all the things we buy. Ironically, however, people seem to look to purchasing storage items as a <u>panacea</u> for a general urge to consume. Americans in particular seem easy victims to a need to buy, to own, to possess. What better way to do so than to buy products using the excuse that these items are needed to maintain order in our over-cluttered households?

    Whatever the cause, the effect seems here to stay for a while. However, critics express concern for the modern yen for cleanliness. It takes more than a one-time shopping binge to maintain a household; most likely people, by buying all this new stuff, are setting themselves up as victims for professional organizers.

13. *The author implies _____.*

    This question is a/an _____ question.

    (A) that the kind of people who are normally interested in leisure magazines are not the type also interested in organizing their houses
    (B) that current American interest in household organization will die away
    (C) that current American interest in household organization will last indefinitely
    (D) that spare, uncluttered houses are worse than sprawling, filled-to-the-brim houses

14. *The word* panacea *can be defined as* _____.

   This question is a/an _____ question.

   (A) something that creates panic
   (B) the idea that refers to paneling
   (C) a phrase that includes everyone
   (D) an answer to one's prayers

15. *The writer's main purpose for writing this passage is* _____.

   This question is a/an _____ question.

   (A) to express a wish that professional organizers would come clean his/her house
   (B) to make an argument for leaving houses messy
   (C) to point out the total money people spent on organization products last year
   (D) to inform the reader about a new fad that has hit American consumers

16. *The author states that which of the following statements is true?*

   This question is a/an _____ question.

   (A) Professional organizers get paid between $50 and $200 for their services.
   (B) People spend on average 15 weeks searching for stuff they own but can't find.
   (C) Home storage products raked in $5.36 in sales last year.
   (D) Sales of home storage products are up 10% since 1988.

> Johnson makes the case that it is ironic that much of what is praiseworthy about humanity and its accomplishments came about not through thoughtful, preplanned intent, but through accident. Johnson then asks the reader to consider the following cases.
>
> He tells how Ancient Egyptians discovered the fermentation process by accident; a store of grain had been allowed to rot due to an abnormally warm season, and spores, blown in on the wind, settled in the grain and began the chemical reaction now known as the fermentation process. Christopher Columbus' discovery of America came about via a botched attempt to locate a quick trade route to the Indies. The discovery of rubber vulcanization occurred when Charles Goodyear, a man with no formal education, accidentally dropped a piece of sulfur-treated rubber on a hot stove and noticed that the previously brittle substance had acquired significant flexibility. Johnson then makes the claim that many other examples, "too numerous to list here," also exist.
>
> Johnson concludes with a rather pessimistic analysis, namely that, since most innovation comes as the result of accident, there exists no reason for trying to achieve anything on one's own. Such an argument strikes me as overly fatalistic. Indeed, I would suggest turning Johnson's argument on its head; humanity, to me, is worthy of praise for its undeniable ability to turn a negative into a positive, to turn <u>dross</u> into gold. One case in point is the crisis of September 11, 2001.

17. *Based on the author's use of the word* dross *in this passage, which of the following definitions is most appropriate?*

   This question is a/an _____ question.

   (A) something valuable
   (B) something worthless
   (C) something hard
   (D) something heavy

18. *The author attributes the discovery of fermentation to which entity?*

    This question is a/an _____ question.

    (A) Christopher Columbus
    (B) Charles Goodyear
    (C) the Egyptians
    (D) Alexander Dumas

19. *The speaker's main purpose in writing this passage is most likely _____.*

    This question is a/an _____ question.

    (A) to call the reader's attention to the good fortune humanity has enjoyed
    (B) to call the reader's attention to little known facts about fermentation and vulcanization
    (C) to criticize humanity for its failures
    (D) to reassure the reader that something positive can be found in even the most negative of situations

20. *The author of this piece will most likely discuss which of the following topics?*

    This question is a/an _____ question.

    (A) A further discussion of inventions that came about by accident.
    (B) A review of the points already made by the passage.
    (C) The 2001 Attack on America.
    (D) A discussion of fatalistic writers, such as Albert Camus.

    Perhaps one of the most captivating true stories of heroism, daring, and determination comes to us in the form of *Running a Thousand Miles for Freedom: The Story of William and Ellen Craft*. This story, lived and told by ex-slave William Craft, dates back to 1848, when William and his wife Ellen risked everything to gain their freedom. Almost any slave narrative has the ability to capture the attention; the story of the Crafts' escape offers even more drama and sensationalism than most. William and Ellen escaped using trickery: by having Ellen dress as an invalid white slave master, traveling to Philadelphia from Georgia for medical reasons, accompanied by her slave, William.

    Why was this story so popular? One reason is because the tale fit so well with the values of its audience. The story pleased Abolitionists and European critics of the American slavery system. Such members of the audience thrilled to hear how two slaves escaped the chains of slavery: outsmarting their masters, finding appropriate and useful loopholes in the South's slavery system, and often traveling disguised in broad daylight under the watchful eyes of their would-be captors. On the other hand, slave owners could not hear the tale often enough, if only due to obsessive self-denigration for having allowed themselves to be tricked.

21. *The story of William and Ellen Craft took place before which of the following?*

    This question is a/an _____ question.

    (A) The Revolutionary War
    (B) The Civil War
    (C) World War I
    (D) World War II

22. *The word* self-denigration *as used by the author most closely means* _____.

    This question is a/an _____ *question.*

    (A) sadness
    (B) happiness
    (C) anger
    (D) self-hatred

23. *This passage most closely resembles which genre of literature?*

    This question is a/an _____ *question.*

    (A) critical review
    (B) book report
    (C) statistical analysis
    (D) philosophical treatise

24. *The passage deals mainly with* _____.

    This question is a/an _____ *question.*

    (A) explaining why slave narratives in general are interesting
    (B) explaining why the story of William and Ellen Craft in particular is interesting
    (C) explaining why the South opted for a slave system in the first place
    (D) explaining why the North hated the Craft's story so much

Baseball players use hand signals all the time; hand signals are so commonly used during games that observers might be oblivious to their presence in the game. However, hand signals were not always part of baseball.

In the 1880s, pitchers and managers communicated via one-on-one conferences on the pitcher's mound and verbal calls across the diamond. Discussing strategy secretly was crucial; sometimes, teammates covered their mouths and whispered in one another's ears so as to prevent the opposing team from overhearing.

One season, however, William "Dummy" Hoy signed on to play for the Cincinnati Reds. Hoy was an incredible pitcher who ended his career having played for 5 different teams in 15 seasons from 1888 to 1902. He led the National League with 82 stolen bases in his rookie year with the Cincinnati Reds. He stole 30 or more bases in his first 12 years of his career. He scored 100 runs nine times, and his on base average was over .400 four times. Hoy's lifetime batting average was .292, and he had 2,057 hits.

Such a brilliant career began, however, with a rocky start; Hoy was deaf. He couldn't hear verbal signals, nor could he reliably keep up with the game's progress due to his inability to hear team chatter.

In response to this obstacle, however, Hoy's manager showed creativity and innovation. He ordered his entire team to learn the American Universal Sign Language, the language of hand signals created for and used by deaf people. Now, all of Hoy's teammates could communicate with Hoy, and he with them, without the other team being able to infiltrate team strategy.

Other teams, impressed with this silent form of communication, followed the Reds' lead. Now, one cannot attend a baseball game without seeing these familiar hand signals.

25. *The reason why people gave William Hoy the nickname "Dummy" is most likely because* _____.

    This question is a/an _____ question.

    (A) he had no formal education
    (B) he got all C's in school
    (C) he was deaf and therefore hard to talk to
    (D) he was blind but brilliant at math

26. *The best title for this passage would be* _____.

    This question is a/an _____ question.

    (A) Three Strikes and You're Out!
    (B) Star Struck
    (C) From Mouth to Hand
    (D) Manners on the Mound

27. *The author uses the word* infiltrate *in this passage to mean* _____.

    This question is a/an _____ question.

    (A) contaminate
    (B) discover
    (C) invade
    (D) prepare

28. *The use of hand signals in baseball dates back to the* _____.

    This question is a/an _____ question.

    (A) 1990s
    (B) 1890s
    (C) 1980s
    (D) 1880s

Edgar Allan Poe (1809–1849) is best known for his spooky stories and dark poetry. However, modern literary critics now look to him for his insight into human nature. Despite himself, Poe has gained a reputation as a social commentator.

At first glance, Poe's world view appears to be one of fear and mistrust, especially toward women. Consider a very brief account of Poe's work. His protagonists are almost <u>invariably</u> delicate, highly educated males, who prefer to study in their candle-lit salons rather than interact with other people. They seem fearful of all people, particularly women. Yet despite their apparent fear of women, they nevertheless seek out the secrets women possess. In "Ligea," the protagonist cannot quench his intense desire to look into her eyes, the windows of her soul; in "Berenice," the protagonist obsessively seeks to possess Berenice's teeth.

Hidden beneath these generalizations is a strict division between male and female personality traits. One of Poe's best short stories, "The Fall of the House of Usher," illustrates this relationship between men and women. In this story, Poe's protagonist, Usher, tries to rid himself of his sister. He fails, and his ancestral mansion falls down around him. Modern critics look to this tale as an allegory of the human mind, with Usher representing the male/scientific/left-brained side of the human personality and Usher's sister representing the female/artistic/right-brained side. The inference: Usher tries to bury the half of himself that makes him uncomfortable.

Upon first reading, one might be tempted to infer that Poe advocates such a world view. However, reading between the lines leads to exactly the opposite conclusion. Almost invariably, those of Poe's protagonists who insist upon dividing their personalities between left- and right-brained functions end up mad, incarcerated, or otherwise destroyed.

29. *What is the best concluding sentence for this passage?*

    This question is a/an _____ question.

    (A) Clearly then, Poe is arguing for a strict separation of the male-female impulses.
    (B) Clearly then, Poe is arguing for a balance of the male-female impulses.
    (C) Clearly then, the reader can see that Poe himself feared women.
    (D) Clearly then, one can see that we all share the same world view.

30. *What did the writer not list as one of the characteristics of a Poe protagonist?*

    This question is a/an _____ question.

    (A) Possessing a great degree of education
    (B) Being heavily addicted to opium
    (C) Being obsessive about women
    (D) Possessing a delicate temperament

31. *Which of the following definitions most closely fits the word* invariably?

    This question is a/an _____ question.

    (A) unchangingly
    (B) sporadically
    (C) never
    (D) oddly

32. *The passage mainly discusses _____.*

    This question is a/an _____ question.

    (A) Poe's use of bizarre and strange detail in his work
    (B) the effect of extreme intelligence and intense education on the human personality
    (C) using literature to point out a relationship between human psychology and literature
    (D) a survey of literature typical of the late 19th century

Zelda Fitzgerald, superstar of her generation, set a high standard for madness during an already mad decade. She came from a prominent Alabama family, a fact that became glaringly obvious to those who met her; her wealth and breeding simply radiated from her. Attractive, with red-gold hair, delicate features, and assured body language, she became accustomed to public attention early on.

Eager to maintain her spot in the limelight, she often invented ways of remaining in it. Once, as a young child, she stole away in the family car, enjoying a brief but wild ride before being recaptured. Not much later on a particularly boring day, she phoned the police and alerted them to a young child stranded atop a high rooftop in need of rescue—then she promptly climbed to the roof of her own house to await the excitement.

Her love of chaos continued into her adult life. She intentionally married "beneath her" by accepting the wedding proposal of F. Scott Fitzgerald, a gifted but penniless writer, burned by the amorality of 1920 society. She and Fitzgerald threw wild, lavish, drunken parties, often topping off the evening's revels with a dip in the water fountain or a marital spat or two. Once, jealous that Fitzgerald paid too much attention to a visiting actress, Zelda silently climbed to the top of a stair banister, caught Fitzgerald's attention, and stepped off into the abyss.

Zelda's increasingly dangerous and disturbing <u>antics</u> finally caused people to conclude she was slipping into real insanity. She was institutionalized in 1934 and spent the remainder of her life in and out of asylums. Nevertheless, her beauty, her spirit, and her tragic fall from orbit illustrate perfectly the social culture surrounding her.

33. *Why did Zelda call the police?*

    This question is a/an _____ question.

    (A) She wanted to be rescued from her abusive home life.
    (B) She had gotten stuck accidentally on the roof of her house.
    (C) She wanted to impress her grandmother.
    (D) She was bored and wanted excitement.

34. *When did Zelda get institutionalized?*

    This question is a/an _____ question.

    (A) 1914
    (B) 1924
    (C) 1934
    (D) 1944

35. *Which of the following best defines the word* antics?

    This question is a/an _____ question.

    (A) tantrums
    (B) stunts
    (C) confusion
    (D) dementia

36. *The title that best expresses the ideas of this passage is _____.*

    This question is a/an _____ question.

    (A) Limelight
    (B) Once More into the Breach
    (C) Prohibition and Women
    (D) Portrait of a Lost Lady

Answers to "More Practice Sessions"

(beginning on page 174)

1. Main Idea	D	13. Inference	B	25. Inference	C
2. Word in Context	B	14. Word in Context	D	26. Main Idea	C
3. Fact	B	15. Main Idea	D	27. Word in Context	B
4. Inference	C	16. Fact	A	28. Fact	D
5. Fact	D	17. Word in Context	B	29. Inference	B
6. Inference	A	18. Fact	C	30. Fact	B
7. Word in Context	D	19. Main Idea	D	31. Word in Context	A
8. Main Idea	B	20. Inference	C	32. Main Idea	C
9. Word in Context	C	21. Fact	B	33. Inference	D
10. Main Idea	D	22. Word in Context	D	34. Fact	C
11. Fact	D	23. Inference	A	35. Word in Context	B
12. Inference	A	24. Main Idea	B	36. Main Idea	D

Answer Explanations to "More Practice Sessions"

Note: We at Barron's want to help you feel confident that you can identify the type of reading comprehension question that will be asked of you. We, therefore, strongly recommend you verify which type of question is being asked with a quick reference to the chart at the beginning of this chapter (page 164). Then check out our explanations of why certain answers are wrong and others are right. Good luck!

1. **Main Idea: D.** Any time you see a question that asks that you come up with a title for a selection, you are being asked to identify the main idea of that passage; this is a main-idea reading comprehension question. Break down the three-paragraph reading passage by identifying the main idea (or topic sentence) for each paragraph. Your breakdown should read something like the following:

   Paragraph One: Historically, people have desired speed.

   Paragraph Two: People desire speed in many areas of life—whether it be speedy travel or speedy medical recovery.

   Paragraph Three: Quick fixes, in particular placebos, increasingly do not work effectively.

   Now, check out the titles. The title suggestion of "Doctor Knows Best" asks you to think about the patient-doctor relationship but gives no insight into how speed of recovery or effectiveness of certain drugs might come into play. Neither does the title "Go Ask Alice" refer to either of these subjects; the best you can say for it is that it makes a clever reference to a pop song from the seventies ("White Rabbit" by the Jefferson Airplane). Choice B, "Placebos: The Miracle Drug," at least mentions the idea of placebos (as discussed briefly in the third paragraph), so you might be tempted to choose it. But consider choice D, which mentions both a desire for quick solutions to problems as well as disappointment in the result of attempting to use those quick-fix methods. A quick comparison with the paragraph breakdown shows this choice to be the best.

2. **Word in Context: B.** The question clearly asks you to define *placebo*; therefore, this is a word-in-context question. The reading passage states that "doctors sometimes prescribe actual drugs for some patients, while prescribing placebos for others." The construction of this phrase implies a contrast with opposites (prescribing one thing for one group and the opposite of that thing for another). The first thing being prescribed is described as being "actual drugs," which means doctors are giving real medication that will have a documentable effect on the person(s) taking it. Therefore the second thing being described—the placebos—must be something opposite of actual drugs, or something that does not have an effect on the user. In short, you can infer from the use of the word in context that a placebo has no effect on the user. A quick scan of the selections reveals that choice B is the only selection that describes a "drug" that has no effect on the user—because it contains no medicine.

3. **Fact: B.** This question is asking that you locate the factual answer to a factual question; therefore, it is a fact question. You need to find out which of the cities on the list is mentioned in the reading passage. Using your memory is best, but if you need to, quickly scan the article again; you discover that Lexington is the only city in the selection list that also appears in the reading passage.

4. **Inference: C.** Any time you see the word *implied* in a reading comprehension question, you can be sure that you are being asked an inference question. Using what you have read—and not what you know (or think you know) about the topic—consider your four options. Be careful; you are trying to find the sentence that contains a true implication about *any portion of the reading passage.* Several choices can be ruled out from the first. Rule out, for example, choice A. Nowhere in the paragraph are you given any evidence to believe (or infer) that people who crave speed are more likely to be depressed than any-

one else; the only people who you might infer would get depressed more often than others based on this reading passage might be people who keep trying quick-fix drug therapy without results. Choice B also presents a problem: While one might make the case that the use of placebos to treat certain medical conditions successfully is proof that a positive mental attitude is key to recovery, one cannot fully infer this; one might as easily infer that all drug therapy is as likely to work as not to work. You can also reject choice D. Nothing in the paragraph gives any inclination that money is being lost (or gained, for that matter) in the cities attempting experimental drug therapy. In short, choice C is the only sentence that can fully be inferred. Paragraph one states that a postcard sent from Kentucky to Louisiana can travel farther than a human once could; one can definitively infer, therefore, that travel speeds have significantly increased over time; otherwise, people and postcards would still be traveling at the same slow rate.

5. **Fact: D.** This question is asking for a fact you recall from your reading the selection in conjunction with a fact you should probably know from your other studies. Comparing the dates tells you that choice D, Edgar Degas who died in 1917, died just before the end of World War I (1918).

6. **Inference: A.** Again, notice the key word *implies*; this is an inference question. You can immediately rule out choice D; the reading passage clearly indicates that Monet created more than one work of art (one of gardens, another of water lilies). You can also rule out choice B; the article does not go on long enough for you to make any inferences regarding what the author thinks about post-Impressionist art. Choice C is tempting, since the author seems to think it very important to Degas' work that he was influenced by Japanese art forms, but nowhere does the author imply that all Impressionist artists were influenced by Japanese art—without a "mass movement" in which most Impressionist artists give credit to Japanese art forms for inspiration, you simply cannot infer that Japanese art forms had that much influence on Impressionism. Your only real inference lies in choice A. Paragraph one indicates by comparison that Impressionism was more exciting and fantastic than the art that came before it; therefore, you can infer that the pre-Impressionist art was more realistic and more "normal" (or conventional) than Impressionist art.

7. **Word in Context: D.** Since the question asks you to define how a particular word is used in this reading selection, you can easily identify the question as a word-in-context type. Paragraph three details all of the typical things that Degas' work included; therefore, you can assume that most of the verbs being used in this paragraph will fit the basic definition of *include*. Judging from the list of choices, you can only select choice D as a synonym for *include*. The others simply do not fit (*denies, leaves behind,* and *obscures* all basically fit the definition of *excludes*).

8. **Main Idea: B.** The question's key phrase "main purpose" essentially means main idea. Breaking down the paragraph structure, much as we did in question 1, yields the following result:

   Paragraph One: This paragraph defines Impressionism and gives an impression of popular response to it.

   Paragraph Two: This paragraph introduces Monet and gives examples of his style of Impressionism.

   Paragraph Three: This paragraph introduces a contrasting example of Impressionism, that of the artist Degas.

   All three paragraphs give descriptive, informative, and factual evidence regarding the subject of Impressionism. The piece does not attempt to persuade the reader toward a particular opinion or point of view; therefore, you can rule out choices A, C, and D, which all contain vocabulary that implies an attempt to convince or persuade ("convince" in choice A, "Impressionist art is better than" in choice C, and "encourage the reader" in choice D).

9. **Word in Context: C.** The question asks you to select the best definition for a word used in the passage; this is clearly a word-in-context question. Paragraph one tells the reader

that the reason Ryan and Sue cannot find babysitters for their kids is because of the bad behavior their kids display; paragraph two shows Ryan and Sue trying to discipline their children. One can infer from the use of the word *insubordinate* that the behavior displayed by Ryan and Sue's kids is bad; therefore *insubordinate* must mean bad. Scanning the list of choices, you notice that Choice D is obviously not the answer; ridiculous behavior can be amusing, which might actually work to encourage babysitters to take care of Ryan and Sue's kids. Choices A and B are equally unsuitable; neither aggressive (acting out) nor passive (quiet but stubborn resistance) behavior is necessarily bad behavior, and sometimes it is quite necessary—witness the tactics used by Civil Rights activists in the 1960s. However, unruly behavior is by definition bad behavior; therefore choice C is the correct response.

10. **Main Idea: D.** The question uses a glaring hint here—"main point" is basically another way of saying main idea. Break down the reading selection as follows:

    Paragraph One: Ryan and Sue's kids act so badly no one will babysit them.

    Paragraph Two: Ryan and Sue are confused about how to get their kids to behave.

    Paragraph Three: Ryan and Sue give the kids an allowance.

    Paragraph Four: Ryan and Sue tie good behavior with rewards (keeping their allowance) and bad behavior with discipline that the kids respect (revoking the allowance).

    Paragraph Five: Ryan and Sue are rewarded by well-behaved kids (and frequent babysitting).

    Essentially, then, the selection outlines the way one set of parents copes with badly behaved kids. Nowhere does the article evaluate the quality of babysitters from which Ryan and Sue hired babysitting help; rule out choice A. Nowhere, too, does the selection imply that Ryan and Sue are troubled with badly behaving kids or an inability to fix the situation because of their age; rule out choice B. Finally, paragraph two clearly states that threats did not work; rule out choice C. The main point of the passage is to persuade parents that the key to good parenting is to find rules and disciplinary action that kids respect and respond to; the correct answer is choice D.

11. **Fact: D.** This question asks for a simple fact recalled from reading; clearly then this is a fact question. Use your short-term memory (or quickly check the passage again); Ryan and Sue have three kids.

12. **Inference: A.** The phrase "What would most likely take place next" tells you that you must guess (or infer), based on the facts in the selection, what will happen next—this is an inference question. Refer to the paragraph breakdown; if the parents set up a cause-effect relationship with their kids in which good behavior gets financial reward, and, upon the completion of the evening, the kids behaved well, then we know that the kids will receive their reward. Therefore the only correct choice offered is Choice A. Choice B must be rejected (unless Ryan and Sue are hypocritical parents). We have no reason to think that Ryan and Sue will test their system again so soon; in fact, they should not, so as to retain the power of their new disciplinary system. Rule out choice C. The skill of the babysitter had nothing to do with the behavior of the kids—the power of the situation rested entirely in the power of the kids to desire money more than they desire to behave badly; therefore, rule out choice D.

13. **Inference: B.** The phrase "The author implies…" tells you that this question will be an inference question. Now you just need to figure out which inference is one the author actually makes. Rule out choice A, since the author does not discuss any details about the reading habits possessed by people who are currently caught up in the push to get their houses clean. Rule out choice D also, since the author really tries hard not to praise one kind of house over another. Now, you're down to choices B and C. These state opposite sides of the same question, so if you can rule one out, you can figure out the answer. Look to the final paragraph, which has a dismal tone that intensifies the author's closing comment that Americans will yet again be disappointed by their efforts to find the answers to their troubles. So you want to pick choice B.

14. **Word in Context: D.** The question asks you to define a word; clearly then this is a word-in-context question. The word *panacea* refers to something that answers the needs of everyone. Therefore you want to choose choice D. The other choices are included to trick you into selecting them—notice they all play off some mismatched association with part of the word *panacea*. The *pan* in *panacea* means all, not panic or paneling; so you can rule out choices A and B. Yet, you don't want to choose choice C, despite the fact that the *pan* in *panacea* means all; the word *panacea* doesn't merely mean all. Choosing choice C is too simplistic.

15. **Main Idea: D.** By now you should be recognizing the synonym of "main purpose"; this is a main-idea question. Now, make sure you know what the article is trying to say. Break down the paragraphs.

    Paragraph One introduces the topic, making an observation about what people are reading and watching nowadays.

    Paragraph Two begins telling the reader about the specific facts associated with this new obsession—money spent, products bought, etc.

    Paragraph Three begins giving reasons why people are so interested in cleaning their houses.

    Paragraph Four concludes with a dismal speculation regarding whether getting their houses clean will really satisfy people in the long run.

    Based on this breakdown, the reader will notice that the author does not express any wish that people would come help clean his/her house; rule out choice A. Nor does the author make any case for leaving things messy; rule out choice B. The author does tell the reader how much people are spending on cleaning up, but this is not the focus of the article; rule out choice C. Choice D is the only one that encompasses the entirety of the article.

16. **Fact: A.** Finding out "which of the following statements is true" tells you that you are looking for facts from the reading selection. All of these statements refer to details from the reading: the only problem is that three of the statements relate incorrect information. People only lose twelve weeks of time searching for stuff; people spent $4.36 billion last year; and sales have increased 10% since 1998 (not 1988). The only correct answer is the fact that professional organizers can get big bucks ($50–$200) for helping you clean up your own mess.

17. **Word in Context: B.** This question asks you to look at how the author uses a word in the passage; this is a word-in-context question. Rereading the last paragraph of the passage reveals the following phrase: "to turn a negative into a positive, to turn <u>dross</u> into gold." The phrase is based on the principle of the appositive: to give an example of something in close succession to the thing just discussed. You know that gold is a good thing, and you know that "something good" is being discussed; you can equate these two topics. By contrast and by the process of elimination, you can then link up "something bad" with *dross*, even if you don't know what dross is. Finally, you can set up the phrase like an equation:

something negative = dross
something positive = gold

Therefore, if *dross* means something negative, scan the selections to see what matches up. The choice that best fits is choice B.

18. **Fact: C.** The question asks you to figure out who the author states is responsible for the discovery of fermentation; this is a fact question. Based on your recollection of the passage—or a quick scan—you discover that the author states the Egyptians discovered the fermentation process; the other names are there as red herrings, to confuse you. Select choice C.

19. **Main Idea: D.** Again, your brain should automatically be signaling that "main purpose" is really code for main idea. Break it down!

Paragraph One: Johnson (who he really is doesn't matter) talks about how ironic it is that great things come about through accident more often than through intentional human action.

Paragraph Two: Johnson (by implication) gives an example of the fermentation of alcohol by the Egyptians or the accidental discovery of rubber by Charles Goodyear.

Paragraph Three: Johnson argues that since good things come about through accident, why attempt to shape the world or the future? The author then starts to give an opposing viewpoint and seems to be about to discuss the crisis of 9/11.

Choices A, B, and C can all be ruled out; after all, the passage refers to examples of good fortune (choice A) as well as bad (choice C). While the passage makes brief mention of the fermentation process, no careful reader would argue that the entire passage is intended to discuss fermentation. The only possible option is choice D, which says that something positive can come out of bad situations—and all examples supplied by the passage support this view. Alcohol comes from mold; rubber came from accidental burning; and, as the author will now set out to prove, some good came out of the 9/11 attacks.

20. **Inference: C.** Of the passages we give you for practice, this is an especially tough one; yet challenge is essential to academic success—so stick to it! The phrase "will most likely discuss" should tell you that you are dealing with a possibility, rather than a fact; therefore, this is an inference question. Knowing what the breakdown of the passage is will help; we do this for you in question 19, so we refrain from redoing so here. Check out question 19's explanation if you need to. Essentially, the author is explaining to the reader what someone named Johnson has argued in the past, an argument that the author will then attempt to shoot down. The author ends this passage with the intent of elaborating on his or her opposing argument. The author does not get to explain his or her argument in full. What will he or she argue next? Consider the options. The author has already discussed a series of inventions, and, given the breakdown of the passage, it seems illogical that the reader would consider discussing more inventions at this point. So, rule out choice A. The author clearly seems to be switching topics; therefore, a review or recap of the major points discussed thus far seems to be inappropriate. So, rule out choice B. Nothing about the discussion implies that the next topic would be Albert Camus; rule out choice D. However, the article ends with a brief reference to the infamous 9/11 attacks—attack against the Twin Towers in New York and against the Pentagon in Washington, D.C. Most likely, then, the author will turn to this topic next. The phrase, "one case in point" also implies that the discussion of whatever case is in point will follow. The correct answer is C.

21. **Fact: B.** The passage asks you to identify a specific fact in the reading passage: when something happened in comparison to when something else happened in history. Knowing your dates helps: the Revolutionary War dates back to the 1770s; the Civil War dates back to the 1860s; and both the First and Second World Wars date back to the 1900s. Paragraph one tells you that William and Ellen Craft's story happens circa 1848; therefore, you can rule out choices C and D. You can also rule out choice A, since the Revolutionary War was long over by 1848. The correct answer is B.

22. **Word in Context: D.** Since the question refers to the definition of a word, you can be sure that this is a words-in-context question. Naturally, it's best for one of these questions that you know the vocabulary from studying in school already. But, check out paragraph two again, if you don't already know the word *self-denigration*. You can tell that the paragraph is setting up a contrast—(1) telling reasons why slaves and abolitionists liked the story of William and Ellen Craft's escape and (2) telling reasons why even slaveholders (who would have been very upset by the tale) listened to the story again and again. The passage states that the slaveholders felt as if they had been tricked— usually something we associate with negative feelings. Scan the list for options that suggest negative feelings. You can rule out choice B, then, since happiness is not a negative feeling. Choice A might work, but slave owners who had been tricked (or imagined themselves being tricked) probably wouldn't be sad—they'd be angry. Narrow your selections

to choices C and D. Check out the word *self-denigration* again; the word refers specifically to the self, so choose D, "self-hatred." (You'll be right!)

23. **Inference: A.** This question asks you to compare the reading selection you have just finished to other types of books or reading passages you have read. You are using personal judgment; therefore, you are making inference. This is an inference question. Scan your options, and rule out obvious wrong answers, like choices C and D. Statistics involves numbers—this passage offers no numbers, aside from the occasional date, at any point; nor does the author talk about philosophy at any point. Consider choices A and B. Do you see any attempt by the author to *evaluate* how good the book is? Or does the reading selection try to "sell" you interesting aspects of the book and its plot? A quick scan reveals that the passage seems to be trying to make you interested in reading the book but is not trying to evaluate the writing style or the author's intent in writing; therefore, the answer is B.

24. **Main Idea: B.** The question uses the word "mainly," which by now should be a strong hint that you are dealing with a main-idea question. You can rule out Choices C and D right off. The short reading passage does not even mention reasons why the South decided to build itself on a foundation of slave trade. Additionally, while Southern slave owners may have hated the Crafts for tricking them, according to the passage, the article specifically paints Northern readers as being just as obsessed with the story of William and Ellen Craft as their Southern counterparts (and without discussing motivation for that obsession). So, look again at choices A and B. Clearly the reading passage tells about slave narratives, but does it discuss the 100 or more slave narratives that came out of this time period? Or just the slave narrative telling about William and Ellen Craft? A quick scan again verifies that this passage only discusses the Crafts. Therefore, you must select choice B.

25. **Inference: C.** This question asks you to make a judgment based on facts in the passage; therefore, it is an inference question. Nowhere in the passage does the author discuss Italy's education; therefore, you can quickly eliminate Choices A, B, and D. Your only answer left is C. (Sometimes a quick answer like this one can help you catch up on your pacing later.)

26. **Main Idea: C.** Being asked to select the best title is a clue that you are looking for the main idea. Eliminate choice B, since it really is too vague to be the best answer for this question. Eliminate choice A for the same reason; it's clearly appropriate for most baseball-related stories, but we want a title that is appropriate for *this* baseball related story. Choice D just doesn't really fit—manners on the mound could mean a variety of things—and we are not shown people acting rudely and being told to reform their manners (not even in the case where people made up the insensitive nickname of "Dummy" for Hoy). Your best selection is choice C, since the passage talks about how players quit talking with their mouths and started talking with their hands.

27. **Word in Context: B.** Since you're being asked to define a word, this is clearly a word-in-context question. Probably you know the word *infiltrate* already, especially if you are at all interested in spy stories, shows, or games. The passage discusses a situation in which two teams use strategy to beat the other, strategy that depends upon each side keeping its plans secret from the "enemy." Words like those in choice A (that deal with contamination) or choice D (that deal with preparation) do not fit the situation, so rule them out. Words like those in choice C also do not really fit, since players are trying to figure out something, not physically invade a territory. Your best selection is choice B, which fits the meaning and the tone of a passage in which trying to figure out secrets is the goal.

28. **Fact: D.** This question asks you to identify a fact from the reading; hence, it is a fact question. Based on memory (or a quick glance up) you find out that paragraph two tells you that hand signals date back to the 1880s; you need to select choice D.

29. **Inference: B.** The question asks you to read the passage, identify the author's train of thought, and then complete that train of thought by choosing a sentence from the list of

options. This is asking you to infer; therefore, this is an inference question. You should break down the passage to make sure you understand the author's train of thought:

Paragraph One: Poe, usually known for his poetry, also gives great insight into human nature.

Paragraph Two: Poe creates male characters who fear women, mostly because they desire something the woman possesses.

Paragraph Three: We can apply this observation to psychology; Poe is saying that some people fear secret, intuitive parts of their own personalities and try to destroy these things they fear.

Paragraph Four: Poe seems to approve of people who try to bury half of their personalities, but actually he steadfastly disapproves.

Now that we know the line of thought, finding the correct response shouldn't be too hard. You can rule out choice D, since the author is talking about Poe in particular, not people in general. You can also rule out choice C, since, even though the author does imply that Poe was obsessed by women, this is not the main point of the argument. And, you can rule out choice A, since paragraph four states exactly the opposite view. Your answer should be choice B.

30. **Fact: B.** This question is asking you to consider a list of options and figure out which one is inappropriate; you can only do so by remembering the data given you in the article and making a checklist. Therefore, this is a fact question. You can find choices A, C, and D discussed in paragraph two; therefore, the only characteristic not discussed anywhere in the text is choice B.

31. **Word in Context: A.** This question asks you to define a word; it is a word-in-context question. Knowing some synonyms for the options listed helps here; you can essentially break them down as follows:

unchangingly	=	always
sporadically	=	sometimes
never	=	never
oddly	=	weirdly

Since the passage, specifically paragraph two, is making a general comment about Poe's writing over time, you are looking for a word that implies something that does not change. The only word in the list that fits this description is choice A.

32. **Main Idea: C.** The key word "mainly" should raise a red flag in your brain; this is a main-idea question. You can rule out choice D, since the passage only discusses Poe's writing; the author makes no attempt to discuss all other Dark Romantic writers of the 19th century, as one might expect in a survey of literature. Choices A and B are equally appealing, since you can point to paragraphs in this passage that do hint at these points. But the best answer is choice C, since the article tries, especially in paragraphs three and four, to make the point that readers can read literature and gain psychological insight into human nature.

33. **Inference: D.** This question asks you to consider what you know about Zelda Fitzgerald's personality and make a judgment; this is, therefore, an inference question. Using your memory (or remembering the author's discussion of the event), create a quick character sketch of Zelda. She was highly intelligent and in great need of entertainment; paragraph two states she was extremely bored that day. Therefore, your best choice would be choice D, which fits well with both things we know about Zelda. The other choices simply have no basis in fact that we know; the article does not say whether her early life was abusive (choice A) nor whether she had a need to impress authority figures around her (choice C). And the selection clearly states that she went onto the roof of her own free will.

34. **Fact: C.** The question asks you to single out a particular fact; therefore, this is a fact question. Paragraph four clearly states that Zelda was institutionalized in 1934. Therefore, your correct answer is C.

35. **Word in Context: B.** Again, the question asks you about a word; this is a word-in-context question. Some of the choices listed are designed to catch sloppy thinkers. Choices C and D, in particular, refer to symptoms a mental patient might exhibit. Just because Zelda eventually became a mental patient does not mean these answers are correct; in fact, they are not correct. Your best answers are choices A and B, since tantrums and antics are superficially very similar; both involve someone trying to get the attention of another person. Knowing the connotations of these words definitely helps. While both definitions are appropriate to this reading passage, tantrums involve inelegant, angry, loud lashing out, usually of two-year-olds against their parents; antics, on the other hand, generally are silly, witty, if occasionally dangerous, and usually only affect the person performing the antic. Since Zelda wanted attention, but usually without causing harm to others, and since she usually showed great wit in her actions, your best choice would be B.

36. **Main Idea: D.** Finding the best title means you are also stating the main idea; this is a main-idea question. You can rule out certain options immediately. While, judging from Zelda's dates, you can clearly see that Prohibition was taking place, the article does not focus on that fact; this passage is clearly written about Zelda, in an almost autobiographical manner. Therefore, choice B simply doesn't make much sense, given what you know about the article. Now, Zelda wanted attention, so you might be drawn to choice A, but the passage talks about more than just her need for attention, so keep looking. The best answer is D, since Zelda, for all her wit and wealth, was indeed "lost."

Model Exams

Answer Sheet
Practice Cooperative Admissions Examination 1

TEST 1   SEQUENCES

1. Ⓐ Ⓑ Ⓒ Ⓓ	5. Ⓐ Ⓑ Ⓒ Ⓓ	9. Ⓐ Ⓑ Ⓒ Ⓓ	13. Ⓐ Ⓑ Ⓒ Ⓓ	17. Ⓐ Ⓑ Ⓒ Ⓓ
2. Ⓕ Ⓖ Ⓗ Ⓙ	6. Ⓕ Ⓖ Ⓗ Ⓙ	10. Ⓕ Ⓖ Ⓗ Ⓙ	14. Ⓕ Ⓖ Ⓗ Ⓙ	18. Ⓕ Ⓖ Ⓗ Ⓙ
3. Ⓐ Ⓑ Ⓒ Ⓓ	7. Ⓐ Ⓑ Ⓒ Ⓓ	11. Ⓐ Ⓑ Ⓒ Ⓓ	15. Ⓐ Ⓑ Ⓒ Ⓓ	19. Ⓐ Ⓑ Ⓒ Ⓓ
4. Ⓕ Ⓖ Ⓗ Ⓙ	8. Ⓕ Ⓖ Ⓗ Ⓙ	12. Ⓕ Ⓖ Ⓗ Ⓙ	16. Ⓕ Ⓖ Ⓗ Ⓙ	20. Ⓕ Ⓖ Ⓗ Ⓙ

TEST 2   ANALOGIES

1. Ⓐ Ⓑ Ⓒ Ⓓ	5. Ⓐ Ⓑ Ⓒ Ⓓ	9. Ⓐ Ⓑ Ⓒ Ⓓ	13. Ⓐ Ⓑ Ⓒ Ⓓ	17. Ⓐ Ⓑ Ⓒ Ⓓ
2. Ⓕ Ⓖ Ⓗ Ⓙ	6. Ⓕ Ⓖ Ⓗ Ⓙ	10. Ⓕ Ⓖ Ⓗ Ⓙ	14. Ⓕ Ⓖ Ⓗ Ⓙ	18. Ⓕ Ⓖ Ⓗ Ⓙ
3. Ⓐ Ⓑ Ⓒ Ⓓ	7. Ⓐ Ⓑ Ⓒ Ⓓ	11. Ⓐ Ⓑ Ⓒ Ⓓ	15. Ⓐ Ⓑ Ⓒ Ⓓ	19. Ⓐ Ⓑ Ⓒ Ⓓ
4. Ⓕ Ⓖ Ⓗ Ⓙ	8. Ⓕ Ⓖ Ⓗ Ⓙ	12. Ⓕ Ⓖ Ⓗ Ⓙ	16. Ⓕ Ⓖ Ⓗ Ⓙ	20. Ⓕ Ⓖ Ⓗ Ⓙ

TEST 3   QUANTITATIVE REASONING

1. Ⓐ Ⓑ Ⓒ Ⓓ	5. Ⓐ Ⓑ Ⓒ Ⓓ	9. Ⓐ Ⓑ Ⓒ Ⓓ	13. Ⓐ Ⓑ Ⓒ Ⓓ	17. Ⓐ Ⓑ Ⓒ Ⓓ
2. Ⓕ Ⓖ Ⓗ Ⓙ	6. Ⓕ Ⓖ Ⓗ Ⓙ	10. Ⓕ Ⓖ Ⓗ Ⓙ	14. Ⓕ Ⓖ Ⓗ Ⓙ	18. Ⓕ Ⓖ Ⓗ Ⓙ
3. Ⓐ Ⓑ Ⓒ Ⓓ	7. Ⓐ Ⓑ Ⓒ Ⓓ	11. Ⓐ Ⓑ Ⓒ Ⓓ	15. Ⓐ Ⓑ Ⓒ Ⓓ	19. Ⓐ Ⓑ Ⓒ Ⓓ
4. Ⓕ Ⓖ Ⓗ Ⓙ	8. Ⓕ Ⓖ Ⓗ Ⓙ	12. Ⓕ Ⓖ Ⓗ Ⓙ	16. Ⓕ Ⓖ Ⓗ Ⓙ	20. Ⓕ Ⓖ Ⓗ Ⓙ

TEST 4   VERBAL REASONING—WORDS

1. Ⓐ Ⓑ Ⓒ Ⓓ	5. Ⓐ Ⓑ Ⓒ Ⓓ	9. Ⓐ Ⓑ Ⓒ Ⓓ	13. Ⓐ Ⓑ Ⓒ Ⓓ	17. Ⓐ Ⓑ Ⓒ Ⓓ
2. Ⓕ Ⓖ Ⓗ Ⓙ	6. Ⓕ Ⓖ Ⓗ Ⓙ	10. Ⓕ Ⓖ Ⓗ Ⓙ	14. Ⓕ Ⓖ Ⓗ Ⓙ	18. Ⓕ Ⓖ Ⓗ Ⓙ
3. Ⓐ Ⓑ Ⓒ Ⓓ	7. Ⓐ Ⓑ Ⓒ Ⓓ	11. Ⓐ Ⓑ Ⓒ Ⓓ	15. Ⓐ Ⓑ Ⓒ Ⓓ	19. Ⓐ Ⓑ Ⓒ Ⓓ
4. Ⓕ Ⓖ Ⓗ Ⓙ	8. Ⓕ Ⓖ Ⓗ Ⓙ	12. Ⓕ Ⓖ Ⓗ Ⓙ	16. Ⓕ Ⓖ Ⓗ Ⓙ	20. Ⓕ Ⓖ Ⓗ Ⓙ

TEST 5   VERBAL REASONING—CONTEXT

1. Ⓐ Ⓑ Ⓒ Ⓓ	3. Ⓐ Ⓑ Ⓒ Ⓓ	5. Ⓐ Ⓑ Ⓒ Ⓓ	7. Ⓐ Ⓑ Ⓒ Ⓓ	9. Ⓐ Ⓑ Ⓒ Ⓓ
2. Ⓕ Ⓖ Ⓗ Ⓙ	4. Ⓕ Ⓖ Ⓗ Ⓙ	6. Ⓕ Ⓖ Ⓗ Ⓙ	8. Ⓕ Ⓖ Ⓗ Ⓙ	10. Ⓕ Ⓖ Ⓗ Ⓙ

TEST 6   READING AND LANGUAGE ARTS

1. Ⓐ Ⓑ Ⓒ Ⓓ   11. Ⓐ Ⓑ Ⓒ Ⓓ   21. Ⓐ Ⓑ Ⓒ Ⓓ   31. Ⓐ Ⓑ Ⓒ Ⓓ
2. Ⓕ Ⓖ Ⓗ Ⓙ   12. Ⓕ Ⓖ Ⓗ Ⓙ   22. Ⓕ Ⓖ Ⓗ Ⓙ   32. Ⓕ Ⓖ Ⓗ Ⓙ
3. Ⓐ Ⓑ Ⓒ Ⓓ   13. Ⓐ Ⓑ Ⓒ Ⓓ   23. Ⓐ Ⓑ Ⓒ Ⓓ   33. Ⓐ Ⓑ Ⓒ Ⓓ
4. Ⓕ Ⓖ Ⓗ Ⓙ   14. Ⓕ Ⓖ Ⓗ Ⓙ   24. Ⓕ Ⓖ Ⓗ Ⓙ   34. Ⓕ Ⓖ Ⓗ Ⓙ
5. Ⓐ Ⓑ Ⓒ Ⓓ   15. Ⓐ Ⓑ Ⓒ Ⓓ   25. Ⓐ Ⓑ Ⓒ Ⓓ   35. Ⓐ Ⓑ Ⓒ Ⓓ
6. Ⓕ Ⓖ Ⓗ Ⓙ   16. Ⓕ Ⓖ Ⓗ Ⓙ   26. Ⓕ Ⓖ Ⓗ Ⓙ   36. Ⓕ Ⓖ Ⓗ Ⓙ
7. Ⓐ Ⓑ Ⓒ Ⓓ   17. Ⓐ Ⓑ Ⓒ Ⓓ   27. Ⓐ Ⓑ Ⓒ Ⓓ   37. Ⓐ Ⓑ Ⓒ Ⓓ
8. Ⓕ Ⓖ Ⓗ Ⓙ   18. Ⓕ Ⓖ Ⓗ Ⓙ   28. Ⓕ Ⓖ Ⓗ Ⓙ   38. Ⓕ Ⓖ Ⓗ Ⓙ
9. Ⓐ Ⓑ Ⓒ Ⓓ   19. Ⓐ Ⓑ Ⓒ Ⓓ   29. Ⓐ Ⓑ Ⓒ Ⓓ   39. Ⓐ Ⓑ Ⓒ Ⓓ
10. Ⓕ Ⓖ Ⓗ Ⓙ   20. Ⓕ Ⓖ Ⓗ Ⓙ   30. Ⓕ Ⓖ Ⓗ Ⓙ   40. Ⓕ Ⓖ Ⓗ Ⓙ

TEST 7   MATHEMATICS

1. Ⓐ Ⓑ Ⓒ Ⓓ   11. Ⓐ Ⓑ Ⓒ Ⓓ   21. Ⓐ Ⓑ Ⓒ Ⓓ   31. Ⓐ Ⓑ Ⓒ Ⓓ
2. Ⓕ Ⓖ Ⓗ Ⓙ   12. Ⓕ Ⓖ Ⓗ Ⓙ   22. Ⓕ Ⓖ Ⓗ Ⓙ   32. Ⓕ Ⓖ Ⓗ Ⓙ
3. Ⓐ Ⓑ Ⓒ Ⓓ   13. Ⓐ Ⓑ Ⓒ Ⓓ   23. Ⓐ Ⓑ Ⓒ Ⓓ   33. Ⓐ Ⓑ Ⓒ Ⓓ
4. Ⓕ Ⓖ Ⓗ Ⓙ   14. Ⓕ Ⓖ Ⓗ Ⓙ   24. Ⓕ Ⓖ Ⓗ Ⓙ   34. Ⓕ Ⓖ Ⓗ Ⓙ
5. Ⓐ Ⓑ Ⓒ Ⓓ   15. Ⓐ Ⓑ Ⓒ Ⓓ   25. Ⓐ Ⓑ Ⓒ Ⓓ   35. Ⓐ Ⓑ Ⓒ Ⓓ
6. Ⓕ Ⓖ Ⓗ Ⓙ   16. Ⓕ Ⓖ Ⓗ Ⓙ   26. Ⓕ Ⓖ Ⓗ Ⓙ   36. Ⓕ Ⓖ Ⓗ Ⓙ
7. Ⓐ Ⓑ Ⓒ Ⓓ   17. Ⓐ Ⓑ Ⓒ Ⓓ   27. Ⓐ Ⓑ Ⓒ Ⓓ   37. Ⓐ Ⓑ Ⓒ Ⓓ
8. Ⓕ Ⓖ Ⓗ Ⓙ   18. Ⓕ Ⓖ Ⓗ Ⓙ   28. Ⓕ Ⓖ Ⓗ Ⓙ   38. Ⓕ Ⓖ Ⓗ Ⓙ
9. Ⓐ Ⓑ Ⓒ Ⓓ   19. Ⓐ Ⓑ Ⓒ Ⓓ   29. Ⓐ Ⓑ Ⓒ Ⓓ   39. Ⓐ Ⓑ Ⓒ Ⓓ
10. Ⓕ Ⓖ Ⓗ Ⓙ   20. Ⓕ Ⓖ Ⓗ Ⓙ   30. Ⓕ Ⓖ Ⓗ Ⓙ   40. Ⓕ Ⓖ Ⓗ Ⓙ

Practice COOP Exam One

#1–20   *15 minutes*

> DIRECTIONS: Choose the letter than will continue the pattern or sequence.

1.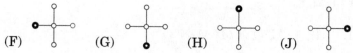

    (A)   (B)   (C)   (D)

2.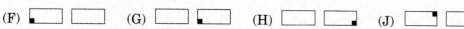

    (F)   (G)   (H)   (J)

3.

    (A)    (B)   (C)    (D)

4.

    (F)   (G)   (H)   (J)

5.

    (A)   (B)   (C)   (D)

6.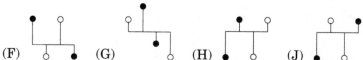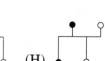

    (F)   (G)   (H)   (J)

7.  _____

8. W V U | S R Q | O N M | _ _ _

(F) J K L   (G) K J I   (H) G F E   (J) G L I

9. *a c f* | *g i l* | *m o r* | *s _ x*

(A) *t*   (B) *u*   (C) *v*   (D) *w*

10. B M D | C M E | J M L | _ _ _

(F) L M N   (G) J K L   (H) L M O   (J) M N O

11. A B D | B D H | C F L | D H _

(A) L   (B) J   (C) P   (D) R

12. $A_4B_5C_6$ | $D_6E_7F_8$ | $G_8H_9I_{10}$ | _____ | $M_{12}N_{13}O_{14}$

(F) $J_{10}K_{11}L_{12}$ (G) $I_9J_{10}K_{11}$ (H) $K_{10}L_{11}M_{12}$ (J) $J_9K_{10}L_{11}$

13. Z Y X | V U T | R Q P | _____ | J I H

(A) G F E   (B) N M L   (C) M N L   (D) H G F

14. $A_1B_2D_3$ | $F_4G_5I_6$ | $K_7L_8N_9$ | $P_{10}Q_{11}$ —

(F) S_{12} (G) R_{11} (H) T_{11} (J) S_{11}

15. 15 17 20 | 43 45 48 | 9 11 _

(A) 13   (B) 14   (C) 17   (D) 29

16. XXIV | XXIX | XXXIV | _____ | XLIV

(F) XXXVII   (G) XLIV   (H) KXXXIV   (J) XXXIX

17. 4 7 6 | 8 11 10 | 15 18 17 | 17 __ 19

   (A) 17   (B) 18   (C) 15   (D) 20

18. 1 1 1 | 2 4 8 | 3 9 27 | 4 16 __

   (F) 125   (G) 50   (H) 100   (J) 75

19. 6 3 1.5 | 8 4 2 | __ 2.5 1.25

   (A) 7   (B) 9   (C) 6   (D) 5

20. 21 25 30 | 17 21 26 | 19 __ 28

   (F) 22   (G) 21   (H) 23   (J) 27

STOP

IF YOU FINISH BEFORE TIME IS UP, CHECK OVER YOUR WORK ON THIS TEST ONLY. DO NOT GO ON TO THE NEXT TEST UNTIL THE SIGNAL IS GIVEN.

TEST 2   ANALOGIES

> DIRECTIONS: Select the picture that will fill the empty box so that the two lower pictures are related to each other in the same manner as the two upper pictures.

1.

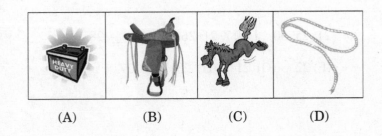

(A)   (B)   (C)   (D)

2.

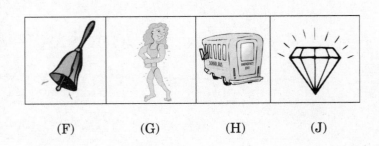

(F)   (G)   (H)   (J)

3.

(A)   (B)   (C)   (D)

4.

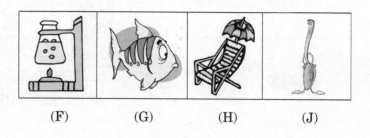

(F) (G) (H) (J)

5.

(A) (B) (C) (D)

6.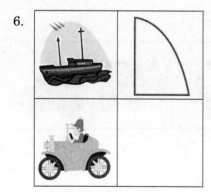

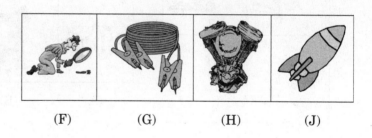

(F) (G) (H) (J)

7.

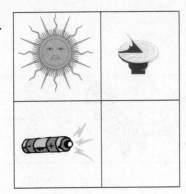

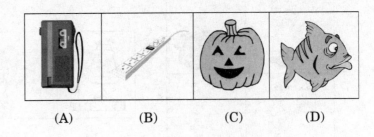

(A)   (B)   (C)   (D)

8.

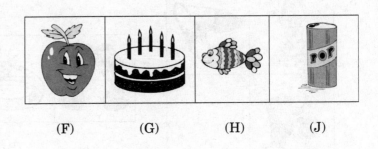

(F)   (G)   (H)   (J)

9.

(A)   (B)   (C)   (D)

10.

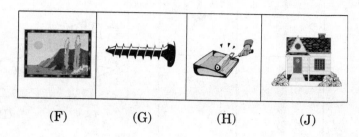

(F)   (G)   (H)   (J)

11.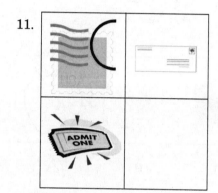

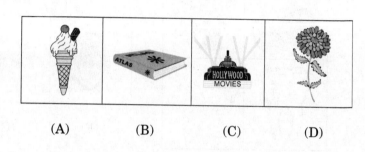

(A)   (B)   (C)   (D)

12.

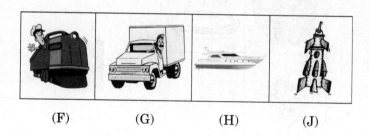

(F)   (G)   (H)   (J)

13.

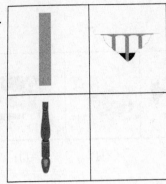

(A)   (B)   (C)   (D)

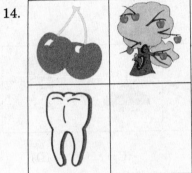

14.

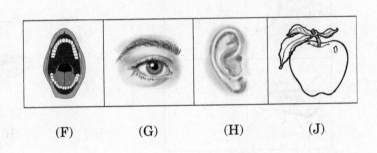

(F)   (G)   (H)   (J)

15.

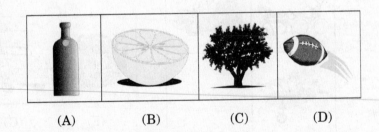

(A)   (B)   (C)   (D)

16.

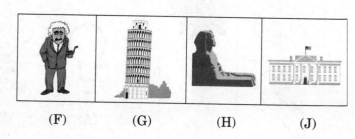

(F)   (G)   (H)   (J)

17.

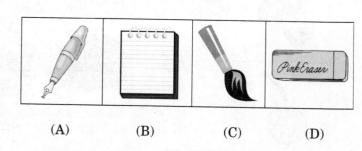

(A)   (B)   (C)   (D)

18.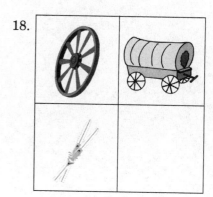

(F)   (G)   (H)   (J)

19.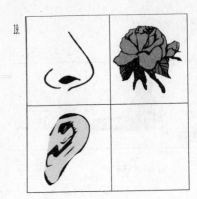

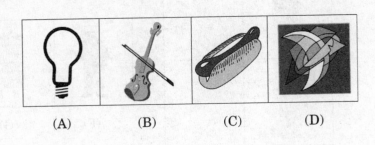

(A)   (B)   (C)   (D)

20.

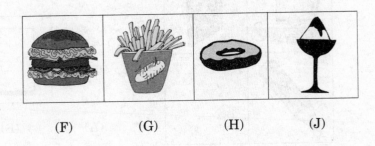

(F)   (G)   (H)   (J)

STOP

IF YOU FINISH BEFORE TIME IS UP, CHECK OVER YOUR WORK ON THIS TEST ONLY. DO NOT
GO ON TO THE NEXT TEST UNTIL THE SIGNAL IS GIVEN.

TEST 3   QUANTITATIVE REASONING

#1–20

5 minutes

DIRECTIONS: For questions 1–7, find the mathematical operation that is applied to the first number in each set so as to arrive at the second number. Then apply that operation to find the missing number. Select the correct answer.

---

1. 2 → ___ → 4
    6 → ___ → 12
    5 → ___ → ?
    (A) 12
    (B) 9
    (C) 10
    (D) 18

2. 10 → ___ → 2
    15 → ___ → 3
    20 → ___ → ?
    (F) 5
    (G) 10
    (H) 4
    (J) 6

3. 6 → ___ → 2
    8 → ___ → 4
    5 → ___ → ?
    (A) 6
    (B) 4
    (C) 2
    (D) 1

4. 2/5 → ___ → 2
    3 → ___ → 15
    3/5 → ___ → ?
    (F) 5
    (G) 4
    (H) 2
    (J) 3

5. 7 → ___ → 2
    9 → ___ → 4
    4 → ___ → ?
    (A) −1
    (B) 0
    (C) 3
    (D) 1

6. 3/4 → ___ → 1/4
    1 → ___ → 1/2
    3/2 → ___ → ?
    (F) 1/2
    (G) 1
    (H) 3/4
    (J) 1/4

7. 24 → ___ → 6
    16 → ___ → 4
    6 → ___ → ?
    (A) 2
    (B) 2.5
    (C) 1.5
    (D) 3

DIRECTIONS: For questions 8–14, express the part of the grid that is dark.

8.  (F) 3/9 (G) 4/8 (H) 3/10 (J) 3/8

9. (A) 1/3 (B) 3/10 (C) 3/12 (D) 4/9

10. (F) 4/9 (G) 3/10 (H) 4/11 (J) 2/5

11. (A) 4/12 (B) 2/5 (C) 1/6 (D) 1/3

12. (F) 1/5 (G) 3/7 (H) 2/9 (J) 4/9

13. (A) 3/8 (B) 3/4 (C) 5/8 (D) 1/2

14.   (F) 3/10 (G) 1/3 (H) 5/9 (J) 4/9

DIRECTIONS: For questions 15–20, check the balanced scale at the left and see which weights are balanced. From the results, determine which weights are balanced on the right.

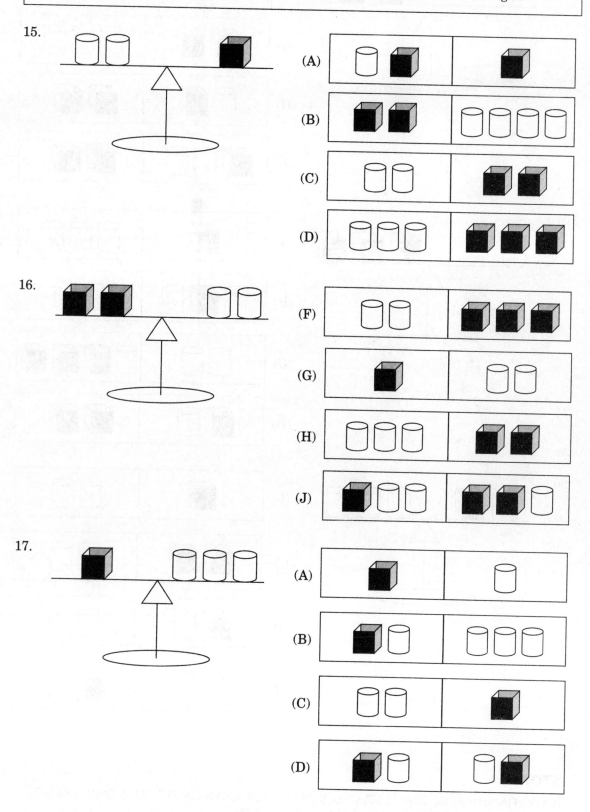

18.

19.

20.

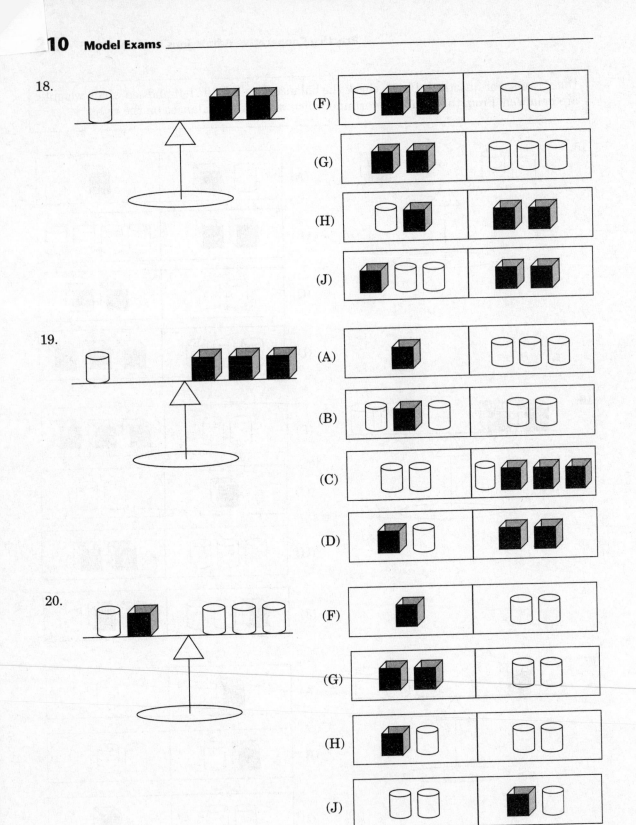

STOP
IF YOU FINISH BEFORE TIME IS UP, CHECK OVER YOUR WORK ON THIS TEST ONLY. DO NOT
GO ON TO THE NEXT TEST UNTIL THE SIGNAL IS GIVEN.

TEST 4   VERBAL REASONING—WORDS

#1–20   *15 minutes*

DIRECTIONS: For questions 1–5, find the word that names a necessary part of the underlined word.

1. <u>painting</u>

   (A) brush
   (B) color
   (C) paint
   (D) canvas

2. <u>university</u>

   (F) dormitory
   (G) students
   (H) organizations
   (J) tower

3. <u>tuxedo</u>

   (A) jacket
   (B) dance
   (C) corsage
   (D) black

4. <u>imagination</u>

   (F) thought
   (G) books
   (H) pictures
   (J) stories

5. <u>music</u>

   (A) notation
   (B) strings
   (C) song
   (D) sound

DIRECTIONS: For questions 6–10, choose the word that is most like the underlined words.

6. <u>telephone</u>   <u>radio</u>   <u>megaphone</u>

   (F) telegraph
   (G) microphone
   (H) fax
   (J) e-mail

7. <u>physics</u>   <u>chemistry</u>   <u>biology</u>

   (A) botany
   (B) plants
   (C) theory
   (D) science

8. <u>photograph</u>   <u>painting</u>   <u>movie</u>

   (F) portrait
   (G) novel
   (H) song
   (J) radio

9. <u>cream</u>   <u>milk</u>   <u>cheese</u>

   (A) lemonade
   (B) butter
   (C) cow
   (D) skim

10. <u>address</u>   <u>recite</u>   <u>lecture</u>

   (F) debate
   (G) narrate
   (H) display
   (J) perform

DIRECTIONS: For questions 11–15, choose the word that does *not* belong.

11.

(A) foe
(B) rival
(C) enemy
(D) spy

12.

(F) pigeon
(G) bird
(H) cardinal
(J) dove

13.

(A) break
(B) fraction
(C) piece
(D) section

14.

(F) discard
(G) reject
(H) acquire
(J) eliminate

15.

(A) employ
(B) job
(C) use
(D) hire

DIRECTIONS: In questions 16–20, the words in the top row are related. The words in the bottom row are related in a similar way. Choose the word that completes the sequence in the bottom row.

16.

Grizzly	Polar	Black
Orange	Lemon	

(F) panda
(G) grapefruit
(H) banana
(J) apple

17.

Baseball	Bowling ball	Basketball
Bicycle	Truck	

(A) tricycle
(B) bus
(C) car
(D) taxi cab

18.

Rooster	Hen	Chick
_____	Goose	Gosling

(F) drake
(G) gander
(H) swan
(J) gooster

19.

Teenager	Toddler	Infant
Delta	Beta	_____

(A) alpha
(B) epsilon
(C) pi
(D) omega

20.

Zebra	Tiger	Skunk
Cheetah	Leopard	_____

(F) Dalmatian
(G) referee
(H) toucan
(J) clown fish

STOP

IF YOU FINISH BEFORE TIME IS UP, CHECK OVER YOUR WORK ON THIS TEST ONLY. DO NOT GO ON TO THE NEXT TEST UNTIL THE SIGNAL IS GIVEN.

TEST 5 VERBAL REASONING—CONTEXT

> DIRECTIONS: For these questions, find the statement that is true according to the given information.

1. Mrs. Julian listens to country music on her car radio. When Mr. Julian borrowed her car, he switched the radio to a classical station. Mrs. Julian switched it back to country the next day.

   (A) Mr. Julian's car needed repairs.
   (B) Mr. and Mrs. Julian have different tastes in music.
   (C) Mr. Julian is in trouble.
   (D) Mrs. Julian dislikes having her radio station changed.

2. Mel enjoys watching cartoons in the morning. *The Roadrunner Show* comes on at 7:00. Mel slept until 8:00.

   (F) *The Roadrunner Show* does not run on Saturday.
   (G) Mel did not feel well that morning.
   (H) Mel did not watch *The Roadrunner Show*.
   (J) Mel does not like *The Roadrunner Show*.

3. Tina is writing a book. She is trying to find someone to illustrate it. She has not found an appropriate illustrator yet.

   (A) Tina is a published author.
   (B) Tina is writing a children's book.
   (C) Tina does not consider herself an appropriate illustrator.
   (D) Tina's book does not require illustrations.

4. Anna takes French, Jeanna takes Spanish, and Nora takes Latin. Their father is a mathematician. Their mother and brother are musicians.

   (F) Anna, Jeanna, and Nora do not like math or music.
   (G) Their father is a math teacher.
   (H) Anna, Nora, and Jeanna are sisters.
   (J) Their brother is a singer.

5. Mrs. Greene bakes birthday cakes for our staff. Charlie gets his cake from her every September. His favorite is chocolate.

   (A) Mrs. Greene baked a chocolate cake for Charlie.
   (B) Charlie's birthday is in September.
   (C) Mrs. Greene is a professional baker.
   (D) Only one member of our staff got a cake in September.

6. Michael's favorite book is *Cheaper by the Dozen*. His teacher read it to his class in seventh grade. He did not enjoy the new movie version.

   (F) The movie version of the book had a sad ending.
   (G) The movie and the book are different.
   (H) Michael no longer likes the story.
   (J) Michael always thinks the book versions are superior.

7. Mrs. Donne is having a baby. If it's a girl, she's going to name her Emily Elizabeth. If it's a boy, she wants to name him John.

    (A) Mrs. Donne is having twins.
    (B) Mrs. Donne does not know whether she is having a girl or a boy.
    (C) Mrs. Donne prefers to be surprised when her baby is born.
    (D) Mrs. Donne is always prepared.

8. All Alphas wear gray clothing all the time. All Deltas wear khaki exclusively. Lenina makes a point to wear green.

    (F) Lenina is not an Alpha or a Delta.
    (G) Lenina is rebellious.
    (H) Lenina looks best in green.
    (J) Lenina is a Beta.

9. Barbara and Ernest go for a walk every day at 6:00. We often see them when we walk our dog. Our dog loves to visit Barbara.

    (A) Barbara babysits our dog.
    (B) Ernest enjoys exercise.
    (C) We often walk around 6:00.
    (D) We all walk after dinner.

10. Amanda is scheduled to volunteer one day a week at a daycare center. On Wednesday, she and the toddlers played with clay. The week before, she helped the children paint.

    (F) Amanda is an artist.
    (G) Amanda's volunteer day is Wednesday.
    (H) Amanda has several jobs.
    (J) Amanda loves clay and paint.

STOP

IF YOU FINISH BEFORE TIME IS UP, CHECK OVER YOUR WORK ON THIS TEST ONLY. DO NOT GO ON TO THE NEXT TEST UNTIL THE SIGNAL IS GIVEN.

TEST 6   READING AND LANGUAGE ARTS

> DIRECTIONS: For questions 1–40, read each passage and the questions following that passage. Find the answer.

PASSAGE FOR QUESTIONS 1–6

In 2002, Americans spent a whopping $6.6 billion on kitchen renovations. They also spent a total of $433 million on cookbooks that specialized in making dishes out of specialized items like berries, cherries, and lemons. Increasingly people <u>patronized</u> food stores that offered gourmet items such as cilantro, jicama, chorizo, fresh ginger, and dried chilis. TV networks catered to the new culinary fad by adding cable stations that offered lessons on how to prepare filet mignon and other fancy dishes 24/7.

Yet, despite their purchases and alleged interest in home cooking, America is becoming a "take-out nation." Americans are more likely to read their cookbooks at bedtime than use them to prepare meals. People gaze fondly at the carefully arranged rows of jicama and ginger on their way to the deli counter where they purchase store-brand meals—like fried chicken and mashed potatoes or rotisserie chicken with potato salad. Or, they hop over to a restaurant, or even a fast food joint, and skip the supermarket altogether.

People vigorously defend their paradoxical actions. Some people claim they want to try adventurous foods—like sushi—that they don't trust themselves to prepare at home. Others point to differing gustatory tastes of their family members: mom and dad like it spicy, but the kids like it bland; takeout easily accommodates all diners. Those who are single argue that cooking for themselves is simply not cost-effective. Some simply say despairingly that they don't have the time to do their own cooking. Still others grow defiant; they point out that they can afford to have others prepare food for them.

For whatever reasons, now more than ever, Americans seem to desire the luxury of the home-cooked meal—but not so greatly that they will set aside time to prepare it.

1. Which of the following would publish the above article?

   (A) the newest edition of Betty Crocker's Cookbook
   (B) the Leisure and Popular Culture section of weekly news magazines like *Newsweek*
   (C) *Popular Science Magazine*
   (D) the *TV Guide*

2. The author of this piece intends _____.

   (F) to make fun of Americans
   (G) to praise Americans
   (H) to reform Americans
   (J) to point out an ironic paradox about Americans

3. What is the best definition of the word <u>patronized</u>, based on the use of the word in the reading passage?

   (A) to look down upon the person with whom you are speaking
   (B) to support a cause, usually with monetary donations
   (C) to use the services of, usually in connection with acquiring supplies
   (D) It is impossible to answer this question based on the information in the passage.

4. What does the author say is ironic about America's recent food purchases?

   (F) Americans, by and large, support super-sized fast food meals despite the threat to their waistline.

   (G) Americans like to try different foods—like sushi—but are worried about preparing them at home.

   (H) Americans have bought supplies that would allow them to prepare nutritious, gourmet meals at home, yet they continue to buy fast food and prepackaged items.

   (J) Americans keep buying items like jicama without knowing what these items are.

5. Which of the following sentences is written correctly?

   (A) Many American's get their recipes from the backs of boxes.

   (B) One of my favorite recipes are the apple pie made without apples.

   (C) Whom has ever tried this recipe?

   (D) Someday when I have time, I will make this pie.

Read the following baking directions and answer the question that follows.

A   Bake in a 350-degree oven for 50 minutes.

B   Boil the water and sugar until it forms a syrup.

C   Add this to the crust and crackers, along with butter, cinnamon, and your favorite spices.

D   Break the crackers into the pie crust.

6. What is the best order for these directions?

   (F) A, B, C, D

   (G) D, B, C, A

   (H) B, A, D, C

   (J) B, C, A, D

PASSAGE FOR QUESTIONS 7–13

As early as 1786, people set off in search of the great and <u>lucrative</u> Northwest Passage. This fabled water route allegedly connected the Atlantic and Pacific Oceans, and people hoped that such a passage would open up valuable trade markets. A Northwest Passage, after all, would make travel from East to West much easier, safer, and more affordable. Explorers like Christopher Columbus, Ferdinand Magellan, and Ponce de Leon all spent their lives searching fruitlessly for the Northwest Passage, although they did find substitute good stuff along the way—like the rich land west of the Mississippi prime for America settlement. Eventually, people gave up on ever finding a Northwest Passage.

Finally, when people least expected it, Norwegian Roald Mundsen discovered a Northwest Passage. He found it less than a century ago, at about the same time the U.S. government was making plans to dig the Panama Canal. Unfortunately, what Mundsen found was not an answer to travelers'—and merchants'—prayers. The Passage, nestled between Canada's mainland and some of its Arctic islands, still remained inconvenient, and ice often blocked the way. Easy travel remained nearly impossible. Once and for all, therefore, people at last abandoned the idea of using a Northwest Passage. Instead, they chose to create the initially costly, but ultimately practical, water route now known as the Panama Canal.

7. Which of the following sentences is written correctly?

   (A) Marco Polo brought spices from China to europe in the 13th century, starting a great demand for more.
   (B) Spices were not simply ingredients for food, they were used for medicine, perfume, and even currency.
   (C) Finding a quick water route to China, Japan, and India.
   (D) Christopher Columbus found great inspiration in the writings of Marco Polo.

8. According to the author, which of the following people actually discovered the Northwest Passage?

   (F) Christopher Columbus
   (G) Ferdinand Magellan
   (H) Ponce de Leon
   (J) Roald Mundsen

9. The author's main purpose in writing is to _____.

   (A) belittle the contributions of men like Columbus, Magellan, and de Leon
   (B) illustrate how dangerous and inconvenient travel routes once were
   (C) explain where the designer label for Northwest Passage clothing came from
   (D) point out that when we finally found the great Northwest Passage, we no longer wanted it

10. We can infer, based on the passage above, that the author thinks that _____.

    (F) had people never discovered the Northwest Passage, it would not have greatly affected human activity
    (G) because we finally discovered the Northwest Passage, we at last became able to realize our highest trade-based hopes
    (H) using the Panama Canal turned out to be one of the worst decisions ever made by Americans
    (J) we wasted a great deal of time exploring the Americas for the Northwest Passage

11. The author's use of the word <u>lucrative</u> is best described as _____.

    (A) filthy
    (B) creepy
    (C) wealthy
    (D) slow

12. Which sentence is written correctly?

    (F) Many explorers spent their lives searching fruitlessly for the Northwest Passage.
    (G) Many explorers spent they're lives searching fruitlessly for the Northwest Passage.
    (H) Many explorers spend his or her lives searching fruitlessly for the Northwest Passage.
    (J) Many explorers spend their lives searching fruitless for the Northwest Passage.

13. What is the best way to combine the following two sentences?

The bluish glow of electricity that appears on ships during storms is called Saint Elmo's Fire. Saint Elmo is the patron saint of sailors.

(A) Named for the patron saint of sailors, Saint Elmo's Fire is the bluish glow of electricity that appears on ships during storms.
(B) The bluish glow that appears on ships during storms is called Saint Elmo's Fire, moreover Saint Elmo is the patron saint of sailors.
(C) The patron saint of sailors, St. Elmo, has a fire on ships during storms that is actually an electric bluish glow.
(D) The electric bluish glow on ships during storms is called Saint Elmo's Fire, the patron saint of sailors.

DIRECTIONS: Read the following paragraph and answer the questions that follow.

_____. A good example of a palindrome is the following slogan: A man, a plan, a canal—Panama! The very first palindrome is purported to have been uttered by the first man to the first woman: "Madam, I'm Adam."

14. What is the best topic sentence for the above paragraph?

(F) Palindromes!
(G) What is a palindrome?
(H) Sentences that read the same backwards and forward are called palindromes.
(J) Many people are searching for an example of a palindrome.

15. What is the best way to write the following sentence?

(A) The first palindrome is purported to be uttered by the first man to the first woman.
(B) The first palindrome was purported to had been uttered by the first man to the first woman.
(C) The first palindrome is purportedly uttered by the first man to the first woman.
(D) The first palindrome is purported to have been uttered by the first man to the first woman.

16. Which of the following sentences is written correctly?

(F) We do not have the original journal of Christopher Columbus; what we do have is a summary made from a copy.
(G) Its filled with errors and inconsistencies; some people think Columbus wrote it in code to hide his discoveries.
(H) No one seems to consider that the journal could of been a forgery.
(J) Regardless, it seems that Columbus was neither saint or villain.

PASSAGE FOR QUESTIONS 17–21

Current writers of American history seem determined to prove that our Founding Fathers were not as nice as we always thought they were. College freshmen are soon told, for example, that the Pilgrims did more than fight for the right to worship God their way—they also committed fraud and kidnapping to ensure that right. Students convinced of the noble, hard-working nature of early American settlers soon discover that many such colonists came from the <u>dregs</u> of British society (some from prisons, others from brothels), that many came to America merely to find gold, and that some ruthlessly <u>desecrated</u> Native American graves (which often held food offerings) when supplies ran short.

But even young children are getting the harsh news these days. Booksellers report a spike in purchases of children's history books—the type that tell the nitty gritty details. Children as young as 10 and 11 now have access to tales that relate interesting details like the fact that William Howard Taft was so fat that he needed a specially built oversized bathtub or that George Washington was toothless and required ivory dentures. These kids also can easily find out that many American presidents owned slaves (George Washington attempted to avoid the dentures by transplanting nine teeth—extracted from his slaves' mouths—first) and had affairs (like Thomas Jefferson, who somehow produced six kids after the death of his wife).

Some parents support the idea of raising children on fact rather than fantasy. But perhaps the real on-going debate should center around not whether people should know the truth about popular cultural figures—but when they should be told and by whom.

17. Which opinion do you think the author holds?

(A) Children need to be sheltered from the truth, even when the truth needs to be told.
(B) Children need to be told the truth, at as early an age as possible.
(C) Children need to be told the truth, but careful attention should be paid to determining when to tell them.
(D) Children can never accept the truth, given their inability to understand deep topics.

18. Based on the context of this passage, to which of the following words is the word <u>dregs</u> similar?

(F) upper class
(G) middle class
(H) lower class
(J) criminal class

19. According to the passage, which person removed teeth from slaves in an attempt to make dentures?

(A) Taft
(B) Washington
(C) Jefferson
(D) Bush

20. The author most likely intends _____.

(F) to challenge children to find out as much as they can about the "dirty" side of history
(G) to challenge parents to reevaluate their child-rearing habits
(H) to convince people to cover up uncomfortable details about our past
(J) to revise current definitions of historical accuracy in research

21. Based on the use of the word in this passage, how would one best define the word <u>desecrated</u>?

(A) ransacked
(B) opened
(C) plowed
(D) moved

PASSAGE FOR QUESTIONS 22–26

Doctors have frequently enjoyed a reputation of being miracle workers—and no wonder. Their very lives are miraculous, when you consider the hours they work. Residency interns, for example, have historically shouldered a workload averaging 90 hours (or more) per week, a burdensome total by most people's standard. Johns Hopkins Hospital set these expectations back in 1899, although they were not seen as particularly abusive. Back then, after all, the term *residency* meant what it implied—that doctors in training actually lived on hospital premises. But, times have changed. Doctors no longer live at hospitals; they commute, often long distances.

Our exhausted doctors find themselves having to care for increasingly delicate patients. As recently as the 1960s, people visited the hospital and endured long periods of observation and treatment when stricken by illnesses we now consider "outpatient" cases. Newly delivered mothers, for example, stayed in the hospital for a week; now they stay a maximum of two days. Heart attack patients stayed for observation for three weeks; nowadays, they rarely stay three hours. Today, patients who stay in the hospital for long periods of time are far more ill than their counterparts back in the 1960s.

Administrators became concerned that sleep deprivation among the doctors coupled with the more precarious state of the patients themselves was resulting in more, often deadly, mistakes in hospital care. Therefore, the Accreditation Council for Graduate Medical Education has decided medical residents can only work an eighty-hour work-week with no one working more than thirty hours at a stretch. While these hours may still seem abusive, they represent a decided improvement over the past.

22. The word <u>residency</u>, as used in this passage, refers to the fact that _____.

    (F) doctors have always commuted to work
    (G) doctors in training traditionally lived at their place of study
    (H) doctors have always suffered from sleep deprivation
    (J) doctors need more medical reform to assist them in helping others

23. The main idea of this passage can best be described as _____.

    (A) sleep deprivation among medical staff has quadrupled since 1910
    (B) medical training dates back to the 1890s at Johns Hopkins Hospital
    (C) everyone is concerned that the safety of patients is in the hands of exhausted nursing staff
    (D) no one is totally satisfied with current medical regulations, but they are an improvement over the past

24. One can infer from the message of paragraph three that _____.

    (F) people recover faster from illness
    (G) people are forced to leave hospitals at a faster rate than at any other time in history
    (H) people are no longer forced to stay in hospitals longer than advances in treatment require
    (J) people no longer consider illnesses such as heart attacks deadly

25. According to the passage, the Accreditation Council for Graduate Medical Education requires a(n) ___ hour work-week with no one working more than ___ hours at a stretch.

    (A) 90 . . . 36
    (B) 36 . . . 90
    (C) 30 . . . 80
    (D) 80 . . . 30

26. How long, according to the passage, do doctors hold heart attack victims for observation?

    (F) 3 days
    (G) 3 hours
    (H) depends on the seriousness of the case
    (J) The article does not state.

PASSAGE FOR QUESTIONS 27–32

American parents have grown increasingly anxious to help their kids succeed in life. They provide classical music for the fetus *in utero*, buy specially constructed educational toys for preschool kids, and start working with flashcards as early as age five. Is all the fuss paying off?

Many child experts say no, that there appears to be "no advantage" to pushing kids to achieve ahead of schedule. Despite our best intentions, they say, we are in fact teaching them to be perfectionists focused on the future who lack the ability to enjoy the present.

For those who remain unconvinced, consider the (granted, extreme) case of John Stuart Mill, a child pushed by the age of three to learn to read and speak Latin and Greek and who wrote a compelling dissertation by the age of eight. He won himself a stint in a padded cell before he reached adulthood.

27. The author most likely meant to express which of the following statements?

    (A) We should push our kids to achieve great things—no matter what the cost.
    (B) Kids need time to learn, grow, and experience life, without being forced to follow a schedule.
    (C) While kids need discipline and education, they also need balance with paid, skilled activity.
    (D) There is no advantage to rush the development of children; indeed there are many severe disadvantages to doing so.

28. Why does the author use the example of John Stuart Mill in the last paragraph?

    (F) as an example of how pushing children too hard can create severe complications in the child
    (G) as an example of how pushing children to achieve can greatly enhance their life experiences
    (H) as an example of how not interfering with the natural course of child-rearing can benefit all involved
    (J) as an example of how waiting until the teen years to begin educating the child is a sensible plan of action

29. What does the phrase *in utero* mean?

    (A) It refers to an album by the group Nirvana.
    (B) It refers to the gestational growth required by the human birthing process spent in the human uterus.
    (C) It refers to the Latin phrase "for the sake of usefulness."
    (D) We cannot tell from the information given.

30. By what age did John Stuart Mill learn Greek?

    (F) 2
    (G) 3
    (H) 4
    (J) 5

31. Choose the sentence that is written correctly.

    (A) John Stuart Mill, and Jeremy Bentham devoted their life to social improvement.
    (B) Their philosophy centered on one goal; happiness for the greatest number of people.
    (C) Ironically, Mill found that he himself was not happy.
    (D) After a nervous breakdown, poetry brought him comfort.

32. Choose the best combination of the following sentences.

    John Stuart Mill wrote *The Subjection of Women*. In it, he argues passionately for equality for women in all aspects of life.

    (F) In John Stuart Mill's *The Subjection of Women*, he argues passionately for equality for women in all aspects of life.
    (G) John Stuart Mill, author of *The Subjection of Women*, argues passionately in his book for equality for women in all, not just some, aspects of life.
    (H) Equality for women (in all aspects of life) is argued passionately in John Stuart Mill's *The Subjection of Women*.
    (J) In John Stuart Mill's *The Subjection of Women*, he argues passionate that, in all aspects of life, equality is for women.

PASSAGE FOR QUESTIONS 33-37

Ask teens today what they think of kids' sports, and their answers might surprise you. Most of today's teens have been through kids' sports since they were in kindergarten. They've gone through the little leagues and the YMCA recreational leagues. Some of them were so talented they won positions in the more competitive teams, often called "travel clubs." By the time these players reach high school, one might expect them to see sports as a way of instilling good values, a way of staying in shape, or even a way of paying for college using skills <u>honed</u> over years of competitive sport.

Yet 70 percent of kids who play sports yearn to get out of sports altogether. They're tired of the competition, tired of the practice and game schedules, tired of the commitment required by participation. And, increasingly, they're tired of the parents.

Yes, parents.

These guys have seen it all. They've seen adults fight, in rare cases to the death, over umpire calls and referee rulings. They've endured parental threats and emotional blackmail regarding performance on the playing field. They've been told by their "protectors" that playing while hurt is appropriate because "this is a man's game." They've been manipulated by win-hungry coaches (usually parents themselves) who care more about winning than about instilling values like good sportsmanship. If you think these kids are exaggerating, consider these statistics: a survey of 500 adults conducted in 1999 concluded that 82 percent of respondents thought parents were too aggressive generally; 56 percent claimed to have witnessed aggressive adult behavior. 45 percent claimed that, as players, they had been verbally insulted; 22 percent said they had been pressured into playing injured; and 18 percent claimed they had been "hit, kicked, or slapped while participating."

Luckily kids have some adults advocating their position. People like Cal Ripken, Jr., former Baltimore Orioles shortstop, for example, have made it their mission to "fix" kids' sports. Ripken, aided by lay people like Fred Engh, has put together a program designed to remove what they see as "legalized child abuse" from competitive sports. The program requires mandatory participation in coach training, use of specially designed coaching manuals, and rigorously enforced rules of adult conduct.

Even though the success of programs like the ones advocated by Ripken and Engh remain to be seen, they at least have been able to make the point that kids no longer have to put up with abuse on the sportsfield. That in itself is a great victory.

33. The title that best expresses the ideas in this piece would be _____.

  (A) You're in the Big Leagues Now
  (B) There's No Crying in Baseball!
  (C) Why Johnny Hates Sports
  (D) Fixing Kids' Sports

34. Most likely, based on the reading passage, this author _____.

  (F) agrees with the point of view s/he is making in the article
  (G) disagrees with the point of view s/he is making in the article
  (H) remains completely neutral regarding the point of view s/he is making in the article
  (J) We cannot tell from the information given in the passage

35. According to the passage, what percentage of people surveyed claim to have been hit while participating in sports?

  (A) 28 percent
  (B) 22 percent
  (C) 18 percent
  (D) 45 percent

36. The word <u>honed</u> in the text can be best defined as _____.

  (F) a low murmuring, to the point of being inaudible
  (G) dulled, to the point of uselessness
  (H) refined, sharpened to the point of perfection
  (J) sweet, to the point of setting one's teeth on edge

37. According to the passage what percentage of kids want to drop out of sports?

  (A) 50 percent
  (B) 60 percent
  (C) 70 percent
  (D) 80 percent

PASSAGE FOR QUESTIONS 38–40

There's nothing new under the sun. Apparently Shakespeare was right. Again. Some scientists claim, for example, that the West Nile virus, so frightening to so many recently, is no new thing.

Almost 3,000 years ago, Alexander the Great died a feverish death; until now, scientists had put out various theories—that he had died from malaria, from typhoid, or from poisoning. But recent study of the West Nile virus has many scientists putting out the theory that he died from the West Nile virus.

The facts are rather persuasive. Alexander was living in an area <u>plagued</u> by mosquitoes, a common carrier of the West Nile virus. Apparently Alexander witnessed a large number of ravens and "some of them fell dead before him"; we know that the West Nile virus can be fatal to and carried by crows, a relation of ravens. Finally, Alexander the Great was said to have suffered fever and paralysis prior to his death, both symptoms of the West Nile virus.

38. In what sort of publication are you most likely to find this article?

(F) almanac
(G) *Guinness Book of World Records*
(H) the popular science section of your local newspaper
(J) a journal that publishes articles about Greek and Latin literature

39. The word <u>plagued</u>, based on its use here, is best defined as _____.

(A) lacking in
(B) inhabited
(C) overrun
(D) made free of

40. Of which of the following have people thought Alexander the Great died?

(F) malaria
(G) polio
(H) strangulation
(J) AIDS

STOP

IF YOU FINISH BEFORE TIME IS UP, CHECK OVER YOUR WORK ON THIS TEST ONLY. DO NOT GO ON TO THE NEXT TEST UNTIL THE SIGNAL IS GIVEN.

TEST 7   MATHEMATICS

#1–40   *35 minutes*

DIRECTIONS: Select the best answer from the given choices.

1. Find the value of $\dfrac{3^9}{4 \cdot 3^7}$.

    (A) 2.25   (B) 2.15
      (C) 3.25   (D) 3^2

2. Find the value of the expression
    $4xy + 5z^2$ when $x = 4$, $y = -3$, and
    $z = -2$.

    (F) –6   (G) 18
      (H) –18   (J) –28

3. Represent the area of a triangle with a
    base of $2x + y$ and a height of $4z$.

    (A) $2z(2x + y)$ (B) $2x(z + y)$
      (C) $2xyz$ (D) $z(2x + y)$

4. What is the product of the greatest
    common factor and the least common
    factor of 30 and 70?

    (F) 10   (G) 7
      (H) 15   (J) 28

5. Dwayne was on a diet. When he
    weighed himself at the start of his
    diet, Dwayne weighed 215 pounds.
    At the end of three months, Dwayne
    weighed 175 pounds. What fraction
    of his original weight did he lose?
    Reduce to lowest terms.

    (A) 8/43   (B) 9/36
      (C) 7/29   (D) 9/35

6. Find the value of x in the figure below.

    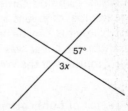

    (F) 57°   (G) 41°
      (H) 39°   (J) 3°

7. $6\dfrac{2}{3} \times 5\dfrac{1}{4} =$

    (A) $5\dfrac{1}{2}$ (B) 16

    (C) 23   (D) 35

8. The Kanakee Eagles scored 12, 7, 10,
    6, and 9 runs in their last 5 games.
    If they want to maintain an average
    of 9 runs per game for 6 games, how
    much do they have to score on their
    next game?

    (F) 4   (G) 10
      (H) 8   (J) 6

9. Which of the the following expressions
    is the **smallest**?

    (A) $4^2 + 5(9 - 3)$
    (B) $3 \cdot 17 - 4 \cdot 6$
    (C) $7 + 9 \cdot 4 - 6(9 - 7)^3$
    (D) $6 - 2 + 48/6$

10.

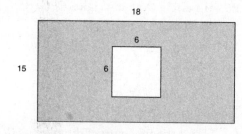

Find the shaded area.

(F) 234   (G) 123
    (H) 342   (J) 188

11. A ticket to the movies is $8 right now. If the price increases 7% this year and 5% the following year, how much will a movie ticket cost at the end of two years? Round off to the nearest cent.

(A) $10.18   (B) $10.82
    (C) $9.85   (D) $8.99

12. Two-fifths of what number subtracted from 18 is equal to 4 more than two-thirds of 6?

(F) 4   (G) 12
    (H) 25   (J) 32

13. Melissa drives from Central City to Marbury, a distance of 154 miles. If she leaves Central City at 8 A.M. and arrives in Marbury at 10:45 A.M., what is her average rate of speed?

(A) 56 mph   (B) 39 mph
    (C) 48 mph   (D) 62 mph

14. Find the missing number in the following expression: $6(? + 5) - 3 = 135$.

(F) 12   (G) 23
    (H) 18   (J) 15

15. Six times a certain number is 24.72. What is the result if we divide that original number by 4?

(A) 2.4   (B) 1.03
    (C) 2.35   (D) 1.8

16. The perimeter of a ranch is 23,760 feet. If Lois walks at the rate of 3 miles per hour, how long will it take for her to walk around the ranch?

(F) 2 hours   (G) 2.5 hours
    (H) 1 hour   (J) 1.5 hours

17. Hector is putting together a package that weighs 5 pounds 6 ounces. If he removes several items and reduces the weight of the package by 2 pounds 9 ounces, how much does the new package weigh?

(A) 3 pounds 4 ounces
(B) 2 pounds 13 ounces
(C) 3 pounds 8 ounces
(D) 4 pounds 7 ounces

18. Two centimeters are what part of a meter?

(F) 3%   (G) 2%
    (H) 1/500   (J) 1/25

19. Tanika receives a base salary of $300 per week plus an 8% commission on sales over $2,000 for the week. If she sold $3,500 for the week, what was her total salary?

(A) $460   (B) $560
    (C) $480   (D) $420

20. The average monthly prices for a gallon of regular gasoline are shown in the graph.

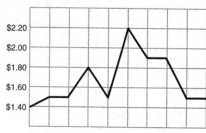

Find the average price of a gallon of gasoline for the months of April and August.

(F) $0.90   (G) $1.85
    (H) $1.20   (J) $1.35

21. Estimate the product of 34 and 68.

    (A) 2,600   (B) 2,300
      (C) 2,400   (D) 2,100

22. Compare the areas of the following figures.

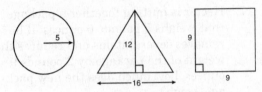

    (F) The area of the square is greater than the area of the triangle.
    (G) The area of the triangle is greater than the area of the circle.
    (H) The difference between the area of the triangle and the area of the circle is greater than the area of the square.
    (J) The area of the circle is less than the area of the triangle.

23. Simplify $82 + \dfrac{6}{10} + \dfrac{8}{100} + \dfrac{7}{1000}$.

    (A) 82.687   (B) 82.786
      (C) 82.147   (D) 8.2678

24. What is the distance from point A (5,4) to point B (5,−3)?

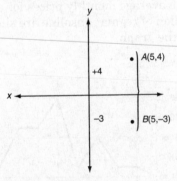

    (F) 2   (G) 4
      (H) 5   (J) 7

25. In circle O at the right, $CO = 3a$.

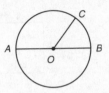

Find the measure of diameter AB.

    (A) 3a   (B) a
      (C) 6a   (D) 2a

26. The bar graph summarizes the numbers of cartoons, dramas, and comedies produced in the United States in the years 2001–2003. Use the information provided in the bar graph to determine which of the following statements is false.

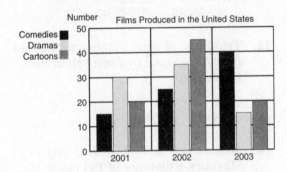

    (F) The number of cartoons in 2003 is fewer than the number of dramas in 2001.
    (G) The number of cartoons in 2001 is fewer than the number of dramas in 2002.
    (H) The number of dramas in 2003 is greater than the number of comedies in 2001.
    (J) The number of comedies in 2002 is greater than the number of cartoons in 2003.

27. Find the value of $5.3 \times 10^3 - 1.3 \times 10^2$.

    (A) 345 (B) 5,310
    (C) 5,170 (D) 540

28. What happens to the volume of a cube when each side is doubled?

    (F) multiplied by 8
    (G) doubled
    (H) tripled
    (J) quadrupled

29. Examine these three figures and choose the best answer.

    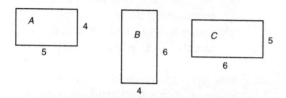

    (A) Area C is smaller than area A.
    (B) Area A is larger than area B.
    (C) Area B is smaller than area C.
    (D) Area C is smaller than area A.

30. Ruben, Shelly, and Malcolm have recorded a hit song. If Ruben gets 2/5 of the income and Shelly gets 1/3 and they earn $300,000, how much does Malcolm get?

    (F) $80,000 (G) $250,000
    (H) $210,000 (J) $90,000

31. Sides AB and BC in isosceles $\triangle ABC$ are equal in measure. If the exterior angle at C measures 96°, find the measure of angle B.

    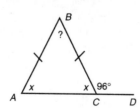

    (A) 18° (B) 24°
    (C) 12° (D) 16°

32. In the following diagrams, circle O has a radius of 5 and triangle RST has sides of 5 and 12 and a hypotenuse of 13. The circumference of a circle, C, is equal to $2\pi r$ and the area of a circle, A_C, is equal to πr^2. In both of these cases, $\pi = 3.14$ and r = the radius. The area of a triangle, A_T, is equal to $\frac{1}{2}bh$, where b = base and h = height.

    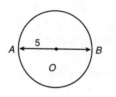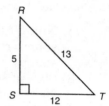

    Which of the following statements is true?

    (F) The area of triangle $RST < \frac{1}{2}$ area of circle O.
    (G) The circumference of the circle < the perimeter of triangle RST.
    (H) The area of the circle + the area of the triangle < 100.
    (J) The circumference of the circle – the perimeter of the triangle > 2.

33. If x and y are negative integers and $y > x$, which of the following statements is true?

    (A) $xy < 0$ (B) $x + y > 0$
    (C) $xy > 0$ (D) $y - x < 0$

34. What is the difference between the sum of the prime factors of 35 and 30?

    (F) 5 (G) 4
    (H) 2 (J) 3

35. Find $16\frac{2}{3}\%$ of 360.

    (A) 45 (B) 60
    (C) 40 (D) 35

36. The area of a circle inscribed in a square is approximately $\frac{3}{4}$ of the area of the square. Estimate the area of a circle inscribed in a square whose side is 6.2.

    (F) 29   (G) 27
       (H) 30   (J) 32

37. Which one of the following statements is true?

    (A) Nine $0.15 stamps plus six $0.37 stamps cost more than five $0.65 stamps.
    (B) Sixteen $0.15 stamps plus eight $0.37 stamps is less than seven $0.30 stamps plus nine $0.24 stamps.
    (C) Four $0.30 stamps plus five $0.37 stamps cost more than thirteen $0.15 stamps and eight $0.24 stamps.
    (D) Seven $0.24 stamps plus twelve $0.30 stamps cost $0.45 less than four $0.37 stamps

38. Find the total number of interior degrees in the angles of an octagon.

    (F) 540°   (G) 360°
       (H) 720°   (J) 1080°

39. From the Venn diagram below, what conclusion can we draw?

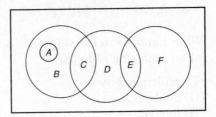

    (A) All members of set F are members of set E.
    (B) All members of set C are members of set E.
    (C) Some members of set D are members of set F.
    (D) Some members of set B are members of set E.

40. The circle graph indicates how the average high school student spends her/his 24-hour day. How many hours does the average student spend on personal items?

    (F) 4.2 hours   (G) 2.7 hours
    (H) 1.9 hours   (J) 3.6 hours

STOP

IF YOU FINISH BEFORE TIME IS UP, CHECK OVER YOUR WORK ON THIS TEST ONLY.

Answers to Practice Cooperative Admissions Examination 1

TEST 1 SEQUENCES

1. B	6. J	11. C	16. J
2. H	7. B	12. F	17. D
3. D	8. G	13. B	18. F
4. F	9. A	14. F	19. D
5. C	10. F	15. B	20. H

TEST 2 ANALOGIES

1. C	6. H	11. C	16. H
2. G	7. A	12. J	17. B
3. A	8. G	13. A	18. H
4. F	9. A	14. F	19. B
5. D	10. J	15. D	20. J

TEST 3 QUANTITATIVE REASONING

1. C	6. G	11. C	16. J
2. G	7. C	12. H	17. D
3. D	8. J	13. A	18. F
4. J	9. A	14. G	19. C
5. A	10. J	15. B	20. F

TEST 4 VERBAL REASONING—WORDS

1. C	6. G	11. D	16. G
2. G	7. A	12. G	17. B
3. A	8. F	13. A	18. G
4. F	9. B	14. H	19. A
5. D	10. G	15. B	20. F

TEST 5 VERBAL REASONING—CONTEXT

1. B	3. C	5. B	7. B	9. C
2. H	4. H	6. G	8. F	10. G

TEST 6   READING AND LANGUAGE ARTS

1. B	11. C	21. A	31. C
2. J	12. F	22. G	32. F
3. C	13. A	23. D	33. D
4. H	14. H	24. H	34. F
5. D	15. D	25. D	35. C
6. G	16. F	26. G	36. H
7. D	17. C	27. D	37. C
8. J	18. J	28. F	38. H
9. D	19. B	29. B	39. C
10. F	20. G	30. G	40. F

TEST 7   MATHEMATICS

1. A	11. D	21. D	31. C
2. J	12. H	22. J	32. F
3. A	13. A	23. A	33. C
4. F	14. C	24. J	34. H
5. A	15. G	25. C	35. B
6. G	16. J	26. H	36. G
7. D	17. B	27. C	37. A
8. G	18. G	28. J	38. J
9. C	19. D	29. C	39. C
10. F	20. G	30. F	40. J

Answer Explanations

TEST 1   SEQUENCES

1. **(B)** The objects move left, one at a time.
2. **(H)** The dark circle moves clockwise.
3. **(D)** The objects are arranged in size: small, large, small, large, small
4. **(F)** The small black rectangles move clockwise, only within the large left rectangle.
5. **(C)** The polygons are arranged in order of sides (three sides), quadrilateral (four sides), hexagon (six sides).
6. **(J)** The open and closed circles reverse after being flipped over the horizontal line.
7. **(B)** The dark triangle moves counterclockwise.
8. **(G)** The letters are listed in backwards alphabetical order, with one letter skipped between groups.
9. **(A)** The letters are listed in alphabetical order. One letter is skipped between the first and second letters of each group and two letters are skipped between the second and third letters in each group.
10. **(F)** M is the middle letter in each group and one letter is skipped between the first and third letter in each group.
11. **(C)** List the letters in alphabetical order and assign each letter a corresponding number:

a b c d e f g h i j k l m n
1 2 3 4 5 6 7 8 9 10 11 12 13 14

o p q r s t u v w x y z
15 16 17 18 19 20 21 22 23 24 25 26

Let's list the letters in the problem as well as their corresponding number.

A B D | B D H | C F L | D H _
1 2 4 | 2 4 8 | 3 6 12 | 4 8 _

From this numerical pattern, we can determine that each preceding number

is doubled, so that the last letter should be (2×8) the 16th letter in the alphabet, namely P.

12. **(F)** The letters are in alphabetical sequence. The subscripts are increasing and the last subscript in the earlier group is repeated in the following group.
13. **(B)** The letters are listed in backwards-alphabetical sequence, and one letter is skipped between each group.
14. **(F)** Skip one letter between groups and one letter between the second and third letters within each group. The subscripts are increasing by one.
15. **(B)** The numerical sequence is $+ 2, + 3$.
16. **(J)** Just add 5 to the preceding Roman numeral.
17. **(D)** The sequence is $+ 3, - 1$.
18. **(F)** The sequence is $1^1, 1^2, 1^3, 2^1, 2^2, 2^3, 3^1, 3^2, 3^3, 4^1, 4^2, 4^3 (= 64)$.
19. **(D)** To derive the second and third members of each group, divide the preceding number by 2.
20. **(H)** The sequence in each group is $+ 4, + 5$.

TEST 2   ANALOGIES

1. **(C)** Tire is to car as horseshoe is to horse. A car rides along tires, and a horse must be shod.
2. **(G)** Brick is to building as cell is to human. A building is constructed from bricks, and a human is made of cells.
3. **(A)** Announcer is to radio as actress is to the Broadway stage. The announcer is the chief character on the radio, and the actress is the heart of the Broadway stage.
4. **(F)** Chef is to soup as scientist is to chemical experiment. A chef makes soup, and a scientist develops an experiment.
5. **(D)** Dancer is to shoes as magician is to wand. A dancer needs a pair of shoes, and a magician needs a wand.

6. **(H)** Boat is to sail as car is to motor. A sail helps power a boat, and a motor helps power a car.

7. **(A)** Sun is to sundial as battery is to cassette recorder. The sundial and the recorder are dependent upon the sun and battery, respectively.

8. **(G)** Snowflake is to snowman as egg is to cake. A snowman is made of snowflakes, and one of the ingredients in a cake is eggs.

9. **(A)** Mouse is to cat as worm is to fish. Cats eat mice, and fish eat worms.

10. **(J)** Coat is to woman as paint is to house. A coat covers a woman, and paint covers a house.

11. **(C)** Stamp is to envelope as ticket is to movies. A stamp is the price of mailing an envelope, and a ticket is the price of admission to a movie.

12. **(J)** Horse and buggy is to car as piper cub airplane is to rocket. The horse and buggy preceded the car, and the piper cub airplane preceded the rocket.

13. **(A)** Support is to bridge as leg is to chair. A support upholds a bridge, and a leg supports a chair.

14. **(F)** Cherries are to trees as tooth is to mouth. Cherries are found on a tree, and teeth are found in a mouth.

15. **(D)** Apples are to pie as grapes are to wine (in bottle). A pie is made of apples, and wine is made of grapes.

16. **(H)** Napoleon is to the Eiffel Tower as Cleopatra is to the Sphinx. The Eiffel Tower represents France, and Napoleon was the emperor of that country. The Sphinx represents Egypt, and Cleopatra was the queen of that country.

17. **(B)** Computer is to disk as pencil is to a notebook. A computer writes on a disk, and a pencil writes on a notebook.

18. **(H)** Wheel is to wagon as skis are to skier. A wagon moves on wheels, and a skier moves on skis.

19. **(B)** Nose is to a rose as ear is to a violin. A nose can smell a rose, and an ear can hear a violin.

20. **(J)** Mushrooms are to pizza as a cherry is to ice cream. Mushrooms are toppings for pizza, and cherries are toppings for ice cream.

TEST 3   QUANTITATIVE REASONING

1. **(C)** Multiply each given number by 2: $5 \times 2 = 10$.

2. **(G)** Divide each given number by 5: $20/5 = 4$.

3. **(D)** Subtract 4 from each given number: $5 - 4 = 1$.

4. **(J)** Multiply each given number by 5: $(3/5) \times 5 = 3$.

5. **(A)** Subtract 5 from each given number: $4 - 5 = -1$.

6. **(G)** Subtract $\frac{1}{2}$ from each given number: $\left(\frac{3}{2}\right) - \left(\frac{1}{2}\right) = 1\frac{1}{2} - \frac{1}{2} = 1$.

7. **(C)** Divide each given number by 4: $\left(\frac{6}{4}\right) = 1\frac{1}{2} = 1.5$.

8. **(J)** Three out of eight squares are dark: 3/8.

9. **(A)** Three out of nine squares are dark: $3/9 = 1/3$.

10. **(J)** Four out of ten squares are dark: $4/10 = 2/5$.

11. **(C)** Four half squares are shaded: $4 \times (1/2) = 2$. That makes two out of twelve squares shaded: $2/12 = 1/6$.

12. **(H)** One square plus two half-squares are shaded: $1 + 2 \times (1/2) = 1 + 1 = 2$. That makes two out of nine squares shaded: 2/9.

13. **(A)** Six half-squares are shaded: $6 \times (1/2) = 3$. That makes three out of eight squares shaded: 3/8.

14. **(G)** Two squares plus two half-squares are shaded: $2 + 2 \times (1/2) = 2 + 1 = 3$. That makes three out of nine squares shaded: $3/9 = 1/3$.

15. **(B)** 1 cube = 2 cylinders. So, 2 cubes = 4 cylinders.

16. **(J)** 2 cubes = 2 cylinders. So, 1 cube = 1 cylinder. And 1 cube + 2 cylinders = 2 cubes + 1 cylinder.

17. **(D)** 1 cube = 3 cylinders. This information is irrelevant because 1 cube + 3 cylinders = 1 cube + 1 cylinder.

18. (**F**) 1 cylinder = 2 cubes. So, 1 cylinder + 2 cubes = 1 cylinder + 1 cylinder or 1 cylinder + 2 cubes = 2 cylinders.

19. (**C**) 1 cylinder = 3 cubes. So, 2 cylinders = 1 cylinder + 1 cylinder or 2 cylinders = 3 cubes + 1 cylinder.

20. (**F**)
$$
\begin{array}{rl}
1\text{ cylinder} + 1\text{ cube} = & 3\text{ cylinders} \\
- 1\text{ cylinder} \quad\quad\quad = & -1\text{ cylinder} \\
\hline
1\text{ cube} = & 2\text{ cylinders}
\end{array}
$$

TEST 4 VERBAL REASONING— WORDS

1. (**C**) Obviously, paint is necessary for a painting. You don't really need a brush or canvas, and the painting could be all black.

2. (**G**) A university could function without certain buildings and organizations. Students are necessary.

3. (**A**) Picture a tuxedo. Take away the dance, and it's still a tuxedo. Take away the corsage, take away the black, and it's still a tuxedo. Take away the jacket, and it's a pair of pants and a frilly shirt.

4. (**F**) Imagination requires only thought.

5. (**D**) Music does not have to be notated; it does not need strings or song. However, it does need sound.

6. (**G**) All of these require sound, too.

7. (**A**) These are all *specific* sciences.

8. (**F**) A photograph, a painting, a movie, and a portrait are all visual media.

9. (**B**) These are all dairy products.

10. (**G**) These are all verbs relating to speech. Moreover, they are speeches made by a single person, so it cannot be a debate. A performance does not necessarily involve speech.

11. (**D**) A spy is not necessarily an enemy.

12. (**G**) The other choices are specific types of birds.

13. (**A**) The other choices are synonyms for a portion.

14. (**H**) This is the only choice that concerns receiving something rather than throwing it away.

15. (**B**) The word *job* is related to some of the others, but it is a noun. The others are verbs meaning to use.

16. (**G**) Grizzly, polar, and black are types of bear. Orange, lemon, and grapefruit are types of citrus fruit.

17. (**B**) These increase in size.

18. (**G**) The relationship is male, female, and offspring. A male goose is a gander.

19. (**A**) The choices here are in reverse order. Teenager comes after toddler, which comes after infant. The second group is in reverse alphabetical order: delta, beta, alpha.

20. (**F**) Zebras, tigers, and skunks have stripes. Cheetahs, leopards, and Dalmatians have spots.

TEST 5 VERBAL REASONING— CONTEXT

1. (**B**) Mrs. Julian prefers country music, while Mr. Julian prefers classical. We are not told the reasons why Mr. Julian borrowed the car, nor are we told how well they get along otherwise.

2. (**H**) For whatever reason (and on whatever day), Mel did not watch this particular cartoon.

3. (**C**) We don't know if Tina has ever written a book before or what type she is writing now. We do know that she is not considering herself as an illustrator.

4. (**H**) With all the facts about their brother and parents, we know that the girls are sisters.

5. (**B**) Since Charlie got "his" cake in September, that must be his birthday month. We don't know the flavor he got or how many cakes Mrs. Greene baked that month.

6. (**G**) If Michael liked the book but not the movie, they must be different. We don't know how, though.

7. (**B**) Since Mrs. Donne has chosen both male and female names, she does not know if she is having a boy or a girl. We have no facts to back up the other choices. They would be guesses.

8. (**F**) Since we know that "all" Alphas and Deltas wear particular colors all of the time, we can say with certainty that Lenina is not a member of either group.

9. (**C**) We see one another on our walks, so we must all walk at the same time: around 6:00.

10. (**G**) We are told that Amanda volunteers one day a week at the center; we are told that she was there on a Wednesday. This choice simply puts those two facts together.

TEST 6   READING AND LANGUAGE ARTS

1. (**B**) The text discusses food, and so one might be tempted to say that a cookbook would be the logical place to find this article; however, the article also talks about people's buying habits, making it unlikely that a cookbook would print it. So rule out choice A. A science magazine also would not publish such an article (rule out choice C). Choice D might, under certain circumstances, publish such an article, but only on a rare occasion. Choice B is much more likely, for *Newsweek,* like most weekly news magazines, devotes a section of its page count to talking about popular trends. The best answer is choice B.

2. (**J**) The author does not obviously praise Americans for their decisions (since it is illogical—and possibly ridiculous—to buy things for which you have no use); rule out choice G. The author, similarly, does not make fun of Americans for their actions, since were s/he doing so, s/he could have been a lot more biting in her/his comments; rule out choice F. Neither is the author apparently trying to reform anyone, since the article is mostly phrased using neutral language. Your best answer is J; the author does point out a paradox—that Americans routinely spend their money on items they do not intend to use.

3. (**C**) Choice D is not useful to you; if a word is used in a sentence, then you have information at your disposal to

help you figure out its meaning. The remaining definitions all apply to the topic, but since the article does not talk about thinking ourselves better than others (choice A) or giving donations to a worthy cause (choice B), rule out choices that deal with these topics. That leaves choice C, and, indeed, the article does discuss buying the services of particular markets to get supplies.

4. (**H**) The author does not discuss whether people are concerned with obesity when they make food-purchasing decisions; rule out choice F. The author does mention that Americans like to try strange new foods but worry about making them themselves (choice G), but this is not the focal point of the piece. The article, moreover, makes it clear that Americans do not purchase strangely named foods often—they will consider doing so but usually do not follow through (paragraph two), so rule out choice J. The whole point of the article revolves around choice H.

5. (**D**) Choice D is written correctly, with no errors in tense. Choice A uses an apostrophe to form the plural of American. (Instead of *American's*, it should be *Americans*). Choice B should read **One** of my favorite recipes is the apple pie made without apples. Choice C uses the object form *whom* instead of the subject *who*.

6. (**G**) This is the only logical sequence. You know you will have to end with A (baking), so the other choices can be eliminated. If you go through the other sequences, you will see that they make no sense.

7. (**D**) The word Europe should be capitalized in choice A. Choice B contains a comma splice; the comma can be replaced with a semicolon. Choice C is a fragment.

8. (**J**) The article mentions all of the people listed as options, but only one is defined as the person who actually found the Northwest Passage.

9. (**D**) This question builds on the previous one; the author is bringing new information to light for most readers, the exception being historians who have

learned about Roald Mundsen in their studies. But the author shows no inclination to mock early explorers (choice A) or discuss the dangers of early travel (choice B) or explain how the term Northwest Passage became a popular clothing label. The best answer is D.

10. **(F)** The article states that people have accommodated the lack of a Northwest Passage for so long, in part by constructing the Panama Canal, so that by the time the Northwest Passage was discovered, we no longer required it. That implies that we no longer needed an alternate route. So, we can rule out choice G, since no one uses the Northwest Passage for anything lucrative; we can also rule out choice H, since we use the Panama Canal constantly. One might be tempted to select J, but the article does not dwell on negatives; the best choice is F.

11. **(C)** Lucrative is a word that comes from the Latin *lucre* which refers to money. Most people know this word, and they will select the word automatically. But, when in doubt, substitute. Choice C is the best.

12. **(F)** Choice G uses the contraction *they're* instead of the possessive *their*. Choice H uses incorrect pronoun-antecedent agreement. (Explorers spend *their* lives . . . .) Choice J uses the adjective *fruitless* instead of the adverb *fruitlessly* to describe how they search.

13. **(A)** This is the most accurate and concise combination. Choice B uses a comma splice; the word *moreover* is not a conjunction. Choice C is awkward and wordy, and choice D is inaccurate. (The patron saint's name is not St. Elmo's Fire.)

14. **(H)** This sentence contains essential information. The paragraph doesn't make sense without it.

15. **(D)** The sentence is accurate as it appears in the original essay. It uses the accurate tense (it *is purported to have been uttered*) rather than the construction in choice B (it *was purported to had been uttered*). Choices A and C make little sense in present tense.

16. **(F)** Choice G uses the possessive *Its* rather than the contraction *It's*. Choice H uses the incorrect usage *could of* instead of *could have*. Choice J uses the paired *neither/or* instead of *neither/nor*.

17. **(C)** The author's opinion really seems to come out in the final paragraph of this reading selection. Judging from that paragraph, one would reject choice D, since the author does seem to think that kids can handle tough issues early on. You can also reject choices A and B, since the author refuses to specify exactly when a child "ought" to be informed about life. Your best answer, therefore, is C; here the author makes her/his opinion clear—that kids can handle tough issues—but that the parent has the right—and the responsibility—to disseminate that truth at the appropriate time.

18. **(J)** You may have heard the word dregs used before—the dregs (or bottom leftovers) of a cup of coffee or tea. Generally speaking, dregs means bottom of the barrel. Judging from the list of options, criminal classes would be at the very bottom of most people's social scale.

19. **(B)** Re-reading (or memory) tells you that the author claims it was Washington who tried to use slaves' teeth as replacements for his own.

20. **(G)** You can reject option one, since this author seems in favor of the *responsible* passing down of information; therefore, this author would likely not favor random dirt-seeking by kids. You can also rule out choice H, since this statement stands diametrically opposed to the author's point of view on the matter. Option J really has no relevance at all. Your only real choice is G.

21. **(A)** You've probably heard the word *desecrated* before and have a good sense of the meaning; if not, break it down into syllables: *de*, meaning not, and *sacred*, meaning holy. So, if something has been desecrated, it is no longer holy. Now consider the list of choices and the question (which involves graves). All four could take place in the process of making a grave no longer holy. Rank

them in order of seriousness of offense—merely opening a grave seems less offensive than moving a grave; both seem less offensive than plowing under a grave. But probably the worst thing you could do is ransack a grave.

22. **(G)** You have heard the word residency before—every time you move you must establish residency wherever you end up. So residency has something to do with living arrangements. The only option that has anything to do with living arrangements is option G; sure enough, the passage defines the term for you, backing up your guess, in paragraph two.

23. **(D)** The main point of the passage appears in the final paragraph of the piece; the remaining paragraphs merely trace the logical steps the author takes toward this conclusion. Therefore, have a look at the final paragraph and make some connections with the list of options. Nothing in the passage supports choice A. Choice B is true, and even mentioned in the selection, but it is the starting point for the piece, not its ending point. Choice C is true but does not match with the statements of the final paragraph. Your correct answer, therefore, is D.

24. **(H)** Paragraph three talks about how doctors no longer keep heart attack victims in the hospital for long and gives a reason why that is the case: namely that we know more about heart attacks, and, in many cases, we don't require the three-day observation period any longer. Therefore, you can rule out choices F, G, and J, since they give faulty reasons why heart attack victims are released more quickly than they once were.

25. **(D)** Re-reading (or your memory) reveals that new medical legislation demands that doctors only work an 80-hour work-week with no one working more than 30 hours in a shift—an improvement, hard as it may be to realize.

26. **(G)** Again, re-reading (or your memory) reminds you that hospitals tend to keep heart attack patients around for observation for only three hours (or fewer).

27. **(D)** Breaking down the paragraphs to find their logical order helps here. In the first paragraph, you learn that some parents are trying to teach their kids at extremely young ages—even while still in the womb. Paragraph two states that child psychologists claim such tactics are a waste of time, that *in utero* education has no significant effect on developing kids. Finally, paragraph three holds up an example of a child pushed too far. The message is clear: pushing kids to develop according to some sort of predetermined, fast-paced agenda is wrong and ineffective anyway. So, the answer that best matches this stance is D. You might be momentarily attracted to option B, but the phrasing of the answer is too vague to be satisfactory. After all, referring to a schedule can mean many things, and sometimes schedules are good (even necessary) to follow. You are looking for a statement that links the two main points of the article; that would be D.

28. **(F)** The author, as discussed in the last answer explanation, uses Mill as an example of good intentions gone very bad. Choices G, H, and J simply do not address the issue. Your only real option is F.

29. **(B)** Rule out choice D; whenever a word is used, you can figure out the meaning through context—sometimes it's just harder to do so than at other times. The other three options all have some basis in truth, although clearly choice A is out of the question. Since we're talking about children and their development, it's better to choose the option dealing with the uterus rather than any other. The best answer is B.

30. **(G)** Re-reading (or your memory) tells you that Mill learned Greek by the age of three.

31. **(C)** Choice C correctly uses the intensifier *himself*. Choice A uses an unnecessary comma between the subjects *Mill* and *Bentham*. It also refers to *their life* (singular), when it should read *their*

lives (plural). Choice B should use a colon rather than a semicolon to introduce the information. The modifier in choice D is awkwardly placed; the poetry did not have a nervous breakdown. It should read *After a nervous breakdown, he found comfort in poetry.*

32. (**F**) Choice G is wordy. Choice H is passive. Choice J uses the adjective *passionate* rather than the adverb *passionately* to describe how he argues.

33. (**D**) Break down the article if you need to.

Paragraph One: The piece begins by setting up false expectations regarding the reader's opinion of how kids view participation in sports.

Paragraph Two: This paragraph undermines the expectations set up in paragraph one, saying that kids actually want out of group sports.

Paragraph Three: A fragment intentionally used to underscore a point, rhetorically.

Paragraph Four: This paragraph provides evidence that kids have seen adults acting badly.

Paragraph Five: The information here describes what some adults are doing to fix sports.

Paragraph Six: In the conclusion, the author applauds the attempts of Ripken and Engh to fix kids' sports.

This question asks you to identify the main idea by selecting an appropriate title. Consider all the choices. Choices A and B are too general to make a good fit for the passage. Choice C is quite appropriate for half of the article, but not the entire piece, since the article discusses both flaws with kids' sports *and* ways to improve it. Your best choice is choice D, which addresses both parts of the article.

34. (**F**) Most of the time when an author holds an opinion, s/he finds it difficult to keep that opinion from slipping into the text. This author has not done a good job keeping his/her bias out of the piece. It is clear from the tone of the piece, as well as the last paragraph, that the author approves of changes made to kids' sports; no reader would be able to make a good argument that the author approves of adults berating

kids. Therefore, the best answer is F.

35. (**C**) Re-reading (or memory) makes it clear that 18% of people surveyed claim to have been hit during sports participation.

36. (**H**) The word *honed*, as you might know from working through vocabulary lessons in school, means to sharpen—as one would a knife. So, you want to select choice H, which is the only definition offered you that fits this description.

37. (**C**) Re-reading (or memory) tells you that the article claims 70% of kids want to drop out of organized sports.

38. (**H**) The article talks about how recent thought about the scary West Nile virus makes people think that disease may have been what struck down Alexander the Great. This is interesting but is hardly "real" science; it's chatty and informational rather than rigorously scientific. Therefore, you must consider these facts when you try to guess which text might publish this piece. Almanacs discuss what the weather will be like on certain days; the *Guiness Book of World Records* documents people doing odd things for extremely long periods of time; neither text seems the appropriate place to read about Alexander the Great or the West Nile virus. On the other hand, a journal that publishes articles about Greek and Latin literature is likely to have a very different tone from that in the above piece; such articles are rigorous, full of lofty and difficult jargon, and don't usually discuss topical events like the West Nile virus. So, your best option is H.

39. (**C**) A plague is a bad thing, usually a disease, that takes over an area and makes everyone miserable (or kills everything in its path). Therefore, the definition of *overrun* is the best match here. *Inhabited* is too tame a word, and the other two choices both refer to a *lack*, rather than a presence, of plague.

40. (**F**) Re-reading (or memory) tells you that the author lists several possible causes of Alexander the Great's death; of the options listed here, only malaria is one of those enumerated by the author.

TEST 7   MATHEMATICS

1.

ANALYSIS

Simplify $3^9/3^7$ and then divide by 4.

WORK

$$\frac{3^9}{4\times 3^7} = \frac{\overset{3^2}{\cancel{3^9}}}{4\times\underset{1}{\cancel{3^7}}} = \frac{9}{4} = 2\frac{1}{4} = 2.25$$

ANSWER: (A)

2.

ANALYSIS

Substitute the values for x, y, and z into the given expression.

WORK

$$x = 4, y = -3, z = -2:$$

$$4xy + 5z^2$$
$$4(4)(-3) + 5(-2)^2$$
$$16(-3) + 5(-2)(-2)$$
$$-48 + 5(4)$$
$$-48 + 20$$
$$-28$$

ANSWER: (J)

3.

ANALYSIS

Use the formula $A = (1/2)bh$, where A = the area, b = the base, and h = the height of the triangle.

WORK

$$A = \frac{1}{2}bh$$

$$b = 2x + y,$$
$$h = 4z: \qquad = \frac{1}{\cancel{2}}(2x + y)(\overset{2}{\cancel{4}}z) = 2z(2x + y)$$

ANSWER: (A)

4.

ANALYSIS

Find the greatest and the least common factors of 70 and 14 and multiply.

WORK

$$\left.\begin{array}{l} 70 = 2 \cdot 5 \cdot 7 \\ \\ 14 = 2 \cdot 7 \end{array}\right\} \quad \begin{array}{l}\text{greatest common factor} = 7 \\ \text{least common factor} = 2\end{array}$$

The product of 7 and 2 is 14.

ANSWER: (F)

5.

ANALYSIS

Determine how much weight Dwayne lost and then let the result be the numerator of a fraction with the original weight the denominator.

WORK

Weight Lost:
   215 pounds − 175 pounds = 40 pounds

Weight Lost: $\dfrac{40}{215} = \dfrac{\overset{1}{\cancel{5}}\times 8}{\underset{1}{\cancel{5}}\times 43} = \dfrac{8}{43}$
Original Weight:

ANSWER: (A)

6.

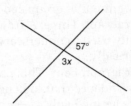

ANALYSIS

The two angles lie on a straight line, so they add up to 180°.

WORK

$$3x + 57 = 180$$
Subtract 57: $3x = 123$
Divide by 3: $x = 41$

ANSWER: (G)

7.

ANALYSIS

Change to improper fractions and multiply.

$$6\frac{2}{3} \times 5\frac{1}{4} = \frac{\overset{5}{\cancel{20}}}{\underset{1}{\cancel{3}}} \times \frac{\overset{7}{\cancel{21}}}{\underset{1}{\cancel{4}}} = 35$$

ANSWER: (D)

8.

ANALYSIS

Let y = the number of runs the team has to score on the last game, and set up an equation to solve for the mean.

WORK

$\bar{x}$ = mean: $\bar{x} = \dfrac{12 + 7 + 10 + 6 + 9 + y}{6}$

$\bar{x} = 9$: $9 = \dfrac{44 + y}{6}$

Multiply by 6: $54 = 44 + y$
Subtract 44: $10 = y$

ANSWER: (G)

9.

WORK

(A) $4^2 + 5(9 - 3) = 16 + 5 \cdot 6 = 16 + 30 = 46$
(B) $3 \cdot 17 - 4 \cdot 6 = 51 - 24 = 27$
(C) $7 + 9 \cdot 4 - 6(9 - 7)^3 = 7 + 36 - 6(2)^3 =$
    $43 - 6(8) = 43 - 48 = -5$
(D) $6 - 2 + 48/6 = 4 + 8 = 12$

ANSWER: (C)

10.

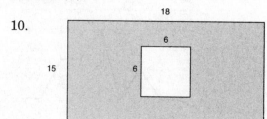

ANALYSIS

Subtract the area of the inner square from the area of the outer rectangle.

WORK

Area of outer rectangle	= base × height (or bh)
$b = 18, h = 15$:	= 18×15
	= 270

Area of inner square	= s^2
$s = 6$:	= 6^2
	= 36

Area of outer rectangle	= 270
− Area of inner square	= −36
Shaded area	= 234

ANSWER: (F)

11.

ANALYSIS

The price of the ticket at the end of this year will be 107% of the price at the beginning of the year. Then, to find the price at the end of two years, find 105% of the price at the end of this year.

WORK

Change 107% to a decimal and multiply:

$$1.07 \times \$8 = \$8.56$$
$$1.05 \times \$8.56 = \$8.988 \approx \$8.99$$

ANSWER: (D)

12.

ANALYSIS

Let x = the unknown number.

WORK

$$8 - \frac{2}{5}x = \frac{2}{3} \cdot 6 + 4$$

$$18 - \frac{2}{5}x = 4 + 4$$

Multiply by 5: $5 < 18 - \dfrac{2}{5}x = 8$

$$90 - 2x = 40$$

Subtract 90: $-2x = -50$
Divide by −2: $x = 25$

ANSWER: (H)

13.

ANALYSIS

Distance (D) = Rate $(R) \cdot$ Time (T)
$D = 154$

There are 2 hours and 45 minutes $\left(2\dfrac{45}{60}\right)$

or $2\dfrac{3}{4}$ hours of time between 8 A.M. and 10:45 A.M.

$$T = 2\frac{45}{60} = 2\frac{3}{4}$$

Divide 154 miles by $2\dfrac{3}{4}$ in order to obtain the average speed.

WORK

$$154 \div 2\frac{3}{4} = 154 \div \frac{11}{4} = 154 \times \frac{4}{11} = \frac{616}{11} = 56$$

ANSWER: (A)

14.

ANALYSIS

Let x = the unknown number.

WORK

$$6(? + 5) - 3 = 135$$
$$6(x + 5) - 3 = 135$$
$$6x + 30 - 3 = 135$$
$$6x + 27 = 135$$

Subtract 27: $6x = 108$

Divide by 6: $x = 18$

ANSWER: (C)

15.

ANALYSIS

Let x = the original number. Find that number and then divide by 4.

WORK

$$6x = 24.72$$

Divide by 6: $x = 4.12$

Divide by 4: $4.12 \div 4 = 1.03$

ANSWER: (G)

16.

ANALYSIS

There are 5,280 feet in a mile. Change both units of distance to the same measure. In this case, let's just change 3 miles per hour to feet per hour and then divide.

Work

3 miles per hour $= 3 \times 5{,}280$ feet per hour

                    $= 15{,}840$ feet per hour

$$\frac{23{,}760}{15{,}840} = 1.5$$

ANSWER: (J)

17.

ANALYSIS

Subtract 2 pounds 9 ounces from 5 pounds 6 ounces. Borrow one pound (16 ounces) from 5 pounds and add it to the 6 ounces.

WORK

$$
\begin{array}{r}
4 \qquad 16+6 = 22 \text{ ounces} \\
\cancel{5} \text{ pounds} \quad \cancel{6} \text{ ounces} \\
- 2 \text{ pounds} \quad 9 \text{ ounces} \\
\hline
2 \text{ pounds} \quad 13 \text{ ounces}
\end{array}
$$

ANSWER: (B)

18.

ANALYSIS

There are 100 centimeters in one meter.

WORK

1 centimeter = 1/100 of a meter

2 centimeters = 2/100 = 1/50 of a meter

          $1/50 = 0.02 = 2\%$

ANSWER: (G)

19.

ANALYSIS

Find 8% of the excess money over $2,000 and add the result to the $300 base salary.

WORK

$$\$3{,}500 - \$2{,}000 = \$1{,}500$$
$$8\% = 0.08$$
$$0.08 \times \$1{,}500 = \$120$$
$$\$300 + \$120 = \$420$$

ANSWER: (D)

20.

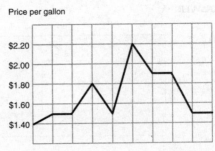

Price per gallon

Jan. Feb. Mar. Apr. May Jun. Jul. Aug. Sep. Oct.

ANALYSIS

Add the April and August prices and divide by 2.

WORK

$$\frac{\$1.80 + \$1.90}{2} = \frac{\$3.70}{2} = \$1.85$$

ANSWER: (G)

21.

ANALYSIS

To get a rough estimate, let's round off 32 to 30 and 68 to 70.

WORK

$$30 \times 70 = 2{,}100$$

ANSWER: (D)

22.

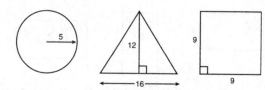

ANALYSIS

Find the areas of all three figures and then substitute into the given choices. To simplify calculations, round off π to 3.

WORK

Circle: $A_C = \pi r^2$, where A_C = area of circle, r = radius

$\pi = 3, r = 5$: $A_C = (3)(5)^2 = (3)(25) = 75$

Triangle: $A_T = \left(\dfrac{1}{2}\right)bh$, where

A_T = area of triangle,
b = base,
h = height

$b = 16, h = 12$: $A_T = \left(\dfrac{1}{2}\right)(16)(12) = 96$

Square: $A_S = s^2$, where A_S = area of square, s = side of square

$s = 9$: $A_S = (9)^2 = 81$

The area of the circle is less than the area of the triangle.

$$75 < 96 \ \checkmark$$

ANSWER: (J)

23.

ANALYSIS

Simplify the fractions by turning them into decimals and then do the arithmetic.

WORK

$$82 + 6/10 + 8/100 + 7/1000 =$$
$$82 + 0.6 + 0.08 + 0.007$$

$$
\begin{array}{r}
82.000 \\
0.600 \\
0.080 \\
+\ \ 0.007 \\
\hline
82.687
\end{array}
$$

ANSWER: (A)

24.

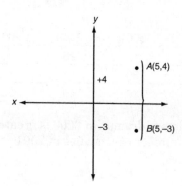

ANALYSIS

The total distance from -3 to $+4$ is 7 units.

ANSWER: (J)

25.

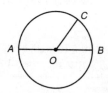

ANALYSIS

A diameter is equal to twice the measure of its radius.

WORK

$$AB = 2 \times CO$$
$$AB = 2 \times 3a = 6a$$

ANSWER: (C)

26.

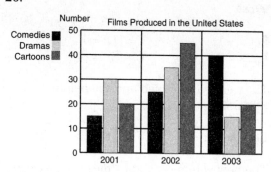

ANALYSIS

First make a table indicating the numbers of cartoons, dramas, and comedies produced in each of the indicated years. Then you're in a position to check the given statements for their validity. Each horizontal line represents 10 films.

WORK

	2001	2002	2003
Comedies	15	25	40
Dramas	30	35	15
Cartoons	20	45	20

The number of dramas in 2003 is greater than the number of comedies in 2001

$$15 > 15 \ \text{✗}$$

ANSWER: (H)

27.

ANALYSIS
Simplify the expression and then subtract.

WORK

$5.3 \times 10^3 = 5.3 \times 10 \times 10 \times 10 = 5.3 \times 1,000 = 5,300$
$-1.3 \times 10^2 = -1.3 \times 10 \times 10 \quad = -1.3 \times 100 \ = -130$

$$= 5,170$$

ANSWER: (C)

28.

ANALYSIS
The best approach to this problem is to substitute some small positive integers for the radius and the height and then to see what happens to the volume. We can leave π alone.

WORK

$$V = s^3$$
Let s = 1: $\quad V = (1)^3 = 1$
Let s = 2: $\quad V = (2)^3 = 8$

The radius is doubled and the height remains the same.

Let $r = 2, h = 2$: $\quad V = \dfrac{1}{3}\pi(2)^2(2) = \dfrac{8}{3}\pi$

The new volume is eight times the measure of the old volume.

ANSWER: (J)

29.

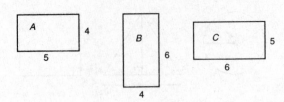

ANALYSIS
Find all the areas and then substitute the results into the four inequalities.

WORK

$$\text{Area A} = bh = 5 \cdot 4 = 20$$
$$\text{Area B} = bh = 4 \cdot 6 = 24$$
$$\text{Area C} = bh = 6 \cdot 5 = 30$$

Area B is less than area C.
$$24 < 30 \ \text{✔}$$

ANSWER: (C)

30.

ANALYSIS
Add 2/5 and 1/3 and then subtract the result from 1 (the total amount). The answer is Malcolm's portion. Once we determine Malcolm's portion, multiply that fraction by $300,000, the total income.

WORK

$$\dfrac{2}{5} = \dfrac{6}{15} \qquad 1 = \dfrac{5}{15}$$

$$+\dfrac{1}{3} = \dfrac{5}{15} \qquad -\dfrac{11}{15} \qquad \dfrac{4}{15} \times 300,000 = 80,000$$

$$\dfrac{11}{15} \qquad\qquad \dfrac{4}{15}$$

ANSWER: (F)

31.

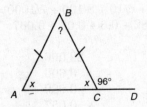

ANALYSIS
Step 1: The measure of $\angle BCA$ + the measure of $\angle BCD = 180°$ because the angles lie

on a straight line and, together, add up to a straight angle. Find m∠BCA.

Step 2: Since the triangle is isosceles, interior angles *A* and *BCA* are the same measure, so let m∠A = x and let m∠BCA = x. Then add up all three interior angles of △ABC, and set the sum equal to 180°.

Step 3: Now find the measure of ∠B.

WORK

Step 1:
$$m\angle BCA + m\angle BCD = 180$$
$$x + 96 = 180$$

Subtract 96: $x = 84$

Step 2: $m\angle A + m\angle B + m\angle BCA = 180$

m∠A =

m∠BCA = x: $x + m\angle B + x = 180$
$$2x + m\angle B = 180$$

x = 84: $2(84) + m\angle B = 180$
$$168 + m\angle B = 180$$

Step 3: $m\angle B = 12$

ANSWER: (C)

32.

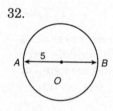

ANALYSIS

Find the areas and perimeters of the circle and the triangle and then substitute into the preceding statements. Let π = 3.14.

WORK

Circumference of
  circle *O*: $C = 2\pi r$
π = 3.14, r = 5: $= 2(3.14)(5) = 31.4$

Area of circle *O*: $A_c = \pi r^2$
π = 3.14, r = 5: $= (3.14)(5)^2 = 78.5$

Perimeter of
  triangle *RST*: $P = 5 + 12 + 13 = 30$

Area of triangle
  RST: $A_T = \frac{1}{2}bh$

b = 12, h = 5: $= \frac{1}{2}(12)(5) = 30$

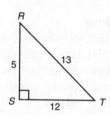

Area of triangle $RST < \frac{1}{2}$ Area of circle *O*

$$30 < \frac{1}{2}(78.5)$$

$$30 < 39.52 \ ✔$$

ANSWER: (F)

33.
ANALYSIS

In cases when we are given a generalized statement, make the problem concrete by using actual numbers. The two unknowns, *x* and *y*, are negative and y > x, so let's try using x = –2 and y = –1.

WORK

$$xy > 0$$
Let x = –2, y = –1: $(-2)(-1) = +2$
$$+2 > 0 \ ✔$$

ANSWER: (C)

34.
ANALYSIS
Determine the prime factors of 35 and 30. Then find the difference of their sums.

WORK

$35 = 7 \cdot 5$ $30 = 2 \cdot 5 \cdot 3$
$7 + 5 = 12$ $2 + 5 + 3 = 10$
$$12 - 10 = 2$$

ANSWER: (H)

35.
ANALYSIS
In a case like this, if we want an exact answer, convert the percentage to a fraction and then multiply.

WORK

$$16\frac{2}{3}\% = 16\frac{2}{3} \div 100 = 16\frac{2}{3} \div \frac{100}{1}$$

$$= \frac{\overset{1}{\cancel{50}}}{3} \times \frac{1}{\underset{2}{\cancel{100}}} = \frac{1}{6}$$

$$16\frac{2}{3}\% = 1/6$$

$$1/6 \times 360 = 60$$

ANSWER: (B)

36.

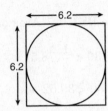

ANALYSIS
Round off 6.2 to 6. Then find the area of the square and find $\frac{3}{4}$ of the answer.

WORK
Area of square = (side)² = (6)² = 36

Approximate area of circle = $\frac{3}{4} \times 36 = 27$

ANSWER: (G)

37.
WORK
Nine $0.15 stamps plus six $0.37 stamps cost more than five $0.65 stamps.

$$9 \times \$0.15 + 6 \times \$0.37 > 5 \times \$0.65$$
$$\$1.35 + \$2.22 > \$3.25$$
$$3.57 > \$3.25 ✔$$

ANSWER: (A)

38.
ANALYSIS
One method is to first divide the octagon into a number of triangles. Then, since we know that there are 180° in the angles of a triangle, just multiply the number of triangles by 180°.

A second method is to use the formula for determining the number of interior degrees in any polygon: $N_D = (n-2)180$, where N_D = the number of interior degrees and n = the number of sides of the polygon.

Either way, the solution is the same.

WORK
Method 1

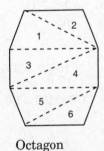

Octagon

6 triangles: $6 \times 180° = 1,080°$
$$N_D = 1,080°$$

Method 2 $\quad N_D = (n-2)180$
$$= (8-2)180$$
$$= 6 \times 180$$
$$= 1,080°$$

ANSWER: (J)

39.

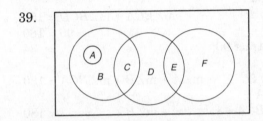

ANALYSIS
All elements of set A are members of set B. Some elements of set D are in set B, some are in set F, and some are independent of both sets B and F. We'll have to check each statement to determine its truth value.

WORK
Some members of set D are members of set F. Set D is represented by the middle circle. Some elements in set D (those elements of set E) are members of set F, so the statement is **true**.

ANSWER: (C)

40.

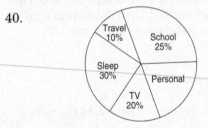

ANALYSIS
To determine the number of hours spent on personal items, add up the various percentages and then subtract from 100%. Then multiply the answer by 24 hours.

WORK
$$30\% + 10\% + 25\% + 20\% = 85\%$$
$$100\% - 85\% = 15\%$$
$$0.15 \times 24 = 3.6$$

ANSWER: (J)

Answer Sheet
Practice Cooperative Admissions Examination 2

TEST 1 SEQUENCES

1. Ⓐ Ⓑ Ⓒ Ⓓ	5. Ⓐ Ⓑ Ⓒ Ⓓ	9. Ⓐ Ⓑ Ⓒ Ⓓ	13. Ⓐ Ⓑ Ⓒ Ⓓ	17. Ⓐ Ⓑ Ⓒ Ⓓ
2. Ⓕ Ⓖ Ⓗ Ⓙ	6. Ⓕ Ⓖ Ⓗ Ⓙ	10. Ⓕ Ⓖ Ⓗ Ⓙ	14. Ⓕ Ⓖ Ⓗ Ⓙ	18. Ⓕ Ⓖ Ⓗ Ⓙ
3. Ⓐ Ⓑ Ⓒ Ⓓ	7. Ⓐ Ⓑ Ⓒ Ⓓ	11. Ⓐ Ⓑ Ⓒ Ⓓ	15. Ⓐ Ⓑ Ⓒ Ⓓ	19. Ⓐ Ⓑ Ⓒ Ⓓ
4. Ⓕ Ⓖ Ⓗ Ⓙ	8. Ⓕ Ⓖ Ⓗ Ⓙ	12. Ⓕ Ⓖ Ⓗ Ⓙ	16. Ⓕ Ⓖ Ⓗ Ⓙ	20. Ⓕ Ⓖ Ⓗ Ⓙ

TEST 2 ANALOGIES

1. Ⓐ Ⓑ Ⓒ Ⓓ	5. Ⓐ Ⓑ Ⓒ Ⓓ	9. Ⓐ Ⓑ Ⓒ Ⓓ	13. Ⓐ Ⓑ Ⓒ Ⓓ	17. Ⓐ Ⓑ Ⓒ Ⓓ
2. Ⓕ Ⓖ Ⓗ Ⓙ	6. Ⓕ Ⓖ Ⓗ Ⓙ	10. Ⓕ Ⓖ Ⓗ Ⓙ	14. Ⓕ Ⓖ Ⓗ Ⓙ	18. Ⓕ Ⓖ Ⓗ Ⓙ
3. Ⓐ Ⓑ Ⓒ Ⓓ	7. Ⓐ Ⓑ Ⓒ Ⓓ	11. Ⓐ Ⓑ Ⓒ Ⓓ	15. Ⓐ Ⓑ Ⓒ Ⓓ	19. Ⓐ Ⓑ Ⓒ Ⓓ
4. Ⓕ Ⓖ Ⓗ Ⓙ	8. Ⓕ Ⓖ Ⓗ Ⓙ	12. Ⓕ Ⓖ Ⓗ Ⓙ	16. Ⓕ Ⓖ Ⓗ Ⓙ	20. Ⓕ Ⓖ Ⓗ Ⓙ

TEST 3 QUANTITATIVE REASONING

1. Ⓐ Ⓑ Ⓒ Ⓓ	5. Ⓐ Ⓑ Ⓒ Ⓓ	9. Ⓐ Ⓑ Ⓒ Ⓓ	13. Ⓐ Ⓑ Ⓒ Ⓓ	17. Ⓐ Ⓑ Ⓒ Ⓓ
2. Ⓕ Ⓖ Ⓗ Ⓙ	6. Ⓕ Ⓖ Ⓗ Ⓙ	10. Ⓕ Ⓖ Ⓗ Ⓙ	14. Ⓕ Ⓖ Ⓗ Ⓙ	18. Ⓕ Ⓖ Ⓗ Ⓙ
3. Ⓐ Ⓑ Ⓒ Ⓓ	7. Ⓐ Ⓑ Ⓒ Ⓓ	11. Ⓐ Ⓑ Ⓒ Ⓓ	15. Ⓐ Ⓑ Ⓒ Ⓓ	19. Ⓐ Ⓑ Ⓒ Ⓓ
4. Ⓕ Ⓖ Ⓗ Ⓙ	8. Ⓕ Ⓖ Ⓗ Ⓙ	12. Ⓕ Ⓖ Ⓗ Ⓙ	16. Ⓕ Ⓖ Ⓗ Ⓙ	20. Ⓕ Ⓖ Ⓗ Ⓙ

TEST 4 VERBAL REASONING—WORDS

1. Ⓐ Ⓑ Ⓒ Ⓓ	5. Ⓐ Ⓑ Ⓒ Ⓓ	9. Ⓐ Ⓑ Ⓒ Ⓓ	13. Ⓐ Ⓑ Ⓒ Ⓓ	17. Ⓐ Ⓑ Ⓒ Ⓓ
2. Ⓕ Ⓖ Ⓗ Ⓙ	6. Ⓕ Ⓖ Ⓗ Ⓙ	10. Ⓕ Ⓖ Ⓗ Ⓙ	14. Ⓕ Ⓖ Ⓗ Ⓙ	18. Ⓕ Ⓖ Ⓗ Ⓙ
3. Ⓐ Ⓑ Ⓒ Ⓓ	7. Ⓐ Ⓑ Ⓒ Ⓓ	11. Ⓐ Ⓑ Ⓒ Ⓓ	15. Ⓐ Ⓑ Ⓒ Ⓓ	19. Ⓐ Ⓑ Ⓒ Ⓓ
4. Ⓕ Ⓖ Ⓗ Ⓙ	8. Ⓕ Ⓖ Ⓗ Ⓙ	12. Ⓕ Ⓖ Ⓗ Ⓙ	16. Ⓕ Ⓖ Ⓗ Ⓙ	20. Ⓕ Ⓖ Ⓗ Ⓙ

TEST 5 VERBAL REASONING—CONTEXT

1. Ⓐ Ⓑ Ⓒ Ⓓ	3. Ⓐ Ⓑ Ⓒ Ⓓ	5. Ⓐ Ⓑ Ⓒ Ⓓ	7. Ⓐ Ⓑ Ⓒ Ⓓ	9. Ⓐ Ⓑ Ⓒ Ⓓ
2. Ⓕ Ⓖ Ⓗ Ⓙ	4. Ⓕ Ⓖ Ⓗ Ⓙ	6. Ⓕ Ⓖ Ⓗ Ⓙ	8. Ⓕ Ⓖ Ⓗ Ⓙ	10. Ⓕ Ⓖ Ⓗ Ⓙ

TEST 6   READING AND LANGUAGE ARTS

1. Ⓐ Ⓑ Ⓒ Ⓓ
2. Ⓕ Ⓖ Ⓗ Ⓙ
3. Ⓐ Ⓑ Ⓒ Ⓓ
4. Ⓕ Ⓖ Ⓗ Ⓙ
5. Ⓐ Ⓑ Ⓒ Ⓓ
6. Ⓕ Ⓖ Ⓗ Ⓙ
7. Ⓐ Ⓑ Ⓒ Ⓓ
8. Ⓕ Ⓖ Ⓗ Ⓙ
9. Ⓐ Ⓑ Ⓒ Ⓓ
10. Ⓕ Ⓖ Ⓗ Ⓙ

11. Ⓐ Ⓑ Ⓒ Ⓓ
12. Ⓕ Ⓖ Ⓗ Ⓙ
13. Ⓐ Ⓑ Ⓒ Ⓓ
14. Ⓕ Ⓖ Ⓗ Ⓙ
15. Ⓐ Ⓑ Ⓒ Ⓓ
16. Ⓕ Ⓖ Ⓗ Ⓙ
17. Ⓐ Ⓑ Ⓒ Ⓓ
18. Ⓕ Ⓖ Ⓗ Ⓙ
19. Ⓐ Ⓑ Ⓒ Ⓓ
20. Ⓕ Ⓖ Ⓗ Ⓙ

21. Ⓐ Ⓑ Ⓒ Ⓓ
22. Ⓕ Ⓖ Ⓗ Ⓙ
23. Ⓐ Ⓑ Ⓒ Ⓓ
24. Ⓕ Ⓖ Ⓗ Ⓙ
25. Ⓐ Ⓑ Ⓒ Ⓓ
26. Ⓕ Ⓖ Ⓗ Ⓙ
27. Ⓐ Ⓑ Ⓒ Ⓓ
28. Ⓕ Ⓖ Ⓗ Ⓙ
29. Ⓐ Ⓑ Ⓒ Ⓓ
30. Ⓕ Ⓖ Ⓗ Ⓙ

31. Ⓐ Ⓑ Ⓒ Ⓓ
32. Ⓕ Ⓖ Ⓗ Ⓙ
33. Ⓐ Ⓑ Ⓒ Ⓓ
34. Ⓕ Ⓖ Ⓗ Ⓙ
35. Ⓐ Ⓑ Ⓒ Ⓓ
36. Ⓕ Ⓖ Ⓗ Ⓙ
37. Ⓐ Ⓑ Ⓒ Ⓓ
38. Ⓕ Ⓖ Ⓗ Ⓙ
39. Ⓐ Ⓑ Ⓒ Ⓓ
40. Ⓕ Ⓖ Ⓗ Ⓙ

TEST 7   MATHEMATICS

1. Ⓐ Ⓑ Ⓒ Ⓓ
2. Ⓕ Ⓖ Ⓗ Ⓙ
3. Ⓐ Ⓑ Ⓒ Ⓓ
4. Ⓕ Ⓖ Ⓗ Ⓙ
5. Ⓐ Ⓑ Ⓒ Ⓓ
6. Ⓕ Ⓖ Ⓗ Ⓙ
7. Ⓐ Ⓑ Ⓒ Ⓓ
8. Ⓕ Ⓖ Ⓗ Ⓙ
9. Ⓐ Ⓑ Ⓒ Ⓓ
10. Ⓕ Ⓖ Ⓗ Ⓙ

11. Ⓐ Ⓑ Ⓒ Ⓓ
12. Ⓕ Ⓖ Ⓗ Ⓙ
13. Ⓐ Ⓑ Ⓒ Ⓓ
14. Ⓕ Ⓖ Ⓗ Ⓙ
15. Ⓐ Ⓑ Ⓒ Ⓓ
16. Ⓕ Ⓖ Ⓗ Ⓙ
17. Ⓐ Ⓑ Ⓒ Ⓓ
18. Ⓕ Ⓖ Ⓗ Ⓙ
19. Ⓐ Ⓑ Ⓒ Ⓓ
20. Ⓕ Ⓖ Ⓗ Ⓙ

21. Ⓐ Ⓑ Ⓒ Ⓓ
22. Ⓕ Ⓖ Ⓗ Ⓙ
23. Ⓐ Ⓑ Ⓒ Ⓓ
24. Ⓕ Ⓖ Ⓗ Ⓙ
25. Ⓐ Ⓑ Ⓒ Ⓓ
26. Ⓕ Ⓖ Ⓗ Ⓙ
27. Ⓐ Ⓑ Ⓒ Ⓓ
28. Ⓕ Ⓖ Ⓗ Ⓙ
29. Ⓐ Ⓑ Ⓒ Ⓓ
30. Ⓕ Ⓖ Ⓗ Ⓙ

31. Ⓐ Ⓑ Ⓒ Ⓓ
32. Ⓕ Ⓖ Ⓗ Ⓙ
33. Ⓐ Ⓑ Ⓒ Ⓓ
34. Ⓕ Ⓖ Ⓗ Ⓙ
35. Ⓐ Ⓑ Ⓒ Ⓓ
36. Ⓕ Ⓖ Ⓗ Ⓙ
37. Ⓐ Ⓑ Ⓒ Ⓓ
38. Ⓕ Ⓖ Ⓗ Ⓙ
39. Ⓐ Ⓑ Ⓒ Ⓓ
40. Ⓕ Ⓖ Ⓗ Ⓙ

Practice COOP Exam Two

#1–20   *15 minutes*

DIRECTIONS: Choose the letter than will continue the pattern or sequence.

1. ○＿□△∖｜＿○□△∖｜＿□○△∖｜＿＿＿＿

   (A) □○△＿   (B) □△＿○   (C) △＿○□   (D) ＿□△○

2. ⊕ ⊖ ⊙ ⊕｜⊖ ⊙ ⊕ ⊙｜⊕ ⊖ ⊕ ⊖｜＿＿＿

   (F) ⊖ ⊕ ⊖ ⊙   (G) ⊖ ⊙ ⊖ ⊙   (H) ⊖ ⊖ ⊕ ⊙   (J) ⊙ ⊖ ⊕ ⊖

3. ▭ ○ □ △｜○ □ △ ▭｜○ △ ▭ ○｜＿＿＿

   (A) ○ ▭ □ △   (B) ○ □ △ ▭   (C) △ ▭ ○ □   (D) △ □ ○ ▭

4. ○ □ ○ ▫｜◇ ▱ ▽ ▫｜○ □ ○ △｜＿＿＿

   (F) □ ○ ◺ ▽   (G) ▫ ○ ▫ △   (H) ○ ◇ ▱ ▽   (J) ▫ ○ △ ▱

5.

   (A)   (B)   (C)   (D)

6. ＊｜＊｜＊｜＊｜＊｜＿＿＿

   (F)   (G)   (H)   (J)

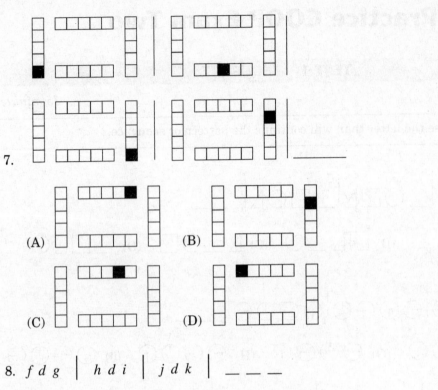

7. (A) (B) (C) (D)

8. *f d g* | *h d i* | *j d k* | _ _ _

(F) *k o m*   (G) *l d m*   (H) *n o p*   (J) *o d p*

9. D F H | J L N | P R T | _ _ _

(A) U V X   (B) S U W   (C) U V W   (D) V X Z

10. a c f | g i l | m o r | _ _ _

(F) s u x   (G) r t v   (H) s t u   (J) u w x

11. X V T | R P N | L J H | _ _ _

(A) G F C   (B) F D B   (C) G E D   (D) F E C

12. XXX | XXVII | XXIV | _ _ _ | XVIII

(F) XX   (G) XXII   (H) XXIII   (J) XXI

13. A R B | C R D | _ _ _ | G R H

(A) E R F   (B) G R F   (C) I R J   (D) K L M

14. 1 1 1 | 2 4 8 | 3 __ 27 | 4 16 64

    (F) 10   (G) 8   (H) 18   (J) 9

15. 20 5 1.25 | 16 4 1 | 60 __ 3.75

    (A) 6   (B) 10   (C) 15   (D) 20

16. 9 7 14 | 4 __ 4 | 8 6 12

    (F) 3   (G) 1   (H) 2   (J) 6

17. 1 3 9 | 2 6 __ | 4 12 36

    (A) 12   (B) 18   (C) 9   (D) 8

18. 36 32 28 | 24 20 16 | 12 __ 4

    (F) 9   (G) 5   (H) 10   (J) 8

19. 2 4 3 | 3 5 4 | 7 9 __

    (A) 8   (B) 6   (C) 10   (D) 11

20. $C_{12} E_{12} H_{12}$ | $I_{10} K_{10} N_{10}$ | $O_8 Q_8 T_8$ | __ __ __

    (F) $T_6 U_6 W_6$ (G) $U_5 W_4 X_2$ (H) $U_6 W_6 Z_6$ (J) $T_6 V_4 Z_2$

STOP

IF YOU FINISH BEFORE TIME IS UP, CHECK OVER YOUR WORK ON THIS TEST ONLY. DO NOT GO ON TO THE NEXT TEST UNTIL THE SIGNAL IS GIVEN.

TEST 2   ANALOGIES

#1–20   *7 minutes*

DIRECTIONS: Select the picture that will fill the empty box so that the two lower pictures are related to each other in the same manner as the two upper pictures.

1.

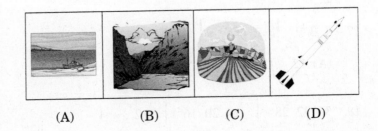

(A)   (B)   (C)   (D)

2.

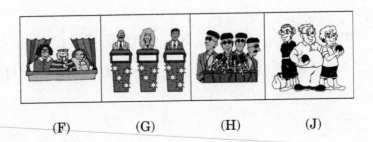

(F)   (G)   (H)   (J)

3.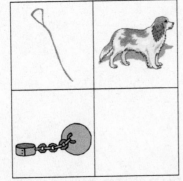

(A)   (B)   (C)   (D)

4.

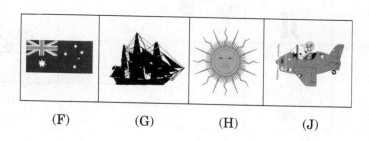

(F)   (G)   (H)   (J)

5.

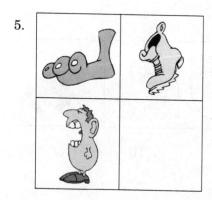

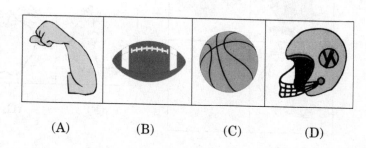

(A)   (B)   (C)   (D)

6.

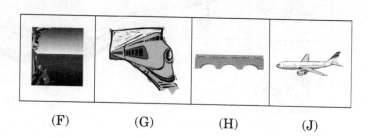

(F)   (G)   (H)   (J)

7.

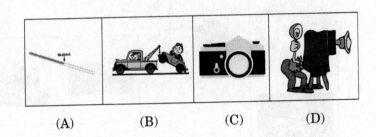

(A)　　　　(B)　　　　(C)　　　　(D)

8.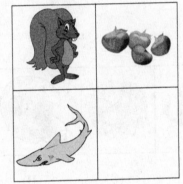

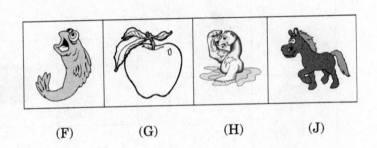

(F)　　　　(G)　　　　(H)　　　　(J)

9.

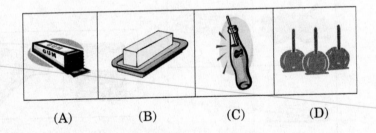

(A)　　　　(B)　　　　(C)　　　　(D)

10.

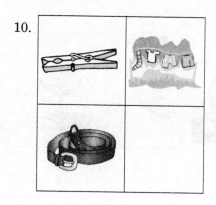

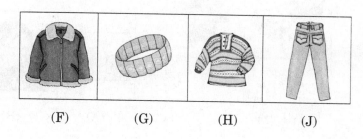

(F) (G) (H) (J)

11.

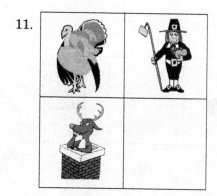

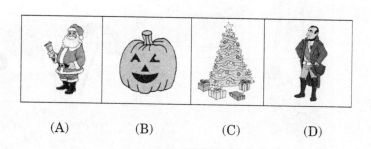

(A) (B) (C) (D)

12.

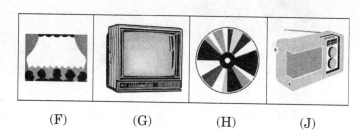

(F) (G) (H) (J)

13.

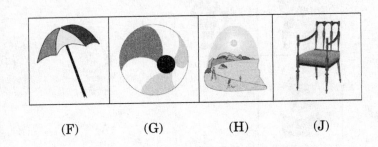

(A)   (B)   (C)   (D)

14.

(F)   (G)   (H)   (J)

15.

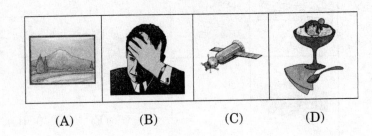

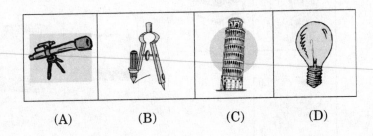

(A)   (B)   (C)   (D)

16.

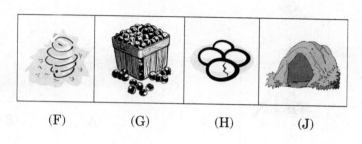

(F) (G) (H) (J)

17.

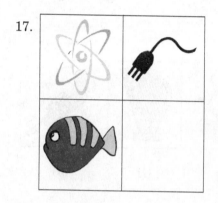

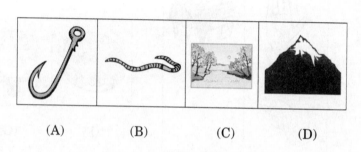

(A) (B) (C) (D)

18.

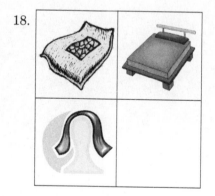

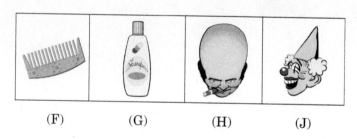

(F) (G) (H) (J)

19.

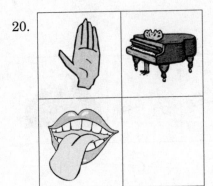

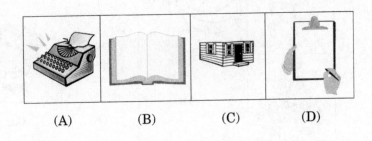

(A) (B) (C) (D)

20.

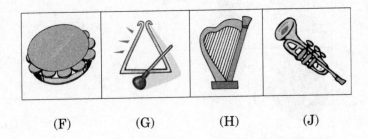

(F) (G) (H) (J)

STOP

IF YOU FINISH BEFORE TIME IS UP, CHECK OVER YOUR WORK ON THIS TEST ONLY. DO NOT GO ON TO THE NEXT TEST UNTIL THE SIGNAL IS GIVEN.

TEST 3   QUANTITATIVE REASONING

#1–20

5 minutes

DIRECTIONS: For questions 1–7, find the mathematical operation that is applied to the first number in each set so as to arrive at the second number. Then apply that operation to find the missing number. Select the correct answer.

---

1. 8 → ___ → 5
    9 → ___ → 6
    5 → ___ → ?
    (A) 0
    (B) 1
    (C) 4
    (D) 2

2. 4 → ___ → 8
    3 → ___ → 6
    6 → ___ → ?
    (F) 12
    (G) 10
    (H) 9
    (J) 6

3. 12 → ___ → 4
    9 → ___ → 3
    6 → ___ → ?
    (A) 1
    (B) 2
    (C) 3
    (D) 4

4. 4/9 → ___ → 4
    2/3 → ___ → 6
    1/3 → ___ → ?
    (F) 2
    (G) 6
    (H) 3
    (J) 9

5. 1/2 → ___ → 1
    2 → ___ → 2.5
    1.5 → ___ → ?
    (A) 2
    (B) 3.5
    (C) 3
    (D) 2.5

6. 5 → ___ → 3
    1 → ___ → −1
    4.5 → ___ → ?
    (F) −2.5
    (G) 4
    (H) 2.5
    (J) 4.5

7. 14 → ___ → 7
    10 → ___ → 5
    8 → ___ → ?
    (A) 4
    (B) 16
    (C) 3
    (D) 10

DIRECTIONS: For questions 8–14, express the part of the grid that is dark.

8. 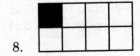   (F) 3/8   (G) 1/2   (H) 1/4   (J) 1/8

9.   (A) 3/5   (B) 3/8   (C) 1/2   (D) 5/8

10. 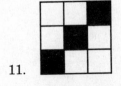   (F) 2/3   (G) 1/4   (H) 1/3   (J) 2/5

11.    (A) 1/2   (B) 1/3   (C) 3/7   (D) 3/10

12.   (F) 1/2   (G) 1/3   (H) 2/3   (J) 3/4

13. 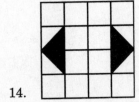   (A) 2/5   (B) 3/5   (C) 1/3   (D) 3/8

14. 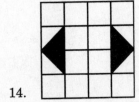   (F) 1/4   (G) 1/8   (H) 4/9   (J) 1/3

DIRECTIONS: For questions 15–20, check the balanced scale at the left and see which weights are balanced. From the results, determine which weights are balanced on the right.

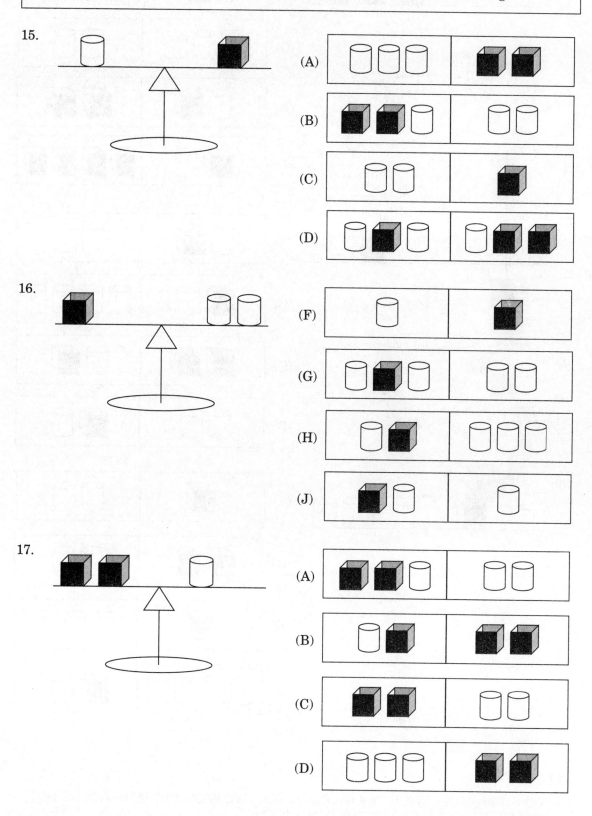

15.

16.

17.

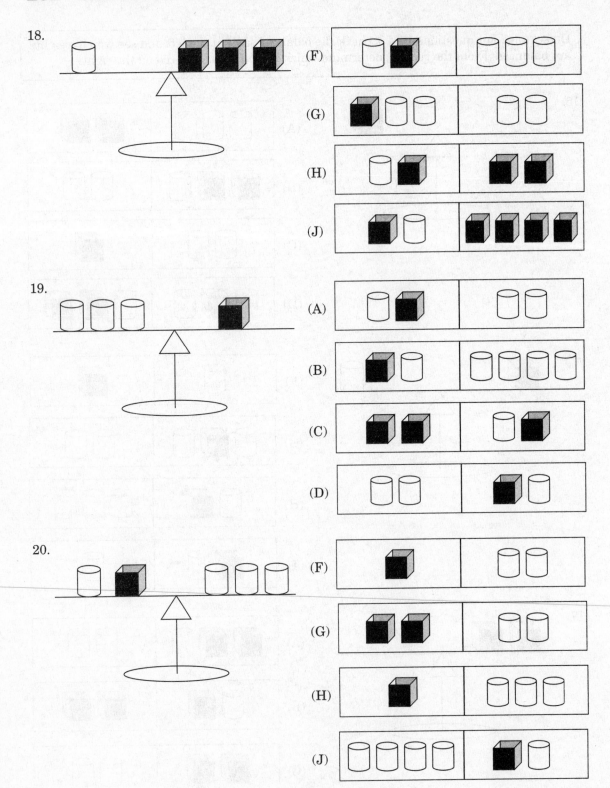

18.

(F)

(G)

(H)

(J)

19.

(A)

(B)

(C)

(D)

20.

(F)

(G)

(H)

(J)

STOP

IF YOU FINISH BEFORE TIME IS UP, CHECK OVER YOUR WORK ON THIS TEST ONLY. DO NOT
GO ON TO THE NEXT TEST UNTIL THE SIGNAL IS GIVEN.

TEST 4   VERBAL REASONING—WORDS

#1–20   *15 minutes*

> DIRECTIONS: For questions 1–5, find the word that names a necessary part of the underlined word.

1. shoe

   (A) sole
   (B) leather
   (C) laces
   (D) heel

2. bath

   (F) soap
   (G) water
   (H) tub
   (J) towel

3. library

   (A) building
   (B) books
   (C) chairs
   (D) computers

4. movie

   (F) sound
   (G) picture
   (H) popcorn
   (J) theater

5. pencil

   (A) wood
   (B) lead
   (C) paper
   (D) idea

> DIRECTIONS: For questions 6–10, choose the word that is most like the underlined words.

6. sport   play   recreation

   (F) tease
   (G) game
   (H) volleyball
   (J) fishing

7. pack   bag   parcel

   (A) suitcase
   (B) sleeper
   (C) bottle
   (D) ice

8. parade   march   pageant

   (F) procession
   (G) circus
   (H) band
   (J) float

9. record   document   transcribe

   (A) manuscript
   (B) chronicle
   (C) history
   (D) inscription

10. content   pleased   happy

    (F) substance
    (G) stoic
    (H) ambivalent
    (J) satisfied

DIRECTIONS: For questions 11–15, choose the word that does *not* belong.

11.
- (A) music
- (B) noise
- (C) sound
- (D) ear

12.
- (F) soup
- (G) milk
- (H) ice
- (J) juice

13.
- (A) balanced
- (B) fair
- (C) beautiful
- (D) pretty

14.
- (F) shade
- (G) darken
- (H) cover
- (J) discover

15.
- (A) conflict
- (B) contrast
- (C) battle
- (D) combat

DIRECTIONS: In questions 16–20, the words in the top row are related. The words in the bottom row are related in a similar way. Choose the word that completes the sequence in the bottom row.

16.

Influence	Power	Omnipotence
Comma	Semicolon	

- (F) quotation
- (G) period
- (H) parentheses
- (J) hyphen

17.

Valley	Hill	Mountain
	2	5

- (A) 0
- (B) 1
- (C) −1
- (D) 3

18.

Italy	France	Spain
Panama	Nicaragua	_____

(F) Canada
(G) Guatemala
(H) Russia
(J) Uganda

19.

Key	Lock	Door
_____	Field	Computer

(A) password
(B) file
(C) web site
(D) menu

20.

spaghetti	macaroni	lasagna
maple	oak	_____

(F) shrub
(G) cedar
(H) furniture
(J) chair

STOP

IF YOU FINISH BEFORE TIME IS UP, CHECK OVER YOUR WORK ON THIS TEST ONLY. DO NOT GO ON TO THE NEXT TEST UNTIL THE SIGNAL IS GIVEN.

TEST 5   VERBAL REASONING—CONTEXT

#1–10   *7 minutes*

DIRECTIONS: For these questions, find the statement that is true according to the given information.

1. Cookies were on sale at the grocery store. Carlo went in to buy cookies, but he came out with fruit, instead.

   (A) Carlo did not have enough money for cookies.
   (B) Carlo is on a diet.
   (C) The store was out of cookies.
   (D) Carlo changed his mind.

2. David and I shared a locker last year. This year I wanted to share a locker with Steven, but he is not in my homeroom. I ended up sharing a locker with John.

   (F) David and I no longer get along.
   (G) David moved away.
   (H) John is in my homeroom.
   (J) Steven is sharing a locker with David.

3. Mrs. Stevens hired Mrs. Hall in April. She hired Mrs. Wheat in June. Mrs. Hall and Mrs. Wheat are good friends.

   (A) Mrs. Hall recommended Mrs. Wheat for a job.
   (B) Mrs. Hall, Mrs. Wheat, and Mrs. Stevens are very good friends.
   (C) Mrs. Hall and Mrs. Wheat met on the job.
   (D) Mrs. Hall, Mrs. Wheat, and Mrs. Stevens all work for the same organization.

4. Brandi has appeared in many plays in many roles. She especially enjoys Shakespeare. Although she prefers comedies, her favorite play is *Romeo and Juliet*.

   (F) Brandi is an actress.
   (G) Brandi only likes Shakespearean plays.
   (H) *Romeo and Juliet* is a comedy.
   (J) Brandi's favorite role is Juliet.

5. The film crew caught Andy's fancy dribbling on videotape. It played on the eleven o'clock news program. Kristen saw it, but Kelsay couldn't stay awake that late.

   (A) Kelsay is too young to stay up until 11:00.
   (B) Kelsay had to watch Andy on tape.
   (C) Andy is a professional basketball player.
   (D) Kelsay didn't watch the eleven o'clock news that night.

6. Otto has seven siblings. Three of them are boys, and four of them are girls. He still keeps in touch with all of them, and they all visit their mother and father on holidays.

   (F) Otto is extremely organized.
   (G) Otto's family has four sons.
   (H) All seven children in Otto's family visit their parents.
   (J) Otto's family is very religious.

7. Cathy and her husband both speak Latin. They attended the same college and got married while they were in school. Now they write books together.

   (A) Cathy and her husband have a lot in common.
   (B) Cathy and her husband write books in Latin.
   (C) They both received degrees in Latin.
   (D) Their children speak Latin.

8. Tamara grew up in the eastern part of the state. After a few years in the city, she moved back to the mountains. She missed the country.

(F) Tamara does not like cities.
(G) The eastern part of Tamara's state has mountains.
(H) Tamara's family still lives in the country.
(J) The city is located in the mountains.

9. Rhonda and Debbie used to be neighbors and best friends. Rhonda moved to another state when they were in high school. Debbie moved away when she went to nursing school.

(A) Rhonda and Debbie live near each other again.
(B) Debbie is a registered nurse.
(C) Rhonda and Debbie are no longer in contact.
(D) Rhonda and Debbie are no longer neighbors.

10. Billy lives on the top floor of his apartment building. When he gets on the elevator on the first floor, he presses the button for the 11th floor. When he arrives, he walks the rest of the way up.

(F) Billy is not tall enough to reach the elevator buttons higher than 11.
(G) Billy is trying to get more exercise.
(H) The elevator in Billy's building does not go past the 11th floor.
(J) Billy's building has more than 11 stories.

STOP

IF YOU FINISH BEFORE TIME IS UP, CHECK OVER YOUR WORK ON THIS TEST ONLY. DO NOT GO ON TO THE NEXT TEST UNTIL THE SIGNAL IS GIVEN.

TEST 6   READING AND LANGUAGE ARTS

#1–40   *40 minutes*

DIRECTIONS: For questions 1–40, read each passage and the questions following that passage. Find the answer.

PASSAGE FOR QUESTIONS 1–4

The outbreak of World War II brought about changes at all levels of American society. Young men from all over the states, fresh from school and farms, enlisted to serve their country in the war abroad—often losing their lives in the process. Even those not allowed to join the military found ways to contribute to the war effort. Retirees and those unable to serve for a variety of physical reasons manned amateur ham radios, monitoring radio waves for new information. Housewives contributed to the war effort by growing their own food in "victory gardens" and by staining their legs with coffee and tea to mimic the color of nylon stockings—sacrificing the actual nylon to the production of needed war supplies. By 1943, even 16-year-old females got a chance to get involved. Dubbed "gunpowder girls," these young women performed various duties for the military. These jobs ranged from painting aircraft wings with "dope," a thick, noxious liquid that protected them from rain and snow, to tearing apart mangled plane engines.

The demands that World War II made on American society forced young people to grow up fast and to shoulder responsibilities they hadn't thought possible. Returning GIs faced quite a different home front following World War II. Society lacked the luxuries to which the soldiers had been accustomed before the war; women wore rugged clothes and carried themselves with pride, knowing they had helped the military cause in important ways. At first people tried to return to the old behavioral patterns. Fashion catalogs, for example, displayed frilly, feminine clothes for women to wear as they returned to their domestic chores of raising children and cooking hot meals. But Rosie the Riveter, and those like her who had manned the home front, resisted returning to the roles of wife, nursemaid, and cook. Few of those who had experienced the satisfaction of doing a demanding job well and earning a fair wage could peaceably allow themselves to be so <u>constrained</u> again.

1. Which of the following would be the best title for this selection?

   (A) Uncle Sam Wants YOU to Contribute
   (B) 1001 Tips for Old Coffee
   (C) Rosie the Riveter Unriveted by Domestic Duties
   (D) Women: Dutiful in All Ways

2. All but which of the following appears in the reading passage above as an example of a job that nonmilitary people could do to contribute to the World War II cause?

   (F) monitoring radio waves to keep aware of current events
   (G) growing a victory garden to provide cheap but nutritious food
   (H) staining one's legs with coffee to save nylon
   (J) walking instead of driving to save gas

3. What kind of publication would print this article?

   (A) *Glamour Magazine*
   (B) *National Geographic*
   (C) *Popular Science*
   (D) *Tiger Beat*

4. Based on the use of the word in the passage, what is the best definition of <u>constrained</u>?

   (F) free
   (G) imprisoned
   (H) adventurous
   (J) angry

PASSAGE FOR QUESTIONS 5–8

American society, hot to try any new method for staying slim (other than a sensible diet and increased exercise), finds itself taken with a new nutritional fad—the low-carb, high-protein diet. But some doctors maintain that such diets are not successful at helping the dieter maintain long-term weight loss. These doctors also point out that such diets are especially dangerous for young kids.

Modern nutritionists debate over what is the cause of American obesity. On the one hand, some claim that genetics are to blame; they say that some people are simply predisposed toward fatness. On the other hand, some claim that individual choice is to blame; they say that if people simply made better nutritional and activity choices, they wouldn't be overweight. Neither choice is entirely satisfying. Focusing on individual responsibility makes it easier to blame people for their own well-being and allows those with self control a certain smug satisfaction. But focusing the debate on genetics brings up uncomfortable implications elsewhere—like whether or not certain populations are genetically more adept at athletics or dancing or intelligence.

The question will probably never be settled until a reliable set of statistics can be generated. So long as we study the question of "nature vs. nurture" by studying children in their domestic situations, being reared by their biological parents, scientists won't be able to distinguish which factors are constant and which are not. Perhaps the best way to answer the question would be to monitor how <u>adoptive</u> children mature and record their level of obesity. Then we could compare the results to the fitness level of the biological parents. Such a study would be expensive—and require scientists to have access to adoptive information (which is currently illegal)—but might finally answer our questions regarding weight.

5. Which of the following statements is true for this author?

   (A) Problems like obesity clearly stem from lack of self-discipline and issues of free will.
   (B) Problems like obesity clearly stem from genetic codes that predetermine our lives.
   (C) Problems like obesity stem from a combination of free will and genetic tendency.
   (D) We cannot, at this stage of human development, determine exactly whether free will or genetic tendency causes obesity.

6. Why did the author write this piece?

   (F) to document the history of the debate over whether free will or genetic predetermination rules human behavior
   (G) to confuse the debate over free will vs. genetics with unnecessary detail
   (H) to suggest a way that the debate of free will vs. genetics might be resolved
   (J) to outline several stances by authority figures that contribute to the recurring debate over free will vs. genetic predisposition

7. Which of the following is the best definition of <u>adoptive</u>?

    (A) able to adapt well to new situations
    (B) adults who adopt children into their household
    (C) children who are adopted into a household
    (D) being good at a skill

8. Which of the following is a claim made in the course of this paper?

    (F) People who exercise a lot and eat very little tend to gain the most weight.
    (G) A high-carb, high-protein diet is fast becoming the diet most recommended by doctors.
    (H) People who exercise a lot and eat nutritiously always maintain a healthy weight.
    (J) A low-carb, high-protein diet is dangerous for kids.

PASSAGE FOR QUESTIONS 9–12

For a long time, publishers have tried to provide high-quality reading material for readers aged 13–18. This has proven to be an unsurprisingly difficult task given all the competition, ranging from hula hoops in the 1950s to roller skates in the 1970s to DVDs and video games offered by 21st century popular culture. One option marketers have tried is hiring new authors to create age- and values-appropriate texts that cater to modern tastes; currently such authors as J. K. Rowling, author of the ever popular Harry Potter series, serve up literary works designed to fit this <u>niche</u>.

Nevertheless, marketers have learned that one does not always have to reinvent the wheel. Sometimes one just has to give it a new coat of paint.

Recently the publishers of old favorites like Nancy Drew and the Hardy Boys have <u>gotten out their paint brushes</u>. Originally published by the Edward R. Stratemeyer syndicate, the Nancy Drew and Hardy Boy series have always tried to provide wholesome, PG-rated entertainment that taught good moral values through the actions of admirable and age-appropriate heros. These texts, written since the 1930s by a series of ghost writers, continue to be produced today. Until the 2000s, the main differences among these texts has come in the form of fashion and historical details. Nancy Drew, for example, is still 18, strawberry-blonde, and dating Ned Nickerson—but she now wears designer jeans and cool sweaters rather than neat dresses with white collars, and she volunteers for animal rights rallies rather than running the local Meals-on-Wheels program. Producers of the Hardy Boys, however, have allowed the series to "pump up the excitement" even more. In book one of the updated version, Joe Hardy's girlfriend becomes the victim of a fatal car bombing.

9. The main idea of this reading passage would be _____.

    (A) to show how kids are getting bored with old-fashioned children's books

    (B) to show how writers, because they recycle old material, are not as clever and creative as they used to be.

    (C) to show how marketers have reacted to changing literary taste by updating old favorites from previous decades.

    (D) to show that people still enjoy pastimes like hula hoops and roller skates despite how long ago they were invented.

10. How, according to the reading passage above, does Joe Hardy's girlfriend die?

    (F) strangled at the movie theater

    (G) blown up at an animal rights rally

    (H) victim of a car bombing

    (J) poisoned during her Meals-on-Wheels job

11. What does the author of this piece mean when s/he uses the expression "gotten out their paint brushes"?

    (A) These old books got new cover art but left the stories the same in order to win over new audiences and keep old fans.

    (B) The publishers and marketers of the Nancy Drew and Hardy Boys series have begun updating old material in hopes of capturing a new audience.

    (C) Many publishers and markets have decided to change professions.

    (D) The publishers and marketers of the Nancy Drew and Hardy Boys series have decided to reject old formulas in favor of concentrated additions of immorality and violence.

12. Based on the use of the word in the passage above, which of the following is the best definition of niche?

    (F) market

    (G) genre

    (H) notch

    (J) tires

DIRECTIONS: The following student essay can be improved. Read it and answer the questions that follow.

(1) My father has alot of old Hardy Boys books down in the basement. (2) I like reading them. (3) They represent a more innocent time. (4) The boys don't have to worry about terrorist bombs; their more concerned with finding gold doubloons or following a secret passageway. (5) And you can always tell who the villains are because they always drive black sedans.

13. What is the best way to write the first sentence?

   (A) My father has a lot of old Hardy Boys books down in the basement.
   (B) My father has a lot of old, Hardy Boys books down in the basement.
   (C) My father have a lot of old Hardy Boys books down in the basement.
   (D) My father he has alot of old Hardy Boys books down in the basement.

14. What is the best way to combine sentences 2 and 3?

   (F) I like reading them unless they represent a more innocent time.
   (G) I like reading them, moreover, they represent a more innocent time.
   (H) I like reading them because they represent a more innocent time.
   (J) I like reading them, representing a more innocent time than they do.

15. What is the best way to write this section of sentence 4?

   (A) Their more concerned, concerning finding gold doubloons and secret passageways.
   (B) They're more concerned with finding gold doubloons and secret passageways.
   (C) Finding gold doubloons and secret passageways is something about which they are more concerned.
   (D) They're most concerned with finding gold doubloons than with secret passageways.

16. What is the best concluding sentence for this paragraph?

   (F) They seem a bit corny, but I really enjoy them.
   (G) I don't know why my father kept all of those old books.
   (H) The Hardy Boys books were published by the Stratemeyer syndicate.
   (J) My mother has a lot of Nancy Drew books, too.

17. Which of the following sentences is written correctly?

   (A) Nancy Drew originally drove a red roadster, however, when the book was revised, it was changed into a convertible.
   (B) The Hardy brothers owned a convertible, of course, as well as twin motorcycles.
   (C) There friend Chet Morton owned a yellow jalopy that he nicknamed "The Queen".
   (D) The villains always seemed to drive black sedans; they must of all shopped at the same dealership.

PASSAGE FOR QUESTIONS 18–23

Few would deny that American society craves things that are new, fast, and exciting. One such example is auto racing. But as the media reports increasing numbers of fatalities and injuries due to such activities, the demand for more rigorous safety regulations increases just as fast as public interest in such sports.

NASCAR's research and development facilities in North Carolina are trying to keep up with the safety trend as best they can. They have produced spectacular changes in car safety design just since 2001. Race tracks now provide steel-and-foam cushioning around the track walls that better absorb impact. The cars themselves have benefited from increased R&D. Cars now come equipped with escape hatches through which drivers can wriggle if their side exits get blocked or crushed. Air filters that remove carbon monoxide from cockpits are now <u>SOP</u>. Cars also carry black boxes, just like the ones in airplanes, that record crash characteristics—like G-forces that can be studied following impact. And cars use Kevlar straps to keep wheels from flying off and causing collateral damage to other racers during crashes. While racecars can never be 100 percent safe, they can always be a little bit safer than they were last year.

18. What would be the best title for the above reading selection?

   (F) Relationship between NASCAR and Military Equipment Explored
   (G) Technology Innovations at NASCAR Move at Sonic Speed
   (H) The Dangers of Carbon Monoxide
   (J) Speed First, Safety Second

19. Which of the following relationships is substantiated by the passage?

   (A) NASCAR vehicles are like airplanes because of the equipment they carry.
   (B) NASCAR vehicles are like military vehicles because of their bullet-proof armor.
   (C) NASCAR vehicles are like LA-Z-Boy recliners because of their use of steel-and-foam cushioning at the neck.
   (D) NASCAR vehicles are like houses because they are both totally safe.

20. What does the author mean by using the acronym <u>SOP</u>?

   (F) Security Operating Procedures
   (G) Standard Operating Procedure
   (H) Safe Operating Practice
   (J) Scope Of Practice

21. According to the passage, since when have the changes discussed above taken place?

   (A) 2000
   (B) 2001
   (C) 2003
   (D) 2004

22. According to the passage, what is removed from the cockpits of NASCAR vehicles?

   (F) carbon dioxide
   (G) oxygen
   (H) carbon monoxide
   (J) steel

23. Choose the sentence that is written correctly.

   (A) After an accident, the black box contained important data.
   (B) The wheels of a NASCAR vehicle is designed not to fly off.
   (C) Every design improvement affects the dynamics of racing.
   (D) Racing fans want innovation, adrenaline, and to feel speed.

DIRECTIONS: Read the following paragraph and answer the questions that follow.

PASSAGE FOR QUESTIONS 24–26

The idea that automobiles were the exclusive playthings of the wealthy ended in 1908. In that year, Henry Ford, the American industrialist and founder of the Ford Motor Company, successfully applied the principles of mass production to the manufacture of automobiles. His Model T car (nicknamed the "Tin Lizzie" or the "Flivver") was the first automobile built on an assembly line with interchangeable parts (available "in any color—so long as it's black").

24. What is the best way to write the opening sentence?

   (F) The idea that automobiles were the exclusive playthings of the wealthy ended in 1908.
   (G) Automobiles, as the exclusive playthings of the wealthy, is an idea that ended in 1908.
   (H) In 1908, the automobile as wealthy plaything ended.
   (J) Before 1908, the automobile was a wealthy plaything; after that date, this ends.

25. What is the best conclusion to this paragraph?

   (A) Henry Ford invented the assembly line.
   (B) This lowered the cost enough to make the car available to the general public.
   (C) This led to the development of NASCAR.
   (D) Black must have been a popular color.

26. Which of the following sentences is written correctly?

   (F) The success of Henry Ford's assembly line delighted many people but it frightened many others.
   (G) Some people feared that growing technology would deprive people of their identities.
   (H) The novel, *Brave New World*, explores the consequences of this technological system.
   (J) In the book, the factories of the future creates people on an assembly line.

PASSAGE FOR QUESTIONS 27–30

The popular culture produced by a society reflects the fears, passions, and obsessions of that society. In the 1950s, for example, the increase of technology in popular culture, especially the use of <u>standardized</u> procedures like the Xeroxing machine and the assembly line, led to a rise in science fiction that warned against losing one's identity to a machine. Stories like *Invasion of the Body Snatchers*, for example, took hold of the nation's imagination; the story told of fear of being replaced and no one either noticing the difference or, worse, not caring about the replacement.

Again, in the 1970s, we see pop culture reflecting the values of society. The 1970s encouraged people to find a passion for things that represented the country or, better yet, other cultures. Beads, flowers, face painting, and musical references to setting up a community on a farm where people could share life in peace and communistic harmony abound then. Such references mirror the Hippies' cultural revolt against "<u>straight</u>" society's respect for paying taxes, obeying the rules, going to war, and acting conservatively.

Now, in the 21st century, we can detect the same pattern forming again. Current mass markets show a cultural obsession with reality TV—shows that mirror real life in all its boring realism . . .

27. The author's use of the word <u>standardized</u> can be best defined as meaning _____.

   (A) automated
   (B) streamlined
   (C) fearful
   (D) efficient

28. The author makes the point that popular culture mirrors cultural beliefs. Based on that fact, the author might agree with which of the following statements?

   (F) People in the 1930s, which followed hard on the Great Depression, valued expensive home furnishings.
   (G) People in the 1940s, which were engrossed in the military campaigns of World War II, were not patriotic.
   (H) People in the 1960s, with its fear of prolonged military commitment in Vietnam, respected the government.
   (J) People in the 1980s, with its love of technology, revered jewelry made from used technology (like O-rings and car gaskets).

29. The author's use of the word <u>straight</u> is not typical; which definition fits the author's use of this word?

   (A) legal
   (B) efficient
   (C) normal
   (D) sober

30. Which of the following restates a fact discussed in the reading?

   (F) People in the 1950s watched lots of movies.
   (G) People in the 1970s liked being in nature and wore things to remind them of nature.
   (H) People are always aware of fads and popular trends in their world.
   (J) People currently find themselves obsessed with nature, just like in the 1970s.

PASSAGE FOR QUESTIONS 31–35

As of 2004, college <u>remediation</u> classes cost the state $15 million; 28 percent of the student body signed up for remedial classes in math, reading, and writing. Why, in this modern era of public education, should this be the case?

Some experts say that the problem is the student, but far more of the experts point the finger at the educational system itself. They call our current K-12 programs old-fashioned, unchallenging, and unable to prepare students for college. The problem is due to not only lack of student performance or lack of teacher expertise but also to an unwillingness to treat high school kids as the adults they are.

Senior year, according to popular wisdom, is <u>going the way of the dinosaur</u>. Finished with the core graduation requirements, struck by senioritis, and demoralized by turning 18 without gaining what they perceive as the proper respect, students lose their motivation to learn. And, perhaps the senior year *should* be sacrificed to social Darwinism. After all, grades earned past the fall semester of the senior year very rarely count toward any concrete goal; GPAs needed for entrance exams or scholarships are typically turned in by November of the fall semester. About the only way that spring semester grades can hurt a graduating senior is by causing them to fail a core requirement class—like English or math.

Whatever the reason, kids aren't paying attention to senior year classes, which severely weakens their academic skills by the time they enter the college scene. But try telling that to a graduating senior. After 11 years of (in some cases) hard work, they feel entitled to a rest—and are willing to risk their initial success at university to do so.

31. What does the author mean by the use of the word <u>remediation</u>?

   (A) redo
   (B) revise
   (C) resubmit
   (D) reevaluate

32. What percentage of the student body enrolled in remedial classes their first year at college?

   (F) 26 percent
   (G) 27 percent
   (H) 28 percent
   (J) 29 percent

33. With which of the following statements would the author most likely agree?

   (A) The education system should remain as it is.
   (B) The education system should be modified.
   (C) The education system should be done away with.
   (D) We cannot tell based on the tone of the passage.

34. What does the author mean when s/he uses the phrase <u>going the way of the dinosaur</u>?

   (F) Something is evolving into a new form.
   (G) Something is becoming extinct.
   (H) Something is becoming a habit.
   (J) Something is being promoted.

35. What would be a good title for this passage?

   (A) Why Johnny Won't Read
   (B) From College to High School: Ten Steps Backwards
   (C) How to Survive in College
   (D) Saving Senior Year

PASSAGE FOR QUESTIONS 36–40

Jeremy often told his mother about the bad little boy at school. His name was Scott. And was Scott terrible! He ate chalk. He scribbled on other kids' papers. He even hit girls. He spent a long time in the corner or in "time out."

Every day Jeremy came home with a new story about Scott. Today, Scott unrolled all the rolls of toilet paper in the school bathroom. This time, he stepped on the flag. Jeremy's mother came to look forward to the time, every day after school, when Jeremy would tell her the latest bad news. They would laugh together over what Scott had done—and <u>speculate</u> as to what Scott would do next.

One day Jeremy's mother went to the school for a parent-teacher conference. She was surprised when the teacher sat down, a worried look on her face. "I'm a little concerned," said the teacher, "why you haven't answered any of my written notes or telephone messages."

"What notes? What telephone messages?" said Jeremy's mother.

36. Why is the teacher likely having the parent-teacher conference with Jeremy's mother?

   (F) to praise Jeremy for being such a good student
   (G) to ask Jeremy's mother to volunteer for a field trip
   (H) to discuss why Jeremy is acting so terribly at school
   (J) in response to a note Jeremy's mother has sent previously

37. What does the author mean by using the word <u>speculate</u>?

   (A) watch
   (B) argue about
   (C) guess
   (D) list

38. Where might you find this text published?

   (F) an elementary school reader
   (G) a romance novel
   (H) a study guide for *Gone with the Wind*
   (J) the comics section of the newspaper

39. What did Scott do in school?

   (A) flushed the toilet a million times
   (B) stepped on the American flag
   (C) stole money
   (D) pulled Jeremy's hair

40. What can you infer about Jeremy?

   (F) He is afraid of Scott.
   (G) Scott makes Jeremy angry.
   (H) He is Scott.
   (J) He thinks that Scott is funny.

STOP

IF YOU FINISH BEFORE TIME IS UP, CHECK OVER YOUR WORK ON THIS TEST ONLY. DO NOT GO ON TO THE NEXT TEST UNTIL THE SIGNAL IS GIVEN.

TEST 7   MATHEMATICS

> DIRECTIONS: Select the best answer from the given choices.

1. What does the digit 6 represent in the number 346,782?

   (A) tens   (B) hundreds
   (C) thousands   (D) ten-thousands

2. Of the numbers 911, 34, 8, 243, and 274, which is greater than 548 but less than 8,243?

   (F) 274   (G) 8,234
   (H) 243   (J) 911

3. Simplify the following powers and then select the correct answer.

   (a) 5^2 (b) 2^5 (c) 2^3

   (A) a > b or c > a
   (B) c = a or b < c
   (C) c > b and a = b
   (D) b < a or c < b

4. If $a < 0$, list the following terms, from smallest to largest: $a, a^2, a^3, -a, -a^2, a^0$.

   (F) $-a^2 > a^2 > -a > a^3 > a^0 > a$
   (G) $a^3 < -a^2 < a < a^0 < -a < a^2$
   (H) $a^2 < a^0 < -a < a < a^3 < -a^2$
   (J) $a^3 < a^0 < a^2 < a < -a^2 < -a$

5. The Aztec Chemical Company wants to repackage 1,159 ounces of one of their chemicals into one-pound containers. How many ounces remain after all the chemicals are repackaged?

   Sixteen ounces equals one pound.

   (A) 7 ounces   (B) 48 ounces
   (C) 64 ounces   (D) 72 ounces

6. Malcolm filled a bag with some cashew nuts. He then added 2 ounces of cashews and weighed the total, which was 13 ounces. Select the correct answer from the following choices.

   (F) The original weight of the cashews was more than 5 times the weight of the added cashews.
   (G) The final weight of the cashews was less than 6 times the weight of the added cashews.
   (H) The original weight of the cashews was less than 4 times the weight of the added cashews.
   (J) The final weight of the cashews was less than 4 times the weight of the added cashews.

7. The temperature is 90 degrees at 3 P.M. If it decreases by 40 percent by midnight and then increases by 26 percent by 10 A.M. the next day, what is the temperature at 10:01 A.M.? Round off to the nearest degree.

   (A) 68   (B) 54   (C) 66   (D) 42

8. What number multiplied by 8 is 18 more than 5 times the number?

   (F) 3   (G) 6   (H) 7   (J) 8

9. If $x = 4/5$, $y = 2/3$ and $z = \sqrt{3}$, find the value of $10x - 9y - 4z^2$.

   (A) –6   (B) –8   (C) –10   (D) 4

10. If a is a negative integer and b is a positive integer, which of the following statements is true?

    (F) $a^2 < 0$ (G) $b^2 < 0$
       (H) $a^2 + b^2 > 0$ (J) $ab^2 > 0$

11. Simplify $-2|5| \cdot 3 \ |-4|$.

    (A) –120   (B) 100
       (C) –80   (D) 140

12. The height of the front door in a blueprint of a one-family house measures $\frac{3}{4}''$. If the actual door is 8 feet tall, what is the ratio of the blueprint to the actual dimensions of the house?

    (F) 1/128   (G) 2/5
       (H) 3/32   (J) 1/64

13. If a is a positive even integer, and b and c are the following consecutive positive integers, which of the following statements is false?

    (A) ab is even   (B) $a + b$ is odd
       (C) ac is odd   (D) $b + c$ is odd

14. Find the measure of the angle between the hour hand and the minute hand when a clock reads 9:05. Select the best answer.

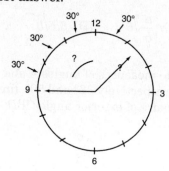

    (F) 90°   (G) 150°
       (H) 120°   (J) 110°

15. $\overleftrightarrow{AB}$ and $\overleftrightarrow{CD}$ intersect at point E. If m$\angle DEA = 87°$ and m$\angle CEB = 2y + 19$, find the value of y.

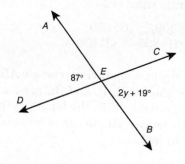

    (A) 34°   (B) 23°
       (C) 19°   (D) 65°

16. If $ABCD$ is a square, which statement is false?

    (F) Angle B is a right angle.
    (G) The measure of angle B equals the measure of angle C.
    (H) The measure of angle B plus the measure of angle A equals 180°.
    (J) BC is perpendicular to AD.

17. Let k represent the length of a rectangle. Represent the perimeter when the width is 8 less than the length.

    (A) $6k - 6$ (B) $2k + 16$
       (C) $4k - 10$ (D) $4k - 16$

18. Each of the equal sides of an isosceles triangle is 7 and its base is 2 more than the base of an equilateral triangle. If the perimeters of the two triangles are equal, find a side of the equilateral triangle.

    (F) 8   (G) 5   (H) 9   (J) 6

19. The areas of a rectangle and a square are equal. If one side of the square is twice the width of the rectangle and the length of the rectangle is 16, find the width of the rectangle.

    (A) 6   (B) 10   (C) 4   (D) 8

20. The volume of a sphere enclosed in a cube is approximately 1/2 the volume of the cube. Estimate the volume of a sphere enclosed in a cube, each of whose sides is 10.8.

    (F) 300   (G) 550
      (H) 800   (J) 650

21. In the accompanying triangle *ABC*, the lengths of *AC* and *BC* are 5 and 7, respectively. Find the length of the hypotenuse, *AB*, to the nearest tenth of an inch.

    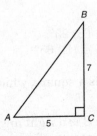

    (A) 7.4   (B) 4.5   (C) 8.6   (D) 5.8

22. In a triangle, the sum of any two sides is always greater than the third side. Select the best choice to represent the three sides of a triangle.

    (F) 3, 4, 7   (G) 4, 5, 8
      (H) 5, 6, 12   (J) 10, 5, 5

23. Round off 1,147,690 to the nearest thousand.

    (A) 1,147,200   (B) 1,150,000
      (C) 1,148,000   (D) 1,149,000

24. Change 0.054% to a decimal.

    (F) 0.0054   (G) 5.4
      (H) 0.054   (J) 0.00054

25. Find the value of the expression $3rs - 2t$ when $r = 2$, $s = 3$ and $t = 4$.

    (A) 4   (B) 6   (C) 8   (D) 10

26. Simplify $-4(-2)^3$, and choose the correct answer.

    (F) +32   (G) −32
      (H) +24   (J) −16

27. Of the following expressions, which is the smallest?

    (A) $5 \times 3 - (2 + 7)$
    (B) $5(3) - 48/6$
    (C) $14 - 5 + 30/6$
    (D) $18/2 - 3(4 - 6) + 54/9$

28. If we let U = the set of all countries of South America, P = {Uruguay, Chile, Brazil}, and Q = {Argentina, Columbia, Paraguay}, find the intersection of P and Q.

    (F) Paraguay   (G) null set
      (H) Brazil   (J) Columbia

29. Simplify $\dfrac{a\sqrt{42}}{b\sqrt{7}}$

    (A) $\dfrac{a}{b}\sqrt{7}$ (B) $\sqrt{\dfrac{6a}{7b}}$

    (C) $\dfrac{a}{b}\sqrt{6}$ (D) $6a\sqrt{b}$

30. If the measures of angles A and C are respectively 32° and 59°, find the measure of exterior angle *CBD*.

    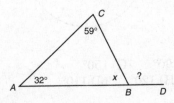

    (F) 59°   (G) 91°   (H) 89°   (J) 98°

31. *O* is the center of the circle.

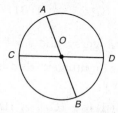

Which of the following statements is true?

(A) $AB > CD$
(B) $OC < OB$
(C) $AB - OB = OD$
(D) $CD - OB < OD$

32. In the two diagrams, which of the following statements is true?

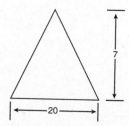

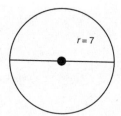

(F) Three fifths of the area of the triangle is greater than the area of the circle.
(G) The area of the triangle is greater than half the area of the circle.
(H) One half the area of the circle is equal to the area of the triangle.
(J) The area of the circle is greater than twice the area of the triangle.

33. The circle graph on the right indicates the types of goods a factory produces. If the factory received $30,000,000 in orders last year, which of the following statements is true?

(A) The military orders exceeded the airplane orders by more than $5,000,000.
(B) The difference between the bicycle and the auto orders was less than $3,000,000.
(C) Bicycle and auto orders together were equal to $15,000,000.
(D) Airplane orders were $6,000,000 less than bicycle orders.

34. An urn contains 4 blue, 3 green, 5 white, and 6 red marbles. What is the probability of selecting a green marble without looking?

(F) 2/9   (G) 5/18
   (H) 1/6   (J) 1/3

35. The bar graph represents the average temperature in Alaska during the indicated months. Check the graph and then select the correct answer.

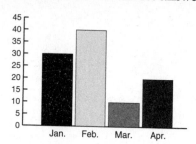

(A) Mar. + Apr. = 60
(B) Jan. − Mar. = 20
(C) Feb. − Mar. > 40
(D) Apr. + Feb. > 50

36. Michelle spends $t + 4$ hours per day watching television. Carmen spends t hours and Henry watches television $t - 2$ hours per day. Find the average number of hours of TV time for the three students.

    (F) $(3t + 2)/3$ (G) $(4t/3) + 2$
    (H) $2t + 4$ (J) $(4t - 2)/3$

37. Arrange in order, from smallest to largest: 24 ounces, 0.8 of a kilogram, and 1.09 pounds?

    There are 16 ounces in one pound and 1 kilogram weighs 2.2 pounds.

    (A) 1.2 pounds $< 1\frac{1}{4}$ pounds < 24 ounces

    (B) 1.2 pounds < 24 ounces $< 1\frac{1}{4}$ pounds

    (C) 24 ounces < 1.2 pounds $< 1\frac{1}{4}$ pounds

    (D) $1\frac{1}{4}$ pounds < 24 ounces < 1.2 pounds

38. Estimate 8% of 232.

    (F) 50   (G) 23   (H) 31   (J) 47

39. For all integers x and y, $x \# y = \dfrac{x+y}{2}$.
    If $5 \# y$ is an integer, what is a possible value for y?

    (A) 2   (B) 6   (C) 7   (D) 4

40. Find the coordinates of the point formed by the intersection of a line parallel to the y-axis and two units to the right of it and a second line parallel to the x-axis and 4 units above it.

    (F) (4,2)   (G) (2,4)
    (H) (0,4)   (J) (2,3)

STOP

IF YOU FINISH BEFORE TIME IS UP, CHECK OVER YOUR WORK ON THIS TEST ONLY.

Answers to Practice Cooperative Admissions Examination 2

TEST 1   SEQUENCES

1. D	6. G	11. B	16. H
2. F	7. C	12. J	17. B
3. C	8. G	13. A	18. J
4. J	9. D	14. J	19. A
5. B	10. F	15. C	20. H

TEST 2   ANALOGIES

1. C	6. G	11. A	16. F
2. J	7. B	12. H	17. C
3. A	8. F	13. B	18. H
4. G	9. B	14. H	19. C
5. D	10. J	15. D	20. J

TEST 3   QUANTITATIVE REASONING

1. D	6. H	11. B	16. H
2. F	7. A	12. F	17. A
3. B	8. J	13. D	18. J
4. H	9. C	14. G	19. B
5. A	10. H	15. D	20. F

TEST 4   VERBAL REASONING—WORDS

1. A	6. G	11. D	16. G
2. G	7. A	12. H	17. C
3. B	8. F	13. A	18. G
4. G	9. B	14. J	19. A
5. B	10. J	15. B	20. G

TEST 5   VERBAL REASONING—CONTEXT

1. D	3. D	5. D	7. A	9. D
2. H	4. F	6. G	8. G	10. J

TEST 6   READING AND LANGUAGE ARTS

1. C	11. B	21. B	31. A
2. J	12. F	22. H	32. H
3. B	13. A	23. C	33. D
4. G	14. H	24. F	34. G
5. D	15. B	25. B	35. A
6. H	16. F	26. G	36. H
7. C	17. B	27. A	37. C
8. J	18. G	28. J	38. F
9. C	19. A	29. C	39. B
10. H	20. G	30. G	40. H

TEST 7   MATHEMATICS

1. C	11. A	21. C	31. C
2. J	12. F	22. G	32. J
3. D	13. C	23. C	33. C
4. G	14. H	24. J	34. H
5. A	15. A	25. D	35. D
6. F	16. J	26. F	36. F
7. A	17. D	27. A	37. A
8. G	18. F	28. G	38. G
9. B	19. C	29. C	39. C
10. H	20. J	30. G	40. G

Answer Explanations

TEST 1   SEQUENCES

1. (**D**) The circle moves to the right, one position at a time.

2. (**F**) In each succeeding diagram, the arrow turns 90° counterclockwise.

3. (**C**) The objects move left, one at a time.

4. (**J**) The objects are arranged in terms of size: small, large, large, small.

5. (**B**) In the six-box rectangle, the X moves down one column and then up the next column and down again. In the square, the perimeter is darkened, in order from the inner figure to the outer figure.

6. (**G**) The dark line is rotated counterclockwise, first two units, then one unit.

7. (**C**) In each succeeding diagram, the shaded box moves three units counterclockwise.

8. (**G**) D is always the middle letter. The other letters are in ascending alphabetical order.

9. (**D**) One letter is skipped between each letter in the sequence.

10. (**F**) One letter is skipped between the first and second letters in each group and two letters are skipped between the second and third letters in each group.

11. (**B**) One letter is skipped in backwards alphabetical order.

12. (**J**) The Roman numerals are descending by 3.

13. (**A**) R is the middle letter in each group. The other letters are in alphabetical order.

14. (**J**) The numbers are in the order x, x^2, x^3, where x is a whole number.

15. (**C**) To get to the second number in each group, divide the first number by 4. To get to the third number, divide the second number by 4.

16. (**H**) To find the second number in each group, subtract 2 from the first number. To find the third number, multiply the second by 2.

17. (**B**) To get to the succeeding number in each group, multiply the preceding number by 3.

18. (**J**) Subtract 4 from each preceding number.

19. (**A**) In order to find the second number in each group, add 2 to the first number. To get to the third number, subtract 1 from the second.

20. (**H**) One letter is skipped between the first and second letters in each group and two letters are skipped between the second and third letters in each group. The subscripts in each succeeding group are decreased by 2.

TEST 2   ANALOGIES

1. (**C**) Scissors is to hair as lawnmower is to grass. Scissors cut hair, and a lawnmower cuts grass.

2. (**J**) Musician is to band as bowler is to team. A musician is a part of a band, and a bowler is part of a team.

3. (**A**) Leash is to dog as ball and chain is to convict. A leash restrains a dog as a ball and chain restrains a convict.

4. (**G**) Stop sign is to a car as skull and crossbones is to a ship. A stop sign signals stop to a driver, and a skull and crossbones signals a pirate ship to a seaman.

5. (**D**) Foot is to shoe as head is to helmet. A shoe protects the foot, and a helmet protects the head.

6. (**G**) Car is to road as ship is to ocean. A car drives along a road, and a ship sails across the ocean.

7. (**B**) Doctor is to patient as mechanic is to car wreck. A doctor heals a patient, and a mechanic repairs a car.

8. (**F**) Squirrel is to nuts as shark is to fish. Squirrels eat nuts, and sharks eat fish.

9. (**B**) Cloud is to rain as cow is to butter. A cloud produces rain, and a cow produces butter.

10. **(J)** Clothespin is to wash as belt is to jeans. A clothespin holds up clothes, and a belt supports jeans.

11. **(A)** Turkey is to Pilgrim as reindeer is to Santa Claus. Turkeys and Pilgrims are associated together, and reindeer and Santa Claus are associated together.

12. **(H)** Writer is to book as singer is to record. A writer notes his thoughts in a book as a singer records her words on a CD.

13. **(B)** Money is to happiness as car collision is to headache. We usually think money brings happiness, and a car collision brings headaches.

14. **(H)** Stool is to kitchen as beach chair is to beach. A stool is found in a kitchen, and a beach chair is found on the beach.

15. **(D)** Scale is to person as meter is to light bulb. People measure themselves on a scale, and a meter measures the electricity used by a light bulb.

16. **(F)** Monkey is to banana as bear is to honey. Monkeys eat bananas, and bears eat honey.

17. **(C)** Electron is to electric wire as fish is to water. Electrons travel through an electric wire, and fish travel through water.

18. **(H)** Blanket is to bed as hairpiece is to bald head. A blanket covers a bed, and a hairpiece covers a bald head.

19. **(C)** Pot cover is to pot as roof is to house. A pot cover covers a pot, and a roof covers a house.

20. **(J)** Hand is to piano as mouth is to trumpet. A hand plays the piano, and the mouth plays the trumpet.

TEST 3   QUANTITATIVE REASONING

1. **(D)** Subtract 3 from each given number: $5 - 3 = 2$.

2. **(F)** Multiply each given number by 2: $6 \times 2 = 12$.

3. **(B)** Divide each given number by 3: $6/3 = 2$.

4. **(H)** Multiply each given number by 9: $\frac{1}{3} \times 9 = 3$.

5. **(A)** Add $\frac{1}{2}$ to each given number:
$1\frac{1}{2} + \frac{1}{2} = 2$.

6. **(H)** Subtract 2 from each given number: $4.5 - 2 = 2.5$.

7. **(A)** Divide each given number by 2: $8/2 = 4$.

8. **(J)** One out of eight squares is dark: 1/8.

9. **(C)** Three out of six squares are dark: $3/6 = 1/2$.

10. **(H)** Two out of six squares are dark: $2/6 = 1/3$.

11. **(B)** Three out of nine squares are dark: $3/9 = 1/3$.

12. **(F)** One half of the entire figure is dark: 1/2.

13. **(D)** Two full squares plus two half-squares are dark: $2 + 2 \times \frac{1}{2} = 2 + 1 = 3$. That makes a total of three out of eight dark squares: 3/8.

14. **(G)** Four half-squares are shaded: $4 \times \frac{1}{2} = 2$. That makes a total of two out of sixteen dark squares: $2/16 = 1/8$.

15. **(D)**

1 cylinder	=	1 cube
+ 1 cylinder + 1 cube	=	+ 1 cylinder + 1 cube
2 cylinders + 1 cube	=	1 cylinder + 2 cubes

16. **(H)**

1 cube	=	2 cylinders
+ 1 cylinder	=	+ 1 cylinder
1 cube + 1 cylinder	=	3 cylinders

17. **(A)**

2 cubes	=	1 cylinder
+ 1 cylinder	=	+ 1 cylinder
2 cubes + 1 cylinder	=	2 cylinders

18. **(J)**

1 cylinder	=	3 cubes
+ 1 cube	=	+ 1 cube
1 cylinder + 1 cube	=	4 cubes

19. **(B)**

3 cylinders	= 1 cube
+ 1 cylinder	= + 1 cylinder
4 cylinders	= 1 cube + 1 cylinder

or

1 cube + 1 cylinder = 4 cylinders

20. (**F**)

1 cylinder + 1 cube	=	3 cylinders
– 1 cylinder	=	– 1 cylinder
1 cube	=	2 cylinders

TEST 4 VERBAL REASONING—WORDS

1. (**A**) A shoe does not *need* to be made of leather, nor does it need a heel or laces. The sole is the essential part of a shoe.

2. (**G**) Water is essential for a bath. You can bathe without soap or a towel, and you can bathe in other places besides a tub.

3. (**B**) A library needs books. A bookmobile does not have a building or chairs, for instance, and libraries have not always had computers.

4. (**G**) Silent movies did not have sound, obviously, and you can watch a movie at home and without popcorn. The picture is essential.

5. (**B**) While ideas are important, the pencil itself needs lead in order to write.

6. (**G**) These are all general words for recreation.

7. (**A**) These are all containers for solid items.

8. (**F**) These are all synonyms. The other choices are related, but they don't mean the same.

9. (**B**) The first three words are verbs meaning "*to* record." Only choice (B) can be a verb; the other choices are nouns meaning "*a* record."

10. (**J**) *Happy, content, pleased*, and *satisfied* are synonyms for a pleasant feeling. *Stoic* and *ambivalent* do not indicate happiness.

11. (**D**) You hear music, noise, and sound *with* your ear.

12. (**H**) The other choices are all liquids.

13. (**A**) The other choices describe something visually pleasant.

14. (**J**) *Discover* is the opposite of the other words, which indicate covering.

15. (**B**) A contrast does not necessarily indicate fighting or argument.

16. (**G**) Omnipotence is most powerful, while influence is less powerful. The strongest stopping point listed is a period.

17. (**C**) A valley is below level ground, a hill is higher than level, and a mountain is highest. The choice below zero is negative one.

18. (**G**) The top row lists countries in Europe. The bottom row lists countries in Central America.

19. (**A**) You use a key in a lock to open a door. You use a password in a field to access a computer.

20. (**G**) The top row lists types of pasta; the bottom row lists types of trees.

TEST 5 VERBAL REASONING—CONTEXT

1. (**D**) Carlo must have changed his mind. We are not told why.

2. (**H**) We can infer that being in the same homeroom is required in order to share a locker. If John and I share a locker, we must be in the same homeroom.

3. (**D**) If Mrs. Stevens hired Mrs. Hall and Mrs. Wheat, they must all work for the same organization. We don't know how they met, how they were hired, or how they may have become friends.

4. (**F**) If Brandi has appeared in many plays, then she is an actress. We are never told that she *exclusively* likes Shakespeare plays. (She especially enjoys them.) We can easily infer that *Romeo and Juliet* is not a comedy. (Brandi enjoys that play *even though* she prefers comedies.) Furthermore, we are not told that she played Juliet. (That *play* is her favorite.)

5. (**D**) All we know for certain is that Kelsay did not watch the news program that night.

6. (**G**) Otto and his three brothers comprise the four sons in the family. Choice (H) is incorrect because the family has *eight* siblings in total (including Otto).

7. (**A**) Cathy and her husband have a lot in common. However, we are never

specifically told that they share the other choices.

8. **(G)** We are told that Tamara moved *back* to the mountains. Therefore, the eastern part of her state (where she lived before) must be mountainous.

9. **(D)** We are told that these women *used* to be neighbors.

10. **(J)** If Billy must continue walking upstairs after the 11th floor, his building must have more than 11 stories. The rest of the choices *could* be true, but they are not *necessarily* true.

TEST 6 READING AND LANGUAGE ARTS

1. **(C)** The article discusses various ways in which World War II affected American society. In particular, however, the piece focuses the reader's attention on the effect the war had on women (see paragraph three). The main point of the article, as described in paragraph three, runs thus: Rosie the Riveter . . . resisted their return to the roles of wife, nursemaid, and cook." Therefore you are looking for a title that communicates this point of view. Choice A can be ruled out because it is too general a call for help, and it addresses no consequences that stem from that help. Choice B is incorrect, simply because the article discusses far more important topics than giving advice on how to use old coffee. And choice D is incorrect, because the women discussed in this piece are not dutiful—even though they love their families, they are nevertheless growing more independent.

2. **(J)** Rereading (or memory) tells you that the only statement not listed in the article as a fact is J.

3. **(B)** Of the four publications options you are given, only one targets subject matter that might address the issues of the aftereffects of World War II. *Glamour* magazine focuses on fashion and beauty tips, *Popular Science* focuses on scientific issues, and *Tiger Beat*

focuses on popular culture topics interesting to teens—for example, Brittany Spears's newest stunt. None of these subjects really fit with the topic of the article; therefore, if only through process of elimination, you can work your way to the correct answer—which is B.

4. **(G)** The final sentence of the piece sets up an opposing situation—women who have enjoyed adventure and freedom will not willingly go back to boredom. So, substitute the words for constrained and see which word fits the tone of the statement best. You will find that choice G is the best fit. (Although you might be briefly tempted by choice J, and even though many women forced to return to the domestic scene after World War II may well have been angry, the word is simply too limited to convey the author's intent.)

5. **(D)** The author strives to keep a neutral balance throughout the presentation of this piece. In fact, s/he offers a solution that s/he feels might settle the issue in a documented, reliable manner in paragraph three. So, you should reject any statements that connote an opinion or biased view of the debate. Therefore, rule out choices A and B. You might be tempted by choice C, but it is really a cop-out. The author makes it very clear that s/he thinks we simply cannot tell whether nature or nurture is stronger; hence s/he offers the solution in paragraph three.

6. **(H)** The author, as discussed in the previous question, seems to be writing primarily to present a new idea regarding how to settle the debate of nature vs. nurture. Check to see whether you can rule out the other options. Choice F is wrong; to discuss an entire history would take considerable space and more fact than this author has chosen to include. Similarly, choice J is unacceptable, since the author does not reference any claims by authority figures—indeed, the author mentions no one by name, and were s/he attempting to make points by calling our attention to authority figures, surely s/he would

have done so. Choice G is wrong, since the author is trying to make things clearer, not more confusing. The only correct answer is H.

7. **(C)** The choices here are intended to make sure you know what you're talking about. Choices A and D, for example, are trying to trick you into thinking you've read the word *adaptive* (able to change) rather than the word *adoptive*. Only choices B and C refer to adoption—the act of parents taking into their family children who are not biologically theirs. But the word *adoptive* in the reading passage is linked to the word children—so you can rule out choice B.

8. **(J)** Re-reading (or memory) proves to you that only J is discussed in the passage.

9. **(C)** Choice D may be true, but the passage does not make this clear; in fact it implies just the opposite. Choice B is not discussed—the creativity of the authors does not come into the discussion except perhaps indirectly in paragraph three when the author questions the bombing of Joe's girlfriend. Choice A is implied in the article, for if kids weren't bored with traditional reading materials, then there would be no need to update or modernize or replace them. But the article does not simply state that kids are bored and gives several examples proving that statement; the article goes on to discuss what people are doing to combat that boredom. The best answer is choice C.

10. **(H)** Re-reading (or memory) proves to you that Joe Hardy's girlfriend was indeed a victim of a car bombing, as ridiculous as that sounds.

11. **(B)** The phrase "gotten out their paint brushes" is indeed meant to convey a message—but not that writers of kids' books are suddenly turning to painting as a profession; rule out choice C. Choice A, B, and D refer to the author's discussion of how writers are adapting to changing kids' tastes. Choice A is clearly wrong, since the piece talks about changes to the plot; naturally, then, the writing has changed in addition to whatever art work has changed.

Choice D might be right, but it is such a biased opinion that we cannot be certain; I certainly feel that blowing up Joe Hardy's girlfriend shows the marketers giving in too much to the 21st-century taste for violence, but you may not—you may think it's just plain exciting, and you were tired of her character anyway. The only legitimate answer, therefore, is B.

12. **(F)** A niche can be a market and a type of tires, but the author is trying to trick you with choices G and H; genre refers to a category of book, but is not really the same thing as a niche, and giving you notch is just trying to get you to read the question incorrectly. Tires as a definition for niche simply doesn't fit, so you are left with F (and, given the context of the passage, creating or tapping into new markets makes perfect sense).

13. **(A)** This is the most direct way of writing the sentence. Choice B has an unnecessary comma between the words *old* and *Hardy*. Choice C contains an error in subject-verb agreement (My **father** has . . .), and choice D repeats the subject and uses the incorrect usage of *alot* for *a lot*.

14. **(H)** This is the only choice that clearly indicates a reason why the writer enjoys the books.

15. **(B)** This choice is the most concise. Choice A is awkward, and it uses the possessive *Their* instead of the contraction *They're* (They are). Choice C is wordy and passive. Choice D does not convey the original meaning of the sentence.

16. **(F)** This is the only sentence that reinforces the idea that the writer enjoys the books. Choice G hints that the books are not worthy of attention, and choices H and J change the topic with irrelevant information.

17. **(B)** The interrupter (*of course*) is separated correctly with commas. Choice A incorrectly uses the word *however* as a conjunction. Choice C misuses the word *There,* and it places the period outside of the quotation marks. Choice D uses the expression *must <u>of</u>* instead of *must <u>have</u>*.

18. (**G**) While you can find brief mentions of all four subjects in this piece, you must consider the degree to which they are thoroughly discussed in the selection. The author does show a slight connection between NASCAR technology and military innovation (paragraph two), but this connection is not the focus of the passage; rule out F. Clearly people find carbon monoxide a problem in car racing; otherwise, they would not have developed a device to remove it from NASCAR cockpits (paragraph two). But the dangers of CO_2 poisoning is not mentioned often enough to be considered the main point of this article either; rule out H. And the article seems to emphasize safety at all costs, so J doesn't make sense. Your best option is G.

19. (**A**) Remembering basic facts from the article will help you here; NASCAR vehicles don't carry bullet-proof armor, so rule out B; NASCAR vehicles do carry steel-and-foam cushioning at the neck, but the relationship between cars and recliners stops there. No one, even the biggest fans, would make the claim that NASCAR races are safe; rule out C and D. But you might have been interested to find out that NASCAR vehicles, like planes, carry black boxes that help determine causes of wrecks; this is the best connection available to you. The best answer is A.

20. (**G**) We have all heard the term SOP; it may surprise you that the acronym SOP can be comprised of various words. Substitute the various phrases in the sentence; the best fit is G.

21. (**B**) Re-reading (or memory) tells you that safety precautions really took off since 2001.

22. (**H**) Re-reading (or memory) tells you that now devices remove carbon monoxide gas from NASCAR cockpits.

23. (**C**) The verb *affect* is used correctly. Choice A uses a past tense verb (*contained*) after an introduction that places the time in the future. Choice B contains an error in subject-verb agreement. (It should read *The* **wheels** *are* **designed**.) Choice D contains a list that is not parallel. (The series should be all

nouns: *Racing fans want* _innovation_, _adrenaline_, *and* _speed_.)

24. (**F**) This is the only sentence without grammatical errors. Choice H sounds as if the car itself is wealthy, and choice J mixes past and present tense.

25. (**B**) The paragraph has been leading to this statement that the general public could then afford to buy cars.

26. (**G**) This sentence contains no errors. Choice F is missing a comma to separate the two independent clauses. Choice H separates a restrictive appositive with commas. (If you took out the title of the novel, the sentence would read as follows: *The novel explores the consequences of this technological system.* We wouldn't know which novel.) Choice J should read **factories** _create_.

27. (**A**) Looking again at paragraph one, you notice that the paragraph is talking about how people feared losing their jobs—and their identity—to technological advances. Therefore, check out the list of words under consideration. C describes the emotional state of some people, but it does not describe the word *procedures* in the sentence. Choices B and D both describe the term *procedures*, but they do not explain fully why either streamlined or efficient procedures might adversely affect people so badly. Besides, many types of systems can be streamlined and efficient—and not frightening. Only choice A implies precision and lack of humanity, which is the basis of the fear being discussed in paragraph one.

28. (**J**) Choices A, B, C, and D involve the description of a decade and proposed likely inference based on what the author has told you in that description. You are basically reading four cases of cause-effect relationships. However, three of these cause-effect relationships simply don't work. If a decade is forced to save money, they will not value expensive purchases (choice F); if a decade is devoted to a war, they *will* be patriotic (choice G); if a decade is fearful of a long-term military commitment, they will not respect the government forcing them to engage in the long-term

military engagement (choice H). The only correct cause-effect relationship listed is in choice J.

29. **(C)** The author's use of quotation marks surrounding the word straight in the sentences gives you a clue that the normal definition of the word does not hold true; rule out option B. Substitute the remaining choices one by one; only choice C makes sense.

30. **(G)** Re-reading (or memory) reminds you that only choice G is stated in the article.

31. **(A)** Most test takers have heard the term *remedial*, which in this case refers to non-credited classes students are forced to take to shore up weaknesses in their basic academic skills. If you are taking a remedial class, you are redoing work you should have mastered earlier. Compare this definition to the list of choices—only choice A fits that context.

32. **(H)** Re-reading (or memory) quickly tells you that you are looking for the figure of 28%.

33. **(D)** This author is striving diligently to maintain a neutral tone for the duration of this piece; however, s/he is not succeeding entirely. Looking carefully, you can identify places where the author seems to agree that something needs to be done to revamp the educational system. Therefore, the best answer is B.

34. **(G)** Dinosaurs are extinct; if something follows the example of the dinosaur ("going the way of the dinosaur"), then it, too, is going extinct. Choose choice G. Choice F talks about something changing (and possibly surviving), and choices H and J definitely refer to something surviving; these options simply do not fit the situation.

35. **(A)** Choice B makes no logical sense— you attend college after high school, so the chronological presentation of movement from college to high school in this proposed title does not make sense. The article does not give tips on how to make it in college; rule out choice C. If the article intended to make suggestions on how to make senior high school

year better, the article would contain different facts and a different (persuasive) tone; we have already stated that this selection strives (successfully) for an unbiased tone. Your only option is choice A. And since many students, lately, take remedial classes because they have chosen to be lazy during their senior year, the title makes very good sense—Why Johnny Won't (rather than Can't) Read.

36. **(H)** Paragraph two gives you a clue as to why the teacher and mother are really meeting in conference. Until this point, the reader—and the mother— have been unaware that Jeremy's stories about Scott might be hiding another sort of truth, but the teacher's comment connotes a feeling of foreshadowing that hints trouble might be coming.

37. **(C)** Substitute the words one by one and choose the one that sounds best. Choice A doesn't make much sense; choice B doesn't either—simply because the mother and son seem to be having a good time in their discussion, not arguing. Choice D is tempting—but choice C is better, and your job is to select the best option, not any old option, that works.

38. **(F)** The author gives you a story here, one that strikes you as simplistic; therefore, your best guess as to where it belongs would be in an anthology designed for beginning readers. Choice G is out; there is no mention of romance or dating. Choice H is out; the text never mentions Gone with the Wind. Choice J is out—since comics are visual and this story is not.

39. **(B)** Re-reading (or memory) tells you that Scott stepped on the flag, presumably an American flag.

40. **(H)** By the time you reach paragraph three, you have a pretty strong feeling that Jeremy is Scott. The article gives no indication that Jeremy fears Scott (F) or is angered by Scott (G); you might be tempted into choosing choice J—for clearly, Jeremy (and his mother) think Scott is funny in the beginning. But, given the foreshadowing in paragraphs two and three, you must choose H as the best response.

TEST 7   MATHEMATICS

1.
WORK

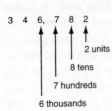

3 4 6, 7 8 2

2 units
8 tens
7 hundreds
6 thousands

ANSWER: (C)

2.
ANALYSIS
First, list the numbers in order, either ascending or descending. In this case, we'll list the numbers from largest to smallest and we'll also include 8,243 and 548.

WORK
8,243 > 911 > 548 > 243 >274 > 34 > 8

When we list them, we can clearly see that 911 is greater than 548 but less than 8,243.

ANSWER: (J)

3.
ANALYSIS
Simplify each expression and then substitute.

WORK
(a) $5^2 = 5 \cdot 5 = 25$
(b) $2^5 = 2 \cdot 2 \cdot 2 \cdot 2 \cdot 2 = 32$
(c) $2^3 = 2 \cdot 2 \cdot 2 = 8$

b < a or c < b
32 < 25 or 8 < 32 ✔

ANSWER: (D)

4.
ANALYSIS
Since $a < 0$, let's use a number less than 0 and substitute into all of the expressions.

WORK
Let $a = -2$. $a = -2$
$a^2 = (-2)(-2) = +4$
$a^3 = (-2)(-2)(-2) = -8$
$-a = -(-2) = +2$
$-a^2 = -(-2)^2 = -(-2)(-2) = -(+4) = -4$
$a^0 = (-2)^0 = +1$

$-8 < -4 < -2 < +1 < +2 < +4$
$a^3 < -a^2 < a < a^0 < -a < a^2$

ANSWER: (G)

5.
ANALYSIS
Since one pound equals 16 ounces, divide 1,159 by 16.

WORK

$$
\begin{array}{r}
7\,2\text{R}7 \\
16\overline{)1,1\,5\,9} \\
\underline{1\,1\,2}\,x \\
3\,9 \\
\underline{3\,2} \\
7
\end{array}
$$

ANSWER: (A)

6.
ANALYSIS
Find the original weight of the cashews by subtracting 2 from 13. Then substitute into the statements.

WORK

Original weight of cashews		Final weight of cashews		Added weight
	=		−	

= 13 − 2
= 11

The original weight of the cashews was more than 5 times the weight of the added cashews.

11 > 5(2)
11 > 10 ✔

ANSWER: (F)

7.
ANALYSIS
On the first day, if the temperature decreases by 40%, it still is at 60% of the original temperature (100% − 40% = 60%). The next day, the temperature increases by 26%, so it is now 126% of the midnight temperature.

WORK

$$60\% = 0.60$$
$$0.60 \times 90 = 54$$ } Midnight temperature

$$126\% = 1.26$$
$$1.26 \times 54 = 68.04$$

$$68.04 \approx 68 \quad \text{10 A.M. temperature}$$

ANSWER: (A)

8.

ANALYSIS

Let x = the unknown number.

WORK

$$8x = 5x + 18$$
Subtract $5x$: $\quad 3x = \quad 18$
Divide by 3: $\quad x = \quad 6$

ANSWER: (G)

9.

ANALYSIS

Substitute the values for the variables into the given expression.

WORK

$$10x - 9y - 4z^2$$

$x = 4/5, y = 2/3,$
$z = \sqrt{3}:$

$$10(4/5) - 9(2/3) - 4(\sqrt{3})^2$$
$$8 \quad - \quad 6 \quad -4(3)$$
$$2 \quad\quad\quad -12$$
$$-10$$

ANSWER: (B)

10.

ANALYSIS

Let's substitute -2 for a and 3 for b.

WORK

$$a^2 + b^2 > 0$$
$$(-2)^2 + (3) > 0$$
$$4 + 3 > 0 \checkmark$$

ANSWER: (H)

11.

ANALYSIS

Remove the absolute value signs and then multiply all the numbers.

WORK

$$-2|5| \cdot 3 |-4| = (-2)(5)(3)(4) = -120$$

ANSWER: (A)

12.

ANALYSIS

$$\text{Ratio} = \frac{\text{Height of door in blueprint}}{\text{Height of actual door}}$$

Change 8 feet to inches and then simplify the ratio.

WORK

$$\text{Ratio} = \frac{\frac{3}{4} \text{ in.}}{8 \text{ ft}}$$

$$1 \text{ foot} = 12 \text{ in.:} \quad = \frac{\frac{3}{4}}{8 \times 12} = \frac{\frac{3}{4}}{96} = \frac{3}{4} \div 96$$

$$= \frac{3}{4} \times \frac{1}{96} = \frac{1}{128}$$

ANSWER: (F)

13.

ANALYSIS

The best way to solve an abstract example like this is to substitute some numbers for a, b, and c. Since a is a positive even integer, let $a = 4$. b and c are the following consecutive positive integers, so let $b = 5$ and $c = 6$. Then see which statement is **false**.

WORK

$a = 4, c = 6:$ $\quad ac$ is odd
$$4(6) = 24; 24 \text{ is not odd.} ✖$$

ANSWER: (C)

14.

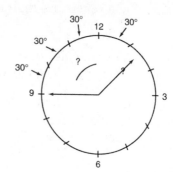

ANALYSIS

There are 360° in a circle and the hours 1–12 divide the circle into 12 parts. If we divide 360° by 12, we find that there are 30° between each two hours. The answer will be approximate since, at 9:05, the hour hand lies a little above the 9.

WORK
As the diagram clearly shows, there are
4 sections between the hands of the clock
at 9:05, so $4 \times 30° = 120°$.

ANSWER: (H)

15.

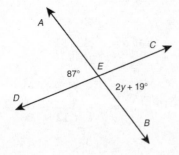

ANALYSIS
Vertical angles are congruent.

WORK

$$2y + 19 = 87$$
Subtract 19: $\quad 2y = 68$
Divide by 2: $\quad y = 34$

ANSWER: (A)

16.

ANALYSIS
Draw a diagram to help out and remember
that all angles in a square are right angles.

WORK
(F) Angle B is a right angle. ✔
(G) The measure of angle B equals the
measure of angle C. ✔
(H) The measure of angle B plus the
measure of angle A equals 180°. ✔
(J) BC is perpendicular to AD. ✘

ANSWER: (J)

17.
ANALYSIS
Let P = the perimeter. Let k = the length of
the rectangle, and let $k - 8$ = the width of
the rectangle.

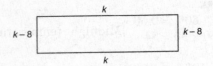

WORK
$P = 2 \cdot$ Length $+ 2 \cdot$ Width
$P = 2(k) + 2(k - 8) = 2k + 2k - 16$
$P = 4k - 16$

ANSWER: (D)

18.
ANALYSIS
Let the base of the equilateral triangle = x.
Since all the sides of an equilateral triangle
are equal, let each side of the equilateral
triangle = x. Let the base of the isosceles
triangle = $x + 2$.

WORK

Equilateral triangle   Isosceles triangle

The perimeters
are equal: $x + 2 + 7 + 7 = 3x$
$x + 16 = 3x$
Subtract x: $16 = 2x$
Divide by 2: $x = 8$

ANSWER: (F)

19.
ANALYSIS
Let A_S = area of the square, and let A_R =
area of the rectangle. Let x = the width of
the rectangle and $2x$ = one side of the
square. Since all sides of a square are
equal, all of the sides are equal to $2x$.

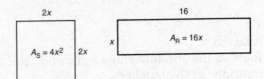

WORK

$$A_S = A_R$$

The areas are equal: $\quad 4x^2 = 16x$

Divide by 4: $\quad\quad\quad x^2 = 4x$

Divide by x: $\quad\quad\quad x = 4$ (width of the rectangle)

ANSWER: (C)

20.

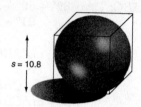

$s = 10.8$

ANALYSIS

Round off 10.8 to 11. Find the volume of the cube and then take $\frac{1}{2}$ of the answer.

WORK

Volume of cube $= s^3 = 11^3 = 1331$

Approximate
volume of sphere $= \frac{1}{2} \times 1331 = 665.5 \approx 666$

Since we rounded 10.8 to 11, the final answer should be less than 666.

ANSWER: (J)

21.

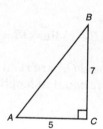

ANALYSIS

Use the PythagoreanTheorem and let $a = 7$, $b = 5$.

WORK

$$a^2 + b^2 = c^2$$
$$7^2 + 5^2 = c^2$$
$$49 + 25 = c^2$$
$$74 = c^2$$
$$c = \sqrt{74}$$
$$c \approx 8.60 \approx 8.6$$

ANSWER: (C)

22.

ANALYSIS

Select the set in which the sum of any two numbers is greater than the third number.

WORK

$$4 + 5 > 8 \;\checkmark$$
$$4 + 8 > 5 \;\checkmark$$
$$5 + 8 > 4 \;\checkmark$$

ANSWER: (G)

23.

ANALYSIS

Look at the hundreds' place and then round to the nearest thousand.

WORK

hundreds' place
↓
1,147,690
↑
add 1 to the thousands' place and round off

$$1,147,690 \approx 1,148,000$$

ANSWER: (C)

24.

ANALYSIS

Move the decimal over two places to the left.

WORK

$$0.054\% = 0.00.054 = 0.00054$$

ANSWER: (J)

25.

ANALYSIS

Substitute the values for r, s, and t in the given expression.

WORK

$r = 2, s = 3, t = 4$:
$$3rs - 2t$$
$$3(2)(3) - 2(4)$$
$$18 - 8$$
$$10$$

ANSWER: (D)

26.

ANALYSIS

Remember, when we multiply two negatives, the result is a positive, and when we multiply a positive and a negative, the result is a negative.

WORK

$-4(-2)^3 = -4(-2)(-2)(-2) = +8(-2)(-2) = -16(-2) = +32$

ANSWER: (F)

27.

ANALYSIS

Simplify expressions within the parentheses and then work from left to right.

WORK

(A) $5 \cdot 3 - (2 + 7) = 15 - (9) = 6$
(B) $5(3) - 48/6 = 15 - 8 = 7$
(C) $14 - 5 + 30/6 = 14 - 5 + 5 = 9 + 5 = 14$
(D) $18/2 - 3(4 - 6) + 54/9 = 9 - 3(-2) + 6 = 9 + 6 + 6 = 21$

ANSWER: (A)

28.

ANALYSIS

There are no elements in common.

ANSWER: (G)

29.

ANALYSIS

Divide the letters (representing rational numbers) and the radicals separately.

WORK

$$\frac{a\sqrt{42}}{b\sqrt{7}} = \frac{a}{b}\sqrt{\frac{42}{7}} = \frac{a}{b}\sqrt{6}$$

ANSWER: (C)

30.

ANALYSIS

The sum of the angles of a triangle equals $180°$, so, in order to determine the measure of angle ABC, add up the two given angles and subtract from $180°$. Then, since the measure of straight angle ABD is $180°$, subtract the answer from $180°$ once again.

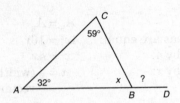

WORK

Let $x = m\angle ABC$:

$$32° + 59° + x = 180°$$
$$91° + x = 180°$$
$$x = 89°$$
$$m\angle ABC = 89°$$

$$m\angle ABC + m\angle CBD = 180°$$

$m\angle B = 89°$:

$$89° + m\angle CBD = 180°$$

Subtract $89°$:

$$m\angle CBD = 91°$$

ANSWER: (G)

31.

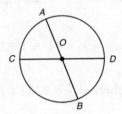

ANALYSIS

OC, OD, OA, and OB are radii and are therefore equal in length. AB and CD are diameters and are also equal in length.

WORK

diameter AB – radius OB = radius OA

OD and OA are radii and are equal in length.

ANSWER: (C)

32.

ANALYSIS

To determine the area of a circle, use the formula $A_C = \pi r^2$. Let $\pi = 22/7$. A_C = the area, and r is the radius. The area of a triangle, A_T, is equal to $\frac{1}{2}bh$, where b = the base and h = the height.

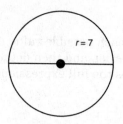

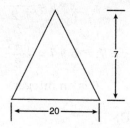

WORK

		Decimal		Final
Order	%	(d)	d × \$30,000,000	answer
Auto	20%	0.20	0.20 × 30,000,000	6,000,000
Airplane	15%	0.15	0.15 × 30,000,000	4,500,000
Bicycle	30%	0.30	0.30 × 30,000,000	9,000,000
Military	35%	0.35	0.35 × 30,000,000	10,500,000

Bicycle and auto orders together were equal to \$15,000,000.

$$\$9,000,000 + \$6,000,000 = \$15,000,000 \checkmark$$

ANSWER: (C)

34.
ANALYSIS
The probability of selecting a green marble is the ratio of the number of green marbles to the total number of marbles.

WORK
$$\frac{\text{Number of green marbles}}{\text{Total number of marbles}} = \frac{3}{18} = \frac{1}{6}$$

ANSWER: (H)

35.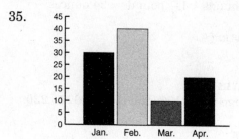

ANALYSIS
Determine the average temperatures for each month and then do the calculations.

WORK
January: 30°
February: 40°
March: 10°
April: 20°

$$\text{Apr.} + \text{Feb.} > 50°$$
$$20° + 40° > 50°$$
$$60° > 50° \checkmark$$

ANSWER: (D)

WORK

Circle

$$A_C = \pi r^2$$
$$A_C = (22/7)(7)^2$$
$$A_C = (22/7)(49)$$
$$A_C = 154$$

Triangle

$$A_T = \frac{1}{2}bh$$
$$A_T = \frac{1}{2}(20)(7)$$
$$A_T = \frac{1}{2}(140)$$
$$A_T = 70$$

Area of the circle > twice the area of the triangle.
$$154 > 2(70)$$
$$154 > 140 \checkmark$$

ANSWER: (J)

33.

ANALYSIS
To make life easier, first develop a chart. Change the percentages to dollars and then substitute into the statements.

36.
ANALYSIS
Add up all the hours and divide by 3, the number of students.

WORK

$$\bar{x} = \frac{(t + 4) + (t) + (t - 2)}{3} = \frac{3t + 2}{3}$$

ANSWER: (F)

37.
ANALYSIS
There are 16 ounces in one pound. Change all the measures to the smallest common unit, ounces.

WORK
24 ounces

1.2 pounds · 16 ounces per pound = 19.2 ounces

$1\frac{1}{4}$ pounds · 16 ounces per pound =
5/4 · 16 = 20 ounces

19.2 ounces < 20 ounces < 24 ounces

1.2 pounds < $1\frac{1}{4}$ pounds < 24 ounces

ANSWER: (A)

38.
ANALYSIS
Change 8% to 10% and round 232 to 230.

WORK
$$.10 \times 230 = 23$$

ANSWER: (G)

39.
ANALYSIS
Substitute each possible value into the given expression and then determine which value makes the full expression into an integer.

WORK

$$x \# y = \frac{x + y}{2}$$

Let $x = 5$, $y = 7$: $5 \# 7 = \frac{5+7}{2} = \frac{12}{2} = 6$

6 is an integer.

ANSWER: (C)

40.
ANALYSIS
From the given information, draw a diagram.

WORK

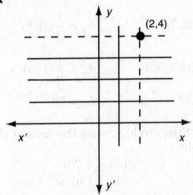

ANSWER: (G)

Answer Sheet
Practice High School Placement Test 1

SUBTEST 1   VERBAL SKILLS

1. Ⓐ Ⓑ Ⓒ Ⓓ	13. Ⓐ Ⓑ Ⓒ Ⓓ	25. Ⓐ Ⓑ Ⓒ Ⓓ	37. Ⓐ Ⓑ Ⓒ Ⓓ	49. Ⓐ Ⓑ Ⓒ Ⓓ
2. Ⓐ Ⓑ Ⓒ Ⓓ	14. Ⓐ Ⓑ Ⓒ Ⓓ	26. Ⓐ Ⓑ Ⓒ Ⓓ	38. Ⓐ Ⓑ Ⓒ Ⓓ	50. Ⓐ Ⓑ Ⓒ Ⓓ
3. Ⓐ Ⓑ Ⓒ Ⓓ	15. Ⓐ Ⓑ Ⓒ Ⓓ	27. Ⓐ Ⓑ Ⓒ Ⓓ	39. Ⓐ Ⓑ Ⓒ Ⓓ	51. Ⓐ Ⓑ Ⓒ Ⓓ
4. Ⓐ Ⓑ Ⓒ Ⓓ	16. Ⓐ Ⓑ Ⓒ Ⓓ	28. Ⓐ Ⓑ Ⓒ Ⓓ	40. Ⓐ Ⓑ Ⓒ Ⓓ	52. Ⓐ Ⓑ Ⓒ Ⓓ
5. Ⓐ Ⓑ Ⓒ Ⓓ	17. Ⓐ Ⓑ Ⓒ Ⓓ	29. Ⓐ Ⓑ Ⓒ Ⓓ	41. Ⓐ Ⓑ Ⓒ Ⓓ	53. Ⓐ Ⓑ Ⓒ Ⓓ
6. Ⓐ Ⓑ Ⓒ Ⓓ	18. Ⓐ Ⓑ Ⓒ Ⓓ	30. Ⓐ Ⓑ Ⓒ Ⓓ	42. Ⓐ Ⓑ Ⓒ Ⓓ	54. Ⓐ Ⓑ Ⓒ Ⓓ
7. Ⓐ Ⓑ Ⓒ Ⓓ	19. Ⓐ Ⓑ Ⓒ Ⓓ	31. Ⓐ Ⓑ Ⓒ Ⓓ	43. Ⓐ Ⓑ Ⓒ Ⓓ	55. Ⓐ Ⓑ Ⓒ Ⓓ
8. Ⓐ Ⓑ Ⓒ Ⓓ	20. Ⓐ Ⓑ Ⓒ Ⓓ	32. Ⓐ Ⓑ Ⓒ Ⓓ	44. Ⓐ Ⓑ Ⓒ Ⓓ	56. Ⓐ Ⓑ Ⓒ Ⓓ
9. Ⓐ Ⓑ Ⓒ Ⓓ	21. Ⓐ Ⓑ Ⓒ Ⓓ	33. Ⓐ Ⓑ Ⓒ Ⓓ	45. Ⓐ Ⓑ Ⓒ Ⓓ	57. Ⓐ Ⓑ Ⓒ Ⓓ
10. Ⓐ Ⓑ Ⓒ Ⓓ	22. Ⓐ Ⓑ Ⓒ Ⓓ	34. Ⓐ Ⓑ Ⓒ Ⓓ	46. Ⓐ Ⓑ Ⓒ Ⓓ	58. Ⓐ Ⓑ Ⓒ Ⓓ
11. Ⓐ Ⓑ Ⓒ Ⓓ	23. Ⓐ Ⓑ Ⓒ Ⓓ	35. Ⓐ Ⓑ Ⓒ Ⓓ	47. Ⓐ Ⓑ Ⓒ Ⓓ	59. Ⓐ Ⓑ Ⓒ Ⓓ
12. Ⓐ Ⓑ Ⓒ Ⓓ	24. Ⓐ Ⓑ Ⓒ Ⓓ	36. Ⓐ Ⓑ Ⓒ Ⓓ	48. Ⓐ Ⓑ Ⓒ Ⓓ	60. Ⓐ Ⓑ Ⓒ Ⓓ

SUBTEST 2   QUANTITATIVE SKILLS

61. Ⓐ Ⓑ Ⓒ Ⓓ	72. Ⓐ Ⓑ Ⓒ Ⓓ	83. Ⓐ Ⓑ Ⓒ Ⓓ	93. Ⓐ Ⓑ Ⓒ Ⓓ	103. Ⓐ Ⓑ Ⓒ Ⓓ
62. Ⓐ Ⓑ Ⓒ Ⓓ	73. Ⓐ Ⓑ Ⓒ Ⓓ	84. Ⓐ Ⓑ Ⓒ Ⓓ	94. Ⓐ Ⓑ Ⓒ Ⓓ	104. Ⓐ Ⓑ Ⓒ Ⓓ
63. Ⓐ Ⓑ Ⓒ Ⓓ	74. Ⓐ Ⓑ Ⓒ Ⓓ	85. Ⓐ Ⓑ Ⓒ Ⓓ	95. Ⓐ Ⓑ Ⓒ Ⓓ	105. Ⓐ Ⓑ Ⓒ Ⓓ
64. Ⓐ Ⓑ Ⓒ Ⓓ	75. Ⓐ Ⓑ Ⓒ Ⓓ	86. Ⓐ Ⓑ Ⓒ Ⓓ	96. Ⓐ Ⓑ Ⓒ Ⓓ	106. Ⓐ Ⓑ Ⓒ Ⓓ
65. Ⓐ Ⓑ Ⓒ Ⓓ	76. Ⓐ Ⓑ Ⓒ Ⓓ	87. Ⓐ Ⓑ Ⓒ Ⓓ	97. Ⓐ Ⓑ Ⓒ Ⓓ	107. Ⓐ Ⓑ Ⓒ Ⓓ
66. Ⓐ Ⓑ Ⓒ Ⓓ	77. Ⓐ Ⓑ Ⓒ Ⓓ	88. Ⓐ Ⓑ Ⓒ Ⓓ	98. Ⓐ Ⓑ Ⓒ Ⓓ	108. Ⓐ Ⓑ Ⓒ Ⓓ
67. Ⓐ Ⓑ Ⓒ Ⓓ	78. Ⓐ Ⓑ Ⓒ Ⓓ	89. Ⓐ Ⓑ Ⓒ Ⓓ	99. Ⓐ Ⓑ Ⓒ Ⓓ	109. Ⓐ Ⓑ Ⓒ Ⓓ
68. Ⓐ Ⓑ Ⓒ Ⓓ	79. Ⓐ Ⓑ Ⓒ Ⓓ	90. Ⓐ Ⓑ Ⓒ Ⓓ	100. Ⓐ Ⓑ Ⓒ Ⓓ	110. Ⓐ Ⓑ Ⓒ Ⓓ
69. Ⓐ Ⓑ Ⓒ Ⓓ	80. Ⓐ Ⓑ Ⓒ Ⓓ	91. Ⓐ Ⓑ Ⓒ Ⓓ	101. Ⓐ Ⓑ Ⓒ Ⓓ	111. Ⓐ Ⓑ Ⓒ Ⓓ
70. Ⓐ Ⓑ Ⓒ Ⓓ	81. Ⓐ Ⓑ Ⓒ Ⓓ	92. Ⓐ Ⓑ Ⓒ Ⓓ	102. Ⓐ Ⓑ Ⓒ Ⓓ	112. Ⓐ Ⓑ Ⓒ Ⓓ
71. Ⓐ Ⓑ Ⓒ Ⓓ	82. Ⓐ Ⓑ Ⓒ Ⓓ			

SUBTEST 3   READING—COMPREHENSION—VOCABULARY

113. Ⓐ Ⓑ Ⓒ Ⓓ	126. Ⓐ Ⓑ Ⓒ Ⓓ	139. Ⓐ Ⓑ Ⓒ Ⓓ	151. Ⓐ Ⓑ Ⓒ Ⓓ	163. Ⓐ Ⓑ Ⓒ Ⓓ
114. Ⓐ Ⓑ Ⓒ Ⓓ	127. Ⓐ Ⓑ Ⓒ Ⓓ	140. Ⓐ Ⓑ Ⓒ Ⓓ	152. Ⓐ Ⓑ Ⓒ Ⓓ	164. Ⓐ Ⓑ Ⓒ Ⓓ
115. Ⓐ Ⓑ Ⓒ Ⓓ	128. Ⓐ Ⓑ Ⓒ Ⓓ	141. Ⓐ Ⓑ Ⓒ Ⓓ	153. Ⓐ Ⓑ Ⓒ Ⓓ	165. Ⓐ Ⓑ Ⓒ Ⓓ
116. Ⓐ Ⓑ Ⓒ Ⓓ	129. Ⓐ Ⓑ Ⓒ Ⓓ	142. Ⓐ Ⓑ Ⓒ Ⓓ	154. Ⓐ Ⓑ Ⓒ Ⓓ	166. Ⓐ Ⓑ Ⓒ Ⓓ
117. Ⓐ Ⓑ Ⓒ Ⓓ	130. Ⓐ Ⓑ Ⓒ Ⓓ	143. Ⓐ Ⓑ Ⓒ Ⓓ	155. Ⓐ Ⓑ Ⓒ Ⓓ	167. Ⓐ Ⓑ Ⓒ Ⓓ
118. Ⓐ Ⓑ Ⓒ Ⓓ	131. Ⓐ Ⓑ Ⓒ Ⓓ	144. Ⓐ Ⓑ Ⓒ Ⓓ	156. Ⓐ Ⓑ Ⓒ Ⓓ	168. Ⓐ Ⓑ Ⓒ Ⓓ
119. Ⓐ Ⓑ Ⓒ Ⓓ	132. Ⓐ Ⓑ Ⓒ Ⓓ	145. Ⓐ Ⓑ Ⓒ Ⓓ	157. Ⓐ Ⓑ Ⓒ Ⓓ	169. Ⓐ Ⓑ Ⓒ Ⓓ
120. Ⓐ Ⓑ Ⓒ Ⓓ	133. Ⓐ Ⓑ Ⓒ Ⓓ	146. Ⓐ Ⓑ Ⓒ Ⓓ	158. Ⓐ Ⓑ Ⓒ Ⓓ	170. Ⓐ Ⓑ Ⓒ Ⓓ
121. Ⓐ Ⓑ Ⓒ Ⓓ	134. Ⓐ Ⓑ Ⓒ Ⓓ	147. Ⓐ Ⓑ Ⓒ Ⓓ	159. Ⓐ Ⓑ Ⓒ Ⓓ	171. Ⓐ Ⓑ Ⓒ Ⓓ
122. Ⓐ Ⓑ Ⓒ Ⓓ	135. Ⓐ Ⓑ Ⓒ Ⓓ	148. Ⓐ Ⓑ Ⓒ Ⓓ	160. Ⓐ Ⓑ Ⓒ Ⓓ	172. Ⓐ Ⓑ Ⓒ Ⓓ
123. Ⓐ Ⓑ Ⓒ Ⓓ	136. Ⓐ Ⓑ Ⓒ Ⓓ	149. Ⓐ Ⓑ Ⓒ Ⓓ	161. Ⓐ Ⓑ Ⓒ Ⓓ	173. Ⓐ Ⓑ Ⓒ Ⓓ
124. Ⓐ Ⓑ Ⓒ Ⓓ	137. Ⓐ Ⓑ Ⓒ Ⓓ	150. Ⓐ Ⓑ Ⓒ Ⓓ	162. Ⓐ Ⓑ Ⓒ Ⓓ	174. Ⓐ Ⓑ Ⓒ Ⓓ
125. Ⓐ Ⓑ Ⓒ Ⓓ	138. Ⓐ Ⓑ Ⓒ Ⓓ			

SUBTEST 4   MATHEMATICS

175. Ⓐ Ⓑ Ⓒ Ⓓ	188. Ⓐ Ⓑ Ⓒ Ⓓ	201. Ⓐ Ⓑ Ⓒ Ⓓ	214. Ⓐ Ⓑ Ⓒ Ⓓ	227. Ⓐ Ⓑ Ⓒ Ⓓ
176. Ⓐ Ⓑ Ⓒ Ⓓ	189. Ⓐ Ⓑ Ⓒ Ⓓ	202. Ⓐ Ⓑ Ⓒ Ⓓ	215. Ⓐ Ⓑ Ⓒ Ⓓ	228. Ⓐ Ⓑ Ⓒ Ⓓ
177. Ⓐ Ⓑ Ⓒ Ⓓ	190. Ⓐ Ⓑ Ⓒ Ⓓ	203. Ⓐ Ⓑ Ⓒ Ⓓ	216. Ⓐ Ⓑ Ⓒ Ⓓ	229. Ⓐ Ⓑ Ⓒ Ⓓ
178. Ⓐ Ⓑ Ⓒ Ⓓ	191. Ⓐ Ⓑ Ⓒ Ⓓ	204. Ⓐ Ⓑ Ⓒ Ⓓ	217. Ⓐ Ⓑ Ⓒ Ⓓ	230. Ⓐ Ⓑ Ⓒ Ⓓ
179. Ⓐ Ⓑ Ⓒ Ⓓ	192. Ⓐ Ⓑ Ⓒ Ⓓ	205. Ⓐ Ⓑ Ⓒ Ⓓ	218. Ⓐ Ⓑ Ⓒ Ⓓ	231. Ⓐ Ⓑ Ⓒ Ⓓ
180. Ⓐ Ⓑ Ⓒ Ⓓ	193. Ⓐ Ⓑ Ⓒ Ⓓ	206. Ⓐ Ⓑ Ⓒ Ⓓ	219. Ⓐ Ⓑ Ⓒ Ⓓ	232. Ⓐ Ⓑ Ⓒ Ⓓ
181. Ⓐ Ⓑ Ⓒ Ⓓ	194. Ⓐ Ⓑ Ⓒ Ⓓ	207. Ⓐ Ⓑ Ⓒ Ⓓ	220. Ⓐ Ⓑ Ⓒ Ⓓ	233. Ⓐ Ⓑ Ⓒ Ⓓ
182. Ⓐ Ⓑ Ⓒ Ⓓ	195. Ⓐ Ⓑ Ⓒ Ⓓ	208. Ⓐ Ⓑ Ⓒ Ⓓ	221. Ⓐ Ⓑ Ⓒ Ⓓ	234. Ⓐ Ⓑ Ⓒ Ⓓ
183. Ⓐ Ⓑ Ⓒ Ⓓ	196. Ⓐ Ⓑ Ⓒ Ⓓ	209. Ⓐ Ⓑ Ⓒ Ⓓ	222. Ⓐ Ⓑ Ⓒ Ⓓ	235. Ⓐ Ⓑ Ⓒ Ⓓ
184. Ⓐ Ⓑ Ⓒ Ⓓ	197. Ⓐ Ⓑ Ⓒ Ⓓ	210. Ⓐ Ⓑ Ⓒ Ⓓ	223. Ⓐ Ⓑ Ⓒ Ⓓ	236. Ⓐ Ⓑ Ⓒ Ⓓ
185. Ⓐ Ⓑ Ⓒ Ⓓ	198. Ⓐ Ⓑ Ⓒ Ⓓ	211. Ⓐ Ⓑ Ⓒ Ⓓ	224. Ⓐ Ⓑ Ⓒ Ⓓ	237. Ⓐ Ⓑ Ⓒ Ⓓ
186. Ⓐ Ⓑ Ⓒ Ⓓ	199. Ⓐ Ⓑ Ⓒ Ⓓ	212. Ⓐ Ⓑ Ⓒ Ⓓ	225. Ⓐ Ⓑ Ⓒ Ⓓ	238. Ⓐ Ⓑ Ⓒ Ⓓ
187. Ⓐ Ⓑ Ⓒ Ⓓ	200. Ⓐ Ⓑ Ⓒ Ⓓ	213. Ⓐ Ⓑ Ⓒ Ⓓ	226. Ⓐ Ⓑ Ⓒ Ⓓ	

SUBTEST 5   LANGUAGE

239. Ⓐ Ⓑ Ⓒ Ⓓ	251. Ⓐ Ⓑ Ⓒ Ⓓ	263. Ⓐ Ⓑ Ⓒ Ⓓ	275. Ⓐ Ⓑ Ⓒ Ⓓ	287. Ⓐ Ⓑ Ⓒ Ⓓ
240. Ⓐ Ⓑ Ⓒ Ⓓ	252. Ⓐ Ⓑ Ⓒ Ⓓ	264. Ⓐ Ⓑ Ⓒ Ⓓ	276. Ⓐ Ⓑ Ⓒ Ⓓ	288. Ⓐ Ⓑ Ⓒ Ⓓ
241. Ⓐ Ⓑ Ⓒ Ⓓ	253. Ⓐ Ⓑ Ⓒ Ⓓ	265. Ⓐ Ⓑ Ⓒ Ⓓ	277. Ⓐ Ⓑ Ⓒ Ⓓ	289. Ⓐ Ⓑ Ⓒ Ⓓ
242. Ⓐ Ⓑ Ⓒ Ⓓ	254. Ⓐ Ⓑ Ⓒ Ⓓ	266. Ⓐ Ⓑ Ⓒ Ⓓ	278. Ⓐ Ⓑ Ⓒ Ⓓ	290. Ⓐ Ⓑ Ⓒ Ⓓ
243. Ⓐ Ⓑ Ⓒ Ⓓ	255. Ⓐ Ⓑ Ⓒ Ⓓ	267. Ⓐ Ⓑ Ⓒ Ⓓ	279. Ⓐ Ⓑ Ⓒ Ⓓ	291. Ⓐ Ⓑ Ⓒ Ⓓ
244. Ⓐ Ⓑ Ⓒ Ⓓ	256. Ⓐ Ⓑ Ⓒ Ⓓ	268. Ⓐ Ⓑ Ⓒ Ⓓ	280. Ⓐ Ⓑ Ⓒ Ⓓ	292. Ⓐ Ⓑ Ⓒ Ⓓ
245. Ⓐ Ⓑ Ⓒ Ⓓ	257. Ⓐ Ⓑ Ⓒ Ⓓ	269. Ⓐ Ⓑ Ⓒ Ⓓ	281. Ⓐ Ⓑ Ⓒ Ⓓ	293. Ⓐ Ⓑ Ⓒ Ⓓ
246. Ⓐ Ⓑ Ⓒ Ⓓ	258. Ⓐ Ⓑ Ⓒ Ⓓ	270. Ⓐ Ⓑ Ⓒ Ⓓ	282. Ⓐ Ⓑ Ⓒ Ⓓ	294. Ⓐ Ⓑ Ⓒ Ⓓ
247. Ⓐ Ⓑ Ⓒ Ⓓ	259. Ⓐ Ⓑ Ⓒ Ⓓ	271. Ⓐ Ⓑ Ⓒ Ⓓ	283. Ⓐ Ⓑ Ⓒ Ⓓ	295. Ⓐ Ⓑ Ⓒ Ⓓ
248. Ⓐ Ⓑ Ⓒ Ⓓ	260. Ⓐ Ⓑ Ⓒ Ⓓ	272. Ⓐ Ⓑ Ⓒ Ⓓ	284. Ⓐ Ⓑ Ⓒ Ⓓ	296. Ⓐ Ⓑ Ⓒ Ⓓ
249. Ⓐ Ⓑ Ⓒ Ⓓ	261. Ⓐ Ⓑ Ⓒ Ⓓ	273. Ⓐ Ⓑ Ⓒ Ⓓ	285. Ⓐ Ⓑ Ⓒ Ⓓ	297. Ⓐ Ⓑ Ⓒ Ⓓ
250. Ⓐ Ⓑ Ⓒ Ⓓ	262. Ⓐ Ⓑ Ⓒ Ⓓ	274. Ⓐ Ⓑ Ⓒ Ⓓ	286. Ⓐ Ⓑ Ⓒ Ⓓ	298. Ⓐ Ⓑ Ⓒ Ⓓ

Practice HSPT Exam 1

SUBTEST 1   VERBAL SKILLS

#1–60   *16 minutes*

Sample:

Which word does *not* belong with the others?

    (A) easy
    (B) interesting
    (C) simple
    (D) facile

---

1. Which word does *not* belong with the others?

    (A) bicycle
    (B) minivan
    (C) automobile
    (D) motorcycle

2. Which word does *not* belong with the others?

    (A) glum
    (B) pleasant
    (C) kindly
    (D) amiable

3. Which word does *not* belong with the others?

    (A) poodle
    (B) greyhound
    (C) working dog
    (D) collie

4. Payton is taller than Jaylin. Kita is taller than Payton. Kita is taller than Jaylin. If the first two statements are true, the third statement is

    _____.

    (A) true
    (B) false
    (C) uncertain

5. Prejudice most nearly means

    _____.

    (A) legality
    (B) bias
    (C) opinion
    (D) decision

6. Dark is to light as clean is to

    _____.

    (A) heavy
    (B) dirty
    (C) soap
    (D) immaculate

7. Which word does *not* belong with the others?

    (A) maintain
    (B) preserve
    (C) support
    (D) neglect

8. Which word does *not* belong with the others?

    (A) blanket
    (B) quilt
    (C) towel
    (D) bedspread

9. Which word does *not* belong with the others?

   (A) close
   (B) near
   (C) shut
   (D) seal

10. *Voracious* most nearly means
    _____.

    (A) hungry
    (B) loud
    (C) foolish
    (D) vast

11. *Malignant* most nearly means
    _____.

    (A) possessive
    (B) deadly
    (C) positive
    (D) parallel

12. *Liberate* most nearly means
    _____.

    (A) weigh
    (B) think
    (C) listen
    (D) free

13. Fire is to smoke as lightbulb is to
    _____.

    (A) brightness
    (B) electricity
    (C) inspiration
    (D) darkness

14. *Reversal* most nearly means
    _____.

    (A) inversion
    (B) agreement
    (C) indecision
    (D) regret

15. Tim runs faster than Cathy. Cathy runs faster than Nathan. Nathan runs faster than John. If the first two statements are true, the third statement is _____.

    (A) true
    (B) false
    (C) uncertain

16. Which word does *not* belong with the others?

    (A) phrase
    (B) clause
    (C) adverb
    (D) sentence

17. Which word does *not* belong with the others?

    (A) creek
    (B) river
    (C) ocean
    (D) peninsula

18. *Biodegrade* most nearly means
    _____.

    (A) reminisce
    (B) investigate
    (C) divulge
    (D) decay

19. Car is to key as television is to
    _____.

    (A) outlet
    (B) sound
    (C) remote control
    (D) cabinet

20. Imprint means the *opposite* of
    _____.

    (A) stamp
    (B) erase
    (C) read
    (D) steal

21. Rain is to umbrella as draft is to
    _____.

    (A) wind
    (B) cold
    (C) thirst
    (D) door

22. All dogs are mammals. The basenji is a breed of dog. The basenji is not a mammal. If the first two statements are true, the third statement is _____.

    (A) true
    (B) false
    (C) uncertain

23. *Sever* most nearly means _____.

    (A) torment
    (B) divide
    (C) repair
    (D) agree

24. Ursola's hair is longer than Jack's. Jack's hair is shorter than Grace's. Grace's hair is longer than Ursola's. If the first two statements are true, the third statement is _____.

    (A) true
    (B) false
    (C) uncertain

25. *Uniformity* most nearly means

    _____.

    (A) sameness
    (B) stubborness
    (C) diversity
    (D) wardrobe

26. Which word does *not* belong with the others?

    (A) desert
    (B) abandon
    (C) run
    (D) leave

27. A philanthropist is _____.

    (A) greedy
    (B) generous
    (C) wasteful
    (D) anonymous

28. *Congenial* most nearly means

    _____.

    (A) suitable
    (B) intelligent
    (C) magical
    (D) supernatural

29. The shoes cost more than the skirt. The blouse costs less than the skirt. The shoes cost more than the blouse. If the first two statements are true, the third statement is _____.

    (A) true
    (B) false
    (C) uncertain

30. Which word does *not* belong with the others?

    (A) sonnet
    (B) haiku
    (C) limerick
    (D) poem

31. Impressive is to inspiring as derogatory is to _____.

    (A) critical
    (B) praiseworthy
    (C) positive
    (D) elevating

32. Which word does *not* belong with the others?

    (A) accept
    (B) command
    (C) decree
    (D) dictate

33. It's a long way to Tipperary. It's a longer way to Gotham. It is longest to Leicester Square. If the first two statements are true, the third statement is _____.

    (A) true
    (B) false
    (C) uncertain

34. Which word does *not* belong with the others?

    (A) search
    (B) explore
    (C) overlook
    (D) investigate

35. Inequitable is not _____.

    (A) fair
    (B) biased
    (C) correct
    (D) worthy

36. Thrifty means the *opposite* of

    _____.

    (A) expensive
    (B) cheap
    (C) wasteful
    (D) conservative

37. Malfunction is not _____.

    (A) failure
    (B) fault
    (C) success
    (D) breakdown

38. Lee weighs 20 more pounds than John. Steven weighs 10 more pounds than Lee. Steven weighs 30 more pounds than John. If the first two statements are true, the third statement is _____.

    (A) true
    (B) false
    (C) uncertain

39. Console means the *opposite* of _____.

    (A) speaker
    (B) comfort
    (C) agitate
    (D) sympathize

40. Roof is to house as head is to _____.

    (A) thought
    (B) body
    (C) brain
    (D) foot

41. Diligence means the *opposite* of _____.

    (A) laziness
    (B) stupidity
    (C) militant
    (D) vigor

42. Moon River is wider than a mile. Pirate Island is less than a mile wide. Pirate Island would fit in Moon River. If the first two statements are true, the third statement is _____.

    (A) true
    (B) false
    (C) uncertain

43. Which word does *not* belong with the others?

    (A) invade
    (B) infiltrate
    (C) trespass
    (D) depart

44. Fork is to eat as pen is to _____.

    (A) paper
    (B) write
    (C) fill
    (D) instruct

45. *Devise* most nearly means _____.

    (A) startle
    (B) bluff
    (C) create
    (D) outwit

46. Which word does *not* belong with the others?

    (A) engine
    (B) motor
    (C) radio
    (D) mechanism

47. Glorious means the *opposite* of _____.

    (A) esteemed
    (B) serious
    (C) exalted
    (D) unimportant

48. Idle is to employed as graceful is to _____.

    (A) elegant
    (B) clumsy
    (C) petite
    (D) slender

49. The science club has more members than the math club. The math club and the chess club combined have fewer members than the science club. The science club has more members than the chess club. If the first two statements are true, the third statement is _____.

    (A) true
    (B) false
    (C) uncertain

50. Dismay means the *opposite* of
    _____.

    (A) dread
    (B) disatisfaction
    (C) courage
    (D) phobia

51. Noise is to irritate as music is to
    _____.

    (A) sing
    (B) intrude
    (C) calm
    (D) contemplate

52. My cat is smaller than Ryanne's cat.
    My cat is not as small as Patsy's cat.
    Patsy's cat is smaller than Ryanne's
    cat. If the first two statements are
    true, the third statement is
    _____.

    (A) true
    (B) false
    (C) uncertain

53. Which word does *not* belong with the
    others?

    (A) secret
    (B) mystery
    (C) puzzle
    (D) information

54. Morose means the opposite of
    _____.

    (A) poison
    (B) cheerful
    (C) safe
    (D) seated

55. Camellia stayed longer than Karol.
    Karol stayed longer than Theresa.
    Theresa stayed longer than Camellia.
    If the first two statements are true,
    the third statement is _____.

    (A) true
    (B) false
    (C) uncertain

56. Which word does *not* belong with the
    others?

    (A) vocalize
    (B) converse
    (C) repress
    (D) articulate

57. A crucial ingredient is _____.

    (A) necessary
    (B) extra
    (C) optional
    (D) rare

58. Bus is to car as whale is to
    _____.

    (A) fish
    (B) mammal
    (C) dolphin
    (D) ocean

59. Carol has read 12 books this year.
    Katie has read 15 books this year.
    Carol and Katie have read at least 10
    of the same books. If the first two
    statements are true, the third state-
    ment is _____.

    (A) true
    (B) false
    (C) uncertain

60. Julie is older than Robbie. Robbie is
    older than Jane. Julie is younger
    than Jane. If the first two statements
    are true, the third statement is
    _____.

    (A) true
    (B) false
    (C) uncertain

STOP

IF YOU FINISH BEFORE TIME IS UP, CHECK OVER YOUR WORK ON THIS TEST ONLY. DO NOT
GO ON TO THE NEXT TEST UNTIL THE SIGNAL IS GIVEN.

SUBTEST 2   QUANTITATIVE SKILLS

#61–112   *30 minutes*

Sample:

What is the sum of 52 and 31?

(A) 21   (B) 83   (C) 84   (D) none of the above   Ⓐ ● Ⓒ Ⓓ

DIRECTIONS: Select the best answer for each question.

---

61. Review the series: 6, 11, 16, 21, 26, ... Find the next number.

    (A) 32   (B) 30   (C) 25   (D) 31

62. The sum of the square of a positive number and 3 is equal to the product of 4 and 7. What is the number?

    (A) 3   (B) 6   (C) 5   (D) 4

63. Given (a), (b), and (c), select the best answer.

    (a) 7(9 − 3)
    (b) 2 × 4 + 72/4
    (c) 48 − 3(5 + 6)

    (A) (a) is less than (b) and less than (c)
    (B) (b) is greater than (c) and less than (a)
    (C) (c) is less than (a) and greater than (b)
    (D) (c) is greater than (a) and greater than (b)

64. The quotient of 48 and 6 added to 2 is equal to the square root of a number. What is the number?

    (A) 5   (B) 25   (C) 50   (D) 100

65. Review the series: 35, 32, 29, 26, ... Find the next number.

    (A) 23   (B) 28   (C) 27   (D) 24

66. Find the cross-hatched area in the diagram below. The area of a circle is equal to πr^2, where $\pi = 3.14$. Round off the answer to the nearest tenth.

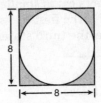

    (A) 12.8
    (B) 13.8
    (C) 13.76
    (D) 12.83

67. Given (a), (b), and (c), select the best answer.

    (a) 45%
    (b) 2/3
    (c) 0.45

    (A) (a) is greater than (b) and less than (c)
    (B) (b) is less than (c) and greater than (a)
    (C) (c) is equal to (a) and less than (b)
    (D) (b) is greater than (a) and less than (c)

68. Review the series: 4, 8, 16, 32, ... Find the next number.

    (A) 28   (B) 36   (C) 64   (D) 40

69. What number is equal to 15 more than two thirds of 30?

    (A) 35   (B) 30   (C) 25   (D) 20

70. Given (a), (b), and (c), select the best answer.

    (a) 3/7 × 42
    (b) 5/8 × 40
    (c) 6/7 × 35

    (A) (a) is less than (b) and less than (c)
    (B) (b) is greater than (c) and greater than (a)
    (C) (c) is greater than (b) and less than (a)
    (D) (a) is less than (c) and greater than (b)

71. Determine the value of x in the equation $62 + 2(8 - x) = 72$.

    (A) 2   (B) 3   (C) 4   (D) 5

72. Review the series: 51, $49\frac{1}{2}$, 48, $46\frac{1}{2}$, ... Find the next number.

    (A) 44   (B) 45
    (C) $43\frac{1}{2}$ (D) $44\frac{1}{2}$

73. Forty-eight divided by what number equals 2/3 × 9?

    (A) 6   (B) 12   (C) 4   (D) 8

74. The product of what number and 5 is equal to 25% of 80?

    (A) 12   (B) 8   (C) 4   (D) 10

75. Review the series: 2, 15, 6, 13, __, 11, 14, ... What number should fill in the blank space.

    (A) 8   (B) 6   (C) 10   (D) 9

76. If the hypotenuse of a right triangle is 13 and one of its legs is 5, find the area of the triangle.

    (A) 20   (B) 40   (C) 45   (D) 30

77. O is the center of the circle.

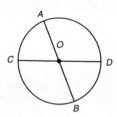

    Which of the following statements is true?

    (A) $AB > CD$
    (B) $CO < OB$
    (C) $AB - OB = DO$
    (D) $CD - OB < OD$

78. A gasoline pump fills an automobile tank at the rate of .7 gallon every 2 seconds. At this rate, how long would it take to fill a 28-gallon tank?

    (A) 1 minute, 20 seconds
    (B) 1 minute, 40 seconds
    (C) 2 minutes, 30 seconds
    (D) 2 minutes, 50 seconds

79. Review the series: 18, 9, $4\frac{1}{2}$, $2\frac{1}{4}$, ... Find the next number.

    (A) 1   (B) $1\frac{1}{2}$
    (C) $1\frac{1}{4}$ (D) $1\frac{1}{8}$

80. Let k represent the length of a rectangle. Represent the perimeter when the width is 8 less than the length.

    (A) $6k - 6$
    (B) $2k + 16$
    (C) $4k - 10$
    (D) $4k - 16$

81. Five times what number equals the difference of 8 squared and 9?

    (A) 8   (B) 9   (C) 11   (D) 12

82. Examine the diagram and select the best choice.

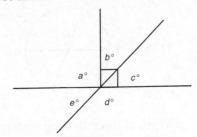

(A) $a° = d° + e°$
(B) $a° = b° + c°$
(C) $c° + d° < a°$
(D) $c° + e° > a°$

83. What number equals four fifths of the average of 18 and 42?

(A) 20   (B) 15   (C) 24   (D) 10

84. Given (a), (b), and (c), find the best answer.

(a) $4.06 × 10^3$
(b) $30 × 10^2$
(c) $52.4 × 10^1$

(A) (a) is greater than (b)
(B) (b) is less than (c)
(C) (c) is greater than (b)
(D) (a) is less than (b)

85. Thirty math books were distributed to an algebra class at the beginning of the semester. Four books were lost and the rest were returned. In simplest terms, what is the ratio of returned books to lost books?

(A) 5/4   (B) 17/9
   (C) 5/13   (D) 13/2

86. Review the series: 2, 4, 5, 10, 11, 22, 23, ... Find the next number.

(A) 34   (B) 36   (C) 44   (D) 46

87. Jocelyn wants to cement the walk to her home. If the walk measures 32 feet by 3.5 feet and costs $12.40 to cement a square foot, what is the total cost of the job?

(A) $456   (B) $392
   (C) $568   (D) $418

88. Examine the figure in which $a > c > d > b$. Then select the best answer.

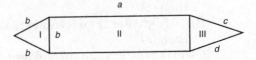

(A) $c + b > a$
(B) $a - b < d$
(C) $d + a < b + a$
(D) $c + d > 2b$

89. Review the series: III, 6, IX, 12, __, 18, ... What number should fill in the blank space?

(A) XII   (B) XV
(C) 16   (D) 15

90. Twenty-four students in a class are right-handed and 6 are left-handed. If these figures represent the entire class, what percent is left-handed?

(A) 15%   (B) 25%
   (C) 20%   (D) 30%

91. Examine right triangle EFG and square $ABCD$ and select the best answer.

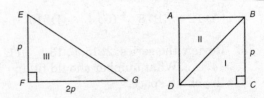

(A) Area △ I + Area △ II = Area △ III
(B) Area △ I = Area △ III
(C) 2 × Area II > Area III
(D) Area $ABCD$ – Area △ I >
   Area △ III

92. Review the series: 3.9, 6.1, 8.3, 10.5, ... Find the next number.

    (A) 12.7   (B) 12.1
       (C) 11.8   (D) 12.6

93. RS is perpendicular to ST. $\angle TSU = 22°$. Find x.

    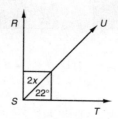

    (A) 68°   (B) 44°
       (C) 28°   (D) 34°

94. Review the series: 2, 1, 3, 2, 6, 5, 15, 14, 42, ... Find the next number.

    (A) 84   (B) 55
       (C) 41   (D) 126

95. Find 15% of 20% of 80.

    (A) 3   (B) 2.4
       (C) 4.6   (D) 3.6

96. Which statement is true?

    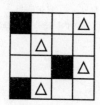

    (A) Total ■ > Total △
    (B) Total △ + Total ■ > Total □
    (C) Total □ − Total △ > Total ■
    (D) Total □ − Total ■ < Total △

97. Review the series: X, T, P, L, ... Find the next letter.

    (A) J   (B) I   (C) H   (D) G

98. Examine the rectangle, the triangle, and the following information; then select the best answer.

    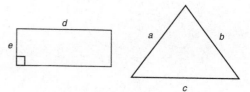

    If $a = 2d$ and $b = 2e$, by how much longer is the perimeter of the triangle than the perimeter of the rectangle?

    (A) b (B) c (C) a (D) d

99. Review the series: 2, 5, 4, 8, 6, 11, ... Find the next number.

    (A) 8   (B) 7   (C) 10   (D) 11

100. If you purchase a soup, a burger, French fries, and a soda and hand in a $10 bill, approximately how much change should you receive?

    $2.85

    $1.89

    $1.37

    $1.16

    (A) $2.75   (B) $2.85
       (C) $2.80   (D) $2.70

101. Examine the following figures and choose the best answer.

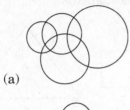

(a)

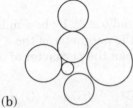

(b)

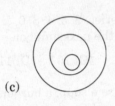

(c)

(A) Figure (a) includes one less circle than figure (c).

(B) Figure (b) includes two more circles than figure (c).

(C) Figure (c) includes two fewer circles than figure (b).

(D) Figure (b) includes three more circles than figure (c).

102. Review the series: 142, 137, 131, 124, __, 107, ... What number should fill in the blank space?

(A) 118   (B) 116
  (C) 109   (D) 111

103. Examine the chart, and then choose the best answer.

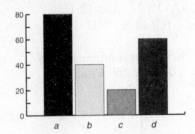

(A) $a - b = c$ (B) $b + c = d$
  (C) $b + c > a$ (D) $d - c < b$

104. Look at the series: 1, 8, 27, 64, 125, ... Find the next number.

(A) 625   (B) 256
  (C) 216   (D) 250

105. Compare (a), (b), and (c).

(a) $4/100 + 5/10 + 3$
(b) $9/100 + 3 + 3/10$
(c) $2/10 + 3 + 3/100$

(A) (c) is greater than (b) and less than (a)

(B) (b) is less than (a) and greater than (c)

(C) (a) is less than (b) and less than (c)

(D) (b) is greater than (a) and greater than (c)

106. *VR* is perpendicular to *VT*, and *VS* is perpendicular to *VU*. Which of the following statements is the best answer?

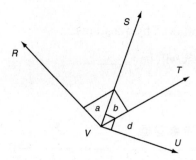

(A) $a + b < b + d$
(B) $d - b = a - b$
(C) $a + b < 90°$
(D) $b + d = 90°$

107. Review the series: 6, 9, 13, 14, 17, 21, 22, __, 29, 30, ... What number should fill in the blank space?

(A) 23   (B) 25   (C) 24   (D) 26

108. Given (a), (b), and (c), select the best answer.

(a) $5/8 \times 40$
(b) $3/4 \times 60$
(c) $2/3 \times 45$

(A) (a) is less than (c) and greater than (b)
(B) (b) is greater than (c) and less than (a)
(C) (c) is less than (b) and greater than (a)
(D) (a) is greater than (b) and greater than (c)

109.

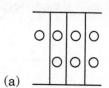

(a)

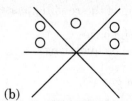

(b)

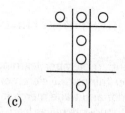

(c)

Which of the following statements is true?

(A) There is one more circle in (b) than lines in (a).
(B) The number of lines in (b) plus the number of circles in (a) is equal to the number of lines in (c) plus the number of circles in (c).
(C) The number of circles in (c) and (a) is less than the number of lines in (a) and (b).
(D) The number of lines in (a) plus the number of circles in (b) is less than the number of lines in (b) and (c).

110. Review the series: 33, 32, 30, 27, 23, ... Find the next number.

(A) 18   (B) 19   (C) 17   (D) 15

111. Review the series: P, P, R, S, P, P, T, U, P, P, V, ... Find the next letter.

(A) W   (B) X   (C) Y   (D) Z

112. Review the series: 128, 125, 120, 113, 104, 93, ... Find the next number.

(A) 77   (B) 86   (C) 80   (D) 78

STOP

IF YOU FINISH BEFORE TIME IS UP, CHECK OVER YOUR WORK ON THIS TEST ONLY. DO NOT GO ON TO THE NEXT TEST UNTIL THE SIGNAL IS GIVEN.

SUBTEST 3   READING—COMPREHENSION—VOCABULARY

#113–174   *25 minutes*

Sample:

The next test has short reading passages, each one is followed by questions.

Correct marking of the reading passages on the next test will be _____.

(A) all on one page
(B) followed by questions
(C) easy to read
(D) very long

PASSAGE FOR QUESTIONS 113–120

Most students remember learning about the European explorer Marco Polo. Polo, among other things, traveled more than 3,000 miles to reach China where he acted as ambassador and trade merchant between two worlds.

But most students never learn about Rabban Sauma, a Mongolian Christian, who traveled 7,000 miles from Beijing to Vienna, Italy. Sauma left China and set out for Baghdad in 1275 A.D., narrowly missing Polo's arrival in Beijing. From Baghdad, Sauma set out for the Vatican, via Paris, where he hoped to arrange a diplomatic relationship that would aid China in its <u>quest</u> to conquer the Middle East. He failed and returned to Baghdad, where he died in 1294 at the age of 75.

Historians claim that had Sauma succeeded in <u>brokering</u> his Mongol-European alliance, his actions would have significantly changed history. Since Jerusalem and Egypt would have fallen into European hands, explorers would not have sailed around looking for a new trade route—and Columbus would never have discovered the Americas.

113. What route did Rabban Sauma follow on his journey to Europe?

   (A) China to France to Italy
   (B) Baghdad to Rome to Paris
   (C) Jerusalem to Egypt to America
   (D) Beijing to Vienna to Versailles

114. In what kind of text would you expect to find this piece?

   (A) in a travel guide
   (B) in a history book
   (C) in a cook book
   (D) in a book of international fairy tales

115. Which of the following definitions best describes the word <u>quest</u> as used in this selection?

   (A) a dangerous, usually magical, journey upon which a person is forced to go
   (B) an elementary school program designed to stimulate gifted and talented students
   (C) a software program for searching the Internet
   (D) a goal, often long term, to which one is especially dedicated

116. The writer's main purpose in writing this selection is _____.

    (A) to reject the idea that people greatly desired a reliable trade route
    (B) to declare without question that Sauma's diplomatic success would have necessarily changed the course of human history
    (C) to challenge the idea that Marco Polo was the only memorable explorer of the 1200s
    (D) to promote the idea that only Italian explorers accomplished anything of any worth

117. The author of this passage implies that _____.

    (A) had Sauma succeeded in his diplomatic mission, the world would be much the same today
    (B) had Sauma failed in his diplomatic mission, the world would be vastly different
    (C) had Sauma convinced Europe to ally itself with China, many explorers would have been out of a job
    (D) had Sauma won over European allies, World War I would have never taken place

118. What was the likely distance of Sauma's trip?

    (A) 3,000 miles
    (B) 7,000 miles
    (C) 10,000 miles
    (D) 14,000 miles

119. The word <u>brokering</u> as used in this passage is best defined as _____.

    (A) arranging
    (B) defeating
    (C) utilizing
    (D) financing

120. Which of the following titles would best suit this selection?

    (A) Rabban! Sauma!
    (B) There and Back Again
    (C) Arabian Nights
    (D) Around the World in 80 Years

PASSAGE FOR QUESTIONS 121–125

Among some of the best war films ever made is John Sturges' movie entitled *The Great Escape*. The film depicts the real life story of how a group of prisoners of war, <u>notorious</u> for their taste for tunneling, struggled to escape from the German POW camp known as Stalag Luft III. Members of the camp worked together to dig three tunnels, nicknamed Tom, Dick, and Harry, through which approximately 55 POWs made their escape. It took more than five million Germans, dispatched from their usual war effort duties, to search out the escapees, detracting significantly from the overall Nazi war effort. Unfortunately, the Germans recaptured and executed all but three of the escapees. In return, the Allies demanded satisfaction; ultimately 21 members of the Gestapo were executed, and 17 were sentenced to prison terms.

121. How many POWs died in the attempt to escape Stalag Luft III?

    (A) 52
    (B) 55
    (C) 3
    (D) 60

122. Which of the following statements can be inferred using information in the passage?

    (A) The POWs of Stalag Luft III generally wasted their time and effort in digging Tom, Dick, and Harry.
    (B) The number of POWs in Stalag Luft III who made it to safety far outnumbered those who were recaptured.
    (C) The POWs of Stalag Luft III outnumbered their German guards, a fact that crucially assisted their successful escape.
    (D) The POWs of Stalag Luft III, despite their inability to escape personally, nevertheless helped the Allies win World War II.

123. The main purpose of this passage would be _____.

    (A) to praise John Sturges for his masterful direction of a difficult story
    (B) to show how diligent German Gestapo were during World War II
    (C) to tell an interesting, and perhaps little known, anecdote about World War II
    (D) to show how Nazi war crimes were resolved during World War II

124. The word <u>notorious</u> can best be defined as _____.

    (A) famous but humble
    (B) wealthy but immoral
    (C) well known but dangerous
    (D) angry but deadly

125. What did the Nazis do to the escapees?

    (A) shipped them to Japan
    (B) executed them
    (C) put them in solitary confinement
    (D) locked them back up again

PASSAGE FOR QUESTIONS 126–133

It's easy to assume that we are all entitled to a childhood; indeed, we feel deprived when we think of various injustices that happen to us during the course of growing up that detract from memories of our "lost innocence."

A popular book, entitled *Centuries of Childhood*, published in 1962 puts such ideas into writing for all to read. The text argues that Victorian culture first began sheltering children from early exposure to the harsh realities of the adult world. This idea of protecting children from the "real world" opposed family practices that took place earlier than the 18th century.

Many writers of other texts pick up where *Centuries of Childhood* leaves off, arguing that 20th century society has extended that period of childhood into longer and longer <u>durations</u>. Consider the hard fact that once a high school graduate could expect to earn a solid living supporting a single-income family; today, it takes a college degree to be a noncommissioned, sales representative at the local mall.

Such authors, like Dr. Benjamin Spock, point to various factors for explanation as to why cultures like ours willingly coddle and handicap their young like this. These authors dispute the wisdom of giving our children a protected childhood. After all, they argue, by encouraging the youth to remain in a state of infancy, we <u>retard</u> the rate at which they can take over adult responsibilities. We, however, would like to put forth an alternate hypothesis.

126. The word <u>durations</u> as used in this selection refers to the concept of _____.

(A) mass
(B) space
(C) sound
(D) time

127. Based on the information in the selection, what kind of text would include this piece?

(A) a science text
(B) a novel
(C) a sociology article
(D) a biography

128. Which of the following titles would best fit this reading passage?

(A) Rocking the Cradle
(B) The Times, They Are a'Changing
(C) Spare the Rod, Spoil the Child
(D) Spock Speaks

129. Which of the following definitions best suits the word <u>retard</u>?

(A) damaged
(B) slowed down
(C) brilliant
(D) advanced

130. In which century does the article state that people first began sheltering children from the harsh realities of the world?

(A) 17th century
(B) 18th century
(C) 19th century
(D) 20th century

131. Based on the information in this selection, what will the author(s) discuss next?

(A) an argument that points out how stupid it is to shelter children from reality
(B) an argument that remains neutral on the topic of sheltering children from reality
(C) an argument that shows the wisdom of sheltering children from reality
(D) We cannot tell from context clues.

132. When does the article state *Centuries of Childhood* was published?

(A) 1920s
(B) 1950s
(C) 1960s
(D) 1980s

133. The author's main purpose in writing this passage is _____.

(A) to discuss the history of child rearing in the United States
(B) to probe psychological reasons behind child rearing in Victorian society
(C) to analyze child-rearing practices of the 17th century
(D) to put forth a theory on the best way to raise children

PASSAGE FOR QUESTION 134–139

Experts in military history often talk about something called the fifth column when they discuss World War II. The term actually comes from a 1936 conflict in Madrid. An invading army, led by Emilo Mola Videl, attacked the city with four columns of armies marching from four directions. As he drew closer to Madrid, Videl boasted of a secret weapon that he would soon <u>deploy</u>—a "fifth" army (or column) that he had previously ordered to infiltrate the city and prepare to attack from the inside.

The term "fifth column," has come to refer to a group of traitors who hide in a targeted area to sabotage that area's defense from within. Military <u>tacticians</u> still use the fifth column in their strategies; for example, Iraqi rebels during the Gulf War and Cuban insurgents in the Bay of Pigs both used the idea in their military planning. The term has also become a favorite concept for writers of spy fiction. Two books that handle the topic particularly well include Ken Follett's *The Eye of the Needle* and Robert Harris's *Fatherland*.

134. The author's purpose in writing this piece is _____.

(A) to define what the term "fifth column" means
(B) to discuss U.S. foreign policy in Cuba
(C) to analyze the spy fiction genre
(D) to document the life of Emilo Mola Videl

135. In what country did the term "fifth column" originate?

(A) United States
(B) Spain
(C) Cuba
(D) Iraq

136. Which of the following options would be most likely to follow the second paragraph in this reading selection?

(A) a discussion of reality-based fiction, specifically those that utilize military tactics
(B) a discussion of famous military leaders, like Castro or Noriega
(C) a discussion of spy fiction, especially those texts that use the "fifth column" as a plot device
(D) a discussion of the phrase, "The eagle has landed"

137. The word <u>tacticians</u> is best defined by which of the following definitions?

(A) people who use strategy to get what they want
(B) people who are very polite
(C) people who organize military actions and battle plans
(D) people who rely on their sense of touch

138. What, based on your reading of the passage, can you infer about the spy novels mentioned in paragraph two?

(A) They will both use Emilo Mola Videl's campaign as a plot device.
(B) They will both use secret weapons as a plot device.
(C) They will both use the idea of weapons of mass destruction as a plot device.
(D) They will both use traitors working within native cities as a plot device.

139. What does the word <u>deploy</u>, as used in this reading passage, mean?

(A) keep in reserve
(B) dismiss
(C) use
(D) hire

PASSAGE FOR QUESTIONS 140–146

Some of the most fascinating creatures on the planet are the tiny planaria. Planaria are flat worms, about ¼ of an inch long, that have oval-like bodies, triangular heads, and what appear to be crossed eyes (although no evidence exists to suggest that these creatures actually see anything). Planaria feed using a little "nose" tube, usually by vacuuming up nutrients that happen to be in the area; they are especially fond of hard-boiled eggs. Generally, they prefer warm environments; living in petri dishes nestled on the low setting of a heating pad helps approximate their preferred natural habitat.

What is especially fascinating about these little creatures is their ability to regenerate lost body parts. If their bodies are damaged, most of the time they can actually regrow the damaged part. As one might expect, total <u>decapitation</u> will kill planaria, but even significant slices to the head can result in the creation of a two-headed planaria. Scientists like to study these creatures in the hopes that doing so will reveal secrets of <u>regeneration</u>—secrets that may one day be successfully applied to humans.

140. Based on your reading of this passage, what kind of worms are planaria?

(A) round
(B) flat
(C) segmented
(D) none of the above

141. In what branch of science does this selection belong?

(A) chemistry
(B) biology
(C) astronomy
(D) physics

142. Which of the following is the best definition of <u>decapitation</u>?

(A) taking off the cap
(B) removing the head
(C) surrender
(D) seeing things that are not really there

143. Based on your reading of the passage, all but which of the following facts are true?

(A) Planaria are ¼ inch long, on average.
(B) Planaria like to live in warm environments.
(C) Planaria absorb nutrients through their nose-tube.
(D) Planaria like to eat scrambled eggs.

144. Why does the author say it is important to study planaria?

(A) Studying planaria may allow us to achieve regeneration in humans.
(B) Planaria are so cute; they are innately fun to study.
(C) Creation of a two-headed planaria is required for most scientific dissertations.
(D) Cultivating planaria allows us to test the effectiveness of the new petri dishes.

145. Based on its usage in the passage, what is the best definition of <u>regeneration</u>?

(A) new growth of cells
(B) regrowth of cells
(C) calculation of cell damage
(D) documentation of cell division

146. Which of the following is the best title for this reading passage?

(A) Decapitation in Planaria
(B) On the Care and Feeding of Planaria
(C) The Potential of Planaria
(D) The Natural Habitat of the Planaria Worm

PASSAGE FOR QUESTIONS 147–152

Most people don't know it, but Valentine's Day began as an annual pagan marriage rite during which men and women chose marriage partners for the upcoming year. Generally, people made their matches randomly, using a lottery system, but on rare occasions a couple could <u>petition</u> to stay together for longer than the usual year. The Catholic Church, which viewed the Valentine's Day lottery as understandably immoral, soon leveled strong pressure against participants to make marriages permanent. Over time, however, most of the political and religious concerns fell away, and the holiday changed its focus away from arranging marriage contracts to simply expressing one's love for one's spouse, fiancé, or significant other.

Accordingly, the holiday has grown increasingly commercialized—and expensive. Everyone has heard of the traditional costs—a card and candy or a dozen red roses (cost: upwards of $25). But, consider recent romantic options. As of February 2004, for a mere $125,000 you could have arranged for the purchase of his and her Mercedes convertibles (to keep), a candle-lit dinner, and an evening of "stars and s'mores" during which you gazed at constellations; this package came with its very own professional astronomer and a butler to roast your marshmallows. Or, if you were on a more limited budget, you could have made reservations at a wide variety of hotels happy to arrange for fireworks displays, romantic messages laid out in rose-petals, and secluded picnics.

In short, Valentine's Day marketers are <u>upping the ante</u> for everyone. Americans spent an average of nearly $100 on Valentine's Day this year, up from $80 last year; unsurprisingly, retailers are out to try to increase that amount for next year.

Why we should feel pressured to express a deep emotion like love using stereotypical and trite methods is a question that should puzzle—and distress—us.

147. One can infer from reading this passage that the author _____.

(A) approves of the way we celebrate Valentine's Day these days
(B) puts forth the opinion that the fertility rites originally connected to Valentine's Day were immoral
(C) thinks that the best Valentine's Day present is a bouquet of flowers and a movie
(D) disapproves of the way some people celebrate Valentine's Day

148. Which of the following would most likely publish this reading passage?

(A) a school text book on holidays and customs
(B) the "Leisure and Arts" section of the daily newspaper
(C) a journal that prints the latest research in biological studies
(D) an encyclopedia

149. What is the best definition of the word <u>petition</u>?

(A) yell
(B) protest
(C) request
(D) demand

150. What is likely to come next in this discussion?

(A) a discussion of St. Valentine's role in the evolution of Valentine's Day
(B) a discussion of how people in the 1800s celebrated Valentine's Day
(C) a discussion of how commercialized Valentine's Day has become
(D) a discussion of how the changes in Valentine's Day celebrations reveals changes in human morals

151. How much does the author say it would cost for a deluxe Valentine package that includes the cars, the astronomy lesson, and the butler-produced s'mores?

    (A) $25
    (B) $80
    (C) $100
    (D) $125,000

152. What does the phrase <u>upping the ante</u> mean, as used in the context of this passage?

    (A) making the playing field equal for those who celebrate Valentine's Day
    (B) increasing the minimum acceptable behavior for celebrating Valentine's Day
    (C) making it more expensive for people to participate in Valentine's Day
    (D) angering those of us who participate in Valentine's Day activities

---

DIRECTIONS: Choose the word that means the same or nearly the same as the underlined word.

---

153. to <u>peruse</u> a text

    (A) underline
    (B) purchase
    (C) read
    (D) ignore

154. to <u>broach</u> a topic

    (A) disprove
    (B) choose
    (C) mention
    (D) research

155. to <u>amass</u> wealth

    (A) accumulate
    (B) spread
    (C) distribute
    (D) detest

156. an anonymous <u>benefactor</u>

    (A) author
    (B) helper
    (C) request
    (D) worker

157. an <u>irate</u> customer

    (A) angry
    (B) loyal
    (C) calculating
    (D) pleasant

158. rough <u>terrain</u>

    (A) land
    (B) water
    (C) justice
    (D) storm

159. a <u>meticulous</u> worker

    (A) sloppy
    (B) manual
    (C) careful
    (D) ridiculous

160. to <u>condone</u> an action

    (A) disapprove
    (B) pardon
    (C) repeat
    (D) hide

161. a <u>candid</u> response

    (A) misleading
    (B) false
    (C) delayed
    (D) straightforward

162. an <u>edible</u> plant

    (A) poisonous
    (B) eatable
    (C) flowering
    (D) medicinal

163. to <u>revere</u> a hero

    (A) follow
    (B) respect highly
    (C) publicize
    (D) antagonize

164. a <u>vigilant</u> guard

    (A) alert
    (B) violent
    (C) professional
    (D) sleeping

165. a human <u>foible</u>

    (A) weakness
    (B) bone
    (C) feeling
    (D) being

166. an unexpected <u>boon</u>

    (A) interruption
    (B) explosion
    (C) gift
    (D) deviation

167. a <u>dubious</u> suggestion

    (A) welcome
    (B) slow
    (C) random
    (D) doubtful

168. closest <u>egress</u>

    (A) exit
    (B) bird
    (C) flower
    (D) garment

169. to <u>proclaim</u> a belief

    (A) support
    (B) hear
    (C) dismiss
    (D) declare

170. a <u>sumptuous</u> banquet

    (A) rich
    (B) paltry
    (C) vegetarian
    (D) hypothetical

171. a <u>whimsical</u> poem

    (A) adaptable
    (B) mechanical
    (C) playful
    (D) difficult

172. a <u>superfluous</u> part

    (A) extra
    (B) large
    (C) attractive
    (D) colorful

173. welcome <u>solace</u>

    (A) decoration
    (B) relief
    (C) anger
    (D) speech

174. a <u>sagacious</u> parent

    (A) wise
    (B) old
    (C) feeble
    (D) healthy

STOP

IF YOU FINISH BEFORE TIME IS UP, CHECK OVER YOUR WORK ON THIS TEST ONLY. DO NOT
GO ON TO THE NEXT TEST UNTIL THE SIGNAL IS GIVEN.

SUBTEST 4   MATHEMATICS

#175–238   *45 minutes*

Sample:

Round 642 to the nearest hundred.

(A) 650   (B) 600   (C) 700   (D) 640   Ⓐ ● Ⓒ Ⓓ

DIRECTIONS: Select the best answer for each question.

---

175. If the length of a rectangle is 4.2″ and its width is 3.65″, find its perimeter.

    (A) 13.6″   (B) 15.7″
        (C) 16.3″   (D) 14.6″

176. Change $5\frac{1}{4}\%$ to a fraction.

    (A) 21/400   (B) 5/100
        (C) 21/100   (D) 25/150

177. Which point lies 4 units above the *x*-axis and 2 units to the left of the *y*-axis?

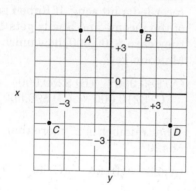

    (A) A   (B) B   (C) C   (D) D

178. A side of a square is 3. If the radius of a circle is 2, compare the perimeter of the square with the circumference of the circle, and choose the best answer. Let $\pi = 3.14$.

    (A) The perimeter of the square is 0.56 more than the circumference of the circle.
    (B) The circumference of the circle is 0.56 less than the perimeter of the square.
    (C) The perimeter of the square is 0.44 less than the circumference of the circle.
    (D) The circumference of the circle is 0.56 more than the perimeter of the square.

179. In a triangle, the sum of any two sides is always greater than the third side. Select the best choice to represent the three sides of a triangle.

    (A) 3, 4, 7   (B) 4, 5, 8
        (C) 5, 6, 12   (D) 10, 5, 5

180. Jesse Patterson has a 0.300 batting average (Hits/Times at bat). If he gets a total of 10 more hits the next 10 times at bat, his batting average jumps to 0.400. Determine how many hits he had originally.

    (A) 12   (B) 10   (C) 14   (D) 18

181. Examine the bar graph, and select the correct answer.

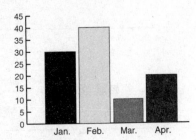

(A) Mar. + Apr. = 60
(B) Jan. – Mar. = 20
(C) Feb. – Mar. > 40
(D) Apr. + Feb. > 100

182. The Gema Corn Flake Company has 2 tons of corn flakes on hand. One ton equals 2,000 pounds and one pound equals 16 ounces. If the company plans to package the corn flakes in 12-ounce boxes, how many boxes will they need? Round the answer to the nearest whole box.

(A) 5,423 boxes   (B) 5,333 boxes
   (C) 5,340 boxes   (D) 5,328 boxes

183. Round off 1,147,690 to the nearest thousand.

(A) 1,147,200   (B) 1,150,000
   (C) 1,148,000   (D) 1,149,000

184. Find the sum of the squares of the prime factors of 42.

(A) 50   (B) 62   (C) 38   (D) 44

185. Determine the perimeter of the triangle.

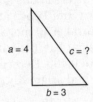

(A) 5   (B) 12   (C) 9   (D) 17

186. The price of a computer dropped from $1,500 to $1,200. What was the percent drop?

(A) 30%   (B) 20%
   (C) 38%   (D) 34%

187. Six times a number reduced by 8 is equal to 58. Find the number.

(A) 8   (B) 6   (C) 11   (D) 9

188. Craymore Electronics sold 81 computers and 52 printers last week. Twenty-five separate customers purchased computers and printers. How many customers purchased only computers?

(A) 39   (B) 42   (C) 49   (D) 56

189. The library has a policy of ordering 5 fiction, 2 historical, 3 biographical, and 3 science books in that order. If 124 books were ordered, what subject was the last book?

(A) fiction   (B) historical
   (C) biographical   (D) science

190. Ruben, Shelly, and Malcolm have recorded a hit song. If Ruben gets 2/5 of the income and Shelly gets 1/3 and they earn $300,000, how much does Malcolm get?

(A) $80,000   (B) $250,000
   (C) $210,000   (D) $90,000

191. What number is 17 more than 5% of 420?

(A) 26   (B) 64   (C) 44   (D) 38

192. Six times a number is 24.72. What is the result if we divide that number by 4?

(A) 2.45   (B) 1.03
   (C) 4.34   (D) 3.82

193. Let X represent the set of multiples of 4, and Y the set of multiples of 10. Which of the following statements is true?

(A) $12 \notin X$ (B) $11 \in X$
   (C) $40 \in Y$ (D) $8 \notin X$

194. The sum of two consecutive odd integers is 156. What is the larger integer?

(A) 75   (B) 77   (C) 78   (D) 79

195. Add: $-3a + 4b - 6c$ and $7b - 4c - 6a$.

(A) $-9a + 11b - 10c$
(B) $3a + 4b - 10c$
(C) $6a - 2b - 6c$
(D) $-7a - 4b + 8c$

196. Find the value of $\dfrac{4 \times 5^8}{2 \times 5^6}$.

(A) 50   (B) 40   (C) 25   (D) 100

197. Which of the following choices will satisfy the inequality $-2 < x < 2.3$?

(A) -5 (B) 3.2   (C) 0   (D) 2.4

198. What percent of 80 is 17.6?

(A) 22%   (B) 79%
(C) 82%   (D) 46%

199. Add: $(-4) + (+9) + (-6) + (+3)$

(A) -4 (B) $+3$ (C) -6 (D) $+2$

200. If x and y are negative integers and $y > x$, which of the following statements is true?

(A) $xy < 0$ (B) $x + y > 0$
(C) $xy > 0$ (D) $y - x < 0$

201. If the perimeter of a rectangle is 44 feet and its width is 7 feet, what is its length?

(A) 12   (B) 11   (C) 15   (D) 14

202. If two interior angles of a triangle are 47° and 58°, select the third angle.

(A) 75°   (B) 43°
(C) 59°   (D) 36°

203. Select the greatest prime factor of 42.

(A) 7   (B) 6   (C) 3   (D) 14

204. The rectangle measures 16 units long and 14 units wide. If each square on the edges of the rectangle measures 3 by 3 units, find the shaded area in the figure below.

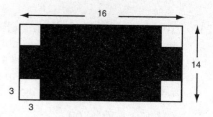

(A) 120   (B) 188
(C) 235   (D) 224

205. Simplify the ratio 2.6/20.8.

(A) 2/3   (B) 1.5
(C) 1/8   (D) 3/7

206. $5(a - 2b) + 6(-2a + 4b) =$

(A) $-7a + 14b$ (B) $9a + 12b$
(C) $33b - 5a$ (D) $-6a - 15b$

207. Change the expression
$7 \times 10^3 + 5 \times 10^2 + 2 \times 10^1 + 6 \times 10^0$
to a four-digit number.

(A) 7,345   (B) 7,890
(C) 7,738   (D) 7,526

208. What happens to the area of a triangle when its height is doubled and its base remains the same?

(A) remains the same
(B) is doubled
(C) is tripled
(D) is multiplied by 2.5

209. Multiply: $3\dfrac{1}{2}$ by $\dfrac{22}{5}$.

(A) $6\dfrac{1}{5}$ (B) $6\dfrac{3}{10}$

(C) 8.4   (D) $8\dfrac{3}{5}$

210. Simplify $\sqrt[3]{64a^3b^9}$

(A) $8ab^3$ (B) $4a^3b^3$
(C) $4a^3b$ (D) $4ab^3$

211. The letters a, b, and c are consecutive odd integers in the given order. If $c = 11$, what is the product of a and b?

    (A) 55   (B) 63   (C) 72   (D) 87

212. In an auto manufacturing plant, the ratio of executives to assembly line workers is 1:15. If there are 480 employees altogether, how many assembly line workers are there?

    (A) 450   (B) 800
       (C) 250   (D) 600

213. Simplify $\dfrac{4\frac{2}{3}}{5\frac{1}{4}}$

    (A) 5/8   (B) 3/5
       (C) 8/9   (D) 5/7

214. BA is perpendicular to BD. Angle ABE measures 17°, and angle DBC measures 54°. Find the measure of angle EBC.

    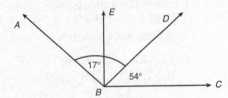

    (A) 125°   (B) 71°
       (C) 127°   (D) 144°

215. In the parallelogram, which two sides are parallel?

    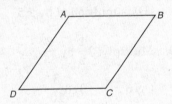

    (A) AB and BC
    (B) BC and CD
    (C) CD and AD
    (D) AD and BC

216. If the two central angles of the adjoining circle are 55° and 115°, find the average of all three central angles.

    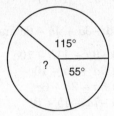

    (A) 55°   (B) 85°
       (C) 120°   (D) 60°

217. If one gallon of iodine is added to a five-gallon, 10% solution of iodine and water, what is the percent of iodine in the new mixture?

    (A) 15%   (B) 25%
       (C) 30%   (D) 20%

218. The average price of a car between the years 1998 and 2005 is given in the chart below.

    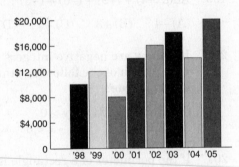

    To the nearest percent, find the increase in the average price of a car from 1999 to 2005.
    (A) 67%   (B) 35%
       (C) 44%   (D) 66%

219. The following table represents the frequency distribution of students' weights. Find the mean weight and round to the nearest tenth.

Pounds, p_i	Frequency, f_i	$p_i f_i$
98	2	
105	1	
109	1	
120	3	
126	2	
132	4	

   (A) 119.3   (B) 119.7
     (C) 119.0   (D) 119.2

220. Simplify $\dfrac{7}{17\frac{1}{2}}$.

   (A) 3/7   (B) 2/5
     (C) 5/9   (D) 7/8

221. Find the value of x in the adjoining diagram.

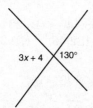

              $3x + 4$ $130°$

   (A) 54°   (B) 38°
     (C) 46°   (D) 42°

222. If the Big Peach Supermarket is selling raisins at $0.20 per ounce, how much would 8 pounds cost?

   (A) $18.40   (B) $24.60
     (C) $25.60   (D) $32.20

223. Madison High School held a junior prom. The total receipts amounted to $3,070. Members of the Student Organization paid $5, while non-members paid $11. If 170 tickets were sold to non-members, how many tickets were sold to Student Organization members?

   (A) 244   (B) 366
     (C) 285   (D) 482

224. Malika wants to build a fence in the shape of a hexagon around her property. The sides of the fence are 49.4 feet, 34.9 feet, 53.6 feet, 65.8 feet, 72.6 feet, and 48.7 feet. If fencing costs $5.30 per foot, find the cost for the complete fence. Round off to the nearest cent.

   (A) $2,340.60   (B) $1,893.60
     (C) $2,342.80   (D) $1,722.50

225. The sides of a pentagon are represented by $x, x + 2, x + 5, 2x + 2,$ and $3x - 1$. If the perimeter is 56, find the length of the longest side.

   (A) 18   (B) 19   (C) 17   (D) 14

226. The area of a square is represented by $4x + 20$. If each side is 8, find x.

   (A) 9   (B) 11   (C) 8   (D) 10

227. Latisha is 5 years older than Wanda. Three years ago Wanda was $8a$ years. How old is Latisha now?

   (A) $8a + 5$ (B) $8a - 3$
     (C) $8a + 8$ (D) $8a + 3$

228. In a two-digit number, the sum of the digits is 11. Three times the tens' digit is 5 more than the units' digit. Find the number.

   (A) 47   (B) 16   (C) 53   (D) 39

229. Thirty math books were distributed to an algebra class at the beginning of the semester. Four books were lost, and the rest were returned. In simplest terms, what is the ratio of returned books to lost books?

   (A) 5/4   (B) 17/9
     (C) 5/13   (D) 13/2

230. Find side BC of the adjoining right angle.

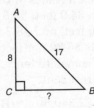

(A) 12 (B) 18 (C) 19 (D) 15

231. Of the following expressions, which is the largest?

(A) $2 \times 5^2 - 9 \div 3$
(B) $3^3 - (18 \div 2) + 7$
(C) $5(8 - 3)^2$
(D) $4 \times 9 + 3(6 - 2)$

232. If $6(a + 2) - 2c = 6$ and $a = 4$, find c.

(A) 15 (B) 18 (C) 12 (D) 17

233. Find the measure of $\angle a$.

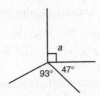

(A) 183° (B) 140°
(C) 230° (D) 130°

234. Which of the following numbers is 8 less than two-thirds of 27?

(A) 10 (B) 8 (C) 6 (D) 4

235. 5 feet 7 inches – 2 feet 9 inches =

(A) 2 feet 2 inches
(B) 3 feet 1 inch
(C) 3 feet 5 inches
(D) 2 feet 10 inches

236. Jack collects tolls. On the average, he collects $5.25 per hour. How much does he collect in two hours?

(A) $460 (B) $540
(C) $400 (D) $630

237. Find the shaded area if the radius of the outer circle is 8 inches and the radius of the inner circle is 5 inches. Let $\pi = 3.14$.

(A) 198.44 (B) 234.82
(C) 122.46 (D) 202.56

238. $5\sqrt{2} \times 3\sqrt{8} =$

(A) $10\sqrt{24}$ (B) $\sqrt{10}\sqrt{16}$
(C) 60 (D) 40

STOP

IF YOU FINISH BEFORE TIME IS UP, CHECK OVER YOUR WORK ON THIS TEST ONLY. DO NOT GO ON TO THE NEXT TEST UNTIL THE SIGNAL IS GIVEN.

SUBTEST 5   LANGUAGE

25 minutes

Samples: Which sentence below contains an error?

   (A) Andrew and he were leaving.
   (B) We was going to the store.
   (C) Josh and Sarah will buy food for us.   Correct marking of samples
   (D) No mistakes.   Ⓐ ● Ⓒ Ⓓ

   (A) Work on the car in here.
   (B) Where will we end up?
   (C) Enter through the front door, please.   Correct marking of samples
   (D) No mistakes.   Ⓐ Ⓑ Ⓒ ●

DIRECTIONS: In questions 239–278, choose the sentence in each group that contains an error in capitalization, punctuation, or usage. If you find no mistake, select D on your answer sheet.

239.
   (A) Alfia and I started our own business.
   (B) Paul can you tell Lisa to come to the party?
   (C) I can hardly contain my enthusiasm.
   (D) No mistakes.

240.
   (A) I attended the St Andrew parish when I was younger.
   (B) Many of his books are set in New Mexico.
   (C) Although the course was difficult, we stayed with it.
   (D) No mistakes.

241.
   (A) Shannon and Ben make a good couple.
   (B) The ingredients include salt, pepper, and nutmeg.
   (C) Merry and Pippin are the taller hobbits in all of the Shire.
   (D) No mistakes.

242.
   (A) Mother sent my sister and me to the store.
   (B) Avery wrote an excellent paper on theology.
   (C) Morgan hardly ever misses class.
   (D) No mistakes.

243.
   (A) One of the men on the team have dropped out of the game.
   (B) Ms. Johns and Mr. Schneider have done a lot of volunteer work.
   (C) Josh's brother's name is Adrian.
   (D) No mistakes.

244.
   (A) Francisco chose the saxophone; David chose the trumpet.
   (B) Would you mind stirring the kettle.
   (C) My friends and I play chess during lunch.
   (D) No mistakes.

245.

(A) Tom, Guy, Sandy, and me, went to the game together.
(B) Vince and Nella walked to the corner and bought some lemon ice.
(C) Gulliver visited many lands during his travels.
(D) No mistakes.

246.

(A) Could you set the package on the chair?
(B) I vowed, therefore, that I would never shop there again.
(C) She returned the textbook to myself.
(D) No mistakes.

247.

(A) What's the frequency, Kenneth?
(B) "I never make exceptions," warned the professor.
(C) Its a difficult problem, but we can handle it.
(D) No mistakes.

248.

(A) The cold medicine had some unpleasant side effects.
(B) Whom is speaking?
(C) For further information on pronunciation, consult your dictionary.
(D) No mistakes.

249.

(A) Its bark is worse than its bite.
(B) In this election, the voter doesn't have enough information to know if they should support the tax.
(C) Sherri, my next door neighbor, volunteered to baby-sit.
(D) No mistakes.

250.

(A) Josh just sits silent in his seat most of the time.
(B) Outside of class, he is very talkative.
(C) In fact, he talks too much.
(D) No mistakes.

251.

(A) Our oldest teacher was born on September, 23, 1960.
(B) No, the color of an airplane's black box is actually orange.
(C) Give the directions to Joseph, Jenny, and me.
(D) No mistakes.

252.

(A) The theme of the story concerned the destructive greed for powerfulness.
(B) Sinon convinced the Trojans to accept the horse.
(C) The revolving door is an efficient way to conserve energy.
(D) No mistakes.

253.

(A) Kat was the meanest manager at the store.
(B) It's hard to believe, but it's true.
(C) Bring the following to class, pen, pencil, paper, and books.
(D) No mistakes.

254.

(A) Theo bought a blanket for his baby sister.
(B) Is Trish getting married in December or in June?
(C) Jake is the truthfullest person I have ever met.
(D) No mistakes.

255.

(A) It is further to Cleveland than to Phildalelphia.
(B) Did you hear Isaac and me come in?
(C) Amanda sings beautifully.
(D) No mistakes.

256.

(A) Meredith was always on time, but John was usually late.
(B) Several of the guests have arrived.
(C) I don't have a lot of free time, nevertheless, I would like the job.
(D) No mistakes.

257.
- (A) No I have never seen a live rhinocerous.
- (B) Our zoo is the smallest in the state.
- (C) I still enjoy visiting, however.
- (D) No mistakes.

258.
- (A) I concluded, therefore, that I'd like to attend the university.
- (B) It's expensive, but I am saving my money.
- (C) Moreover, I plan on earning a scholarship.
- (D) No mistakes.

259.
- (A) You won't have to look for Joe and I.
- (B) We'll be wearing green jackets.
- (C) It's a daring fashion choice, but we're willing to risk it.
- (D) No mistakes.

260.
- (A) Since you're so smart, you won't mind answering a few questions.
- (B) Can you bake some cookies for our sale?
- (C) I realized I had been mistook.
- (D) No mistakes.

261.
- (A) I studied for hours, but the test was still difficult.
- (B) He had already gone before we arrived at the dance.
- (C) One of the teachers had volunteered to coach the bowling team.
- (D) No mistakes.

262.
- (A) I enjoy walking on the beach and to run in the surf.
- (B) Josiah, by the way, is living in Boston now.
- (C) He used to wear a black hat and a long coat.
- (D) No mistakes.

263.
- (A) Really, you're living in a golden age.
- (B) If you arrive late, just blend into the crowd.
- (C) I only have time to eat drink and sleep.
- (D) No mistakes.

264.
- (A) Did you enjoy the skating program?
- (B) Dennis performed good on the ice.
- (C) The music was carefully chosen.
- (D) No mistakes.

265.
- (A) Aunt Wendy often takes Al and I to lunch.
- (A) John Heywood collected and published many famous proverbs; you've probably never heard of him, though.
- (C) Mr. Meyers said—and rightly so—that the rules should apply to all.
- (D) No mistakes.

266.
- (A) The book on the top shelf is too high to reach.
- (B) The deer reared up on it's hind legs.
- (C) You're a mean one, Mr. Grinch.
- (D) No mistakes.

267.
- (A) Derrick listed *The Hobbit* as his favorite book.
- (B) I chose *The Adventures of Sherlock Holmes*.
- (C) I read my first mystery when I was in the third grade.
- (D) No mistakes.

268.
- (A) My favorite Aunt is visiting with my cousin.
- (B) Her sister, an immigrant from Sicily, arrived later.
- (C) They enjoy singing, reading, and cooking.
- (D) No mistakes.

269.
  (A) Everett hardly ever has time for small talk.
  (B) Our school finished first, his school placed second.
  (C) Neither Shannon nor Melissa missed a shot in that game.
  (D) No mistakes.

270.
  (A) Incidentally, amateurs are encouraged to apply.
  (B) My parents are immigrants; they came from Sicily.
  (C) Is that why you named your daughter Cicely?
  (D) No mistakes.

271.
  (A) Shakespeare wrote, "To thine own self be true".
  (B) Lucy received her degree three years ago.
  (C) Mr. White said, "Keep it simple."
  (D) No mistakes.

272.
  (A) Don't loose your tickets, or you won't be able to get in.
  (B) Mrs. Brown kindly offered me a seat.
  (C) The fruit salad consists of the following: cherries, grapes, and peaches.
  (D) No mistakes.

273.
  (A) Neither Jimmy or Tommy has ever been to Canada.
  (B) Fiona is more timid than Martha.
  (C) You'll feel better if you lie down, Griffin.
  (D) No mistakes.

274.
  (A) Larry has always been an excellent pianist.
  (B) He enjoys singing, dancing, and telling jokes.
  (C) I just want to set on my porch and swing.
  (D) No mistakes.

275.
  (A) Is the soup ready yet?
  (B) My least favorite flavor is vanilla.
  (C) Gus transferred here from another school.
  (D) No mistakes.

276.
  (A) I wish I could visit Avonlea.
  (B) You and me are best friends, aren't we?
  (C) Most people are basically kind, aren't they?
  (D) No mistakes.

277.
  (A) Solomon lives across town; nevertheless, we are best friends.
  (B) My neighbors own a german shepherd.
  (C) My leisure time is spent reading classic novels.
  (D) No mistakes.

278.
  (A) Since he started walking.
  (B) Holden has been playing baseball.
  (C) He plays catcher for a team in Rye, New York.
  (D) No mistakes.

DIRECTIONS: For questions 279–288, look for errors in spelling only.

279.
(A) Autumn is the loveliest season of the year.
(B) I doubt we'll ever know the answer to that puzzle.
(C) We rode thorough the tunnel on the way to the shore.
(D) No mistakes.

280.
(A) The monster was portrayed as a mishapen creature.
(B) In the book, he is described as an eloquent man.
(C) We have to ask which character is more monstrous.
(D) No mistakes.

281.
(A) He carfully unwrapped his gifts.
(B) Listen to the surgeon when he speaks.
(C) Matt's techniques are unique in his profession.
(D) No mistakes.

282.
(A) Imagine what the chief could do with that new machine.
(B) Don't interrupt your professor.
(C) Where did you aquire that artifact?
(D) No mistakes.

283.
(A) The first volume is truly useful.
(B) Even though the role was foolish, the actor was not embarassed.
(C) Chris intends to pursue a career in management.
(D) No mistakes.

284.
(A) Gomer was surprised to find himself in that situation.
(B) The warranty on the toaster oven expired long ago.
(C) The hospital discourages visitors after dark.
(D) No mistakes.

285.
(A) She has always been greatly concerned about the enviroment.
(B) Whether or not you attend, I will be there.
(C) The government's foreign policy is flexible.
(D) No mistakes.

286.
(A) Freddy immediately ran to the grocery.
(B) I always go to my science teacher for advise before a new experiment.
(C) Henry's interests are in fantasy books.
(D) No mistakes.

287.
(A) Do you believe in guardian angels?
(B) Too many people use apostrophes to write plurals.
(C) I'll bet I saw that forty times last month.
(D) No mistakes.

288.
(A) Lightening and thunder can be terrifying experiences.
(B) Grammar is an indispensable part of my knowledge.
(C) The bookkeeper resigned from the committee.
(D) No mistakes.

DIRECTIONS: Choose the correct word (or words) to join the thoughts together.

---

289. I couldn't sing in the choir last week _____ I had lost my voice.

    (A) furthermore
    (B) for example
    (C) because
    (D) and

290. Bess wears slippers to bed in the winter; _____, her feet are warm.

    (A) because
    (B) consequently
    (C) nevertheless
    (D) none of these

291. Choose the group of words that best completes this sentence:

    After clearing the dishes, _____.

    (A) a nap can be taken by all
    (B) we can, all of us, take a nap
    (C) we can all take a nap
    (D) a nap will feel good

292. Which of the following expresses the idea most clearly?

    (A) Many stories of the supernatural were written by Nathaniel Hawthorne, the 19th-century American novelist; this is forgotten a lot today.
    (B) Though it is forgotten today, the 19th-century American novelist Nathaniel Hawthorne wrote many stories of the supernatural.
    (C) Hawthorne, a forgotten novelist, wrote supernatural stories, in 19th-century america.
    (D) It is forgotten that Nathaniel Hawthorne, the American novelist who lived in the 19th century, wrote many stories about the supernatural.

293. Which of the following expresses the idea most clearly?

    (A) Since he would not apologize to me, I apologized to him.
    (B) He would not apologize to me. So, therefore, I apologized to him.
    (C) I apologized to him, because no apology was forthcoming from him first.
    (D) I felt that I would apologize to him, after realizing that I would get no apology from him.

294. Which of the following sentences best fits under the topic "Medical Benefits of Garlic"?

    (A) Garlic can give you bad breath, but it tastes good.
    (B) Garlic can lower the risks of some cancers.
    (C) Chicago was named after a strong variety of garlic.
    (D) none of these

295. Which topic is most appropriate for a one-paragraph essay?

    (A) origins of language
    (B) the history of the English dictionary
    (C) the derivation of the word *etymology*
    (D) none of these

296. Which sentence does NOT belong in the following paragraph?

    (1) Stonehenge was built around 5,000 years ago. (2) The monument predates the Celts and the Romans in England. (3) The Irish are descendants of the Celts. (4) No one really knows why Stonehenge was built.

    (A) Sentence 1
    (B) Sentence 2
    (C) Sentence 3
    (D) Sentence 4

297. Which sentence does NOT belong in the following paragraph?

(1) Blowing air over hot soup dissipates the moist vapor over the surface. (2) This allows the soup to cool faster. (3) Putting a lid on soup preserves the vapor, keeping it hot. (4) Some soups, such as gazpacho, are served cold.

(A) Sentence 1
(B) Sentence 2
(C) Sentence 3
(D) Sentence 4

298. Where should the sentence "Medieval Germany had many forests" be placed in the following selection?

(1) In the Middle Ages, many people observed a holiday called Adam and Eve day. (2) On December 24, a tree was displayed, representing the tree of knowledge from the Garden of Eden. (3) This eventually led to the custom of having a Christmas tree in the house.

(A) Between sentences 1 and 2
(B) Between sentences 2 and 3
(C) After sentence 3
(D) The sentence does not fit in this paragraph.

STOP

IF YOU FINISH BEFORE TIME IS UP, CHECK OVER YOUR WORK ON THIS TEST ONLY.

Answers to Practice High School Placement Test 1

SUBTEST 1	VERBAL SKILLS

1. A	11. B	21. D	31. A	41. A	51. C
2. A	12. D	22. B	32. A	42. A	52. A
3. C	13. A	23. B	33. C	43. D	53. D
4. A	14. A	24. C	34. C	44. B	54. B
5. B	15. C	25. A	35. A	45. C	55. B
6. B	16. C	26. C	36. C	46. D	56. C
7. D	17. D	27. B	37. C	47. D	57. A
8. C	18. D	28. A	38. A	48. B	58. C
9. B	19. C	29. A	39. C	49. A	59. C
10. A	20. B	30. D	40. B	50. C	60. B

SUBTEST 2	QUANTITATIVE SKILLS

61. D	71. B	81. C	91. A	101. D	111. A
62. C	72. B	82. B	92. A	102. B	112. C
63. B	73. D	83. C	93. D	103. B	
64. D	74. C	84. A	94. C	104. C	
65. A	75. C	85. D	95. B	105. B	
66. B	76. D	86. D	96. C	106. D	
67. C	77. C	87. B	97. C	107. B	
68. C	78. A	88. D	98. B	108. C	
69. A	79. D	89. B	99. A	109. B	
70. A	80. D	90. C	100. D	110. A	

SUBTEST 3	READING—COMPREHENSION—VOCABULARY

113. A	124. C	135. B	146. C	157. A	168. A
114. B	125. B	136. C	147. C	158. A	169. D
115. D	126. D	137. C	148. B	159. C	170. A
116. C	127. C	138. D	149. C	160. B	171. C
117. C	128. A	139. C	150. D	161. D	172. A
118. D	129. B	140. B	151. D	162. B	173. B
119. A	130. B	141. B	152. B	163. B	174. A
120. A	131. C	142. B	153. C	164. A	
121. A	132. C	143. D	154. C	165. A	
122. D	133. D	144. A	155. A	166. C	
123. C	134. A	145. B	156. B	167. D	

SUBTEST 4 MATHEMATICS

175. **B**	186. **B**	197. **C**	208. **B**	219. **D**	230. **D**
176. **A**	187. **C**	198. **A**	209. **D**	220. **B**	231. **D**
177. **A**	188. **D**	199. **D**	210. **D**	221. **D**	232. **A**
178. **D**	189. **B**	200. **C**	211. **B**	222. **C**	233. **D**
179. **B**	190. **A**	201. **C**	212. **A**	223. **B**	234. **A**
180. **D**	191. **D**	202. **A**	213. **C**	224. **D**	235. **D**
181. **B**	192. **B**	203. **A**	214. **C**	225. **C**	236. **D**
182. **B**	193. **C**	204. **B**	215. **D**	226. **B**	237. **C**
183. **C**	194. **D**	205. **C**	216. **C**	227. **C**	238. **C**
184. **B**	195. **A**	206. **A**	217. **B**	228. **A**	
185. **B**	196. **A**	207. **D**	218. **A**	229. **D**	

SUBTEST 5 LANGUAGE

239. **B**	249. **B**	259. **A**	269. **B**	279. **C**	289. **C**
240. **A**	250. **A**	260. **C**	269. **D**	280. **A**	290. **B**
241. **C**	251. **A**	261. **D**	271. **A**	281. **A**	291. **C**
242. **D**	252. **A**	262. **A**	272. **A**	282. **C**	292. **B**
243. **A**	253. **C**	263. **C**	273. **A**	283. **B**	293. **A**
244. **B**	254. **C**	264. **B**	274. **C**	284. **D**	294. **B**
245. **A**	255. **A**	265. **A**	275. **D**	285. **A**	295. **C**
246. **C**	256. **C**	266. **B**	276. **B**	286. **B**	296. **C**
247. **C**	257. **A**	267. **D**	277. **B**	287. **D**	297. **D**
248. **B**	258. **D**	268. **A**	278. **A**	288. **A**	298. **D**

Answer Explanations

SUBTEST 1 VERBAL SKILLS

1. **(A)** A bicycle is the only vehicle listed without a mechanical engine.

2. **(A)** *Glum* means *sad*. The others are happy, friendly words. If you don't know the word *amiable*, think of the French word for friend—*ami*. Doesn't that sound happy?

3. **(C)** The other words are **specific** breeds of dog.

4. **(A)** True. If you draw the relationship, it should look like this:
   K
   P
   J

5. **(B)** A prejudice is a bias. It can be an opinion (c), but *bias* is closer to the negative connotation of *prejudice*.

6. **(B)** Dirty is the opposite of clean, as light is the opposite of dark.

7. **(D)** *Neglect* is the opposite of all the supportive words.

8. **(C)** These are all similar items, but you don't usually use a towel to keep warm in bed.

9. **(B)** It's getting a bit trickier. The first word *close* has two meanings and two pronunciations. The pronunciation /cloze/ means to shut or seal, so the remaining word, *near*, does not belong.

10. **(A)** If you don't know the word *voracious*, perhaps you can figure out the root *vor* from *carnivore* or *herbivore*. It means to eat.

11. **(B)** *Mal* is one of those "bad" prefixes.

12. **(D)** *Liberate* means to free. Think of the Statue of *Liberty*.

13. **(A)** Fire causes smoke; a lightbulb causes brightness.

14. **(A)** *Reversal* and *inversion* both involve backward movement.

15. **(C)** This one is tricky. We don't hear about John until the last sentence, so we don't know anything about his relationship to the first two.
   T
   C
   N

16. **(C)** Phrases, clauses, and sentences refer to groups of words. An adverb is often a single word.

17. **(D)** Peninsula is the only land mass listed.

18. **(D)** *Bio* means life, and the degradation of life would be *decay*.

19. **(C)** A car is started by a key. A television is started by a remote control. *Outlet* is not quite right, as you are not looking for the power source, but to the instrument that turns it on.

20. **(B)** If you imprint something, you put a mark on it. The opposite is to erase.

21. **(D)** An umbrella keeps out rain. A door keeps out a draft.

22. **(B)** You might draw a box for mammals and put a circle D for dogs inside of that box. A b for basenji would be inside of the circle. Therefore, the third statement is false.

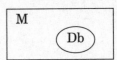

23. **(B)** *Sever* means to cut or separate, which is closest to *divide*.

24. **(C)** We don't know how long Ursola's hair is compared to Grace's. Our diagram might look like this:
   U G?
   J

25. **(A)** You might be tricked into guessing (D) *wardrobe*, but remember that *uni-* means one. *One form* means *sameness*.

26. **(C)** *Run* does not necessarily mean to run *away*, which the other words express.

27. **(B)** *Philo* means *love*, so it's a positive word. Only (B) is positive.

A philanthropist is a person who loves people (*anthropos*) and often donates to charitable organizations.

28. **(A)** *Magic* and *supernatural* are similar, so you can eliminate them; they can't both be the correct choice. *Con* means with or together. Things that go together are *suitable* for one another.

29. **(A)** Shoes
    Skirt
    Blouse

30. **(D)** The other choices are specific kinds of poems.

31. **(A)** Something impressive is inspiring, so you're looking for a synonym for *derogatory*. If you don't know the meaning of *derogatory*, see if you can eliminate some of the choices. The other choices are all positive synonyms, so they can't all be correct. That leaves only the word *critical*, which is a synonym for *derogatory*.

32. **(A)** The other choices are all commands.

33. **(C)** We are not given enough information.

34. **(C)** The other words denote active searching.

35. **(A)** *Not equal* is not fair.

36. **(C)** Thrifty people save their money. They are *not wasteful*.

37. **(C)** *Mal* is one of those negative prefixes, so it is not a success.

38. **(A)** S +10
    L +20
    J

39. **(C)** *Console* (pronounced conSOLE) means to comfort.

40. **(B)** A roof is the top of a house. A head is the top of the body. You wouldn't choose brain (top of the attic) or foot (top of the foundation).

41. **(A)** *Diligence* means hard work.

42. **(A)** Moon River
    mile
    Pirate Island

43. **(D)** The other choices are forward-moving.

44. **(B)** Use a fork to eat. Use a pen to write.

45. **(C)** This is not the noun *device*, but the verb *devise*, which means to make or create.

46. **(D)** The other choices are specific types of machines.

47. **(D)** Glory is important; its opposite is unimportant.

48. **(B)** Someone idle is not employed. Someone graceful is not clumsy.

49. **(A)** S
    M + C

50. **(C)** The other choices are all negative.

51. **(C)** *Noise* irritates you. *Music* calms you. While this may not always be true, it is the only choice that fits logically into your sentence.

52. **(A)** R
    cat
    P

53. **(D)** The other choices indicate a *lack* of information.

54. **(B)** Morose is the opposite of cheerful.

55. **(B)** C
    K
    T

56. **(C)** The other words deal with speaking aloud. Repress means to hold back.

57. **(A)** *Crucial* means necessary.

58. **(C)** A bus is like a large car. A whale is a large <u>sea</u> mammal, such as a dolphin.

59. **(C)** K-15 C-12 We are given no indication that these books overlap.

60. **(B)** Julie
    Robby
    Jane

SUBTEST 2
QUANTITATIVE SKILLS

61.

ANALYSIS

Add 5 to the preceding number.

WORK
$$26 + 5 = 31$$

ANSWER: (D)

62.

ANALYSIS

Let x = the number.

WORK
$$x^2 + 3 = 4 \times 7$$
$$x^2 + 3 = 28$$
Subtract 3: $\quad x^2 = 25$
Take the square root: $\quad x = \pm 5$

ANSWER: (C)

63.

ANALYSIS

Simplify (a), (b), and (c) and then substitute the results into (A), (B), and (C).

WORK
(a) $7(9 - 3) = 7(6) = 42$
(b) $2 \times 4 + 72/4 = 8 + 18 = 26$
(c) $48 - 3(5 + 6) = 48 - 3(11) = 48 - 33 = 15$

(A) (a) is less than (b) and less than (c)
$42 < 26$ and $42 < 15$ ✖
(B) (b) is greater than (c) and less than (a)
$26 > 15$ and $26 < 42$ ✔
(C) (c) is less than (a) and greater than (b)
$15 < 42$ and $15 > 26$ ✖
(D) (c) is greater than (a) and greater than (b)
$15 > 42$ and $15 > 26$ ✖

ANSWER: (B)

64.

ANALYSIS

"Quotient" indicates division. Let x = the unknown number.

WORK
$$48/6 + 2 = \sqrt{x}$$
$$8 + 2 = \sqrt{x}$$
$$10 = \sqrt{x}$$
Square both sides: $\quad 100 = x$

ANSWER: (D)

65.

ANALYSIS

Subtract 3 from each preceding number.

WORK
$$26 - 3 = 23$$

ANSWER: (A)

66.

ANALYSIS

Find the areas of the square and the circle and subtract the two.

The diameter of the circle is 8, so the radius is 4.

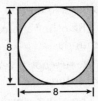

WORK
Area of square, A_S: $\quad A_S = s^2$
$s = 8$: $\quad = 8^2 = 64$

Area of Circle, A_C: $\quad A_C = \pi r^2$
$\pi = 3.14, r = 4$: $\quad = 3.14(4)^2$
$$= 3.14(16)$$
$$= 50.24$$

$$A_S - A_C = 64 - 50.24 = 13.76 \approx 13.8$$

ANSWER: (B) 13.8

67.

ANALYSIS

Change (a), (b), and (c) to decimals and then substitute into (A), (B), (C), and (D).

WORK
(a) $45\% = 0.45$
(b) $2/3 = 0.66\ldots$
(c) $0.45 = 0.45$

(A) (a) is greater than (b) and less than (c)
0.45 > 0.66 and 0.45 < 0.45 ✘
(B) (b) is less than (c) and greater than (a)
0.66 < 0.45 and 0.66 . . . > 0.45 ✘
(C) (c) is equal to (a) and less than (b)
0.45 = 0.45 and 0.45 < 0.66 . . . ✔
(D) (b) is greater than (a) and less than (c)
0.66 > 0.45 and 0.66 . . . < 0.45 ✘

ANSWER: (C)

68.
ANALYSIS
Double each preceding number.

WORK
$$2 \times 32 = 64$$

ANSWER: (C)

69.
ANALYSIS
Let x = the unknown number.

WORK
$$x = \frac{2}{3} \times 30 + 15$$
$$x = 20 + 15$$
$$x = 35$$

ANSWER: (A)

70.
ANALYSIS
Simplify (a), (b), and (c), and substitute into (A), (B), (C), and (D).

WORK
(a) $\frac{3}{7} \times 42 = 18$

(b) $\frac{5}{8} \times 40 = 25$

(c) $\frac{6}{7} \times 35 = 30$

(A) (a) is less than (b) and less than (c)
18 < 25 and 18 < 30 ✔
(B) (b) is greater than (c) and greater than (a)
25 > 30 and 25 > 18 ✘
(C) (c) is greater than (b) and less than (a)
30 > 25 and 30 < 18 ✘
(D) (a) is less than (c) and greater than (b)
18 < 30 and 18 > 25 ✘

ANSWER: (A)

71.
ANALYSIS
First multiply the expression inside the parentheses by 2. Then subtract 78 from both sides of the equation and, finally divide by –2.

WORK
$$62 + 2(8 - x) = 72$$
$$62 + 16 - 2x = 72$$
$$78 - 2x = 72$$
$$\underline{-78 \qquad = -78}$$
$$-2x = -6$$
$$\frac{-2x}{-2} = \frac{-6}{-2}$$
$$x = 3$$

ANSWER: (B)

72.
ANALYSIS
Subtract $1\frac{1}{2}$ from each preceding number.

WORK
$$46\frac{1}{2} - 1\frac{1}{2} = 45$$

ANSWER: (B)

73.
ANALYSIS
Let y = the unknown number.

WORK
$$\frac{48}{y} = \frac{2}{3} \times 9$$

Multiply by y: $\frac{48}{y} = 6$

Divide by 6: $6y = 48$

$$y = 8$$

ANSWER: (D)

74.
ANALYSIS
Let y = the unknown number and let 25% = 0.25.

WORK

$$5y = 0.25 \times 80$$
Divide by 5: $5y = 20$
$$y = 4$$

ANSWER: (C)

75.
ANALYSIS
There are two series here in alternate positions. The first series begins with 2 and increases by 4. The second series begins with 15 and decreases by 2. The missing number is a member of the first series and is thus 4 more than 6.

WORK

$$6 + 4 = 10$$

ANSWER: (C)

76.
ANALYSIS
First find the height of the right triangle by using the Pythagorean Theorem, $a^2 + b^2 = c^2$, where a and b are the legs of the triangle and c is the hypotenuse.

Once we have determined the height of the triangle, we use the formula for the area of a triangle, $A = (1/2)b \cdot h$, where A = area, b = base and h = height.

WORK

$$a^2 + b^2 = c^2$$
$$a^2 + 5^2 = 13^2$$
Subtract 25: $a^2 + 25 = 169$
$$a^2 = 144$$
Take the square root: $a = 12$

Now use the area formula
$$A = (1/2)b \cdot h$$
$b = 5, h = 12$: $A = (1/2)(5)(12)$
$$A = 30$$

ANSWER: (D)

77.

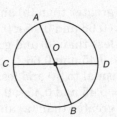

ANALYSIS
$CO, OD, AO,$ and OB are radii and are therefore equal in length. AB and CD are diameters and are also equal in length.

WORK

$$AB - OB = DO$$
diameter AB – radius OB = radius DO

DO is a radius, and all radii in the same circle are equal in length.

ANSWER: (C)

78.
ANALYSIS
First determine the number of .7 gallons there are in 28 gallons. Then multiply your answer by 2 seconds.

WORK

$$\frac{28}{.7} = 40$$

40×2 seconds = 80 seconds = 1 minute, 20 seconds

ANSWER: (A)

79.
ANALYSIS
Take half of the previous number.

WORK

$$\frac{1}{2} \times 2\frac{1}{4} = 1\frac{1}{8}$$

ANSWER: (D)

80.
ANALYSIS
Let P = the perimeter.
Let k = the length of the rectangle and let $k - 8$ = the width of the rectangle.

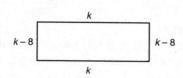

WORK

$P = 2 \cdot \text{length} + 2 \cdot \text{width}$

$P = 2(k) + 2(k - 8) = 2k + 2k - 16$

$P = 4k - 16$

ANSWER: (D)

81.

ANALYSIS

Let y = the unknown number.

WORK

$$5y = 8^2 - 9$$
$$5y = 64 - 9$$
Divide by 5: $5y = 55$
$$y = 11$$

ANSWER: (C)

82.

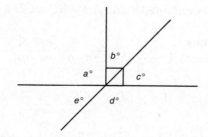

ANALYSIS

$$a° = 90°$$
$$b° + c° = 90°$$

WORK

$$a° = b° + c°$$

ANSWER: (B)

83.

ANALYSIS

Let x = the unknown number.

WORK

$$x = \frac{4}{5} \frac{(18 + 42)}{2}$$

$$x = \frac{4}{5}(30)$$

$$x = 24$$

ANSWER: (C)

84.

ANALYSIS

Simplify (a), (b), and (c) and substitute into (A), (B), and (C).

WORK

(a) $4.06 \times 10^3 = 4.06 \times 1,000 = 4,060$

(b) $30 \times 10^2 = 30 \times 100 = 3,000$

(c) $52.4 \times 10^1 = 52.4 \times 10 = 524$

(A) (a) is greater than (b)
    $4,060 > 3,000$ ✔

(B) (b) is less than (c)
    $3,000 < 524$ ✘

(C) (c) is greater than (b)
    $524 > 3,000$ ✘

(D) (a) is less than (b)
    $4,060 < 3,000$ ✘

ANSWER: (A)

85.

ANALYSIS

Using the number of books lost, find the number of books returned. Then compare both numbers.

WORK

	Original Number of Books:	30
−	Number of Books Lost:	4
	Number of Books Returned:	26

Ratio of returned books to lost books: $\dfrac{26}{4} = \dfrac{13}{2}$

ANSWER: (D)

86.

ANALYSIS

There are three numbers in each group in the series. To find the second number in the group, double the first number. To find the second number in each group, add 1 to the second number.

WORK

$$2 \times 23 = 46$$

ANSWER: (D)

87.

ANALYSIS

To determine the area of the walk, multiply 32 by 3.5. Then, to find the total cost, multiply the answer by $12.40, the cost of cementing a square foot.

WORK

$$32 \text{ ft} \times 3.5 \text{ ft} = 112 \text{ sq ft}$$

$$\begin{array}{r} 1\,1\,2 \\ \times\,3\,.\,5 \\ \hline 5\,6\,0 \\ 3\,3\,6 \\ \hline 3\,9\,2\,.\,0 \end{array}$$

ANSWER: (B)

88.

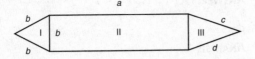

ANALYSIS

Substitute the lengths into (A), (B),(C), and (D).

WORK

(A) $c + b > a$
  We're not certain about the lengths of a, b, and c.

(B) $a - b < d$
  We're not certain about the lengths of a, b, and d.

(C) $d + a > b + a$
  We're not certain about the lengths of a, b, and d.

(D) Given:

$$\begin{array}{r} c > b \\ +\,d > b \\ \hline c + d > 2b \end{array}$$

ANSWER: (D)

89.

ANALYSIS

The series is increasing by 3 and is written in alternate Arabic and Roman numerals.

WORK

15 is the missing number, or, in Roman numerals XV.

ANSWER: (B)

90.

ANALYSIS

Add the right and left-handed numbers of students in order to obtain the total number. Then divide the total into the number of left-handed students.

WORK

Total Number of Students: $6 + 24 = 30$
Left-handed Students/Total: $6/30 = .20$
                             $.20 = 20\%$

ANSWER: (C)

91.

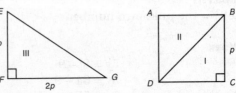

ANALYSIS

The area of a triangle is equal to $\frac{1}{2}$ the product of the base (b) and the height (h).

  Since $ABCD$ is a square, all the sides are of equal length and $AB = BC = CD = p$.

WORK

Area $\triangle$ I $= \frac{1}{2}bh = \frac{1}{2}p \cdot p = \frac{1}{2}p^2$

Area $\triangle$ II $= \frac{1}{2}bh = \frac{1}{2}p \cdot p = \frac{1}{2}p^2$

Area $\triangle$ III $= \frac{1}{2}bh = \frac{1}{2}(2p)(p) = p \cdot p = p^2$

(A) Area $\triangle$ I + Area $\triangle$ II = Area $\triangle$ III

$\frac{1}{2}p^2 + \frac{1}{2}p^2 = p^2$ ✔

(B) Area $\triangle$ I = Area $\triangle$ III

$\frac{1}{2}p^2 = p^2$ ✘

(C) Area $\triangle$ II > Area $\triangle$ III

$2 \times \frac{1}{2}p^2 > p^2$

$p^2 > p^2$ ✘

(D) Area $ABCD$ – Area $\triangle$ I > Area $\triangle$ III

$p \cdot p > p^2$ ✘

ANSWER: (A)

92.

ANALYSIS

The series is increasing by 2.2.

WORK

$$10.5 + 2.2 = 12.7$$

ANSWER: (A)

93.

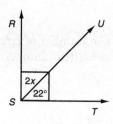

ANALYSIS

The measure of $\angle RST = 90°$, so that $m\angle RSU + m\angle TSU = 90°$.

WORK

$$m\angle RSU + m\angle TSU = 90°$$
$$2x + 22° = 90°$$

Subtract 22°: $\qquad\qquad 2x = 68°$

Divide by 2: $\qquad\qquad\quad x = 34°$

ANSWER: (D)

94.

ANALYSIS

The second number in the series is one less than the first number. The third number is triple the second. And this pattern is repeated.

WORK

$$42 - 1 = 41$$

ANSWER: (C)

95.

ANALYSIS

Change 15% and 20% to 0.15 and 0.20 and then multiply.

WORK

$$0.15 \times 0.20 \times 80 = 2.4$$

ANSWER: (B)

96.

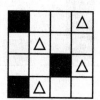

ANALYSIS

Find the totals of ■, □, and △; substitute into (A), (B), (C), and (D).

WORK

Totals: 3 ■, 9 □, 4 △

(A) Total ■ > Total △

$\qquad$ 3 > 4 ✘

(B) Total △ + Total ■ > Total □

$\qquad$ 4 + 3 > 9 ✘

(C) Total □ − Total △ > Total ■

$\qquad$ 9 − 4 > 3 ✔

(D) Total □ − Total ■ < Total △

$\qquad$ 9 − 3 < 4 ✘

ANSWER: (C)

97.

ANALYSIS

The series is listed in backwards alphabetical order, with three letters in between each of the given terms.

WORK

$$L, K, J, I, \mathbf{H}$$

ANSWER: (C)

98.

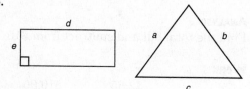

ANALYSIS

Find the perimeters of the triangle and the rectangle, substitute $2d$ for a and $2e$ for b in the perimeter of the triangle, and then compare the two figures.

WORK

Perimeter of the triangle = $a + b + c$

Let $a = 2d$ and $b = 2e$:

Perimeter of the triangle = $2d + 2e + d$

Perimeter of the rectangle = $2d + 2e$

Subtract the perimeter of the rectangle from the perimeter of the triangle:

$$2d + 2e - (2d + 2e + c) = c$$

ANSWER: (B)

99.
ANALYSIS
There are two alternating series here: 2, 4, 6, . . . and 5, 8, 11 . . . .

WORK
The next number = 6 + 2 = 8

ANSWER: (A)

100.

$2.85

$1.89

$1.37

$1.16

ANALYSIS
Find the total bill and subtract from $10.

WORK

$2.85	$10.00
1.89	− 7.27
1.37	$2.73
+ 1.16	
$7.27	

ANSWER: (D)

101.

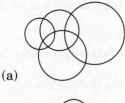

(a)

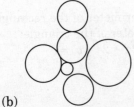

(b)

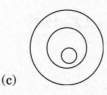

(c)

ANALYSIS
Determine the number of circles in a, b, and c and then substitute into (A), (B), (C), and (D).

WORK
Circles in (a): 4
Circles in (b): 6
Circles in (c): 3

(A) Figure (a) includes one less circle than figure (c).
    4 = 3 − 1 ✖
(B) Figure (b) includes 2 more circles than figure (c).
    6 = 3 + 2 ✖
(C) Figure (c) includes 2 fewer circles than figure (b).
    3 = 6 − 2 ✖
(D) Figure (b) includes 3 more circles than figure (c).
    6 = 3 + 3 ✔

ANSWER: (D)

102.
ANALYSIS
Find the differences between the numbers and look for a pattern.

WORK

←–5→ ←–6→ ←–7→ ←–8→ ←–9→
142   137   131   124   **116**   107

ANSWER: (B)

103.

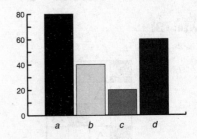

ANALYSIS
Determine a, b, c, and d and then substitute
into (A), (B), (C), and (D).

WORK
$a = 80$
$b = 40$
$c = 20$
$d = 60$

(A) $a - b = c$
$80 - 40 = 20$ ✘
(B) $b + c = d$
$40 + 20 = 60$ ✔
(C) $b + c > a$
$40 + 20 > 80$ ✘
(D) $d - c < b$
$60 - 20 < 40$ ✘

ANSWER: (B)

104.
ANALYSIS
The series is in the form $1^3, 2^3, 3^3, 4^3, 5^3, \ldots$.

WORK
$$6^3 = 6 \times 6 \times 6 = 216$$

ANSWER: (C)

105.
ANALYSIS
Solve (a), (b), and (c) and substitute into (A),
(B), and (C).

WORK
(a) $4/100 + 5/10 + 3 = 0.04 + 0.5 + 3 = 3.54$
(b) $9/100 + 3 + 3/10 = 0.09 + 3 + 0.3 = 3.39$
(c) $2/10 + 3 + 3/100 = 0.2 + 3 + 0.03 = 3.23$

(A) (c) is greater than (b) and less than (a)
$3.23 > 3.39$ and $3.23 < 3.54$ ✘
(B) (b) is less than (a) and greater than (c)
$3.39 < 3.54$ and $3.39 > 3.23$ ✔
(C) (a) is less than (b) and less than (c)
$3.54 < 3.39$ and $3.54 < 3.23$ ✘
(D) (b) is greater than (a) and greater
than (c)
$3.39 > 3.54$ and $3.39 > 3.23$ ✘

ANSWER: (B)

106.

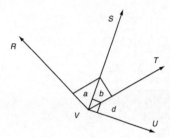

ANALYSIS
Perpendicular lines form right angles.

$$a + b = 90°, b + d = 90°$$

WORK
(A) $a + b < b + d$
$90° + 90° < 90°$ ✘
(B) $d - b = a - b$
(C) $a + b < 90°$
$90° < 90°$ ✘
(D) $b + d = 90°$
$90° = 90°$ ✔

ANSWER: (D)

107.
ANALYSIS
The series is increasing by 3, 4, and 1 units.

WORK
$$22 + 3 = 25$$

ANSWER: (B)

108.
ANALYSIS
Solve for (a), (b), and (c) and substitute into
(A), (B), (C), and (D).

WORK
(a) $5/8 \times 40 = 25$
(b) $3/4 \times 60 = 45$
(c) $2/3 \times 45 = 30$

(A) (a) is less than (c) and greater than (b)
$25 < 30$ and $25 > 45$ ✘
(B) (b) is greater than (c) and less than (a)
$45 > 30$ and $45 < 25$ ✘
(C) (c) is less than (b) and greater than (a)
$30 < 45$ and $30 > 25$ ✔
(D) (a) is greater than (b) and greater
than (c)
$25 > 45$ and $25 > 30$ ✘

ANSWER: (C)

109.

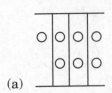

(a)

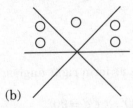

(b)

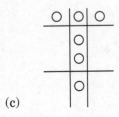

(c)

ANALYSIS
Determine the number of circles and straight lines in (a), (b) and (c) and substitute.

(a) 4 circles, 5 straight lines
(b) 5 circles, 3 straight lines
(c) 6 circles, 4 straight lines

(A) There is one more circle in (b) than lines in (a).
$5 = 5 + 1$ ✘
(B) The number of lines in (b) plus the number of circles in (a) is equal to the number of lines in (c) plus the number of circles in (c).
$3 + 7 = 4 + 6$ ✔
(C) The number of circles in (c) and (a) is less than the number of lines in (a) and (b).
$6 + 4 < 5 + 3$ ✘
(D) The number of lines in (a) plus the number of circles in (b) is less than the number of lines in (b) and (c).
$5 + 5 < 3 + 4$ ✘

ANSWER: (B)

110.
ANALYSIS
The series is decreasing by 1, 2, 3, 4, ...

WORK
$$23 - 5 = 18$$

ANSWER: (A)

111.
ANALYSIS
The letters PP reappear after every two intervening letters. The other letters in the series are increasing in alphabetical order.

WORK
$$V, W$$

ANSWER: (A)

112.
ANALYSIS
The numbers in the series are decreasing in the order −3, −5, −7, −9, −11, ...

WORK
$$93 - 13 = 80$$
ANSWER: (C)

SUBTEST 3 READING

113. (**A**) This question requires you to identify a fact from the reading—simply Sauma's itinerary. While Sauma indeed traveled through all of the locations in choices B and C, he did not do so in the order they list. Choice D is wrong because Sauma never visited Versailles, according to the reading. The correct answer is A.

114. (**B**) This question asks you to guess which kind of book would publish this kind of information and presumes that you are aware of certain genres (or types) of books. The information in the passage makes sense for either choice A or B, since the text talks about geographical locations and travel. The information does not make sense in terms of choices C or D; no mention is made of recipes or ingredients nor typical fairy tale creatures. But your job is to make the *best* choice; while you might find such a

chatty piece in a travel guide, you are more likely to find it in a history book. The correct answer is B.

115. **(D)** All the definitions presented are viable ones for the word *quest*, but only one is appropriate in the context of the sentence. Paragraph two discuses China's long-term intent (another word for goal) to expand its territory. Therefore only choice D is appropriate.

116. **(C)** This question asks you to locate a fact—to identify the main idea in a piece; therefore, you should look for factual information. Choice A is simply wrong; paragraph two states as much. Choice B is also wrong since it uses the phrase "declare without question"; nowhere in the piece does the author definitively state that if X happened (Sauma's treaty) then Y would necessarily follow (a necessary change in world events). Instead, the piece is laced with words that connote hesitation or lack of assurance (claim, may have, would have). Choice D singles out Italian explorers for no apparent reason, despite the fact that the article mentions explorers from several nationalities; choice D essentially makes no sense. The only correct answer is C; the author is trying to bring to light a little known but interesting fact about early human exploration.

117. **(C)** This question is very similar to the previous one, except that it asks you to infer what the author thinks *is likely to have happened* had Sauma got his treaty; asking for inference gives you a great deal more flexibility in your answer. The author seems to attempt being unbiased, but still seems to lean toward a particular opinion on the topic of Sauma's explorations. You can rule out choice D, since the piece does not address the topic of World War II nor does it give you any reason to think that an event taking place in the 1200s could clearly affect an event taking place in the 1940s. Choices A and B give you no help; the article refuses to commit itself to either position. The only

answer left to you is choice C, since, whether or not Sauma's treaty would have had any long-term effects, it would clearly have had a short-term effect—that of shifting the type of explorer likely to go traveling.

118. **(D)** This question asks for a factual answer, although you have to do a little math to get the answer. Just add the distance of Sauma's trip to the Vatican (7,000 miles) to the distance of the trip back home (7,000). The answer is 14,000 or choice D.

119. **(A)** The term *brokering* usually applies to finances, but using that definition in this context does not make sense; rule out choice D. Choices B and C also do not make sense; substitute the words and you will agree. Your only real choice is A.

120. **(A)** This question is meant rather playfully and takes a bit of subtlety on your part. You can rule out C or D; nowhere does the piece specifically refer to Arabia, nor does Sauma attempt to travel the world. Choice B is more compelling and does fit the context. However choice A is best. Think back to your childhood, of your days of playing Marco! Polo! in the pool. Had Marco Polo not gotten all the historical attention, Sauma may well have—we may have been playing Rabban! Sauma! in our pools instead.

121. **(A)** This question asks you to remember a fact, again one which demands a bit of math on your part. This time you should subtract the number of people who actually escaped (3) from the total number of escapees (55); the result is 52. This is the number of people who died (or were executed) for their attempt to escape Stalag Luft III.

122. **(D)** You are asked to make a logical guess here. You can rule out choices B and C, since these questions assume facts that you know, based on your reading, are not true. You must therefore decide between A and D. Based on the tone of the article, you can rule out choice A; the article clearly states toward the end that it took over five million Germans, distracted from

their usual duties, to recapture these escaped men. Since these Germans were away from their posted duties, we can infer they were inefficient at performing those duties; therefore, despite the loss of life and the success of only three men, their efforts did indeed assist the *overall* war effort.

123. (**C**) Choice A is addressed nowhere in the article. The piece only briefly mentions Sturgis, and if the article were supposed to praise his work, his portion of the article should have been longer. The piece makes the argument that the Gestapo were *not* diligent; otherwise Tom, Dick, and Harry would never have been dug, the 55 men would not have escaped, and the Germans would not have needed to deploy such a huge number of people looking for them. Choice D is not addressed in its entirety; we only are told how a few German soldiers are treated in response to executing 52 men, not how Germans were treated for killing six million Jews. The only correct answer is C.

124. (**C**) *Notorious* best fits choice C, both in strict terms of the definition and in context in the sentence. Wealth, anger, and humility simply do not enter the discussion.

125. (**B**) Re-reading (or memory) tells you that the Nazis executed the escaped soldiers, not any of the other options.

126. (**D**) From your schooling (especially in science and math) you should be able to recall that *duration* is a word we associate with time, not mass, space, or sound.

127. (**C**) The article discusses human behavior. That kind of writing tends to appear in many forms. Most often it tends to appear in nonfiction form—either in history texts (because they document human action) or sociology texts (because they discuss how and *why* people perform actions); therefore, you can rule out choices A (because this article is clearly not a scientific discussion), B (since novels, while they can discuss why and how people behave, they discuss such

topics through fictional means), and D (since biographies usually deal with a single person rather than a class of people).

128. (**A**) Of the title choices offered you, choices C and D make the least sense. Dr. Spock (yes, a real person) is mentioned only once throughout the course of the article, and you really are not given enough information about him to justify naming an entire writing sample for him. Choice C seems just too broad for the topic at hand; anything can be discussed under this title. You want something tailor-made for *this* topic. Choices A and B are more persuasive, but arguably choice A is best; rocking has a double meaning here—both rocking (lulling) a child to sleep (which fits with the idea of keeping kids sheltered) and rocking (challenging) society's views (which fits well with the idea of refusing to shelter kids any longer).

129. (**B**) Traditionally the word *retard* means either of the definitions presented in choices A or B. No one argues that the word *retard* means the definitions in choices C or D. But given that the use of the word in the sentence implies a slowing down of progress, your only real choice is B.

130. (**B**) Re-reading (or your memory) brings up the correct fact that historians point to the 18th century for the time when people began sheltering their children (see paragraph two).

131. (**C**) The last sentence of paragraph four gives the answer away: The author clearly states a position in opposition to the statement immediately preceding it. Essentially, then, the author thinks that there are some circumstances in which it is okay to shelter a child from reality. The answer is C.

132. (**C**) Re-reading (or your memory) brings up the correct date—1962.

133. (**D**) The main idea behind this article is to advise parents on the issues of child rearing—specifically how to manage the information flow between

reality and home. Choices A, B, and C are all briefly mentioned throughout the article, but never to such a degree that you should feel comfortable selecting them as the main idea.

134. **(A)** The article mentions briefly all four topics mentioned in the four choices. But the one choice that is most thoroughly covered is choice A.

135. **(B)** This question assumes you know a little bit about world geography. The city of Madrid is located in Spain; therefore, choices A, C, and D are incorrect.

136. **(C)** The tone of the article does not give you much information regarding what will be discussed next. Therefore, you are making an educated guess regarding what might come next. After all, making educated guesses is what inference is all about. Select the option that is most closely linked to the final sentence in the final paragraph—therefore, choice C, which promises to discuss spy fiction that use the "fifth column" as a plot device, is your best answer.

137. **(C)** All of the definitions are related in that they discuss different interpretations of the syllable *tact*. Using knowledge of root words may lead to some confusion, however. The various meanings of tact can apply to any of the choices listed—tact is a form of politeness, it refers to touch (tactile), and so on. You can easily narrow your choices down to A and C, since the sentence makes sense when you consider the need for strategy. But people can use strategy in a multitude of situations; this article discusses the specific use of strategy in a military situation; therefore, choice C is the best response.

138. **(D)** Although this question is intended to function as an inference question, it doesn't take much inference on your part to figure out the answer. The author fairly obviously states in paragraph two that many novelists use the idea of a "fifth column" in their writing; therefore, choice D is the best answer.

139. **(C)** You probably know this word—listening to political speeches by politicians can help you out here. But as a worst-case scenario, substitute the various definitions, and see which one sounds best. The best choice will be C.

140. **(B)** Re-reading (or memory) will help you identify the planaria as belonging to the flat worm family.

141. **(B)** Remembering what you have learned about the various branches of science, you can make a good inference here. Chemistry studies the chemical bonds and structure of the world; astronomy studies planets and stars; and physics studies how things move. None of these are appropriate answers. Biology, however, studies various life forms, and planaria are indeed one version of a life form; therefore, B is your best answer.

142. **(B)** Choices C and D are present to distract you; C really has nothing to do with decapitation, and D is there in case you mistake it for the word *delusion*. Choices A and B are closer to the mark. But the correct answer is B, removing the head.

143. **(D)** This is a typical fact question that reverses the way it asks for information. Three of the four answers are actual facts from the text; you are looking for the single incorrect fact listed. While planaria do indeed like eggs, the article specifies hard-boiled rather than scrambled eggs. The correct choice is D.

144. **(A)** While the author might agree with the opinions expressed by choices B and D, they are not the main point of the passage. The production of a scientific dissertation is full of quite difficult requirements. Creating a two-headed planaria is not difficult; therefore, you can rule out choice C. The best answer is A, in large part because the author practically spells it out for you in paragraph two.

145. **(B)** Break down the word *regeneration* into parts—notice the *re-generation*. *Generation* means birth/growth. *Re* means again. Therefore the best

definition is growth again or regrowth. Your best answer is choice B.

146. **(C)** Questions asking you to pick a title are always a way of asking what the main idea of the passage is. While the passage touches briefly on A, B, and D, they do not constitute the main purpose of the article and, therefore, cannot be considered the main idea of the selection. Your only logical choice is C; the word *potential* is particularly appropriate, since the article states that we study planaria hoping that by doing so we can create potential hope for humanity.

147. **(D)** Since the article ends with a dismal assessment on the way Valentine's Day has turned out, you can infer that the author does not approve.

148. **(B)** A journal on biological subjects would have no interest in publishing a text like the one you have just read. Choices A, B, and D are more compelling, but only choice B is the best. Encyclopedias generally do not express opinions, nor do school books; rule out choices A and D. The best answer is B—newspapers routinely publish this sort of historical trivia-based story that amuses and informs.

149. **(C)** To make a petition is to make a request. The only definition appropriate to this would be choice C.

150. **(D)** The last paragraph in the selection is intended to form a bridge from this topic to another. You can rule out choices A and B since they discuss subjects that the author has already discussed; there is no need to revisit them. Given the tone of the final paragraph, you can assume a criticism of some sort is forthcoming. But, the author has essentially covered choice C. Choice D is the only option that matches the tone and likely topic the author will touch on next.

151. **(D)** Re-reading tells you that the cost of the cars, and other items as revealed by the passage is $125,000.

152. **(B)** The phrase "upping the ante" comes from poker, in which you add to the requirements imposed on people who want to keep playing the game. Therefore, you are not making it easier for people to play (choice A). You may be angering people by raising the ante, but not necessarily. You can rule out choice D. Choices B and C are more tricky. By raising the ante for participation in Valentine's Day, you may or may not be raising the amount of money required—you are certainly raising the level of participation required. So, go with B rather than any other choice.

153. **(C)** To *peruse* a text is to read or look at it carefully. The prefix *per-* usually means very or thoroughly (as in *permanent* or *perfect*).

154. **(C)** To *broach* a topic is to bring it up for the first time. (A brooch is a decorative pin. *I was afraid to broach the subject of her brooch because it was so ugly.*)

155. **(A)** Choices B and C are similar, so they cannot both be correct. To accumulate or amass is to collect something into a mass or pile.

156. **(B)** Remember that the prefix *bene-* means *good*. A *helper* is the most positive choice.

157. **(A)** *Irate* means *angry*.

158. **(A)** The root *terra* means land.

159. **(C)** Choices A and C are opposites, so the answer is likely one of these. A meticulous worker cares for detail.

160. **(B)** Since the prefix *con-* means *together*, we'll choose a positive word. To condone something is to overlook or forgive it.

161. **(D)** Choices A and B are synonyms, so we can eliminate those. A candid response is frank, sincere, and straightforward.

162. **(B)** You can eat something safely if it is edible.

163. **(B)** If you revere someone, you look on him or her with awe.

164. **(A)** Choices A and D are opposites, so look closely at these. A vigilant guard keeps a *vigil*; he is awake and alert. (Have you ever attended "midnight" mass for Easter or Christmas Vigil?)

165. **(A)** The word *foible* is related to the word *feeble*. It's a small defect or weakness.

166. **(C)** A boon is a gift, a benefit, or a blessing.

167. **(D)** *Doubtful* and *dubious* share the same root.

168. **(A)** An egress is an exit. You might be able to guess this from the context. You wouldn't ordinarily have much reason to refer to the closest bird, flower, or garment.

169. **(D)** This one isn't too difficult. If you proclaim something, you declare or announce it.

170. **(A)** You can eliminate choice D, as it doesn't make sense in this context. *Sumptuous* means *expensive*, and choice A is the closest match.

171. **(C)** Whimsy is something humorous or fanciful.

172. **(A)** Since we know the prefix *super-* means *over*, we can narrow our choices to A (*extra*) or B (*large*). Something superfluous is unnecessary—more than sufficient.

173. **(B)** *Solace* is a word worth knowing. It means relief, comfort, or consolation.

174. **(A)** If someone is sage, he or she is wise. This one is tricky because the choices contain a pair of opposites, *feeble* and *healthy*. These choices really don't make much sense in context however; you don't have much cause to discuss a healthy parent, for instance.

SUBTEST 4 MATHEMATICS

175.
ANALYSIS
Add up all four sides of the rectangle.

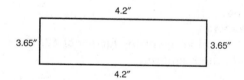

WORK
Perimeter = 4.2″ + 4.2″ + 3.65″ + 3.65″ = 15.7″

ANSWER: (B)

176.
ANALYSIS

$$5\frac{1}{4}\% = \frac{5\frac{1}{4}}{100}$$

WORK

$$\frac{5\frac{1}{4}}{100} = \frac{\frac{21}{4}}{100} = \frac{21}{4} \div \frac{100}{1} = \frac{21}{4} \cdot \frac{1}{100} = \frac{21}{400}$$

ANSWER: (A)

177.

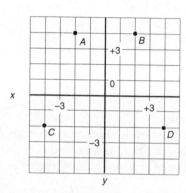

ANALYSIS
The points above the x-axis have positive y values, while the points below the x-axis have negative y values. The points to the left of the y-axis have negative x values, while the points to the right of the y-axis have positive x values.

WORK
Points A and B are both 4 units above the y-axis. Point A is also 2 units to the left of the y-axis.

ANSWER: (A)

178.
ANALYSIS
The perimeter of the square is equal to 4 times one side, s. The circumference of a circle, C, equals 2π times the radius of the circle.

WORK
Perimeter of square: $P = 4s$
$P = 4(3) = 12$

Circumference of circle: $C = 2\pi r$

Let $\pi = 3.14$: $C = 2(3.14)(2) = (4)(3.14) = 12.56$

The circumference of the circle is 0.56 more than the perimeter of the square.
$12.56 = 12 + 0.56$

ANSWER: (D)

179.
ANALYSIS
Select the set in which the sum of any two numbers is greater than the third number.

WORK
(B) $4 + 5 > 8$ ✔
$4 + 8 > 5$ ✔
$5 + 8 > 4$ ✔

ANSWER: (B)

180.
ANALYSIS
Let BA_O = original batting average, H = the number of original hits, and G = the total number of original games played.

$$BA_O = \frac{H}{G}$$

WORK
Original Batting Average
$BA_O = 0.300$: $0.300 = \frac{H}{G}$

$$H = 0.3G$$

New Batting Average = $BA_N = 0.400$:

$$0.400 = \frac{H + 10 \text{ (10 more hits)}}{G + 10 \text{ (10 more games played)}}$$

$$0.4(G + 10) = H + 10$$
$H = 0.3G$: $0.4G + 4 = 0.3G + 10$
$-0.3G, -4$: $0.1G = 6$
Divide by 0.1: $G = 60$
$$H = 0.3G = .3(60) = 18$$

ANSWER: (D)

181.

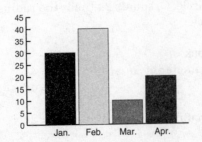

ANALYSIS
Construct a table and select the values for each month. Then substitute into each of the choices.

WORK

	Months		
Jan.	Feb.	Mar.	Apr.
30	40	10	20

(B)   Jan. – Mar. = 20
        $30 - 10 = 20$ ✔

ANSWER: (B)

182.
ANALYSIS
Change 2 tons to pounds and then pounds to ounces. Then divide the answer by 12.

WORK
2 tons = $2 \times 2,000$ pounds =
$2 \times 2,000 \times 16$ ounces = 64,000 ounces

$$\frac{64,000}{12} = 5333.3333 \ldots \approx 5333$$

ANSWER: (B)

183.
ANALYSIS
Find the hundredths' place and then round off to the nearest thousand. If the digit in the hundredth's place is 5 or greater, increase the thousandth's place by 1. Otherwise, leave the thousandth's place alone.

WORK
$$1,147,690 \approx 1,148,000$$
↑
hundredth's place
ANSWER: (C)

184.
ANALYSIS
Determine the prime factors of 42. Then add their squares.

WORK
$$42 = 7 \cdot 6 = 7 \cdot 3 \cdot 2$$
Sum of the
squares: $7^2 + 3^2 + 2^2 = 49 + 9 + 4 = 62$

ANSWER: (B)

185.

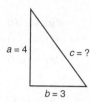

ANALYSIS
Use the Pythagorean Theorem to find the hypotenuse. Then add up all the sides of the triangle.

WORK
$$a^2 + b^2 = c^2$$
$$4^2 + 3^2 = c^2$$
$$16 + 9 = c^2$$
$$25 = c^2$$
$$c = 5$$

Perimeter = 4 + 3 + 5 = 12

ANSWER: (A)

186.
ANALYSIS
The price dropped $300. $300 is what percent of the original price, $1,500?

WORK
$$\frac{300}{1500} = \frac{1}{5} = 0.20 = 20\%$$

ANSWER: (B)

187.
ANALYSIS
Let x = the unknown number.

WORK
$$6x - 8 = 58$$
$$\underline{+ 8 = + 8}$$
$$6x \quad = 66$$

Divide by 6: $\quad 6x \quad = 66$
$$x \quad = 11$$

ANSWER: (C)

188.
ANALYSIS
If 25 customers purchased computers and printers, subtract 25 from 81 to determine how many customers remained who purchased only computers.

WORK
$$81 - 25 = 56$$

ANSWER: (D)

189.
ANALYSIS
Add up all the ratios and divide into 124. Find the remainder and then check to see which is the last book in the remainder.

WORK
$$5 + 2 + 3 + 3 = 13$$
$$\frac{124}{13} = 9\frac{7}{13}$$

There is a remainder of 7. In order, we can purchase 5 fiction and 2 historical books. The historical book is the last book we can order.

ANSWER: (B)

190.
ANALYSIS
Add 2/5 and 1/3 and then subtract the result from 1 (the total amount). The answer is Malcolm's portion. After we determine Malcolm's portion, multiply that fraction by $300,000, the total income.

WORK
$$\frac{2}{5} = \frac{6}{15} \qquad 1 = \frac{15}{15}$$
$$+\frac{1}{3} = \frac{5}{15} \qquad -\frac{11}{15}$$
$$\overline{\qquad} \qquad \overline{\qquad}$$
$$\frac{11}{15} \qquad \frac{4}{15}$$

$$\frac{4}{15} \times \$300,000 = \$80,000$$

ANSWER: (A)

191.
ANALYSIS
Let x = the unknown number. Then find 5% of 420 and add 17.

WORK

$$x = 5\% \cdot 420 + 17$$

$5\% = 0.15$: $\qquad x = 0.05(420) + 17$

$$x = 21 + 17$$

$$x = 38$$

ANSWER: (D)

192.
ANALYSIS
Let x = the unknown number. Then let $x = 24.72$ divided by 6. After we find the number, divide by 4.

WORK

$$x = 24.72/6 = 4.12$$
$$4.12/4 = 1.03$$

ANSWER: (B)

193.
ANALYSIS
Check each statement. There may be more than one statement that is false.

$$X = \{4, 8, 12, 16, \ldots\}$$
$$Y = \{10, 20, 30, 40, \ldots\}$$

WORK

$$10 \in Y$$
$$10 \in \{10, 20, 30, 40, \ldots\} \ ✔$$

ANSWER: (C)

194.
ANALYSIS
Let x = the first consecutive odd integer and let $x + 2$ = the next consecutive odd integer.

WORK

$$x + (x + 2) = 156$$
$$2x + 2 = 156$$
Subtract 2: $\qquad 2x = 154$
Divide by 2: $\qquad x = 77$
$$x + 2 = \underline{\ 79\ } \text{ (larger integer)}$$
$$156$$
Check:

ANSWER: (D)

195.
ANALYSIS
Line up the a's, b's, and c's and then add.

WORK

$$
\begin{array}{r}
-3a + 4b - 6c \\
+\ -6a + 7b - 4c \\
\hline
-9a + 11b - 10c
\end{array}
$$

ANSWER: (A)

196.
ANALYSIS
Divide 5^8 by 5^6 and then simplify.

WORK $\qquad \dfrac{\overset{2}{\cancel{4}} \times \overset{5^2}{\cancel{5^8}}}{\underset{1}{\cancel{2}} \times \underset{1}{\cancel{5^6}}} = 2 \times 25 = 50$

ANSWER: (A)

197.
ANALYSIS
Which of the given numbers is greater than -2 but less than 2.3?

WORK

$$-2 < 0 < 2.3$$

ANSWER: (C)

198.
ANALYSIS
It's sometimes easier to understand this problem if we make it into an equation, so let's represent the answer by the letter x.

WORK

$$x \cdot 80 = 17.6$$
Divide by 80: $\qquad x = \dfrac{17.6}{80}$
$$x = 0.22$$
$$x = 22\%$$

ANSWER: (A)

199.
ANALYSIS
Add the negative and positive numbers separately and then combine the two answers.

WORK

$$(-4) + (-6) = -10$$
$$(+9) + (+3) = \underline{+12}$$
$$+2$$

ANSWER: (D)

200.

ANALYSIS

In cases when we are given a generalized statement, make the problem concrete by using actual numbers fitting the description. The two unknowns, x and y, are negative and $y > x$, so let's try using $x = -2$ and $y = -1$.

WORK

Let $x = -2$, $y = -1$:
$$xy > 0$$
$$(-2)(-1) = +2$$
$$+2 > 0$$

ANSWER: (C)

201.

ANALYSIS

Draw a diagram and label the width. Then length = l, perimeter = P = 44 feet, and width = 7 feet.

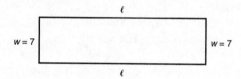

WORK

$P = 44$, $w = 7$:
$$P = 2w + 2l$$
$$44 = 2(7) + 2l$$
$$44 = 14 + 2l$$
Subtract 14: $\quad 30 = 2l$
Divide by 2: $\quad 15 = l$

ANSWER: (C)

202.

ANALYSIS

The sum of the angles of a triangle equals 180°, so add up the two angles and subtract from 180°.

WORK

$$47 + 58 = 105$$
$$180 - 105 = 75$$

ANSWER: (A)

203.

ANALYSIS

Determine all the prime factors of 42. Then select the greatest prime factor.

WORK

$$42 = 2 \times 3 \times 7$$

ANSWER: (A)

204.

ANALYSIS

Find the area of the outer rectangle. Then calculate the total areas of the smaller rectangles and subtract.

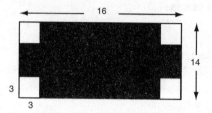

WORK

Area of the larger rectangle $\quad = 16 \times 14 = 224$
$-$ Total areas of the smaller squares $\quad = 4 \times 3 \times 3 = -36$
$$188$$

ANSWER: (B)

205.

ANALYSIS

Reduce to simplest terms.

WORK

$$\frac{2.6}{20.8} = \frac{\overset{1}{\cancel{2}} \times \overset{1}{\cancel{13}}}{\underset{2}{\cancel{4}} \times \underset{4}{\cancel{52}}} = \frac{1}{8}$$

ANSWER: (C)

206.

ANALYSIS

Multiply and then combine like terms.

WORK

$$5(a - 2b) + 6(-2a + 4b) = 5a - 10b - 12a + 24b$$
$$= -7a + 14b$$

ANSWER: (A)

207.

ANALYSIS
Simplify and then combine terms.

WORK

$$
\begin{aligned}
7 \times 10^3 &= 7 \times 10 \times 10 \times 10 = 7 \times 1{,}000 = 7{,}000 \\
5 \times 10^2 &= 5 \times 10 \times 10 \qquad = 5 \times 100 = 500 \\
2 \times 10^1 &= 2 \times 10 \qquad\qquad\qquad\quad = 20 \\
+\; 6 \times 10^0 &= 6 \times 1 \qquad\qquad\qquad\qquad = 6 \\
\hline
&\qquad\qquad\qquad\qquad\qquad\qquad\quad 7{,}526
\end{aligned}
$$

ANSWER: (D)

208.

ANALYSIS
Use the formula for the area of a triangle, $A = bh$, where A = area, b = base, and h = height.

WORK
Area of original triangle,
A_O: $\qquad\qquad\qquad A_O = bh$
Area of new triangle,
A_N, when the height
is doubled: $\qquad\qquad A_N = b(2h) = 2bh$

ANSWER: (B)

209.

ANALYSIS
Change both fractions to improper fractions and then multiply.

WORK

$$
\frac{7}{\cancel{2}_{1}} \times \frac{\cancel{22}^{11}}{5} = \frac{77}{5} = 15\frac{2}{5}
$$

ANSWER: (D)

210.

ANALYSIS
We want to find a monomial that, when multiplied by itself 3 times, is equal to $64a^3b^9$.

WORK

$$
\sqrt[3]{64a^3b^9} = 4ab^3
$$
Check: $\quad 4ab^3 \cdot 4ab^3 \cdot 4ab^3 = 64a^3b^9$ ✔

ANSWER: (D)

211.

ANALYSIS
The letter c is the last odd integer in the series. Find the two preceding odd integers and multiply.

WORK

$$
c = 11,\, b = 9,\, a = 7
$$
$$
a \cdot b = (7)(9) = 63
$$

ANSWER: (B)

212.

ANALYSIS
Let x = the number of executives, and let $15x$ = the number of assembly line workers. The total number of employees is 480, so let $15x + x = 480$.

WORK

$$
\begin{aligned}
15x + x &= 480 \\
16x &= 480 \\
x &= 30 \\
15x &= 15(30) = 450
\end{aligned}
$$

ANSWER: (A)

213.

ANALYSIS
Divide $4\frac{2}{3}$ by $5\frac{1}{4}$.

WORK

$$
4\frac{2}{3} \div 5\frac{1}{4}
$$

$$
\frac{14}{3} \div \frac{21}{4}
$$

$$
\frac{\cancel{14}^{2}}{3} \times \frac{4}{\cancel{21}_{3}} = \frac{8}{9}
$$

ANSWER: (C)

214.

ANALYSIS
First, find the measure of angle EBD. Then add the result to $54°$ (measure of angle DBC) to find the measure of angle EBC.

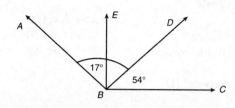

WORK

$$m(\angle DBE) = 90° - 17° = 73°$$
$$m(\angle EBC) = 73° + 54° = 127°$$

ANSWER: (C)

215.
ANALYSIS
In a parallelogram, the opposite sides are parallel.

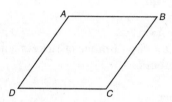

WORK
AD is parallel to BC.

ANSWER: (D)

216.
ANALYSIS
All the central angles add up to 360°, so find the missing third angle (call it x) and then find the average of all three angles.

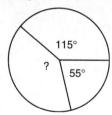

WORK

$$x + 55 + 115 = 360$$
$$x + 170 = 360$$

Subtract 170: $$x = 190$$

Find the average of the three central angles:

$$(55 + 115 + 190)/3 = 360/3 = 120$$

ANSWER: (C)

217.
ANALYSIS
To determine the percent of iodine in the new mixture, first determine the total amount of iodine in the new mix. To do this, add one gallon of iodine to 10% of five gallons, the amount of iodine in the original mix. We have the total amount of iodine in the new mix. Now divide the total amount of iodine in the new mix by the total amount of liquid in the new mix (5 + 1 gallons).

WORK

Amount of iodine in the original mix:	$.10 \times 5 = .5$ gallons
Added iodine:	1.0 gallons
Total amount of iodine in new mix:	1.5 gallons

Percent of iodine in new mix:

$$\frac{\text{total iodine in new mix}}{\text{total liquid in new mix}} = \frac{1.5}{6} = .25 = 25\%$$

ANSWER: (B)

218.

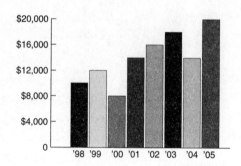

ANALYSIS
Find the increase in price between 1999 and 2005 and then divide that increase by the base price in 1998.

WORK

Price in 2005:	$20,000
− Price in 1999:	$12,000
Price increase:	$8,000

$$\frac{\text{Price Increase:}}{\text{Price in 1999:}} = \frac{\$8,000}{\$12,000} = .6666... \approx .67 = 67\%$$

ANSWER: (A)

219.
ANALYSIS
Multiply the pounds, p_i, by the frequencies, f_i, and then divide by the total frequencies.

WORK

Pounds, p_i	Frequency, f_i	$p_i f_i$
98	2	$2 \times 98 = 196$
105	1	$1 \times 105 = 105$
109	1	$1 \times 109 = 109$
120	3	$3 \times 120 = 360$
126	2	$2 \times 126 = 252$
132	4	$4 \times 132 = 528$
Totals	13	1,550

$$\frac{p_i f_i}{f_i} = \frac{1,550}{13} = 119.23 \approx 119.2$$

ANSWER: (D)

220.
ANALYSIS
Divide 7 by $17\frac{1}{2}$.

WORK

$$7 \div 17\frac{1}{2}$$

$$\frac{7}{1} \div \frac{35}{2}$$

$$\frac{\overset{1}{\cancel{7}}}{1} \times \frac{2}{\underset{5}{\cancel{35}}} = \frac{2}{5}$$

ANSWER: (B)

221.

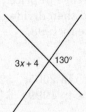

ANALYSIS
Vertical angles are of the same measure, so set $3x + 4$ equal to 130°.

WORK

$$3x + 4 = 130$$
Subtract 4: $\qquad 3x = 126$
Divide by 3: $\qquad x = 42$

ANSWER: (D)

222.
ANALYSIS
One pound is equivalent to 16 ounces, so first change 8 pounds to ounces. Then multiply by $0.20, the price per ounce of raisins.

WORK
8 pounds = 8×16 ounces = 128 ounces
128 ounces $\times$ $0.20 (per ounce) = $25.60

ANSWER: (C)

223. ANALYSIS
Let x = the number of tickets sold to S.O. members.

WORK

	Number, (n)	Price per ticket, (p)	Total price, np
S.O. members	x	$5	$5x$
Nonmembers	170	$11	11(170)

The total revenue from members and nonmembers is $3,700:

$$5x + 11(170) = 3,700$$
$$5x + 1,870 = 3,700$$
Subtract 1,870: $\qquad 5x = 1,830$
Divide by 5: $\qquad x = 366$

ANSWER: (B)

224.
ANALYSIS
A hexagon is a six-sided figure, so, to find the cost of the fence, add up all the sides and multiply by $5.36, the cost per foot of fence.

WORK
$49.4 + 34.9 + 53.6 + 65.8 + 72.6 + 48.7 = 325$

$$325 \times \$5.30 = \$1,722.50$$

ANSWER: (D)

225.

ANALYSIS

A pentagon is a five-sided figure, so add up all the sides and set the sum equal to the perimeter, 56. Find x and then substitute the value of x into the five terms to determine the longest side.

WORK

$$x + (x + 2) + (x + 5) + (2x + 2) + (3x - 1) = 56$$
$$8x + 8 = 56$$
Subtract 8: $\qquad\qquad\qquad\qquad 8x = 48$
Divide by 8: $\qquad\qquad\qquad\quad x = 6$

$$
\begin{aligned}
x + 2 &= 8 \\
x + 5 &= 11 \\
2x + 2 &= 14 \\
+\ 3x - 1 &= 17 \text{ (longest side)} \\
\hline
\end{aligned}
$$
Check: $\qquad\qquad\qquad\quad 56$

ANSWER: (C)

226.

ANALYSIS

To determine the area of a square, multiply two adjacent sides. Then, to determine x, set the result of the multiplication equal to $4x + 20$.

WORK

Area of a square =
side × side: $\qquad 8 \times 8 = 4x + 20$
$\qquad\qquad\qquad\qquad 64 = 4x + 20$
Subtract 20: $\qquad\qquad 44 = 4x$
Divide by 4: $\qquad\qquad 11 = x$

ANSWER: (B)

227.

ANALYSIS

Latisha was always 5 years older than Wanda. Find Latisha's age 3 years ago and then add 3 years.

WORK

Name	Age 3 years ago	Age now
Wanda	$8a$	$8a + 3$
Latisha	$8a + 5$	$8a + 5 + 3$

Latisha is now $8a + 5 + 3 = 8a + 8$ years old.

ANSWER: (C)

228.

ANALYSIS

Let t = the tens' digit, and let u = the units' digit.

WORK

The sum of the
digits is 11: $\qquad$ (i) $\qquad t + u = 11$

Three times the
tens' digit is 5
more than the
units' digit: $\qquad$ (ii) $\qquad 3t = u + 5$

In equation (i),
find t alone: $\qquad$ (i) $\qquad t = 11 - u$

Substitute the
value for t $(11 - u)$
into equation (ii): $\quad$ (ii) $3(11 - u) = u + 5$
$\qquad\qquad\qquad\qquad$ (ii) $33 - 3u = u + 5$
Add $3u$: $\qquad\qquad$ (ii) $\qquad 33 = 4u + 5$
Subtract 5: $\qquad\quad$ (ii) $\qquad 28 = 4u$
Divide by 4: $\qquad\quad$ (ii) $\qquad 7 = u$
$\qquad\qquad\qquad\qquad$ (i) $\quad t + u = 11$
$u = 7$: $\qquad\qquad\quad$ (i) $\quad t + 7 = 11$
Subtract 7: $\qquad\quad$ (i) $\qquad t = 4$

The original number:

$$10t + u = 10(4) + 7 = 40 + 7 = 47$$

ANSWER: (A)

229.

ANALYSIS

Using the number of books lost, find the number of books returned. Then compare both numbers.

WORK

Original number of books:	30
− Number of books lost:	4
Number of books returned:	26

Ratio of returned books to lost books:

$$\frac{26}{4} = \frac{13}{2}$$

ANSWER: (D)

230.

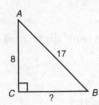

ANALYSIS
Use the Pythagorean Theorem, $a^2 + b^2 = c^2$, where a and b are two legs of a right triangle and c is the hypotenuse.

WORK

$$a^2 + b^2 = c^2$$

$b = 8, c = 17$: $\quad a^2 + 8^2 = 17^2$

$$a^2 + 64 = 289$$

Subtract 64: $\qquad a^2 = 225$

Take the square root: $\qquad a = 15$

ANSWER: (D)

231.
ANALYSIS
Simplify expressions within the parentheses and then work from left to right.

WORK
(A) $2 \times 5^2 - 9 \div 3 = 2 \times 25 - 3 = 50 - 3 = 47$
(B) $3^3 - (18 \div 2) + 7 = 27 - 9 + 7 = 18 + 7 = 25$
(C) $5(8 - 3)^2 = 5(5)^2 = 5(25) = 125$
(D) $4 \times 9 + 3(6 - 2) = 36 + 3(4) = 36 + 12 = 48$

ANSWER: (D)

232.
ANALYSIS
Substitute 4 for a in the given expression.

WORK

$$6(a + 2) - 2c = 6$$
$$6a + 12 - 2c = 6$$

$a = 4$: $\quad 6(4) + 12 - 2c = 6$

$$24 + 12 - 2c = 6$$
$$36 - 2c = 6$$

Subtract 36: $\qquad -2c = -30$

Divide by −2: $\qquad c = 15$

ANSWER: (A)

233.

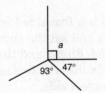

ANALYSIS
All the angles add up to 360°.

WORK

$$m\angle a + 90° + 47° + 93° = 360°$$
$$m\angle a + 230° = 360°$$

Subtract 230°: $\qquad m\angle a = 130°$

ANSWER: (D)

234.
ANALYSIS
Subtract 8 from the product of $\frac{2}{3}$ and 27.

WORK

$$\frac{2}{3} \times 27 - 8 = 18 - 8 = 10$$

ANSWER: (A)

235.
ANALYSIS
1 foot = 12 inches

WORK

$$\begin{array}{r} 4 \qquad 12 + 7 = 19 \\ \cancel{5} \text{ feet } \cancel{7} \text{ inches} \\ - \; 2 \text{ feet } 9 \text{ inches} \\ \hline 2 \text{ feet } 10 \text{ inches} \end{array}$$

ANSWER: (D)

236.
ANALYSIS
Change 2 hours to minutes and multiply by $5.25 per minute.

WORK

$$2 \text{ hours} = 120 \text{ minutes}$$
$$\$5.25 \times 120 = \$630$$

ANSWER: (D)

237.

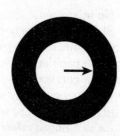

ANALYSIS
Subtract the area of the inner circle from the area of the outer circle.

WORK

$$A = \pi r^2$$

$A_O, r = 8$: $A_O = 3.14 \cdot 8^2 = 3.14 \cdot 64 = 200.96$
$A_I, r = 5$: $-A_I = 3.14 \cdot 5^2 = 3.14 \cdot 25 = 78.50$

Shaded area: 122.46

ANSWER: (C)

238.
ANALYSIS
Multiply the whole numbers and the radicals separately and then simplify.

WORK

$$5\sqrt{2} \times 3\sqrt{8} = 15\sqrt{16} = 15 \times 4 = 60$$

ANSWER: (C)

SUBTEST 5 LANGUAGE

239. **(B)** Paul, can you tell Lisa to come to the party? Use a comma after direct address.

240. **(A)** I attended the St. Andrew parish when I was younger. Use a period for abbreviations.

241. **(C)** Merry and Pippin are the tallest hobbits in *all* of the Shire. Use -*est* when comparing more than two.

242. **(D)** No mistakes.

243. **(A)** **One** [of the men on the team] has dropped out of the game. Subject-verb agreement.

244. **(B)** Would you mind stirring the kettle? This is a question.

245. **(A)** Tom, Guy, Sandy, and I went to the game together. No comma between subject and verb. I is the subject form.

246. **(C)** She returned the textbook to me. Use the object pronoun *me* instead of the reflexive pronoun *myself*.

247. **(C)** It's a difficult problem, but we can handle it. *It's* is the contraction for *It is*.

248. **(B)** Who is speaking? *Who* is the subject form; *whom* is the object form.

249. **(B)** In this election, the voters don't have enough information to know if they should support the tax. Pronoun-antecedent agreement. *They* refers to more than one voter.

250. **(A)** Josh just sits silently in his seat most of the time. The adverb form is silently.

251. **(A)** Our oldest teacher was born on September 23, 1960. Do not use a comma between the month and day.

252. **(A)** The theme of the story concerned the destructive greed for power. Use *power* instead of the awkward *powerfulness*.

253. **(C)** Bring the following to class: pen, pencil, paper, and books. Use a colon before a list.

254. **(C)** Jake is the most truthful person I have ever met. Use *most truthful* rather than *truthfullest*.

255. **(A)** It is farther to Cleveland than to Phildalelphia. *Farther* refers to distance. *Further* refers to degree.

256. **(C)** I don't have a lot of free time; nevertheless, I would like the job. *Nevertheless* is an adverb, not a coordinating conjunction. Use a period or semicolon instead of a comma.

257. **(A)** No, I have never seen a live rhinocerous. Use a comma after a mild interjection.

258. **(D)** No mistakes.

259. **(A)** You won't have to look for Joe and me. The object form is *me*. You won't have to look for me.

260. **(C)** I realized I had been mistaken. The correct past participle is *had been mistaken*, not *had been mistook*.

261. **(D)** No mistakes.

262. **(A)** I enjoy walking on the beach and running in the surf. Use parallel forms of the verb.

263. **(C)** I only have time to eat, drink, and sleep. Use commas in a series.

264. **(B)** Dennis performed well on the ice. *Well* is an adverb.

265. (**A**) Aunt Wendy often takes Al and <u>me</u> to lunch. Use the object form: She often takes <u>me</u>.

266. (**B**) The deer reared up on <u>its</u> hind legs. The possessive form of *it* is *its*. *It's* is the contraction of *it is*.

267. (**D**) No mistakes.

268. (**A**) My favorite <u>aunt</u> is visiting with my cousin. The word *aunt* is not capitalized because it is not part of a specific person's name (such as Aunt Pina).

269. (**B**) Our school finished first<u>;</u> his school placed second. Use a period or semicolon between sentences. Using a comma here is called a comma splice.

270. (**D**) No mistakes.

271. (**A**) Shakespeare wrote, "To thine own self be true." Periods should go <u>inside</u> quotation marks.

272. (**A**) Don't <u>lose</u> your tickets, or you won't be able to get in. Be careful not to confuse the words *lose* and *loose*.

273. (**A**) Neither Jimmy <u>nor</u> Tommy has ever been to Canada. Use *nor* with *neither*.

274. (**C**) I just want to <u>sit</u> on my porch and swing. A person sits.

275. (**D**) No mistakes.

276. (**B**) You and <u>I</u> are best friends, aren't we? *I* is the subject form.

277. (**B**) My neighbors own a German shepherd. Capitalize names of countries.

278. (**A**) Fragment. *Since he started walking* is not a complete sentence.

279. (**C**) *Thorough* should be *through*.

280. (**A**) When you add a prefix, just add it: *mis-shapen* has two *s*'s.

281. (**A**) He <u>carefully</u> unwrapped his gifts.

282. (**C**) Where did you <u>acquire</u> that artifact?

283. (**B**) Even though the role was foolish, the actor was not <u>embarrassed</u>.

284. (**D**) No mistakes.

285. (**A**) She has always been greatly concerned about the <u>environment</u>. This word is a problem if you don't pronounce it correctly.

286. (**B**) I always go to my science teacher for <u>advice</u> before a new experiment. *Advice* is a noun; *advise* is a verb.

287. (**D**) No mistakes.

288. (**A**) <u>Lightning</u> and thunder can be terrifying experiences.

289. (**C**) I couldn't sing in the choir last week <u>because</u> I had lost my voice. Choices A and B are incorrect because they would begin a new sentence. Choice C, *because*, is the only word that indicates a cause/effect relationship.

290. (**B**) Bess wears slippers to bed in the winter; <u>consequently</u>, her feet are warm. The word *consequently* indicates a result.

291. (**C**) After clearing the dishes, we can all take a nap. Choice C is the most concise. Choice A is passive, choice B is wordy, and choice D would result in an awkward modifier.

292. (**B**) This is the only choice that contains all of the information most concisely. Choice C is the shortest, but it contains erroneous information and a capitalization error.

293. (**A**) This is the most direct statement.

294. (**B**) This is the only sentence that deals with medical matters.

295. (**C**) A paragraph should focus on a single idea. The other topics are far too broad.

296. (**C**) All of the sentences except this one are about Stonehenge.

297. (**D**) This sentence is not about how the temperature of soup is regulated.

298. (**D**) The paragraph focuses on the holiday tradition rather than the location of the trees.

Answer Sheet
Practice High School Placement Test 2

SUBTEST 1   VERBAL SKILLS

1. Ⓐ Ⓑ Ⓒ Ⓓ	13. Ⓐ Ⓑ Ⓒ Ⓓ	25. Ⓐ Ⓑ Ⓒ Ⓓ	37. Ⓐ Ⓑ Ⓒ Ⓓ	49. Ⓐ Ⓑ Ⓒ Ⓓ
2. Ⓐ Ⓑ Ⓒ Ⓓ	14. Ⓐ Ⓑ Ⓒ Ⓓ	26. Ⓐ Ⓑ Ⓒ Ⓓ	38. Ⓐ Ⓑ Ⓒ Ⓓ	50. Ⓐ Ⓑ Ⓒ Ⓓ
3. Ⓐ Ⓑ Ⓒ Ⓓ	15. Ⓐ Ⓑ Ⓒ Ⓓ	27. Ⓐ Ⓑ Ⓒ Ⓓ	39. Ⓐ Ⓑ Ⓒ Ⓓ	51. Ⓐ Ⓑ Ⓒ Ⓓ
4. Ⓐ Ⓑ Ⓒ Ⓓ	16. Ⓐ Ⓑ Ⓒ Ⓓ	28. Ⓐ Ⓑ Ⓒ Ⓓ	40. Ⓐ Ⓑ Ⓒ Ⓓ	52. Ⓐ Ⓑ Ⓒ Ⓓ
5. Ⓐ Ⓑ Ⓒ Ⓓ	17. Ⓐ Ⓑ Ⓒ Ⓓ	29. Ⓐ Ⓑ Ⓒ Ⓓ	41. Ⓐ Ⓑ Ⓒ Ⓓ	53. Ⓐ Ⓑ Ⓒ Ⓓ
6. Ⓐ Ⓑ Ⓒ Ⓓ	18. Ⓐ Ⓑ Ⓒ Ⓓ	30. Ⓐ Ⓑ Ⓒ Ⓓ	42. Ⓐ Ⓑ Ⓒ Ⓓ	54. Ⓐ Ⓑ Ⓒ Ⓓ
7. Ⓐ Ⓑ Ⓒ Ⓓ	19. Ⓐ Ⓑ Ⓒ Ⓓ	31. Ⓐ Ⓑ Ⓒ Ⓓ	43. Ⓐ Ⓑ Ⓒ Ⓓ	55. Ⓐ Ⓑ Ⓒ Ⓓ
8. Ⓐ Ⓑ Ⓒ Ⓓ	20. Ⓐ Ⓑ Ⓒ Ⓓ	32. Ⓐ Ⓑ Ⓒ Ⓓ	44. Ⓐ Ⓑ Ⓒ Ⓓ	56. Ⓐ Ⓑ Ⓒ Ⓓ
9. Ⓐ Ⓑ Ⓒ Ⓓ	21. Ⓐ Ⓑ Ⓒ Ⓓ	33. Ⓐ Ⓑ Ⓒ Ⓓ	45. Ⓐ Ⓑ Ⓒ Ⓓ	57. Ⓐ Ⓑ Ⓒ Ⓓ
10. Ⓐ Ⓑ Ⓒ Ⓓ	22. Ⓐ Ⓑ Ⓒ Ⓓ	34. Ⓐ Ⓑ Ⓒ Ⓓ	46. Ⓐ Ⓑ Ⓒ Ⓓ	58. Ⓐ Ⓑ Ⓒ Ⓓ
11. Ⓐ Ⓑ Ⓒ Ⓓ	23. Ⓐ Ⓑ Ⓒ Ⓓ	35. Ⓐ Ⓑ Ⓒ Ⓓ	47. Ⓐ Ⓑ Ⓒ Ⓓ	59. Ⓐ Ⓑ Ⓒ Ⓓ
12. Ⓐ Ⓑ Ⓒ Ⓓ	24. Ⓐ Ⓑ Ⓒ Ⓓ	36. Ⓐ Ⓑ Ⓒ Ⓓ	48. Ⓐ Ⓑ Ⓒ Ⓓ	60. Ⓐ Ⓑ Ⓒ Ⓓ

SUBTEST 2   QUANTITATIVE SKILLS

61. Ⓐ Ⓑ Ⓒ Ⓓ	72. Ⓐ Ⓑ Ⓒ Ⓓ	83. Ⓐ Ⓑ Ⓒ Ⓓ	93. Ⓐ Ⓑ Ⓒ Ⓓ	103. Ⓐ Ⓑ Ⓒ Ⓓ
62. Ⓐ Ⓑ Ⓒ Ⓓ	73. Ⓐ Ⓑ Ⓒ Ⓓ	84. Ⓐ Ⓑ Ⓒ Ⓓ	94. Ⓐ Ⓑ Ⓒ Ⓓ	104. Ⓐ Ⓑ Ⓒ Ⓓ
63. Ⓐ Ⓑ Ⓒ Ⓓ	74. Ⓐ Ⓑ Ⓒ Ⓓ	85. Ⓐ Ⓑ Ⓒ Ⓓ	95. Ⓐ Ⓑ Ⓒ Ⓓ	105. Ⓐ Ⓑ Ⓒ Ⓓ
64. Ⓐ Ⓑ Ⓒ Ⓓ	75. Ⓐ Ⓑ Ⓒ Ⓓ	86. Ⓐ Ⓑ Ⓒ Ⓓ	96. Ⓐ Ⓑ Ⓒ Ⓓ	106. Ⓐ Ⓑ Ⓒ Ⓓ
65. Ⓐ Ⓑ Ⓒ Ⓓ	76. Ⓐ Ⓑ Ⓒ Ⓓ	87. Ⓐ Ⓑ Ⓒ Ⓓ	97. Ⓐ Ⓑ Ⓒ Ⓓ	107. Ⓐ Ⓑ Ⓒ Ⓓ
66. Ⓐ Ⓑ Ⓒ Ⓓ	77. Ⓐ Ⓑ Ⓒ Ⓓ	88. Ⓐ Ⓑ Ⓒ Ⓓ	98. Ⓐ Ⓑ Ⓒ Ⓓ	108. Ⓐ Ⓑ Ⓒ Ⓓ
67. Ⓐ Ⓑ Ⓒ Ⓓ	78. Ⓐ Ⓑ Ⓒ Ⓓ	89. Ⓐ Ⓑ Ⓒ Ⓓ	99. Ⓐ Ⓑ Ⓒ Ⓓ	109. Ⓐ Ⓑ Ⓒ Ⓓ
68. Ⓐ Ⓑ Ⓒ Ⓓ	79. Ⓐ Ⓑ Ⓒ Ⓓ	90. Ⓐ Ⓑ Ⓒ Ⓓ	100. Ⓐ Ⓑ Ⓒ Ⓓ	110. Ⓐ Ⓑ Ⓒ Ⓓ
69. Ⓐ Ⓑ Ⓒ Ⓓ	80. Ⓐ Ⓑ Ⓒ Ⓓ	91. Ⓐ Ⓑ Ⓒ Ⓓ	101. Ⓐ Ⓑ Ⓒ Ⓓ	111. Ⓐ Ⓑ Ⓒ Ⓓ
70. Ⓐ Ⓑ Ⓒ Ⓓ	81. Ⓐ Ⓑ Ⓒ Ⓓ	92. Ⓐ Ⓑ Ⓒ Ⓓ	102. Ⓐ Ⓑ Ⓒ Ⓓ	112. Ⓐ Ⓑ Ⓒ Ⓓ
71. Ⓐ Ⓑ Ⓒ Ⓓ	82. Ⓐ Ⓑ Ⓒ Ⓓ			

SUBTEST 3   READING—COMPREHENSION—VOCABULARY

113. Ⓐ Ⓑ Ⓒ Ⓓ	126. Ⓐ Ⓑ Ⓒ Ⓓ	139. Ⓐ Ⓑ Ⓒ Ⓓ	151. Ⓐ Ⓑ Ⓒ Ⓓ	163. Ⓐ Ⓑ Ⓒ Ⓓ
114. Ⓐ Ⓑ Ⓒ Ⓓ	127. Ⓐ Ⓑ Ⓒ Ⓓ	140. Ⓐ Ⓑ Ⓒ Ⓓ	152. Ⓐ Ⓑ Ⓒ Ⓓ	164. Ⓐ Ⓑ Ⓒ Ⓓ
115. Ⓐ Ⓑ Ⓒ Ⓓ	128. Ⓐ Ⓑ Ⓒ Ⓓ	141. Ⓐ Ⓑ Ⓒ Ⓓ	153. Ⓐ Ⓑ Ⓒ Ⓓ	165. Ⓐ Ⓑ Ⓒ Ⓓ
116. Ⓐ Ⓑ Ⓒ Ⓓ	129. Ⓐ Ⓑ Ⓒ Ⓓ	142. Ⓐ Ⓑ Ⓒ Ⓓ	154. Ⓐ Ⓑ Ⓒ Ⓓ	166. Ⓐ Ⓑ Ⓒ Ⓓ
117. Ⓐ Ⓑ Ⓒ Ⓓ	130. Ⓐ Ⓑ Ⓒ Ⓓ	143. Ⓐ Ⓑ Ⓒ Ⓓ	155. Ⓐ Ⓑ Ⓒ Ⓓ	167. Ⓐ Ⓑ Ⓒ Ⓓ
118. Ⓐ Ⓑ Ⓒ Ⓓ	131. Ⓐ Ⓑ Ⓒ Ⓓ	144. Ⓐ Ⓑ Ⓒ Ⓓ	156. Ⓐ Ⓑ Ⓒ Ⓓ	168. Ⓐ Ⓑ Ⓒ Ⓓ
119. Ⓐ Ⓑ Ⓒ Ⓓ	132. Ⓐ Ⓑ Ⓒ Ⓓ	145. Ⓐ Ⓑ Ⓒ Ⓓ	157. Ⓐ Ⓑ Ⓒ Ⓓ	169. Ⓐ Ⓑ Ⓒ Ⓓ
120. Ⓐ Ⓑ Ⓒ Ⓓ	133. Ⓐ Ⓑ Ⓒ Ⓓ	146. Ⓐ Ⓑ Ⓒ Ⓓ	158. Ⓐ Ⓑ Ⓒ Ⓓ	170. Ⓐ Ⓑ Ⓒ Ⓓ
121. Ⓐ Ⓑ Ⓒ Ⓓ	134. Ⓐ Ⓑ Ⓒ Ⓓ	147. Ⓐ Ⓑ Ⓒ Ⓓ	159. Ⓐ Ⓑ Ⓒ Ⓓ	171. Ⓐ Ⓑ Ⓒ Ⓓ
122. Ⓐ Ⓑ Ⓒ Ⓓ	135. Ⓐ Ⓑ Ⓒ Ⓓ	148. Ⓐ Ⓑ Ⓒ Ⓓ	160. Ⓐ Ⓑ Ⓒ Ⓓ	172. Ⓐ Ⓑ Ⓒ Ⓓ
123. Ⓐ Ⓑ Ⓒ Ⓓ	136. Ⓐ Ⓑ Ⓒ Ⓓ	149. Ⓐ Ⓑ Ⓒ Ⓓ	161. Ⓐ Ⓑ Ⓒ Ⓓ	173. Ⓐ Ⓑ Ⓒ Ⓓ
124. Ⓐ Ⓑ Ⓒ Ⓓ	137. Ⓐ Ⓑ Ⓒ Ⓓ	150. Ⓐ Ⓑ Ⓒ Ⓓ	162. Ⓐ Ⓑ Ⓒ Ⓓ	174. Ⓐ Ⓑ Ⓒ Ⓓ
125. Ⓐ Ⓑ Ⓒ Ⓓ	138. Ⓐ Ⓑ Ⓒ Ⓓ			

SUBTEST 4   MATHEMATICS

175. Ⓐ Ⓑ Ⓒ Ⓓ	188. Ⓐ Ⓑ Ⓒ Ⓓ	201. Ⓐ Ⓑ Ⓒ Ⓓ	214. Ⓐ Ⓑ Ⓒ Ⓓ	227. Ⓐ Ⓑ Ⓒ Ⓓ
176. Ⓐ Ⓑ Ⓒ Ⓓ	189. Ⓐ Ⓑ Ⓒ Ⓓ	202. Ⓐ Ⓑ Ⓒ Ⓓ	215. Ⓐ Ⓑ Ⓒ Ⓓ	228. Ⓐ Ⓑ Ⓒ Ⓓ
177. Ⓐ Ⓑ Ⓒ Ⓓ	190. Ⓐ Ⓑ Ⓒ Ⓓ	203. Ⓐ Ⓑ Ⓒ Ⓓ	216. Ⓐ Ⓑ Ⓒ Ⓓ	229. Ⓐ Ⓑ Ⓒ Ⓓ
178. Ⓐ Ⓑ Ⓒ Ⓓ	191. Ⓐ Ⓑ Ⓒ Ⓓ	204. Ⓐ Ⓑ Ⓒ Ⓓ	217. Ⓐ Ⓑ Ⓒ Ⓓ	230. Ⓐ Ⓑ Ⓒ Ⓓ
179. Ⓐ Ⓑ Ⓒ Ⓓ	192. Ⓐ Ⓑ Ⓒ Ⓓ	205. Ⓐ Ⓑ Ⓒ Ⓓ	218. Ⓐ Ⓑ Ⓒ Ⓓ	231. Ⓐ Ⓑ Ⓒ Ⓓ
180. Ⓐ Ⓑ Ⓒ Ⓓ	193. Ⓐ Ⓑ Ⓒ Ⓓ	206. Ⓐ Ⓑ Ⓒ Ⓓ	219. Ⓐ Ⓑ Ⓒ Ⓓ	232. Ⓐ Ⓑ Ⓒ Ⓓ
181. Ⓐ Ⓑ Ⓒ Ⓓ	194. Ⓐ Ⓑ Ⓒ Ⓓ	207. Ⓐ Ⓑ Ⓒ Ⓓ	220. Ⓐ Ⓑ Ⓒ Ⓓ	233. Ⓐ Ⓑ Ⓒ Ⓓ
182. Ⓐ Ⓑ Ⓒ Ⓓ	195. Ⓐ Ⓑ Ⓒ Ⓓ	208. Ⓐ Ⓑ Ⓒ Ⓓ	221. Ⓐ Ⓑ Ⓒ Ⓓ	234. Ⓐ Ⓑ Ⓒ Ⓓ
183. Ⓐ Ⓑ Ⓒ Ⓓ	196. Ⓐ Ⓑ Ⓒ Ⓓ	209. Ⓐ Ⓑ Ⓒ Ⓓ	222. Ⓐ Ⓑ Ⓒ Ⓓ	235. Ⓐ Ⓑ Ⓒ Ⓓ
184. Ⓐ Ⓑ Ⓒ Ⓓ	197. Ⓐ Ⓑ Ⓒ Ⓓ	210. Ⓐ Ⓑ Ⓒ Ⓓ	223. Ⓐ Ⓑ Ⓒ Ⓓ	236. Ⓐ Ⓑ Ⓒ Ⓓ
185. Ⓐ Ⓑ Ⓒ Ⓓ	198. Ⓐ Ⓑ Ⓒ Ⓓ	211. Ⓐ Ⓑ Ⓒ Ⓓ	224. Ⓐ Ⓑ Ⓒ Ⓓ	237. Ⓐ Ⓑ Ⓒ Ⓓ
186. Ⓐ Ⓑ Ⓒ Ⓓ	199. Ⓐ Ⓑ Ⓒ Ⓓ	212. Ⓐ Ⓑ Ⓒ Ⓓ	225. Ⓐ Ⓑ Ⓒ Ⓓ	238. Ⓐ Ⓑ Ⓒ Ⓓ
187. Ⓐ Ⓑ Ⓒ Ⓓ	200. Ⓐ Ⓑ Ⓒ Ⓓ	213. Ⓐ Ⓑ Ⓒ Ⓓ	226. Ⓐ Ⓑ Ⓒ Ⓓ	

SUBTEST 5   LANGUAGE

239. Ⓐ Ⓑ Ⓒ Ⓓ	251. Ⓐ Ⓑ Ⓒ Ⓓ	263. Ⓐ Ⓑ Ⓒ Ⓓ	275. Ⓐ Ⓑ Ⓒ Ⓓ	287. Ⓐ Ⓑ Ⓒ Ⓓ
240. Ⓐ Ⓑ Ⓒ Ⓓ	252. Ⓐ Ⓑ Ⓒ Ⓓ	264. Ⓐ Ⓑ Ⓒ Ⓓ	276. Ⓐ Ⓑ Ⓒ Ⓓ	288. Ⓐ Ⓑ Ⓒ Ⓓ
241. Ⓐ Ⓑ Ⓒ Ⓓ	253. Ⓐ Ⓑ Ⓒ Ⓓ	265. Ⓐ Ⓑ Ⓒ Ⓓ	277. Ⓐ Ⓑ Ⓒ Ⓓ	289. Ⓐ Ⓑ Ⓒ Ⓓ
242. Ⓐ Ⓑ Ⓒ Ⓓ	254. Ⓐ Ⓑ Ⓒ Ⓓ	266. Ⓐ Ⓑ Ⓒ Ⓓ	278. Ⓐ Ⓑ Ⓒ Ⓓ	290. Ⓐ Ⓑ Ⓒ Ⓓ
243. Ⓐ Ⓑ Ⓒ Ⓓ	255. Ⓐ Ⓑ Ⓒ Ⓓ	267. Ⓐ Ⓑ Ⓒ Ⓓ	279. Ⓐ Ⓑ Ⓒ Ⓓ	291. Ⓐ Ⓑ Ⓒ Ⓓ
244. Ⓐ Ⓑ Ⓒ Ⓓ	256. Ⓐ Ⓑ Ⓒ Ⓓ	268. Ⓐ Ⓑ Ⓒ Ⓓ	280. Ⓐ Ⓑ Ⓒ Ⓓ	292. Ⓐ Ⓑ Ⓒ Ⓓ
245. Ⓐ Ⓑ Ⓒ Ⓓ	257. Ⓐ Ⓑ Ⓒ Ⓓ	269. Ⓐ Ⓑ Ⓒ Ⓓ	281. Ⓐ Ⓑ Ⓒ Ⓓ	293. Ⓐ Ⓑ Ⓒ Ⓓ
246. Ⓐ Ⓑ Ⓒ Ⓓ	258. Ⓐ Ⓑ Ⓒ Ⓓ	270. Ⓐ Ⓑ Ⓒ Ⓓ	282. Ⓐ Ⓑ Ⓒ Ⓓ	294. Ⓐ Ⓑ Ⓒ Ⓓ
247. Ⓐ Ⓑ Ⓒ Ⓓ	259. Ⓐ Ⓑ Ⓒ Ⓓ	271. Ⓐ Ⓑ Ⓒ Ⓓ	283. Ⓐ Ⓑ Ⓒ Ⓓ	295. Ⓐ Ⓑ Ⓒ Ⓓ
248. Ⓐ Ⓑ Ⓒ Ⓓ	260. Ⓐ Ⓑ Ⓒ Ⓓ	272. Ⓐ Ⓑ Ⓒ Ⓓ	284. Ⓐ Ⓑ Ⓒ Ⓓ	296. Ⓐ Ⓑ Ⓒ Ⓓ
249. Ⓐ Ⓑ Ⓒ Ⓓ	261. Ⓐ Ⓑ Ⓒ Ⓓ	273. Ⓐ Ⓑ Ⓒ Ⓓ	285. Ⓐ Ⓑ Ⓒ Ⓓ	297. Ⓐ Ⓑ Ⓒ Ⓓ
250. Ⓐ Ⓑ Ⓒ Ⓓ	262. Ⓐ Ⓑ Ⓒ Ⓓ	274. Ⓐ Ⓑ Ⓒ Ⓓ	286. Ⓐ Ⓑ Ⓒ Ⓓ	298. Ⓐ Ⓑ Ⓒ Ⓓ

Practice HSPT Exam 2

SUBTEST 1 VERBAL SKILLS

#1–60 *16 minutes*

Sample:

Which word does *not* belong with the others?

  (A) easy
  (B) interesting
  (C) simple
  (D) facile

    Ⓐ ● Ⓒ Ⓓ

1. Which word does *not* belong with the others?

  (A) shoes
  (B) socks
  (C) boots
  (D) laces

2. Which word does *not* belong with the others?

  (A) increase
  (B) enlarge
  (C) dilute
  (D) magnify

3. Hero is to villain as antagonist is to _____ .

  (A) character
  (B) protagonist
  (C) mentor
  (D) companion

4. Stationary most nearly means _____ .

  (A) unmoving
  (B) writing
  (C) guarding
  (D) driving

5. Last week, Dr. Zorba saw more patients than Dr. Kildare. Dr. Kildare did not see as many patients as Dr. Casey. Dr. Casey saw more patients than Dr. Zorba. If the first two statements are true, the third statement is _____ .

  (A) true
  (B) false
  (C) uncertain

6. Which word does *not* belong with the others?

  (A) toys
  (B) blocks
  (C) doll
  (D) yo-yo

7. Which word does *not* belong with the others?

  (A) furniture
  (B) chair
  (C) table
  (D) couch

8. Which word does *not* belong with the others?

  (A) display
  (B) uncover
  (C) presentation
  (D) exhibition

9. Resilient most nearly means
   _____ .

   (A) flexible
   (B) rigid
   (C) unmoving
   (D) serene

10. Which word does *not* belong with the others?

   (A) fool
   (B) clown
   (C) deceive
   (D) mislead

11. Donor most nearly means _____ .

   (A) hermit
   (B) doctor
   (C) contributor
   (D) misanthrope

12. Shrill most nearly means _____ .

   (A) piercing
   (B) melodious
   (C) low
   (D) rumbling

13. Drill is to hole as blender is to

   _____ .

   (A) flour
   (B) batter
   (C) eggs
   (D) milk

14. Mr. Quigley has one daughter. Mr. Zuniga has one daughter. The members of the coaching staff have a total of two daughters. If the first two statements are true, the third statement is _____ .

   (A) true
   (B) false
   (C) uncertain

15. Lethargy most nearly means

   _____ .

   (A) inactivity
   (B) speed
   (C) efficiency
   (D) poison

16. Which word does *not* belong with the others?

   (A) philosopher
   (B) sage
   (C) scholar
   (D) solicitor

17. Which word does *not* belong with the others?

   (A) hospital
   (B) schoolhouse
   (C) office tower
   (D) government

18. Scrutiny most nearly means

   _____ .

   (A) revision
   (B) ignorance
   (C) examination
   (D) liability

19. Plunder means the *opposite* of

   _____ .

   (A) rest
   (B) restore
   (C) raid
   (D) steal

20. Coat is to jacket as chair is to

   _____ .

   (A) stool
   (B) table
   (C) couch
   (D) counter

21. Financial is to money as psychological is to _____ .

   (A) mind
   (B) spirit
   (C) body
   (D) academic

22. Jack is three years older than Ralph. Peterkin is two years younger than Ralph. Jack is five years older than Peterkin. If the first two statements are true, the third statement is

   _____ .

   (A) true
   (B) false
   (C) uncertain

23. Punctual most nearly means
    _____ .

    (A) prompt
    (B) late
    (C) rude
    (D) careless

24. Jimmy is younger than Tommy.
    Maria is older than Tommy. Maria is
    older than Jimmy. If the first two
    statements are true, the third
    statement is _____ .

    (A) true
    (B) false
    (C) uncertain

25. Notorious most nearly means
    _____ .

    (A) infamous
    (B) honorable
    (C) hopeful
    (D) fast

26. Obscure most nearly means
    _____ .

    (A) vague
    (B) transparent
    (C) clear
    (D) perfect

27. Which word does *not* belong with the
    others?

    (A) period
    (B) question mark
    (C) comma
    (D) exclamation point

28. A counterfeit is _____ .

    (A) imaginary
    (B) opposite
    (C) false
    (D) ambiguous

29. Perry is a stronger swimmer than
    Ashton. Perry does not swim as well
    as Joey. Joey is a stronger swimmer
    than Ashton. If the first two state-
    ments are true, the third statement
    is _____ .

    (A) true
    (B) false
    (C) uncertain

30. Which word does *not* belong with the
    others?

    (A) biology
    (B) chemistry
    (C) astronomy
    (D) science

31. Cap is to baseball as helmet is to
    _____ .

    (A) soccer
    (B) tennis
    (C) cycling
    (D) golf

32. Which word does *not* belong with the
    others?

    (A) scent
    (B) fragrance
    (C) aroma
    (D) atmosphere

33. Holmes is taller than Watson. Watson
    is taller than Lestrade. Lestrade
    is taller than Holmes. If the first
    two statements are true, the third
    statement is _____ .

    (A) true
    (B) false
    (C) uncertain

34. Which word does *not* belong with the
    others?

    (A) record
    (B) list
    (C) tabulate
    (D) repress

35. Rampant is *not* _____ .

    (A) controlled
    (B) dominant
    (C) common
    (D) difficult

36. Affluent means the *opposite* of
    _____ .

    (A) destitute
    (B) quiet
    (C) speechless
    (D) constructive

37. Earnest is *not* _____ .

    (A) serious
    (B) important
    (C) solemn
    (D) ridiculous

38. Cicely had the highest score in our math class. Luke is in our math class. Cicely scored higher than Luke. If the first two statements are true, the third statement is _____ .

    (A) true
    (B) false
    (C) uncertain

39. Meager means the *opposite* of _____ .

    (A) abundant
    (B) skinny
    (C) rare
    (D) sympathetic

40. Puppy is to paw as colt is to _____ .

    (A) horse
    (B) hoof
    (C) pony
    (D) run

41. Maladroit means the *opposite* of _____ .

    (A) clumsy
    (B) skillful
    (C) inept
    (D) cruel

42. Loren sings lower than Claire. Sarah sings higher than Claire. Sarah sings higher than Loren. If the first two statements are true, the third statement is _____ .

    (A) true
    (B) false
    (C) uncertain

43. Which word does *not* belong with the others?

    (A) room
    (B) den
    (C) kitchen
    (D) office

44. Nose is to face as finger is to _____ .

    (A) foot
    (B) hand
    (C) ear
    (D) head

45. Jeopardy most nearly means _____ .

    (A) game
    (B) peril
    (C) twice
    (D) knowledge

46. Which word does *not* belong with the others?

    (A) depot
    (B) station
    (C) terminal
    (D) vehicle

47. Meticulous means the *opposite* of _____ .

    (A) haphazard
    (B) careful
    (C) precise
    (D) lethargic

48. Modest is to vanity as innocent is to _____ .

    (A) happiness
    (B) reason
    (C) fear
    (D) guilt

49. The *Herald* contains fewer stories than the *Leader*. The *Courier* has more stories than the *Leader*. The *Courier* contains more stories than the *Herald*. If the first two statements are true, the third statement is _____ .

    (A) true
    (B) false
    (C) uncertain

50. Decrepit means the *opposite* of
    _____ .

    (A) weak
    (B) feeble
    (C) slow
    (D) robust

51. Recess is to play as breakfast is to
    _____ .

    (A) dress
    (B) pancakes
    (C) juice
    (D) eat

52. Faust is older than Prospero. Merlin
    is older than Prospero. Merlin is
    older than Faust. If the first two
    statements are true, the third
    statement is _____ .

    (A) true
    (B) false
    (C) uncertain

53. Which word does *not* belong with the
    others?

    (A) calculator
    (B) keyboard
    (C) telephone
    (D) videocassette

54. Hygienic means the *opposite* of
    _____ .

    (A) contaminated
    (B) clean
    (C) safe
    (D) sanitary

55. Bach is more complicated than
    Vivaldi. Handel is simpler than
    Vivaldi. Bach is more complicated
    than Handel. If the first two state-
    ments are true, the third statement
    is _____ .

    (A) true
    (B) false
    (C) uncertain

56. Which word does *not* belong with the
    others?

    (A) excuse
    (B) pardon
    (C) forgive
    (D) accuse

57. A pernicious rumor is _____ .

    (A) harmful
    (B) false
    (C) entertaining
    (D) harmless

58. Willow Court is shorter than
    Greenbriar Drive. Greenbriar Drive
    is not as long as Lexington Street.
    Lexington Street is longer than
    Willow Court. If the first two state-
    ments are true, the third statement
    is _____ .

    (A) true
    (B) false
    (C) uncertain

59. Desert is to arid as rain forest is to
    _____ .

    (A) humid
    (B) dessicated
    (C) dry
    (D) unexplored

60. Corbo's has a larger selection than
    Presti's. Presti's carries more vari-
    eties than Spalding's. Spalding's has
    fewer varieties than Corbo's. If the
    first two statements are true, the
    third statement is _____ .

    (A) true
    (B) false
    (C) uncertain

STOP

IF YOU FINISH BEFORE TIME IS UP, CHECK OVER YOUR WORK ON THIS TEST ONLY. DO NOT
GO ON TO THE NEXT TEST UNTIL THE SIGNAL IS GIVEN.

SUBTEST 2   QUANTITATIVE SKILLS

Sample:
What is the sum of 52 and 31?

(A) 21   (B) 83   (C) 84   (D) none of the above   Ⓐ ● Ⓒ Ⓓ

DIRECTIONS: Select the best answer for each question.

61. Examine the rectangle and the equilateral triangle, and then select the best answer.

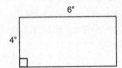
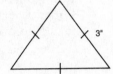

(A) The perimeter of the rectangle is 10″ more than the perimeter of the equilateral triangle.
(B) The perimeter of the equilateral triangle is 8″ less than the perimeter of the rectangle.
(C) The perimeter of the rectangle is 11″ more than the perimeter of the equilateral triangle.
(D) The perimeter of the equilateral triangle is 12″ less than the perimeter of the rectangle.

62. Review the series: 13, 11.6, 10.2, 8.8, ... Find the next number.

(A) 6.8   (B) 7.2
(C) 7.4   (D) 7.6

63. Forty percent of what number is equal to 2 more than the product of $\frac{1}{2}$ and 60?

(A) 24   (B) 80   (C) 32   (D) 60

64. Examine the line graph, and then select the best answer.

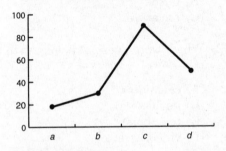

(A) $d > a + b + c$
(B) $d = a + b + c$
(C) $d = a + b$
(D) $c - a < b + c$

65. Review the series: 18, 6, 2, 2/3, ... Find the next number.

(A) 2/9   (B) 1/3
(C) 1/6   (D) 3/8

66. Two thirds of what number is equal to 18 more than 60% of 40.

(A) 27   (B) 33   (C) 36   (D) 63

67. Examine the table, and select the best answer.

	a	b	c	d	e	f
		♠	♥			♥
				♦		
	♥	♦	♦		♣	♦
			♣	♣		
	♥	♦				♠

(A) Column a has one more ♥ than column f.
(B) Column b has two more ♦ than column d.
(C) Column c has one less ♣ than column e.
(D) Column d has one more ♦ than column c.

68. O and O′ are the centers of their respective circles.

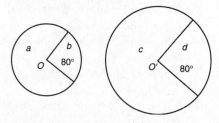

Choose the best answer.

(A) Area *c* > Area *a*
(B) Area *a* + Area *b* > Area *c* + Area *d*
(C) Area *c* − Area *a* > Area *a* + Area *d*
(D) Area *c* − Area *b* = Area *d* + Area *a*

69. Review the series: A, E, I, M, ... Find the next letter.

(A) P   (B) Q   (C) R   (D) O

70. What number is 8 more than two thirds of 60?

(A) 68   (B) 48   (C) 40   (D) 52

71. Review the series: 92, 17, 96, 15, 100, 13, ... Find the next number.

(A) 98   (B) 11   (C) 17   (D) 104

72. Michelle spends *t* + 4 hours per day watching television. Carmen spends *t* hours and Henry watches television *t* − 2 hours per day. Find the average number of hours of TV time for the three students.

(A) (3*t* + 2)/3
(B) (4*t*/3) + 2
(C) 2*t* + 4
(D) (4*t* − 2)/3

73. Review the series: 2, 6, 18, 54, ... Find the next number.

(A) 146   (B) 148
  (C) 162   (D) 152

74. What number is 12 less than $\frac{3}{4}$ of 24?

(A) 10   (B) 8   (C) 14   (D) 6

75. Review the series 7, 11, 10, 14, 13, 17, ... Find the next number.

(A) 21   (B) 16   (C) 19   (D) 22

76. Examine the diagram, and then choose the best answer.

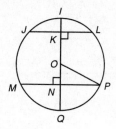

(A) *JL* > *MP*
(B) *ON* < *OK*
(C) *NQ* < *JL*
(D) *OP* > *ON*

77. Based on the information in the diagram, select the best answer.

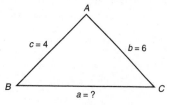

(A) *a* = 10   (B) *a* < 10
  (C) *a* = 11   (D) *a* > 10

78. The formula $d = 16t^2$ represents the distance, d, an object falls in t seconds, where d is in feet. Find the distance an object drops in 3 seconds.

    (A) 144 ft   (B) 96 ft
    (C) 166 ft   (D) 128 ft

79. Review the series: 4, 8, 9, 27, 16, 64, ... Find the next two numbers.

    (A) 96, 192   (B) 32, 96
    (C) 81, 243   (D) 25, 125

80. The difference of what number and 54 is equal to four fifths of the product of 12 and 5?

    (A) 80   (B) 102   (C) 94   (D) 86

81. Review the series: 24, 9, 21, 9, 18, 9, 15, ... Find the next two numbers.

    (A) 9, 12   (B) 7, 9
    (C) 9, 10   (D) 9, 11

82. Given that $c < d$ in the parallelogram, select the best answer.

    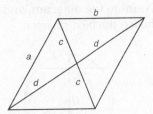

    (A) $a + c > b + d$
    (B) $a + c < a + d$
    (C) $c + d = a + b$
    (D) $b - c = a + d$

83. What number is 9 more than three fifths of 40?

    (A) 33   (B) 24   (C) 37   (D) 49

84. Review the series: 38, 40, 43, 47, 52, 58, ... Find the next number.

    (A) 59   (B) 65   (C) 55   (D) 61

85. Find side BC of the adjoining right angle.

    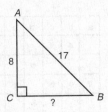

    (A) 12   (B) 18   (C) 19   (D) 15

86. Examine the diagram, and then select the best answer.

    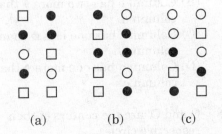

    (a)   (b)   (c)

    (A) There are 2 more ●s in (b) than □s in (c).
    (B) There are 2 fewer □s in (b) than ●s in (a).
    (C) There is 1 less ○ in (c) than □s in (a).
    (D) There are 2 more □s in (a) than ●s in (b).

87. Five eighths of what number is equal to the product of $\frac{1}{3}$ and 60?

    (A) 20   (B) 18   (C) 28   (D) 32

88. Review the series 65, 63, 64, 62, 63, 61, . . . , and find the next number.

    (A) 62   (B) 69   (C) 63   (D) 60

89. Examine the rectangle, and then select the best answer.

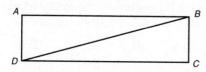

(A) $BD = BC$
(B) $AB > BD$
(C) $BD = AB$
(D) $BD > AB$

90. Review the series: B, E, H, K, N, ... Find the next letter.

(A) O   (B) P   (C) Q   (D) R

91. If ■ = 4, □ = 3 , * = 2, · = multiplication, + = addition, and − = subtraction, find the value of
5 · ■ + 3 · □ − 4 · *.

(A) 23   (B) 34   (C) 21   (D) 18

92. Review the series 4, 8, 9, 18, 19, 38, 39, . . . , and find the next number.

(A) 40   (B) 41   (C) 78   (D) 48

93. Twenty-five subtracted from two thirds of what number is equal to 5 more than 3 times 12?

(A) 99   (B) 100   (C) 98   (D) 96

94. Review the following diagram and information, and then select the best answer.

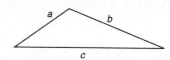

Side c is twice as long as side a, which is 3 inches less than side b.

(A) $c = 2(b − 3)$
(B) $a = b + 3$
(C) $c > a + b$
(D) $b < a − 3$

95. Review the series: 12, 17, 22, 27, __, 37, 42 , ... What number should be in the blank space?

(A) 52   (B) 32   (C) 47   (D) 36

96. The quotient of 36 and a number is equal to the product of five eighths and 80 reduced by 41. Find the number.

(A) 6   (B) 4   (C) 8   (D) 12

97. Review the diagram, and then select the best answer. The squares indicate right angles.

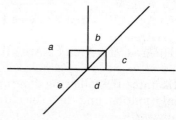

(A) $m\angle c = m\angle b$
(B) $m\angle a + m\angle d < 90°$
(C) $m\angle c = m\angle d$
(D) $m\angle b + m\angle c = 90°$

98. Review the series: 1, 4, 9, 16, . . . , and find the next number.

(A) 10   (B) 20   (C) 36   (D) 25

99. Simplify $−4(−2)^3$ and choose the correct answer.

(A) −16   (B) −32
(C) +24   (D) +32

100. Examine the diagram, and then select the best answer. $m\angle 1 = m\angle 4$, $m\angle 2 = m\angle 6$, $m\angle 3 = m\angle 5$. Circle $O' >$ Circle O.

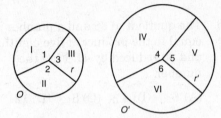

(A) Area I + Area II > Area IV
(B) Area I + Area IV = Area II + Area V
(C) Area IV + Area V > Area I + Area III
(D) Area VI > Area I + Area III

101. Examine the following diagram and information, and then select the best answer.

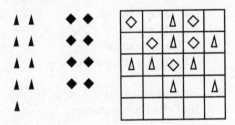

The hollow figures in the table, △ and ◇, have to be filled in with the dark figures, ▲ and ◆. If all the hollow figures are filled in, how many dark figures remain?

(A) 3 ▲ and 2 ◆
(B) 1 ◆ and 1 ▲
(C) 2 ▲ and 1 ◆
(D) 3 ◆ and 1 ▲

102. Review the series: 2, 3, 6, __, 3, 6, 2, 3, 6, ... What number should fill in the blank space?

(A) 6   (B) 2   (C) 8   (D) 3

103. If the product of 8 and a number is reduced by two thirds of 48, the result is equal to the quotient of 160 and 4. Find the number.

(A) 9   (B) 7   (C) 12   (D) 8

104. Review the given information, and then choose the best answer.

(a) 5^2 (b) 3^4 (c) 2^5

(A) (b) < (a) and (c) > (b)
(B) (a) < (b) < (c)
(C) (c) < (a) and c > (b)
(D) (b) > (c) and (b) > (a)

105. Examine the diagram and then select the best answer.

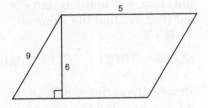

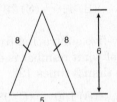

(A) Area of the parallelogram > 2 · Area of the triangle

(B) Area of triangle > $\frac{1}{2}$ · Area of parallelogram

(C) Perimeter of triangle < $\frac{1}{2}$ · Perimeter of parallelogram

(D) Perimeter of parallelogram > Perimeter of triangle + 5

106. Review the series: $24\frac{1}{2}$, 22, $19\frac{1}{2}$, 17, $14\frac{1}{2}$, 12, ... Find the next number.

(A) 10   (B) $10\frac{1}{2}$ (C) 9   (D) $9\frac{1}{2}$

107. Examine the trapezoid, and then select the best answer.

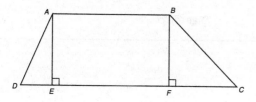

(A) $BC > AE$
(B) $AD = FC$
(C) $DE > FC$
(D) $FC < AB$

108. Examine the diagram, and then select the best answer. Lines a and b are congruent and O is the center of the circle.

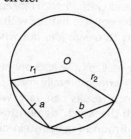

(A) $r_1 + b = a + r_2$
(B) $r_1 + r_2 = a + b$
(C) $r_1 + b < a + r_2$
(D) $r_1 + r_2 < a + b$

109. What number squared is equal to 8 more than the product of 7 and 8?

(A) 7   (B) 8   (C) 9   (D) 10

110. Review the series: XVIII, 3, XV, 5, XII, 7, ..., and find the last number.

(A) IX   (B) 9   (C) VIII   (D) 8

111. Eight times what number is equal to 15 less than the product of 7/9 and 81?

(A) 6   (B) 4   (C) 9   (D) 11

112. Review the series 3, 5, 7, 5, 7, 9, 7, 9, 11, 9, 11, 13, ..., and find the next number.

(A) 11   (B) 13   (C) 9   (D) 15

STOP

IF YOU FINISH BEFORE TIME IS UP, CHECK OVER YOUR WORK ON THIS TEST ONLY. DO NOT GO ON TO THE NEXT TEST UNTIL THE SIGNAL IS GIVEN.

SUBTEST 3   READING—COMPREHENSION—VOCABULARY

#113–174   *25 minutes*

Sample:

The next test has short reading passages, each one is followed by questions.

Correct marking of the reading passages on the next test will be _____.

   (A) all on one page
   (B) followed by questions
   (C) easy to read
   (D) very long   Ⓐ ● Ⓒ Ⓓ

PASSAGE FOR QUESTIONS 113–119

One of the literary texts best known to mankind began as a contest. On a dark and stormy evening, Mary and Percy Bysshe Shelley and their friend Lord Byron, bored with the usual evening entertainments, decided upon a creative challenge. They would each separate and invent a story, then share that story with the others. Dr. Polidori would judge who had made up the best tale.

The result of this literary playtime was *Frankenstein*, a story known by nearly the entire world in one form or another. Numerous versions abound, including the most recent retelling produced and directed by Kenneth Branagh, with Robert DeNiro as the creature himself.

Frankenstein tells of a war being waged between man and God. Victor Frankenstein glories in his intellectual achievements to the extent that he <u>equates</u> himself with God, the creator of man. In his delusion, Frankenstein attempts to create life, but what he ends up creating is both less and more than a man.

The text cleverly calls Frankenstein a monster, but few realize how appropriate the term is. "Monster" comes from the Latin term *monstra*—which literally means only "result," something brought about by a human; but since results can vary, we get multiple words from this term. We get, for example, both the word "demonstration" and the word "monster." The people in the story who surround Frankenstein do not recognize the significance of the *monstra* (a creation intended to astound them); they only see the monster (a menacing creature that frightens them). Ultimately, feared and rejected by society, hunted like a beast, Frankenstein retreats to an icy, watery grave—taking Frankenstein, his creator, with him.

Shelley warns us through her novel that playing with science, toying with knowledge we hardly understand or control, is a dangerous activity. Frankenstein represents that part of humanity that struggles to create and to conquer even those things over which we have (and should have) no control. We should acknowledge her warning—especially when it comes to modern day experimentation with modern day Frankensteins.

113. What will likely follow paragraph five?

 (A) A discussion of the novel *Dracula*.
 (B) An analysis of the term Polydor (which translates into the phrase "many gifts").
 (C) A section of text outlining what is meant by the term "Frankensteins."
 (D) A review of the Kenneth Branagh–Robert DeNiro version of *Frankenstein*.

114. The use of the word <u>equates</u>, as used in this passage, most closely means _____ .

 (A) be superior to
 (B) be equal with
 (C) be inferior to
 (D) be indecisive about

115. How do you think the author likely feels about the question of cloning, based on your reading of this passage?

 (A) S/he thinks it a worthwhile endeavor that deserves funding and resources.
 (B) S/he remains neutral on the topic, refusing to take a side.
 (C) S/he thinks it a dangerous idea because we know so little about what we're doing and the long-term results of practicing it.
 (D) We cannot tell from the passage.

116. According to the passage, the word "monster" comes from _____ .

 (A) the word *monstra*
 (B) the word *remonstrate*
 (C) the word *demonstrate*
 (D) the word *monstrosity*

117. Because Dr. Frankenstein considers himself equal to God, we can best compare him to which of the following?

 (A) Lucifer
 (B) Hitler
 (C) Buddha
 (D) Thomas Edison

118. How does Frankenstein end his existence, according to this passage?

 (A) by fire
 (B) by suffocation
 (C) by drowning
 (D) by starvation

119. Why does the author write this piece?

 (A) to stoke dialog over feminist rights
 (B) to encourage us to write
 (C) to get us to read *Frankenstein*
 (D) to warn us against engaging in activities we may not be able to control

PASSAGE FOR QUESTIONS 120–123

In World War II the Japanese hatched a <u>nefarious</u> plan. They had already planned uses for the military personnel, the planes, and the troops. However, they found a use for nonmilitary personnel as well, especially the women.

Japanese officials commissioned women to create balloons. The women created 9,000 of these balloons, all of them from white paper or rubberized silk. Into each balloon the women then carefully placed a bomb, primed for destruction.

Periodically, weather permitting, the women launched the balloons putting them into the jet stream of air that would allow the deadly "<u>white birds</u>" to sift toward their targets.

As one might have guessed, the target was the United States.

The attack did not come off as well as the Japanese had hoped, however. Many of the bombs drifted astray, eventually landing in the ocean and sinking harmlessly below the waves. Others indeed landed on U.S. soil, carrying duds rather than live bombs. Of all of the potential deathtraps that landed in the United States, few exploded, and fewer hit human targets. Japanese officials ceased launching the balloons in June 1945, having killed only six victims.

120. What does the word <u>nefarious</u> mean, according to the passage?

  (A) neat
  (B) clever
  (C) efficient
  (D) treacherous

121. Why is the author telling you this story?

  (A) to belittle Japanese culture for such a stupid idea
  (B) to tell you of a creative and successful mission
  (C) to relate an interesting but little known true story that took place during World War II
  (D) to illustrate how brave Americans were in the face of danger

122. To what, based on the reading passage, does the term "white birds" most likely refer?

  (A) the white balloons
  (B) the white herons popular in the region
  (C) the white clouds that provided camouflage
  (D) the white stone that flanked the northern shores of Japan

123. Who made the white balloons for the attack, according to the article?

  (A) kamikaze pilots
  (B) nonmilitary women
  (C) children
  (D) soldiers

PASSAGE FOR QUESTIONS 124–127

African culture reveres many ideas that seem foreign to American cultural habits and values. One such idea involves the concept of the "spirit spouse." According to Baule tribal tradition, life is balanced between two worlds: a spirit world from which the soul comes and the "real world" into which everyone is physically born. Everyone in the real world has a spirit spouse whom they have left behind in the spirit world. The spirit spouse awaits the eventual return of the real world spouse to the spirit world after death.

However, sometimes the spirit spouse misses the real world spouse. When this happens, the spirit spouse may become jealous, irritable, and neglected; the spirit spouse may then disrupt the real world life of the real world spouse. As a sign of respect for this spirit spouse, a person will then construct a statue that represents that spirit spouse and keep the sculpture in their home, paying it special attention on a daily basis. However, if the spirit spouse is not <u>placated</u>, then the real world spouse will dedicate one night a week to living with and paying special attention to the spirit spouse. The real world spouse will give the spirit spouse gifts of clothing or jewelry; in return the spirit spouse is supposed to send dream visits from the other world.

124. What is the author's purpose in writing this piece?

    (A) to suggest that we adopt the practice of spirit spouses in America
    (B) to explain the concept of the spirit spouse
    (C) to make fun of African tradition
    (D) to discuss idolatry in foreign countries

125. Based on the author's use of the term, you can tell that *Baule* refers to _____ .

    (A) a round object used in games of sport
    (B) an arid geographical region near India
    (C) an African tribe
    (D) a fancy dress party

126. Which of the following is an example of the kind of thing a real world spouse would present a spirit spouse?

    (A) gifts of food
    (B) gifts of incense
    (C) gifts of clothing
    (D) gifts of money

127. Based on the author's use of the word <u>placated</u>, you can tell that it means _____ .

    (A) appeased
    (B) offended
    (C) obliterated
    (D) angered

PASSAGE FOR QUESTION 128–135

Have you ever been in a multiple-choice test-taking situation? Most people have at some time or other in their lives. By now, you know the routine: read all the choices through, and make your selection. Then work your way through the test, and, if you have time, check through as many answers as you can before time runs out and tests are collected. The question I have always pondered, as you probably have, is this: What if I think I've made an incorrect answer selection? Should I change my answer? Or should I go with my original impulse?

Well, today is your lucky day. Today you find out what the experts advise on this topic.

Psychologists at King's College in Ontario have studied this problem for the past few years and have come up with some surprising results. First, females are more likely than males to change their answers. While this may indicate more flexibility and willingness to admit mistakes on the part of females than males, unfortunately, females are also more likely to make changes from the right answer to the wrong answer. Researches <u>attribute</u> this discovery to the well-documented lower levels of self-esteem under which women seem to labor.

But, you began reading this article because you wanted to know about those changes over which you have been agonizing. Here's the scoop: Of all changes people make to multiple-choice test questions, 50% go from wrong to right, 25% go from right to wrong, and 25% go from wrong to wrong. So, bottom line? Go ahead and make those changes; your first instinct may well have been wrong.

128. Based on the information in this passage, it is better _____ .

    (A) to resist the temptation to change your first answer on a multiple-choice test
    (B) to give in to the temptation to change your first answer on a multiple-choice test
    (C) to change both your first and second answers to multiple-choice test questions
    (D) the article does not give clear enough advice to make a decision

129. Why does the article state women are more likely than men to change their answers?

    (A) Women are more likely to admit they are wrong and accept new instruction.
    (B) Men are more stubborn.
    (C) Women are more likely to second-guess themselves, talking themselves into getting answers wrong.
    (D) Men are more likely to cheat.

130. What percentage of multiple-choice test takers are likely to change an answer from wrong to wrong?

    (A) 100%
    (B) 50%
    (C) 25%
    (D) 0%

131. Where are you most likely to read this kind of article?

    (A) guidance counselor's office
    (B) psychology journal
    (C) *Teen Beat* magazine
    (D) *Reader's Digest*

132. Based on the author's use of the word <u>attribute</u>, which of the following is the best definition?

    (A) blame
    (B) describe
    (C) associate
    (D) refer to

133. Where are the researchers responsible for this human behavior study based?

    (A) Quebec
    (B) Canada
    (C) Ontario
    (D) Newfoundland

134. What would be the best title for this piece?

    (A) Cheating: An Increasing Problem for 21st-Century Students
    (B) Overcoming Indecision
    (C) To Change or Not to Change
    (D) The Times They Are A'changing

135. What percentage of people tend to change their answers from wrong to right?

    (A) 100%
    (B) 50%
    (C) 25%
    (D) 0%

PASSAGE FOR QUESTIONS 136–141

It was a long time since Mrs. Sommers had been fitted with gloves. On rare occasions when she had bought a pair they were always "bargains," so cheap that it would have been preposterous and unreasonable to have expected them to be fitted to the hand.

Now she rested her elbow on the cushion of the glove counter, and a pretty, pleasant young creature, delicate and deft of touch, drew a long-wristed "<u>kid</u>" over Mrs. Sommers's hand. She smoothed it down over the wrist and buttoned it neatly, and both lost themselves for a second or two in admiring contemplation of the little symmetrical gloved hand. But there were other places where money might be spent.

There were books and magazines piled up in the window of a stall a few paces down the street. Mrs. Sommers bought two high-priced magazines such as she had been accustomed to read in the days when she had been accustomed to other pleasant things. She carried them without wrapping. As well as she could she lifted her skirts at the crossings. Her stockings and boots and well fitting gloves had worked marvels in her bearing—had given her a feeling of assurance, a sense of belonging to the well-dressed multitude.

...

The play was over, the music ceased, the crowd filed out. It was like a dream ended. People scattered in all directions. Mrs. Sommers went to the corner and waited for the cable car.

A man with keen eyes, who sat opposite to her, seemed to like the study of her small, pale face. It puzzled him to decipher what he saw there. In truth, he saw nothing—unless he were wizard enough to detect a poignant wish, a powerful longing that the cable car would never stop anywhere, but go on and on with her forever.

(Taken from Kate Chopin's "A Pair of Silk Stockings")

136. Based on the author's use of the word, what does the word <u>kid</u> mean?

   (A) a young child
   (B) a kind of soft material made from goat skin
   (C) a remark made in jest
   (D) a baby goat

137. What can you tell about the woman's spending habits.

   (A) She generally gets to go out and pass a day spending money on herself.
   (B) She generally gets other people to do her shopping.
   (C) She generally has to pinch pennies and be very frugal.
   (D) We cannot tell from the reading passage.

138. How does the woman feel about her day of indulgent spending on herself?

   (A) She revels in the experience, enjoying every moment.
   (B) She cannot wait to return home and share her experiences with her family.
   (C) She feels intense guilt over her actions yet does not quite regret making them.
   (D) We cannot tell from reading this passage.

139. Why does the woman wish that the cable car ride would last forever?

   (A) She is worried about how her husband will react to her spending.
   (B) She has enjoyed her indulgent memory of her former life so much that she hesitates to return to the drudgery of her present life.
   (C) She hates her family and resents their claim on her life.
   (D) We cannot tell from reading the passage.

140. What, according to the passage, gives Mrs. Sommers new poise and self confidence?

   (A) red wine with lunch
   (B) finding a bargain on her cotton stockings
   (C) thinking of how happy her children will be upon her return home
   (D) her enjoyment in wearing her new purchases

141. Why is the author writing this piece?

   (A) She wants to show how spending money can benefit the spender.
   (B) She wants to help women get more money from their husbands to spend on themselves.
   (C) She wants her audience to think Mrs. Sommers is selfish and greedy.
   (D) She wants her audience to sympathize with Mrs. Sommers compulsive "mental health day."

PASSAGE FOR QUESTIONS 142–146

The perceived increase in child abductions has increased the number of self-defense training sessions taking place in many towns. One town in particular has recently helped more than 300 young students protect themselves from possible danger.

Kids, under the <u>tutelage</u> of Lewis Johnson, a 4th degree black belt in tae kwon do, learn to use their most powerful weapon of personal protection: their mouths. Johnson teaches the kids a few moves, sometimes even the cool ones that allow even an 11-year-old to break a wooden board with an open fist.

But most often Johnson teaches kids the kicks that surprise a would-be attacker just long enough to allow the kid to run away. Johnson couples these tricks with good advice on how to scream effectively. Behind him you can hear the practice grow noisy with authoritative volleys of "Stop! You're not my mom! You're not my dad!"

Johnson sees his work as a public service to his community. He plans several more free clinics, likely one per month, over the next year. "I think everyone should learn self-defense. It's not just a kick or a punch—it's also just making smart decisions about how to dress, where to walk, and how to be safe."

142. What kind of publication would include this kind of article?

   (A) *Newsweek* or a similar weekly political news magazine
   (B) an encyclopedia article on martial arts
   (C) a feature article in Johnson's local paper
   (D) *Glamour* magazine

143. The word tutelage, as used in this passage is best defined as _____ .

   (A) training
   (B) abuse
   (C) scholarship
   (D) supervision

144. What degree of black belt does Johnson hold?

   (A) 1st
   (B) 2nd
   (C) 3rd
   (D) 4th

145. According to the article, what has inspired so many people to learn more about self-defense?

   (A) general interest in fitness
   (B) the recent obsession with avoiding obesity
   (C) increased interest in learning about other cultures
   (D) concern over what appears to be an increase in kidnapping cases

146. How much per training session do you think Johnson is paid, based on your reading of the passage?

   (A) $10
   (B) $15
   (C) $20
   (D) free

PASSAGE FOR QUESTIONS 147–152

Even as late as the year 2004, public attention is turning once again to the *Titanic*. The vessel, sunk after its collision with an iceberg in 1912, has historically <u>garnered</u> a large percentage of the public's attention. It has been featured in countless fictional accounts, like the young adult novella entitled *Ghosts I Have Been* by Richard Peck. And, naturally, its demise has been the subject of many films, including the most recent offering by James Cameron starring Leonardo di Caprio and Kate Winslet. Indeed, one can only expect more film representation to come, given the advances in film technology going on.

This time the attention is more historical in intent. Bob Ballard, discoverer of the *Titanic's* underwater grave 19 years ago, is currently trying to <u>drum up</u> public interest over the fact that underwater salvage experts from around the world keep stealing into the *Titanic's* water-logged hulk and removing artifacts for sale in antique markets. Ballard views the *Titanic* as a sort of underwater museum without guards. "Imagine if you could walk into the Louvre and leave with the *Mona Lisa,*" says Ballard. Ballard specifically points an accusatory finger at France and Russia; no private salvagers, he says, can front enough money to support such salvaging missions.

Ballard himself plans to revisit the *Titanic* soon, on a decidedly philanthropic mission. He and his team plan not to plunder but to protect. They will assess damage, locate areas that need buffering, and make plans to paint rust-endangered areas to protect what remains against further corrosion.

147. Why do you think that the author expects more film depictions of the sinking *Titanic* owing to the advances in film technology going on?

(A) Advances in film technology, especially in computer graphics, make filming movies cheaper.
(B) Advances in film technology, especially in computer graphics, make filming movies faster.
(C) Advances in film technology, especially in computer graphics, reduce the need for human actors.
(D) Advances in film technology, especially in computer graphics, allow greater freedom in filming sinking ships realistically.

148. Which of the following would most likely publish this reading passage?

(A) a school text book on the use of historical items in film
(B) the "Leisure and Arts" section of the daily newspaper
(C) a journal that prints the latest research in biological studies
(D) an encyclopedia

149. What is the best definition of the word <u>garner</u> as used in this passage?

(A) tear down
(B) lose
(C) decorate
(D) acquire

150. What is the author's purpose in writing this piece?

(A) to protest Leonardo di Caprio movies
(B) to alert the reader to what's happening in underwater salvage technology
(C) to promote research being conducted by France and Russia in underwater salvage
(D) to alert people to injustices being perpetrated by Bob Ballard

151. When does the article say that Bob Ballard discovered the location of the *Titanic*?

(A) 1982
(B) 1983
(C) 1984
(D) 1985

152. What does the phrase <u>drum up</u> mean, as used in the context of this passage?

(A) beating on a drum
(B) making people forget about an event
(C) getting people interested in a topic
(D) angering people

DIRECTIONS: Choose the word that means the same or nearly the same as the underlined word.

153. an odious task

(A) hateful
(B) attractive
(C) smelly
(D) easy

154. a petty disagreement

(A) loving
(B) serious
(C) violent
(D) unimportant

155. a strict agenda

(A) code
(B) personality
(C) classroom
(D) plan

156. a lucid argument

(A) confusing
(B) clear
(C) weak
(D) irrelevant

157. a gentle zephyr

(A) breeze
(B) caress
(C) whisper
(D) animal

158. to enumerate the reasons

(A) eliminate
(B) list
(C) assign
(D) argue

159. an inopportune moment

(A) untimely
(B) convenient
(C) quick
(D) inconclusive

160. a pungent aroma

(A) sweet
(B) fresh
(C) sharp
(D) subtle

161. to shirk responsibilities

(A) evade
(B) destroy
(C) assume
(D) delegate

162. a credible witness

(A) first-hand
(B) believable
(C) expert
(D) unreliable

163. to feign interest

(A) pretend
(B) encourage
(C) slow
(D) stimulate

164. a thin veneer

(A) liquid
(B) expression
(C) surface
(D) volume

165. lax discipline

(A) loose
(B) strict
(C) oppressive
(D) fair

166. total anarchy

(A) dictatorship
(B) monarchy
(C) democracy
(D) disorder

167.   <u>tangible</u> evidence

   (A) admissible
   (B) irrelevant
   (C) physical
   (D) eyewitness

168.   an interesting <u>lecture</u>

   (A) book
   (B) stand
   (C) reader
   (D) speech

169.   to <u>impede</u> progress

   (A) quicken
   (B) race
   (C) hinder
   (D) support

170.   a strong <u>antipathy</u>

   (A) sympathy
   (B) aversion
   (C) chemical
   (D) opinion

171.   a dedicated <u>pacifist</u>

   (A) swimmer
   (B) soldier
   (C) sports fan
   (D) one opposed to war

172.   published <u>posthumously</u>

   (A) anonymously
   (B) after death
   (C) before midnight
   (D) in a series

173.   the <u>penultimate</u> question

   (A) most difficult
   (B) final
   (C) second to last
   (D) first

174.   <u>verbose</u> directions

   (A) laconic
   (B) specific
   (C) incorrect
   (D) wordy

STOP

IF YOU FINISH BEFORE TIME IS UP, CHECK OVER YOUR WORK ON THIS TEST ONLY. DO NOT GO ON TO THE NEXT TEST UNTIL THE SIGNAL IS GIVEN.

SUBTEST 4 MATHEMATICS

#175–238   *45 minutes*

Sample:

Round 642 to the nearest hundred.

(A) 650   (B) 600   (C) 700   (D) 640   Ⓐ ● Ⓒ Ⓓ

DIRECTIONS: Select the best answer for each question.

175. Review statements a, b, and c, and then select the true statement.

(a) $(24 \cdot 2) / 6$
(b) $(24/6) \cdot 2$
(c) $(24/2) + 6$

(A) $a < b$ and $a < c$
(B) $c > a$ and $a = b$
(C) $b > a$ and $c > b$
(D) $b < a$ and $a > c$

176. If b is a negative number, which of the following terms is the smallest?

(A) b^2
(B) $-b$
(C) b^0
(D) b^3

177. Simplify the following powers, and then select the correct answer.

(a) 5^2 (b) 2^5 (c) 2^3

(A) $a > b$ or $c > a$
(B) $c = a$ or $b < c$
(C) $c > b$ and $a = b$
(D) $b < a$ or $c < b$

178. Find the value of $\dfrac{3^9}{4 \times 3^7}$.

(A) 3   (B) $3\dfrac{1}{2}$

(C) $2\dfrac{1}{4}$ (D) $2\dfrac{3}{4}$

179. Arrange the following expressions in descending order. Use the letters to represent the expressions.

(a) $4^2 + 5(9 - 3)$
(b) $3 \cdot 17 - 4 \times 6$
(c) $7 + 9 \cdot 4 - 6(9 - 7)^3$
(d) $6 + 2 + 42/8 - 2(3 - 1)^2$

Select the correct answer.

(A) $a > b > d > c$
(B) $b > a > d > c$
(C) $d > a > c > b$
(D) $a > d > c > b$

180. Round off 1,742,143 to the nearest hundred.

(A) 1,742,200   (B) 1,742,100
(C) 1,742,000   (D) 1,740,000

181. Malcolm and Dwayne start off running around the track at the same time. If Malcolm can run around the track in 5 minutes and Dwayne can cover the same distance in 3 minutes, when will they again meet at the start of the track?

(A) 12 minutes   (B) 15 minutes
(C) 16 minutes   (D) 18 minutes

182. Perform the indicated operations, and select the correct answer.

    (a) $1\frac{1}{2} \cdot 2\frac{3}{4}$

    (b) $\frac{3}{4} \cdot 4\frac{1}{2}$

    (c) $3\frac{1}{2} \cdot \frac{3}{4}$

    (d) $\frac{1}{2} \cdot 3\frac{1}{4}$

    (A) c < d or c < a
    (B) d < c and d > a
    (C) b > a and b < c
    (D) a > d and a < b

183. Henry drives from Middletown to Rockville, a distance of 206.5 miles. If he leaves Middletown at 2:30 P.M. and drives at the rate of 59 mph, what time will he arrive in Rockville?

    (A) 4:30 P.M.   (B) 5 P.M.
     (C) 5:30 P.M.   (D) 6 P.M.

184. A car uses 12.4 gallons of gasoline in 236.5 miles. To the nearest tenth, how many miles per gallon does the car use?

    (A) 13.8   (B) 23.7
     (C) 32.4   (D) 19.1

185. Twenty-four students in a class are right-handed and 6 are left-handed. If these figures represent the entire class, what percent is left-handed?

    (A) 15%   (B) 25%
     (C) 20%   (D) 30%

186. Which of the following numbers is greater than .77 but less than 7/8?

    (A) 2/3   (B) 3/4
     (C) .82   (D) .913

187. What number is 14 less than two thirds of 54?

    (A) 22   (B) 42   (C) 38   (D) 36

188. Find the cube root of –0.027.

    (A) –0.2   (B) 0.2
     (C) –0.3   (D) 0.3

189. Select a value for x that satisfies the condition $-3 \le |2x + 1| < 2$

    (A) –4   (B) 0   (C) 3   (D) 2

190. Review the following three algebraic expressions, and then select the correct answer.

    (a) $4(r + s)$ (b) $4rs$ (c) $4r + 4s$

    (A) a = c and a = b
    (B) c = b or a ≠ c
    (C) c = a and b ≠ a
    (D) c ≠ a or b = c

191. Mildred weighs $x - 3$ pounds. Her brother Hector weighs 8 pounds more than Mildred, while her sister Stacey weighs 12 pounds less than Hector. Find their total weight.

    (A) $4x - 5$
    (B) $5x + 3$
    (C) $x + 12$
    (D) $3x - 5$

192. Simplify $45| -63 | \div -5 |9|$.

    (A) 63   (B) –12   (C) 9   (D) –14

193. The ratio of a drawing on a blueprint to an actual object is 1:100. If a building is 90 feet high, how long would its image be on the blueprint, in inches?

    (A) 12.4 inches
    (B) 16.8 inches
    (C) 13.6 inches
    (D) 10.8 inches

194. The sum of two consecutive integers is 51. Select the larger integer.

    (A) 19   (B) 21   (C) 25   (D) 26

195. In the diagram, a right angle is formed by the intersection of the vertical and horizontal lines. Determine the value of x.

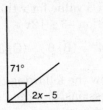

(A) 12°   (B) 18°
   (C) 24°   (D) 32°

196. What is the complement of $a°$?

(A) $(180 - a)°$
(B) $(90 + a)°$
(C) $(90 - a)°$
(D) $(180 + a)°$

197. Find the measure of angle a.

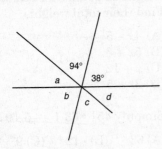

(A) 94°   (B) 48°
   (C) 132°   (D) 58°

198. At how many points do the sides of a septagon intersect?

(A) 8   (B) 6   (C) 5   (D) 7

199. Which of the following is an obtuse triangle?

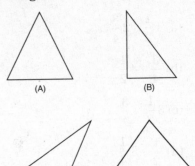

200. The length of a rectangle is 4 more than twice its width. If the width is represented by w, find the perimeter of the rectangle in terms of w.

(A) $6w + 12$
(B) $4w + 8$
(C) $6w - 6$
(D) $6w + 8$

201. $ABCD$ is a rectangle with length 12 and width 4. $RSTU$ is a square, with V and W the midpoints of RS and TU, respectively. RU is 8.

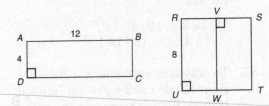

Select the correct statement.

(A) The perimeter of $ABCD$ is greater than the perimeter of $RSTU$.
(B) The perimeter of $ABCD$ is less than the perimeter of $RVWU$.
(C) One half of the perimeter of $ABCD$ is equal to the perimeter of $RVWU$.
(D) One half the perimeter of $ABCD$ is less than the perimeter of $RSTU$.

202. The area of a parallelogram is 114. If its base is 12, find its height.

    (A) 9.5   (B) 8   (C) 11   (D) 10.5

203. The measure of the vertex angle of an isosceles triangle is 50°. Find the measure of an exterior angle to one of the base angles of the triangle.

    (A) 65°   (B) 125°
    (C) 115°   (D) 80°

204. Substitute 2 for r and 5 for s in (a), (b), and (c). Then simplify the following expressions and select the false statement below.

    (a) $(r + 4)^2$
    (b) $9(s - 3)^2$
    (c) $2r^2s$

    (A) a < b and c > b
    (B) a = b or c > a
    (C) b < a or c > b
    (D) c < a and a < b

205. Simplify the ratio of 6 ounces to 3 pounds.

    (A) $\dfrac{1}{2}$ (B) $\dfrac{2}{5}$ (C) $\dfrac{1}{8}$ (D) $\dfrac{3}{8}$

206. Determine the value of x in the equation $62 + 2(8 - x) = 72$.

    (A) 9   (B) 8   (C) 4   (D) 3

207. The distance between cities A and B is 45 miles. On a map, if $\dfrac{1}{2}$ inch represents 9 miles, how many inches represents the distance between the two cities?

    (A) 2″   (B) $3\dfrac{1}{2}$″   (C) 3″   (D) $2\dfrac{1}{2}$″

208. If the circumference of a circle is 62.8, find its radius.

    (A) 6   (B) 10   (C) 7   (D) 4

209. In the following diagrams, circle O has a radius of 5, and triangle RST has sides of 5 and 12 and a hypotenuse of 13. The circumference of a circle, C, is equal to $2\pi r$, and the area of a circle, A_C, is equal to πr^2. In both of these cases, $\pi = 3.14$ and r = the radius. The area of a triangle, A_T, is equal to $\dfrac{1}{2} bh$, where b = base and h = height.

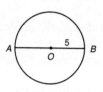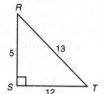

Which of the following statements is true?

    (A) Area of triangle $RST < \dfrac{1}{2}$ Area of circle O
    (B) Circumference of circle < perimeter of triangle RST
    (C) Area of circle + Area of triangle < 100
    (D) Circumference of circle – perimeter of triangle > 2

210. Larisa is pumping oxygen into an emergency room at the rate of 3 cubic meters per minute. If the room is 9 meters long by 6 meters wide by 4 meters high, how long will it take for the room to be filled with oxygen?

    (A) 64 minutes
    (B) 72 minutes
    (C) 86 minutes
    (D) 44 minutes

211. Simplify $\dfrac{56\sqrt{b^3c^4}}{7\sqrt{bc^3}}$

    (A) $8bc$ (B) $8\sqrt{bc}$
    (C) $8b^2\sqrt{c}$ (D) $8b\sqrt{c}$

212. Select the best answer.

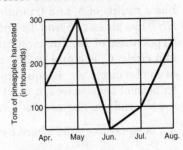

(A) August harvest + July harvest = June harvest
(B) May harvest – April harvest > July harvest
(C) April harvest < August harvest – July harvest
(D) July harvest – June harvest = May harvest

213. If 16 people, with a total weight of 2,560 pounds, are standing on a floor measuring 20 feet by 32 feet, what is the average weight each square foot of the floor is supporting?

(A) 4 lb per sq ft
(B) 2 lb per sq ft
(C) 3 lb per sq ft
(D) 5 lb per sq ft

214. Change $4\frac{3}{4}$ to a percent.

(A) 4.75%   (B) 47.5%
(C) 434%   (D) 475%

215. The formula $d = 16t^2$ represents the distance, d, an object falls in t seconds, where d is in feet. Find the distance an object drops in 3 seconds.

(A) 144 ft   (B) 96 ft
(C) 166 ft   (D) 128 ft

216. Julio earns $13.54 per hour while Shanequa earns $15.93 per hour. In 12 hours, how much more than Julio does Shanequa earn?

(A) $27.26   (B) $191.16
(C) $28.68   (D) $43.36

217. Find the measure of angle 2.

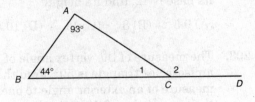

(A) 43°
(B) 44°
(C) 57°
(D) 137°

218. Find the area of the entire figure.

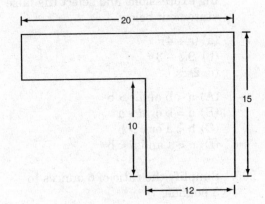

(A) 120   (B) 160
(C) 220   (D) 240

219. What are the coordinates of point A?

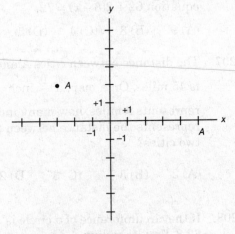

(A) (–2,3)   (B) (–3,2)
(C) (–1,4)   (D) (4,–1)

220. Simplify the ratio 15 seconds to 3 minutes.

    (A) $\dfrac{1}{12}$ (B) $\dfrac{2}{5}$ (C) $\dfrac{1}{4}$ (D) $\dfrac{3}{7}$

221. Find the value of the expression $5x^2 + 2yz$ when $x = 3$, $y = -2$, and $z = 4$.

    (A) 32   (B) 29   (C) 18   (D) 37

222. What is the product of the greatest common factor and the least common factor of 30 and 70?

    (A) 14   (B) 7   (C) 15   (D) 10

223. Find the value of x in the following figure.

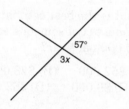

    (A) 57°   (B) 41°
    (C) 39°   (D) 3°

224. $6\dfrac{2}{3} \times 5\dfrac{1}{4} =$

    (A) $5\dfrac{1}{2}$ (B) 16   (C) 23   (D) 35

225. The Buffalo Jaguars scored 12, 7, 10, 6, and 9 runs in their last five games. If they want to maintain an average of 9 runs per game for six games, how much do they have to score in their next game?

    (A) 4   (B) 10   (C) 8   (D) 6

226. The sum of the first and second of four consecutive even integers is 8 more than the fourth. Find the smallest integer.

    (A) 12   (B) 14   (C) 16   (D) 10

227. A magazine costs $6.60 right now. If the price increased 10% two years ago and 20% six months ago, how much did the magazine cost before the first increase two years ago?

    (A) $4.50   (B) $5.00
    (C) $5.50   (D) $6.00

228. Two centimeters are what part of a meter?

    (A) 3%   (B) 2%
    (C) 1/500   (D) 1/25

229. For all real numbers a, b, and c,
    $a\#b!c = \dfrac{a^2}{b} + 3c$. Find c when
    $3\#9!c = 22$.

    (A) 5   (B) 4   (C) 8   (D) 7

230. What percent of 120 is 45? Round off to the nearest percent.

    (A) 24%   (B) 25%
    (C) 38%   (D) 37%

231. Find the perimeter of a rectangle whose area is 36 and whose base is 9.

    (A) 30   (B) 36   (C) 18   (D) 26

232. Solve the inequality $-2.4 < x + 2 \le 3.8$ for x.

    (A) 0   (B) 1   (C) 2   (D) 3

233. Simplify $3\sqrt{7} - 4\sqrt{3} + 11\sqrt{7} - 6\sqrt{3}$.

    (A) $9\sqrt{7} - 10\sqrt{3}$

    (B) $14\sqrt{7} + 7\sqrt{3}$

    (C) $14\sqrt{7} - 10\sqrt{3}$

    (D) $14\sqrt{21} - 10\sqrt{3}$

234. List the prime numbers between 7 and 15.

    (A) 11, 13   (B) 7, 11, 13, 15
    (C) 11, 13, 15   (D) 7, 11, 13

235. Which of the following angles can represent the three angles of a triangle?

    (A) 43°, 56°, 47°
    (B) 58°, 29°, 68°
    (C) 56°, 72°, 38°
    (D) 59°, 53°, 68°

236. The library has a policy of ordering 5 fiction, 2 historical, 3 biographical, and 3 science books in that order. If 124 books were ordered, what subject was the last book?

    (A) fiction   (B) historical
    (C) biographical   (D) science

237. A 25-foot tree casts a shadow of 15 feet. How long is the shadow of a nearby 300-foot building if the tree and its shadow are in the same ratio as the building and its shadow?

    (A) 180 ft   (B) 120 ft
    (C) 200 ft   (D) 140 ft

238. This graph represents the percentage of federal income tax based upon annual income.

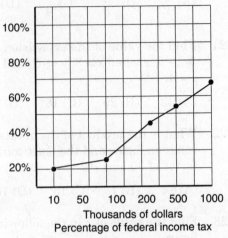

Thousands of dollars
Percentage of federal income tax

What is the best estimate of the income tax of someone earning $90,000 per year?

    (A) $52,000   (B) $23,000
    (C) $9,000   (D) $62,000

STOP

IF YOU FINISH BEFORE TIME IS UP, CHECK OVER YOUR WORK ON THIS TEST ONLY. DO NOT GO ON TO THE NEXT TEST UNTIL THE SIGNAL IS GIVEN.

SUBTEST 5   LANGUAGE

#239–298   *25 minutes*

Samples: Choose the sentence that contains an error.

(A) Andrew and he were leaving.
(B) We was going to the store.
(C) Josh and Sarah will buy food for us.
(D) No mistakes.

Correct marking of samples
Ⓐ ● Ⓒ Ⓓ

(A) Work on the car in here.
(B) Where will we end up?
(C) Enter through the front door, please.
(D) No mistakes.

Correct marking of samples
Ⓐ Ⓑ Ⓒ ●

DIRECTIONS: In questions 239–278, choose the sentence in each group that contains an error in capitalization, punctuation, or usage. If you find no mistake, select D on your answer sheet.

239.
(A) Genny and Rhodes make a cute couple.
(B) Brigid, Becky, and I are inseparable.
(C) Dan and Nazee ate cake, and played at the birthday party.
(D) No mistakes.

240.
(A) Dr. Garcia gave them and me high recommendations.
(B) I don't have problems reading the book but I don't have a lot of time tonight.
(C) Mollie, I'd like you to meet one of my favorite people.
(D) No mistakes.

241.
(A) Patrick knew that Liz wasn't feeling well.
(B) Either Dr. Avery or Dr. Thomas will be on call.
(C) She and i are best friends, and we chat on the Internet often.
(D) No mistakes.

242.
(A) I really enjoyed the first two volumes of *The Lord of the Rings*.
(B) However, I cannot finish the trilogy.
(C) Because the last volume is checked out of the library.
(D) No mistakes.

243.
(A) I could of listened to them sing all day.
(B) Keep off the playground until the mud dries.
(C) We (the students in Lauren's class) all chipped in for a get-well gift.
(D) No mistakes.

244.
(A) I've known Anne's mother, Myra, for many years.
(B) I didn't fall asleep until after he had began speaking.
(C) Let's face the music and dance.
(D) No mistakes.

245.
- (A) With an outline, an author knows what they are going to write next.
- (B) The purple ribbons in Sadie's hair match her dress beautifully.
- (C) Which of the jackets is mine?
- (D) No mistakes.

246.
- (A) To who shall I address this letter?
- (B) I'd like to see these people: Susan, Laura, Chuck, and Ingrid.
- (C) Augie is gracious, intelligent, and moral.
- (D) No mistakes.

247.
- (A) Tell us all about it, Leo.
- (B) Oh my goodness I almost forgot the cake.
- (C) It's never too late to begin studying.
- (D) No mistakes.

248.
- (A) Which of the twins can swim fastest?
- (B) She ran quickly across the court.
- (C) Pass the potatoes, please.
- (D) No mistakes.

249.
- (A) Can you run an errand for Mother?
- (B) Nick is always drumming the desk, tapping his feet, or he bobs his head.
- (C) Jordan, have you met Lydia?
- (D) No mistakes.

250.
- (A) April is the cruelest month.
- (B) The falling leaves of October fill the yard with color.
- (C) Its the humidity that really makes us feel the heat.
- (D) No mistakes.

251.
- (A) I can't tell the difference between oranges and tangerines.
- (B) Sandy taught me to ride without training wheels.
- (C) Dr. Daniel easily recognized her photos.
- (D) No mistakes.

252.
- (A) After the rainstorm, our neighbor washed his car again.
- (B) Daphne doesn't like alot of fuss.
- (C) The colors of the rainbow are red, orange, yellow, green, blue, indigo, and violet.
- (D) No mistakes.

253.
- (A) Your job pays more than Carrie's job.
- (B) My discount card expired last month.
- (C) The groundhog didn't see it's shadow this year.
- (D) No mistakes.

254.
- (A) Eric plays the tuba, and Nora plays the trombone.
- (B) I can't believe I misplaced my keys again.
- (C) The stories of sea adventure always gives me a thrill.
- (D) No mistakes.

255.
- (A) The bus had already departed.
- (B) Neither she or I have missed a day of school this year.
- (C) They're going to be surprised next fall.
- (D) No mistakes.

256.
- (A) After Anastasia left, the party was over.
- (B) "Look out!" cried Sonya.
- (C) Boris accepted the award graciously.
- (D) No mistakes.

257.
- (A) I want to see you rested, relaxed, and tomorrow.
- (B) Do you recall where you were last Saturday afternoon?
- (C) Amy and Lolita are moving to California.
- (D) No mistakes.

258.
- (A) Kelsey sat beside me during the flight.
- (B) Girl Scouts sell cookies; Boy Scouts sell popcorn.
- (C) Sam said, "I know I have something to do.
- (D) No mistakes.

259.
- (A) The director of the play was born in St. Louis.
- (B) Will you call the restaurant for me.
- (C) Branan makes me laugh, but Aaron makes me cry.
- (D) No mistakes.

260.
- (A) The clock in the old, red, tower chimes at noon.
- (B) Calculating the costs will not be difficult.
- (C) We three always travel together.
- (D) No mistakes.

261.
- (A) Doug, our church organist, is the most talented musician I know.
- (B) Include the following in your paragraph, a topic sentence, supporting details, and a closing statement.
- (C) Tom and Joanne walked home together.
- (D) No mistakes.

262.
- (A) I was amazed, and delighted by the music.
- (B) With such talent, the band will go far.
- (C) The rates at the bank change monthly.
- (D) No mistakes.

263.
- (A) Amy had taken piano lessons when she was a child.
- (B) Joe and Joan are happy with they're new business.
- (C) The book that I borrowed is on the third shelf.
- (D) No mistakes.

264.
- (A) Jorge thought about it and said, "I don't recall sugar as one of the ingredients".
- (B) Cameron lives a mile farther down the road
- (C) When the patrons departed, they left their programs in their seats.
- (D) No mistakes.

265.
- (A) Coach Thacker my social studies teacher is a big movie fan.
- (B) Is Charlie always so friendly?
- (C) We had to memorize the poem "Kubla Khan."
- (D) No mistakes.

266.
- (A) Did you receive any exotic gifts, Mrs. Noel?
- (B) On the forth day, he sent me some birds.
- (C) The absentee list (which includes tardies) is distributed before lunch.
- (D) No mistakes.

267.
- (A) Harris told us about the funniest book he has ever read.
- (B) Everyone begged to watch the game, but the teacher went on with class.
- (C) I still enjoy reading childrens' books.
- (D) No mistakes.

268.
  (A) Mary Shelley was a teenager when she wrote her novel "Frankenstein."
  (B) The members of the club talked among themselves until the meeting started.
  (C) After the encounter with the skunk, our yard smelled bad for days.
  (D) No mistakes.

269.
  (A) The fog was so thick that we could hardly see.
  (B) I ordered the buffet: pizza, pasta, breadsticks, and salad.
  (C) Several empty desks stand between you and me.
  (D) No mistakes.

270.
  (A) Spring vacation usually takes place during April.
  (B) Which Doctor did you see?
  (C) How, in your opinion, can we avoid such problems?
  (D) No mistakes.

271.
  (A) I was excepted into the club last year.
  (B) Please sit down and tell me your story.
  (C) My grandmother set up a bank account for me when I was born.
  (D) No mistakes.

272.
  (A) Does anyone collect box tops anymore?
  (B) When I was a little boy, I used to wait patiently for the mailman.
  (C) If Mr. Cerulean would assign less homework, he would have less papers to grade.
  (D) No mistakes.

273.
  (A) Rachel has been planning a trip to Italy.
  (B) The woman who designed the building also has a degree in history.
  (C) The river flowed over the rocks and under the bridge.
  (D) No mistakes.

274.
  (A) Their truck can pull a lot of weight.
  (B) Many members of my family are allergic to milk.
  (C) The special affects in the movie were amazing.
  (D) No mistakes.

275.
  (A) Leah and Jeff were both in my class.
  (B) Josh, Sean and me formed a jazz band.
  (C) Which of these cartons is on sale?
  (D) No mistakes.

276.
  (A) The movie, by the way, was too long.
  (B) She felt sick, so she went to lay down.
  (C) Michael can bowl well when he practices.
  (D) No mistakes.

277.
  (A) For example, most people choose their own screen names.
  (B) "Have you eaten?" asked Richard.
  (C) Lie your head on the pillow and sleep.
  (D) No mistakes.

278.
  (A) Emily is exceptionally polite.
  (B) Of course, we always love to see Julian.
  (C) Both of them are always welcome.
  (D) No mistakes.

DIRECTIONS: For questions 279–288, look for errors in spelling only.

279.
(A) On July 4th, we celebrate Independence Day.
(B) He was to popular to be defeated in the election.
(C) She wore the most exquisite jewelry to the wedding.
(D) No mistakes.

280.
(A) I declined the roll of Hamlet, considering it too demanding on my memory.
(B) The eighth grade is a difficult one, filled with transition.
(C) He used to write a humorous column for the newspaper.
(D) No mistakes.

281.
(A) I don't recall ever having a president who could pronounce the word "nuclear."
(B) The ceiling appeared too low in the apartment.
(C) I never realized how many nickels I had acquired in change.
(D) No mistakes.

282.
(A) His forehead was definitely at least four inches in height.
(B) I hope I'm not mistaken, but aren't you the famous psychologist on television?
(C) I get weary of the cold weather during Febuary, March, and April.
(D) No mistakes.

283.
(A) I try not to be illegible, so people won't think I'm illiterate.
(B) Due to the sheriff's couragous efforts, no one was hurt.
(C) Save your receipts; you can redeem them at school.
(D) No mistakes.

284.
(A) Should we view King Richard as a villain or a conqueror?
(B) Pam said she'd meet me at the libary, but she must have been detained elsewhere.
(C) He viewed computers as unnecessarily complicated.
(D) No mistakes.

285.
(A) The classes joked that the temperature in the room was positively freezing.
(B) We have a lot of atheletes attending our school.
(C) We occasionally have to write summaries of certain books of literature.
(D) No mistakes.

286.
(A) Although I felt confident, I was not arrogant.
(B) The genuine article felt heavier in my grasp.
(C) We can consider the whole controversy as an educational experience.
(D) No mistakes.

287.
(A) I assumed a long speech was unnesessary for this occasion.
(B) Bowing to the sheik was a respectful gesture.
(C) Aren't you curious about what's in the shipment?
(D) No mistakes.

288.
(A) Oh, she can be mischevious when she's in a spunky mood.
(B) The banquet included some of my favorite vegetables.
(C) I predict great success on my exams.
(D) No mistakes.

289. Graymalkin hates to be bathed, _____ she doesn't like to be dirty, either.

    (A) because
    (B) yet
    (C) for instance
    (D) however

290. Sheila wanted to watch the end of the awards program, _____ it was past her bedtime.

    (A) however
    (B) but
    (C) because
    (D) thus

291. Which of the following expresses the idea most clearly?

    (A) She brought brevity, she brought wit, and she brought style to the broadcast.
    (B) Brevity, wit, and style were brought by her to the broadcast.
    (C) To the broadcast she brought brevity, wit, as well as style.
    (D) She brought brevity, wit, and style to the broadcast.

292. Which of the following expresses the idea most clearly?

    (A) Erasmus Darwin was Charles Darwin's grandfather; he excelled in many areas. Some of them were science, philosophy, and poetry.
    (B) Erasmus Darwin, who was the grandfather of Charles Darwin, excelled in many areas: science, philosophy, and poetry.
    (C) Charles Darwin's grandfather, Erasmus Darwin, excelled in many areas, including science, philosophy, and poetry.
    (D) Erasmus Darwin, Charles Darwin's grandfather, excelled in many areas; these included science and philosophy and poetry.

293. Choose the group of words that best completes this sentence:

    According to legend, _____ .

    (A) the Grand Canyon was created by the ax dragging of Paul Bunyan.
    (B) Paul Bunyan created the Grand Canyon by dragging his ax.
    (C) Paul Bunyan dragged his ax, thereby creating what is called the Grand Canyon.
    (D) the Grand Canyon was created by Paul Bunyan, who dragged his ax.

294. Which of the following sentences best fits under the topic "Horse Mythology"?

    (A) Horses are related to the hippopotamus.
    (B) Pegasus is the famed winged horse in Greek legend.
    (C) The Kentucky Derby is the most famous horse race in the United States.
    (D) None of these.

295. Which topic is best suited for a one-paragraph essay?

    (A) Shakespeare and King James
    (B) Neanderthal Man
    (C) World War II
    (D) None of these.

296. Which sentence does NOT belong in the following paragraph?

(1) After a rainfall, we often see earthworms on the sidewalk. (2) This is because worms, like us, have to breathe, and the ground is saturated with water when it rains. (3) In order to survive, the worms have to temporarily leave their homes until some of the water evaporates. (4) Earthworms are also called Night Crawlers or Angleworms.

(A) Sentence 1
(B) Sentence 2
(C) Sentence 3
(D) Sentence 4

297. Where should the sentence "We know it today as the pretzel" fit into this paragraph?

(1) In the Middle Ages, monks would give rewards to children who learned their lessons and prayers. (2) One of these prizes was a snack called a *pretiola,* which is Latin for "little reward." (3) This snack was made of strips of dough, looped around to look like a pair of arms folded in prayer.

(A) between 1 and 2
(B) between 2 and 3
(C) after 3
(D) The sentence does not fit in this paragraph.

298. Where should the sentence "To throw a curve, the pitcher twists his wrist during the throw" fit into this paragraph?

(1) Curve balls are difficult for batters to hit. (2) This spin on the ball creates less air pressure under the ball than on the top. (3) This, in turn, causes the ball to drop faster than it ordinarily would, confusing the batter.

(A) between 1 and 2
(B) between 2 and 3
(C) after 3
(D) The sentence does not fit in this paragraph.

STOP

IF YOU FINISH BEFORE TIME IS UP, CHECK OVER YOUR WORK ON THIS TEST ONLY.

Answers to Practice High School Placement Test 2

SUBTEST 1   VERBAL SKILLS

1. D	11. C	21. A	31. C	41. B	51. D
2. C	12. A	22. A	32. D	42. A	52. C
3. B	13. B	23. A	33. B	43. A	53. D
4. A	14. C	24. A	34. D	44. B	54. A
5. C	15. A	25. A	35. A	45. B	55. A
6. A	16. D	26. A	36. A	46. D	56. D
7. A	17. D	27. C	37. D	47. A	57. A
8. B	18. C	28. C	38. A	48. D	58. A
9. A	19. B	29. A	39. A	49. A	59. A
10. B	20. A	30. D	40. B	50. D	60. A

SUBTEST 2   QUANTITATIVE SKILLS

61. C	71. D	81. A	91. C	101. D	111. A
62. C	72. A	82. B	92. C	102. B	112. A
63. B	73. C	83. A	93. A	103. A	
64. D	74. D	84. B	94. A	104. D	
65. A	75. B	85. D	95. B	105. D	
66. D	76. D	86. A	96. B	106. D	
67. A	77. B	87. D	97. D	107. A	
68. A	78. A	88. A	98. D	108. A	
69. B	79. D	89. A	99. D	109. B	
70. B	80. B	90. C	100. C	110. A	

SUBTEST 3   READING—COMPREHENSION—VOCABULARY

113. C	124. B	135. B	146. D	157. A	168. D
114. B	125. C	136. B	147. D	158. B	169. C
115. C	126. C	137. C	148. B	159. A	170. B
116. A	127. A	138. C	149. D	160. C	171. D
117. A	128. B	139. B	150. B	161. A	172. B
118. C	129. C	140. D	151. D	162. B	173. C
119. D	130. C	141. D	152. C	163. A	174. D
120. D	131. A	142. C	153. A	164. C	
121. C	132. C	143. A	154. D	165. A	
122. A	133. C	144. D	155. D	166. D	
123. B	134. C	145. D	156. B	167. C	

SUBTEST 4   MATHEMATICS

175. B	186. C	197. B	208. B	219. B	230. C
176. D	187. A	198. D	209. A	220. A	231. D
177. D	188. C	199. C	210. B	221. B	232. A
178. C	189. B	200. D	211. D	222. D	233. C
179. A	190. C	201. D	212. B	223. B	234. A
180. D	191. D	202. A	213. A	224. D	235. D
181. B	192. A	203. C	214. D	225. B	236. B
182. A	193. D	204. A	215. A	226. D	237. A
183. D	194. D	205. C	216. C	227. B	238. B
184. D	195. A	206. D	217. D	228. B	
185. C	196. C	207. D	218. C	229. D	

SUBTEST 5   LANGUAGE

239. C	249. B	259. B	269. D	279. B	289. B
240. B	250. C	260. A	269. B	280. A	290. B
241. C	251. D	261. B	271. A	281. D	291. D
242. C	252. B	262. A	272. C	282. C	292. C
243. A	253. C	263. B	273. D	283. B	293. B
244. B	254. C	264. A	274. C	284. B	294. B
245. A	255. B	265. A	275. B	285. B	295. D
246. A	256. D	266. B	276. B	286. D	296. D
247. B	257. A	267. C	277. C	287. A	297. C
248. A	258. C	268. A	278. D	288. A	298. A

Answer Explanations

SUBTEST 1 VERBAL SKILLS

1. **(D)** The other choices *cover* your foot.

2. **(C)** The other words deal with increasing the size or strength. To dilute something is to weaken it.

3. **(B)** A hero is the opposite of a villain; an <u>ant</u>agonist is the opposite of a <u>pro</u>tagonist.

4. **(A)** Station<u>a</u>ry is unmoving.

5. **(C)** Uncertain. Drs. Casey and Zorba are not compared in the first two statements.

    Z C
    K

6. **(A)** The other choices are specific types of toys.

7. **(A)** The other choices are specific types of furniture.

8. **(B)** *Uncover* is a verb. The others are nouns meaning a type of show.

9. **(A)** Something resilient springs back. Choices B and C mean the opposite of this. Choice D means calm.

10. **(B)** The other choices involve deception.

11. **(C)** A donor is a contributor—one who donates.

12. **(A)** A shrill sound is a high-pitched, piercing one.

13. **(B)** A drill makes a hole. A blender makes batter. (It does not *make* flour, eggs, or milk.)

14. **(C)** We are not told that these men are on the coaching staff.

15. **(A)** Something lethargic is slow and drowsy.

16. **(D)** A solicitor is not necessarily a scholar or wise person.

17. **(D)** The government is not a building.

18. **(C)** To scrutinize something is to look closely at it.

19. **(B)** To plunder means to steal; its opposite is to restore.

20. **(A)** A coat is a larger version of a jacket; a chair is a larger version of a stool.

21. **(A)** A financial profile examines money, while a psychological profile examines the mind.

22. **(A)** This is trickier. Your chart may look like this: Jack is three years older than Ralph. Peterkin is two years younger than Ralph.

    J + 3
    R
    P − 2

This can be rewritten showing Ralph as two years older than Peterkin.

    J + 3
    J + 2
    P

23. **(A)** Punctual means on time—prompt.

24. **(A)** M
    T
    J

25. **(A)** Notorious and infamous both mean well known for something bad.

26. **(A)** Choices B and C are synonyms, so they can't both be correct. *Obscure* means unclear.

27. **(C)** A comma cannot end sentences.

28. **(C)** A counterfeit bill is a copy. It is false.

29. **(A)** J
    P
    A

30. **(D)** Choices A, B, and C are *specific* sciences.

31. **(C)** A baseball player wears a cap; a cyclist wears a helmet.

32. **(D)** The other choices are smells.

33. **(B)** H
    W
    L

34. **(D)** The other choices are synonyms for counting or checking.

35. **(A)** Something rampant is out of control.

36. **(A)** *Affluent* means wealthy; its opposite is *destitute*.

37. **(D)** *Earnest* means serious. It is not ridiculous.

38. **(A)**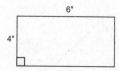

39. **(A)** *Meager* means poor. Its opposite is abundant.

40. **(B)** A puppy's foot is a paw; a colt's foot is a hoof.

41. **(B)** *Mal* is one of those negative prefixes. A maladroit person is not skillful (not adroit).

42. **(A)** S
    C
    L

43. **(A)** The other choices are *specific* rooms.

44. **(B)** Your nose is part of your face; your finger is part of your hand.

45. **(B)** Jeopardy is danger.

46. **(D)** The other choices are places.

47. **(A)** *Meticulous* means careful or precise. Its opposite is *haphazard*.

48. **(D)** Someone who is modest has no vanity; someone who is innocent has no guilt.

49. **(A)** C
    L
    H

50. **(D)** *Decrepit* means weak or feeble. Its opposite is *robust* or *healthy*.

51. **(D)** You play at recess; you eat at breakfast.

52. **(C)** Uncertain. The best we can say is this:

    F M
    P

53. **(D)** A videocassette does not have a keypad.

54. **(A)** *Hygienic* means clean or sanitary. Think of good hygiene.

55. **(A)** B
    V
    H

56. **(D)** Choices A, B, and C are synonyms.

57. **(A)** *Pernicious* means harmful. You might have narrowed this down to choices A and D, since they are opposites.

58. **(A)** L
    G
    W

59. **(A)** A desert is arid; a rain forest is humid.

60. **(A)** C
    P
    S

SUBTEST 2 QUANTITATIVE SKILLS

61.

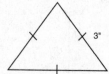

ANALYSIS

All the sides of the equilateral triangle are 3″. The opposite sides of the rectangle are congruent. Find both perimeters and substitute into the choices.

WORK

Perimeter of the rectangle = 6″ + 6″ + 4″ + 4″ = 20″

Perimeter of the triangle = 3″ + 3″ + 3″ = 9″

The perimeter of the rectangle is 11″ more than the perimeter of the equilateral triangle.

$$20'' = 9'' + 11'' \checkmark$$

ANSWER: (C)

62.

ANALYSIS
The series is decreasing by 1.4.

WORK
$$8.8 - 1.4 = 7.4$$

ANSWER: (C)

63.

ANALYSIS
Let x = the unknown number and change 40% to 0.40.

WORK
$$0.40x = \frac{1}{2} \cdot 60 + 2$$
$$0.40x = 30 + 2$$

Multiply by 100: $0.40x = 32$
Divide by 40: $0 \ 40x = 3200$
$$x = 80$$

ANSWER: (B)

64.

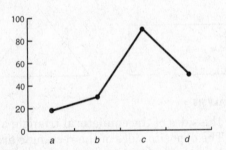

ANALYSIS
Determine the values of $a, b, c,$ and d, and then substitute into (A), (B), (C), and (D).

WORK
$$a \approx 10$$
$$b \approx 30$$
$$c \approx 90$$
$$d \approx 50$$
$$c - a < b + c$$
$$90 - 10 < 30 + 90 \ ✔$$
$$80 < 120$$

ANSWER: (D)

65.

ANALYSIS
Each succeeding number in the series is one third the previous number.

WORK
$$\frac{1}{3} \cdot \frac{2}{3} = \frac{2}{9}$$

ANSWER: (A)

66.

ANALYSIS
Let x = the unknown number, and change 60% to 0.60.

WORK
$$\frac{2}{3}x = 0.60 \cdot 40 + 18$$
$$\frac{2}{3}x = 24 + 18$$

Multiply by 3: $\frac{2}{3}x = 42$

Divide by 2: $2x = 126$
$$x = 63$$

ANSWER: (D)

67.

a	b	c	d	e	f
	♠	♥			♥
			♦		
♥	♦	♦		♣	♦
		♣	♣		
♥	♦				♠

ANALYSIS
Count the number of ♥s, ♠s, ♦s, and ♣s in each column and substitute.

WORK

	a	b	c	d	e	f
♥	2	0	1		0	1
♣	0	0	1	1	1	
♠	0	1	0		0	1
♦	0	2	1	1	0	1

Column a has one more ♥ than column f:
$$2 = 1 + 1 \ ✔$$

ANSWER: (A)

68.

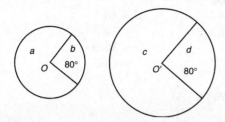

ANALYSIS

Since circle O′ is larger than circle O and the central angles are congruent, Area d > Area b and Area c > Area a.

WORK

Area c > Area a ✔

ANSWER: (A)

69.

ANALYSIS

There are three letters between each two given letters in the series.

WORK

M, N, O, P, Q

ANSWER: (B)

70.

ANALYSIS

Let x = the unknown number.

WORK

Multiply by 3: $x = \dfrac{2}{3} \cdot 60 + 8$

$x = 40 + 8$
$x = 48$

ANSWER: (B)

71.

ANALYSIS

There are two series here: 92, 96, 100, . . . , which increases by 4, and 17, 15, 13, . . . , which decreases by 2.

WORK

100 + 4 = 104

ANSWER: (D)

72.

ANALYSIS

Add up all the hours and divide by 3, the number of students.

WORK

$$\bar{x} = \frac{(t+4)+(t)+(t-2)}{3} = \frac{3t+2}{3}$$

ANSWER: (A)

73.

ANALYSIS

Each succeeding number in the series is three times the previous number.

WORK

$3 \cdot 54 = 162$

ANSWER: (C)

74.

ANALYSIS

Let x = the unknown number.

WORK

$$x = \frac{3}{4} \cdot 24 - 12$$

$x = 18 - 12$
$x = 6$

ANSWER: (D)

75.

ANALYSIS

The series increases by four units and then decreases by one unit.

WORK

17 − 1 = 16

ANSWER: (B)

76.

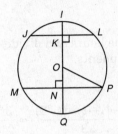

ANALYSIS

OQ, OP, and OI are all radii and are congruent.

WORK

$OP > ON$: OP is a radius, while ON is only a part of radius OQ. Therefore, the statement is true. ✔

ANSWER: (D)

77.

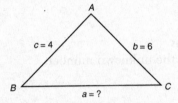

ANALYSIS

The sum of two sides of a triangle are always larger than the third side.

WORK

(A) $a = 10$: If $a = 10$, then $6 + 4$ will form a straight line and will coincide with side a. No triangle will be formed.

(B) $a < 10$: If $a < 10$, then sides 6 and 4 will form a triangle. ✔

(C) $a = 11$: If $a = 11$, then sides 4 and 6 will never meet and no triangle will be formed.

(D) $a > 10$: If $a > 10$, then sides 4 and 6 will never meet and no triangle will be formed.

ANSWER: (B)

78.

ANALYSIS

Substitute 3 for t in the given formula.

WORK

$$d = 16t^2$$
$$t = 3: \quad = 16(3)^2$$
$$= 16(9)$$
$$= 144$$

ANSWER: (A)

79.

ANALYSIS

The series forms the pattern 2^2, 2^3, 3^2, 3^3, 4^2, 4^3, ...

WORK

5^2, 5^3 or 25, 125

ANSWER: (D)

80.

ANALYSIS

Let x = the unknown number.

WORK

$$x - 54 = \frac{4}{5} \cdot 12 \cdot 5$$
$$x - 54 = 48$$
Add 54: $\quad x = 102$

ANSWER: (B)

81.

ANALYSIS

The number 9 is inserted into alternate positions in the series 24, 21, 18, 15, ... Each successive number in the series is reduced by 3.

WORK

24, 9, 21, 9, 18, 9, 15, **9**, **12**, . . .

ANSWER: (A)

82.

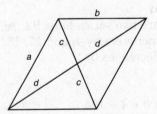

ANALYSIS

The only information we are certain about is that $c < d$.

WORK

$$c < d$$
$$+a = +a$$
$$\overline{a + c < a + d}$$

ANSWER: (B)

83.
ANALYSIS
Let x = the unknown number.

WORK

$$x = \frac{3}{5} \cdot 40 + 9$$
$$x = 24 + 9$$
$$x = 33$$

ANSWER: (A)

84.
ANALYSIS
The numbers are increasing in the pattern +2, +3, +4, +5, +6, ...

WORK
$$58 + 7 = 65$$

ANSWER: (B)

85.

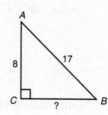

ANALYSIS
Use the Pythagorean Theorem.

WORK

$$a^2 + b^2 = c^2$$
$b = 8, c = 17:$ $\quad a^2 + 8^2 = 172$
$$a^2 + 64 = 289$$
Subtract 64: $\quad\quad a^2 = 225$
Take the square
root of both sides: $\quad\quad a = 15$

ANSWER: (D)

86.

	a	b	c
●	4	5	3
□	4	3	3
○	2	2	4

ANALYSIS

WORK
There are 2 more ●s in (b) than □s in (c).

$$5 = 3 + 2 \quad ✔$$

ANSWER: (A)

87.
ANALYSIS
Let x = the unknown number.

WORK

$$\frac{5}{8}x = \frac{1}{3} \cdot 60$$

Multiply by 8: $\quad \dfrac{5}{8}x = 20$

Divide by 5: $\quad\quad 5x = 160$
$$x = 32$$

ANSWER: (D)

88.
ANALYSIS
The numbers are increasing and decreasing in the pattern −2, +1, −2, +1, −2, ...

WORK
$$61 + 1 = 62$$

ANSWER: (A)

89.

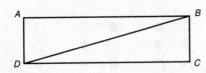

ANALYSIS
The longest side is *BD*, the diagonal.

WORK
$$BD > AB$$

ANSWER: (A)

90.
ANALYSIS
There are two missing letters between each term of the series.

WORK
B, C, D, **E**, F, G, **H**, I, J, **K**, L, M, **N**, O, P, **Q**

ANSWER: (C)

91.
ANALYSIS
Just substitute the given numbers for the symbols in the algebraic expression.

WORK
$$5 \cdot \blacksquare + 3 \cdot \square - 4 \cdot *$$
$\blacksquare = 4, \square = 3$ and $* = 2$:
$$5 \cdot 4 + 3 \cdot 3 - 4 \cdot 2$$
$$20 + 9 - 8$$
$$21$$

ANSWER: (C)

92.
ANALYSIS
The pattern is to double and then increase by one.

WORK
$$2 \times 39 = 78$$

ANSWER: (A)

93.
ANALYSIS
Let x = the unknown number.

WORK
$$\frac{2}{3}x - 25 = 3 \cdot 12 + 5$$

$$\frac{2}{3}x - 25 = 36 + 5$$

$$\frac{2}{3}x - 25 = 41$$

Add 25: $\qquad \frac{2}{3}x = 66$

Multiply by 3: $\qquad 2x = 198$
Divide by 2: $\qquad x = 99$

ANSWER: (A)

94.

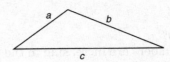

ANALYSIS
Change the words into algebraic form.

WORK
$$c = 2a$$
$$a = b - 3$$
Therefore, $\quad c = 2a = 2(b - 3)$.

ANSWER: (A)

95.
ANALYSIS
The numbers are increasing by 5.

WORK
$$12, 17, 22, 27, \underline{\quad}, 37, 42, 47, \ldots$$

ANSWER: (B)

96.
ANALYSIS
Let x = the unknown number.

WORK

$$\frac{36}{x} = \frac{5}{8} \cdot 80 - 41$$

$$\frac{36}{x} = 50 - 41$$

$$\frac{36}{x} = 9$$

Multiply by x: $36 = 9x$
Divide by 9: $4 = x$

ANSWER: (B)

97.

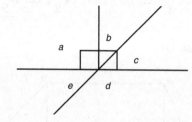

ANALYSIS
From the diagram, $m\angle a° = 90°$ and $m\angle b + m\angle c = 90°$.

WORK
$$m\angle b + m\angle c = 90°$$

ANSWER: (D)

98.
ANALYSIS
The numbers are increasing in squares.

WORK
$$1^2, 2^2, 3^2, 4^2, \underline{5^2}, \ldots$$

ANSWER: (D)

99.
ANALYSIS
Remember, when we multiply two negatives, the result is a positive and when we multiply a positive and a negative, the result is a negative.

WORK
$$-4(-2)^3 = -4(-2)(-2)(-2) = +8(-2)(-2) =$$
$$-16(-2) = +32$$

ANSWER: (D)

100.

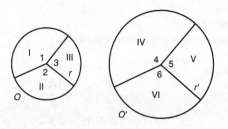

ANALYSIS
Let's eliminate the possible answers, and just select the answer we're certain about.

WORK
Since Circle O′ > Circle O, the corresponding sectors are unequal in the same order.

$$\text{Area IV} + \text{Area V} > \text{Area I} + \text{Area III}$$

ANSWER: (C)

101.

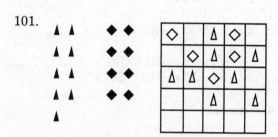

ANALYSIS
Count the number of dark and hollow figures and subtract.

WORK

$$
\begin{array}{cc}
8\blacklozenge & 9\blacktriangle \\
-\;5\diamondsuit & 8\triangle \\
\hline
3\blacklozenge & 1\blacktriangle
\end{array}
$$

ANSWER: (D)

102.
ANALYSIS
The series repeats.

WORK
$$2, 3, 6, \underline{2}, 3, 6, 2, 3, 6, \ldots$$

ANSWER: (B)

103.
ANALYSIS
Let x = the unknown number.

WORK

$$8x - \frac{2}{3} \cdot 48 = \frac{160}{4}$$
$$8x - 32 = 40$$

Add 32: $8x = 72$
Divide by 8: $x = 9$

ANSWER: (A)

104.
ANALYSIS
Simplify (a), (b), and (c), and substitute into (A), (B), (C), and (D).

WORK
(a) $5^2 = 5 \cdot 5 = 25$
(b) $3^4 = 3 \cdot 3 = 9$
(c) $2^5 = 2 \cdot 2 \cdot 2 \cdot 2 \cdot 2 = 32$

(b) > (c) and (b) > (a)
81 > 32 and 81 > 25 ✔

ANSWER: (D)

105.

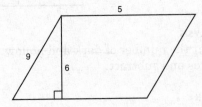

ANALYSIS
The area of a parallelogram is equal to base $(b) \cdot$ height (h). The area of a triangle is equal to $\frac{1}{2}$ base $(b) \cdot$ height (h). The perimeter of any plane figure is equal to the sum of its sides.

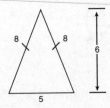

WORK
Perimeter of parallelogram > Perimeter of triangle + 5

$$5 + 5 + 9 + 9 > 21 + 5$$
$$28 > 26 \quad ✔$$

ANSWER: (D)

106.
ANALYSIS
The series is decreasing by $2\frac{1}{2}$.

WORK

$$24\frac{1}{2}, \, 22, \, 19\frac{1}{2}, \, 17, \, 14\frac{1}{2}, \, 12, \, \underline{\mathbf{9\frac{1}{2}}}, \ldots$$

ANSWER: (D)

107.

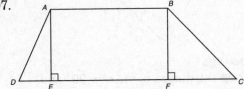

ANALYSIS
From all of the possible answers, select the best answer.

WORK
$$BC > AE$$

ANSWER: (A)

108.

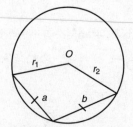

ANALYSIS
All radii in the same circle are congruent. Lines a and b are congruent. Select the best possible answer from the given choices.

WORK
The two radii are congruent, as are the two radii, so $r_1 + b = a + r_2$.

ANSWER: (A)

109.

ANALYSIS

Let x = the unknown number.

WORK

$$x^2 = 7 \cdot 8 + 8$$
$$x^2 = 56 + 8$$
$$x^2 = 64$$

Take the square root: $x = \pm 8$

ANSWER: (B)

110.

ANALYSIS

The Roman numbers are decreasing by 3, while the Arabic numbers are increasing by 2.

WORK

$$XII - III = IX$$

ANSWER: (A)

111.

ANALYSIS

Let x = the unknown number.

WORK

$$8x = \frac{7}{9} \cdot 81 - 15$$

$$8x = 63 - 15$$
$$8x = 48$$

Divide by 8: $x = 6$

ANSWER: (A)

112.

ANALYSIS

The series is divided into groups of three. Within each group, 2 is added to the first and second terms to arrive at the second and third members of the group, respectively. The next group begins with the second member of the previous group and the pattern is repeated.

WORK

3, 5, 7,   5, 7, 9,   7, 9, 11,
9, 11, 13,   **11, 13, 15, . . .**

ANSWER: (A)

SUBTEST 3 READING

113. **(C)** The final paragraph of the reading passage seems to be a transitional piece. Breaking down the organization of the piece supports this claims. Paragraphs one and two catch the reader's attention by telling about the plot of a famous novel. Paragraphs three and four discuss the literary and social significance of that novel. Paragraph five then relates the underlying message of the novel—a warning against engaging in activities we don't really understand. The paragraph ends with a sentence that bridges the discussion from one of the novel to subsequent discussion of examples against which the author will warn us. Therefore it is unlikely that the author will discuss yet another novel (choice A) or analyze random character names (choice B) or return to the (very) brief mention of the movie version of *Frankenstein* (choice D); more likely the discussion will turn to modern topics that define what the author means by "Frankensteins" (choice C).

114. **(B)** You probably know the word *equates*, but even if you don't, you can identify the root word for *equal* within it. Therefore, pick the definitions that best matches with the meaning of equal. Choice B is really your only option.

115. **(C)** Since the author never specifically states his/her opinion on cloning, you do have to make an educated guess (hence the term *inference*). However, since the author seems to agree with Mary Shelley regarding the wisdom of engaging in activity we understand little and control less, it is likely that the author will not be liberal in supporting many controversial topics. Cloning currently raises a great deal of debate, nor do we know much about the repercussions that will stem from experimenting with it. Therefore, C is your best choice.

116. **(A)** Re-reading (or memory) will help you remember that the text specifi-

cally traces back the word monster from the Latin *monstra*.

117. **(A)** The question is asking you to make a connection between the actions of Dr. Frankenstein and that of one of the characters listed. All four of the characters are well known for various reasons, some positive, others negative. However, only one presumed to put himself on par with God, and that is Lucifer.

118. **(C)** Re-reading (or memory) clearly states that Frankenstein dies an "icy, watery" death—in other words drowning.

119. **(D)** The author does not mention feminism (aside from the slight hint, perhaps, by stressing slightly the revelation that the author of *Frankenstein* was a woman), nor does the author say anything overtly to get us to read or write (although s/he does try to interest us in the text, generally speaking). The author *does* in the final paragraph attempt to get us to use good judgment when deciding how to live our lives and explore various new fields. Therefore, D is the correct response.

120. **(D)** You can tell from the context that nefarious is meant to be a negative word; of the four definitional choices, only D can be construed as negative.

121. **(C)** You can rule out choice B, since, by anyone's standards, the balloon bombs were unsuccessful (a dud, if you will). Similarly, you can omit choice D because we Americans didn't get much opportunity to be brave because the mission was not successful. Choice A is not an option because the idea seems clever, resourceful, and cheap—just unlucky. Therefore, the best choice is C.

122. **(A)** The article makes no mention of herons, clouds, or stones; by process of elimination, you can select choice A.

123. **(B)** Re-reading (or memory) helps you pick out the only true fact in the piece—the fact that women made the bombs.

124. **(B)** The article is mostly informational, sincerely interested, and unbiased (not mocking—choice C—or patronizing—choice D—or persuasive—choice A); therefore, you can rule out all choices but B.

125. **(C)** The writers of the test are trying to make sure you do not confuse *Baule* with homonyms (choices A or D). The writers also are testing your knowledge of basic geography (choice B). The only choice backed up by reading the passage is choice C.

126. **(C)** Re-reading (or memory) helps you pick out the correct statement that it is appropriate to give gifts of clothing to the sculpture of the spirit spouse. The other objects may also be appropriate, but the article does not specifically state as much.

127. **(A)** Scanning the word placated, you notice a significant similarity to the word please. Therefore compare the word pleased to the remaining definitions; only A comes close to matching in meaning.

128. **(B)** Re-reading the text (or memory) tells you that the article advises you to go ahead and change your first answer on a multiple-choice test since, statistically speaking, you are probably doing the right thing.

129. **(C)** Re-reading the text (or memory) tells you that the article thinks that because women suffer more than men from low self-esteem, they are more likely to change a right answer to a wrong answer through second-guessing themselves.

130. **(C)** Re-reading the text (or memory) of the article tells you that people change from a wrong answer to a wrong answer 25% of the time.

131. **(A)** The article gives advice on acing multiple-choice tests, and the people most likely to desire such advice are students. Therefore, of the options, students might be most likely to find this information from their school guidance offices. Choices C (teen mag) and D (pop culture mag) are close runners up (because they make their living doling out snippets of wisdom),

but they are not as reliable. Choice B would be the least likely place to find this article.

132. **(C)** You can rule out choice A, since attribute has nothing to do with placing blame on anyone. You might consider choice B, since we all have attributes (characteristics by which we can be described), and that fact might make us think of the word *describe*. But the two best choices are C and D. Nevertheless you are looking for a word that means something like links with or looks to; choice C is your best choice.

133. **(C)** Re-reading the text (or memory) tells you that the article states these researchers are based in Ontario.

134. **(C)** The article discusses the topic of whether or not to change your answers on a multiple-choice test. It does not discuss cheating (rule out choice A) or people's behavior in society (rule out choice D). Choice B is more compelling, but indecision is a broad term that can apply to any aspect of life; choice C is better because it clearly narrows the discussion down to a more manageable level.

135. **(B)** Re-reading the text (or memory) tells you that the article states that 50% of the time people change their first answer on a multiple-choice exam from wrong to right.

136. **(B)** All four definitions of the word *kid* apply, depending on the context. Given the context of this particular article, you can rule out any definition that involves animals or small children (choices A or D). Mrs. Sommers is very serious and sad throughout the piece, so you can also rule out the definition that involves laughter (choice C). Your only option is B, and, given that we are describing gloves and goatskin as a common material for making gloves, the association with B is easy to see.

137. **(C)** Re-reading the text (or memory) tells you that because Mrs. Sommers remembers "the days when she had been accustomed to other pleasant

things," you can see clearly that Mrs. Sommers no longer generally gets to spend money freely; she must instead pinch pennies and be frugal.

138. **(C)** The final paragraph, with its tone of longing and sadness, indicates that Mrs. Sommers feels guilt for her very satisfying day spending money on herself.

139. **(B)** This question builds off of the last one. Mrs. Sommers has enjoyed her time recalling her more wealthy days. Now she faces returning home to her frugal existence, and she is saddened. We cannot know from the passage how she feels about her husband or her family (choices A and C), so we can rule them out. Your best answer is B.

140. **(D)** Re-reading the text (or memory) tells you that the selection tells you her clothing "had given her a feeling of assurance, a sense of belonging." Therefore, the best answer is D.

141. **(D)** By focusing on Mrs. Sommers and making sure to show her intense enjoyment of her day, the author seems to want to point out how everyone needs a day off sometimes. Choice A is incorrect, for although Mrs. Sommers enjoys her spending, she doesn't get any real benefit that we literally see take place. Nor is choice B appropriate for Mrs. Sommers is depicted giving advice to anyone. Nor is choice C appropriate because no one picking up on the tone of the passage would think Mrs. Sommers is just being greedy; she feels too much guilt for her actions.

142. **(C)** The article focuses on a specific trainer in a specific area, and discusses future plans to hold more self-defense sessions; therefore it is unlikely to appear in a country-wide text (like *Newsweek*) or a worldwide text (like the encyclopedia). Since the topic is aimed at helping children in particular defend themselves, it is unlikely to appear in a fashion magazine (like *Glamour*). Therefore your only real option is C—and it makes sense anyway.

143. **(A)** The word *tutelage* refers to learning; the best match to this meaning is A, training. Choices B and D make no sense; choice C comes as the result of learning; therefore, it is not appropriate.

144. **(D)** Re-reading the text (or memory) tells you that the article states that Johnson holds a 4th degree black belt.

145. **(D)** Re-reading the text (or memory) tells you that the selection says that concern over increased kidnapping caused the increase in signing up for self-defense courses (paragraph one).

146. **(D)** Re-reading the text (or memory) tells you that paragraph four talks about how Johnson sees running these types of self-defense courses as a form of public service and volunteerism. Therefore, D is the only possible answer.

147. **(D)** The question itself gives you a clue since it uses the word "think" in its wording. Choices A and B are simply untrue; anyone who follows the film industry's use of computer graphics—in movies like *Shrek* or *Monsters Inc.*—know that use of computer graphics generally increases the cost and time required for movie making. You can also rule out choice C because the article does not state an opinion on the topic at all; most likely, however, mimicking a human using computer graphics would add both to the time and cost of movie making, making it less likely that one would willingly film a movie without humans. The best answer is D—the use of computer graphics has greatly enhanced all kinds of filming, especially adventure films, and has actually lead to an increase in remakes of films that would have benefited from such advances the first time around.

148. **(B)** Choices C and D are unlikely, since biology has little to do with filming, even underwater topics, unless the film focuses specifically on sea life; nor do encyclopedias keep up with current salvaging expeditions. Choice A is also unlikely, since it's simply too specialized to be correct. Your best option is choice B; indeed, it is the location at which this author learned of this topic.

149. **(D)** *Garner* is a special word of which you should be aware, but even if you are not, you can eliminate wrong choices through process of elimination. The sense of the word implies gaining, so you can rule out choices A and B. You might associate *garner* with *garnish* (another word for decoration), but you would be wrong to do so; rule out choice C. The best answer is D—and, indeed, *acquire* is another word for gain.

150. **(B)** Choice B is simply there to distract you; the piece says nothing about Leonardo di Caprio's skills as an actor or as an asset to a film. Choices C and D are also incorrect for they misrepresent facts given in the selection. Neither France or Russia are doing positive things for the *Titanic* and those who respect her; nor is Bob Ballard the villain of the piece—he is the hero. The only true answer is B, to alert the reader to what is going on in the world of underwater salvage.

151. **(D)** Re-reading (or memory) reveals to you the proper answer. Of course, you have to do a little math, but if you do the subtraction correctly, you'll see that the answer is 1985 ($2004 - 19 = 1985$).

152. **(C)** The phrase *drum up* initially meant beating a drum to increase one's interest in an activity—usually going to war. But don't let that mean you relate the phrase to choice A; the meaning is more geared toward raising one's excitement rather than actually beating on a drum. Rule out choice A. Also rule out choice D; anger is indeed a form of excitement, but the context of the passage rules out this option—the author states that Ballard is trying to get people interested, not specifically get them angry. Because B is opposite to getting someone interested, rule it out, too. The best answer is C.

153. **(A)** This is a word you need to know because it can trick you. It doesn't mean what you might think. (It has

nothing to do with odor.) Something odious is detestable, repugnant, and loathsome.

154. **(D)** Something petty is small (think *petite*) and insignificant, so the word *unimportant* is the closest choice.

155. **(D)** An agenda is a plan or a list of things to do. It is related to the words *agent* (a doer) and *agency* (an organization to do something).

156. **(B)** The root *luc* or *luce* means light. Something lucid is bright, light, or clear.

157. **(A)** The ancient Greeks called the west wind Zephyr. It can now refer to any gentle breeze.

158. **(B)** If you thought that *enumerate* has to do with numbers or counting (as in *numerals*), you're correct. The closest word to counting is *to list*.

159. **(A)** The negative prefix *in-* leads us to choices A and D. Something not appropriate or not convenient or not a good opportunity is not at a good time (*untimely*) rather than not with a conclusion (*inconclusive*).

160. **(C)** A pungent aroma is a sharp smell. Pungent is related to *puncture*, *point*, and *punctual* (on time to a point)!

161. **(A)** If you shirk doing your laundry, your shirt may shrink. (Or you can just picture a lazy shark.)

162. **(B)** Remember that the root *cred* means *believe* (as in the Apostle's Creed: "I believe . . ."). Something incredible is unbelievable.

163. **(A)** To *feign* is to simulate or imitate. *Pretend* is the best choice.

164. **(C)** A veneer is a thin face or covering. It's literally the thin wood that covers the surface of some furniture.

165. **(A)** If you think of the word *relax*, you'll choose the correct answer, *loose*. (You can easily eliminate *strict* and *oppressive*.)

166. **(D)** You learned that the suffix *-archy* means rule. Anarchy is without rule. D (*disorder*) is the closest choice.

167. **(C)** *Tangible* means touchable. Something physical is touchable.

168. **(D)** A lectern is a reading stand or desk, and a lector is a reader or lecturer.

169. **(C)** Though it seems strange, you can actually use etymology to figure this one out. *Im-pede* means not foot, right? That would eliminate choices A (*quicken*) and B (*race*). Moreover, because it's negative, it would eliminate D (*support*). If your feet are blocked, you are definitely hindered.

170. **(B)** Etymology works again! *Anti-pathy* means against feeling. It's the opposite of *sym-pathy* (with feeling).

171. **(D)** *Pace* means peace.

172. **(B)** This one is tricky. *Post-humous* literally means after earth/dirt or after burial!

173. **(C)** If the ultimate is the final, the penultimate is the next to last. The ultimate pen was too expensive, so I bought the next best writing utensil, the penultimate pen.

174. **(D)** *Verb* means word. (By the way, *noun* or *nom* means name.)

SUBTEST 4 MATHEMATICS

175.
ANALYSIS
Simplify statements a, b, and c, and then substitute into A, B, C, and D.

WORK
(a) $(24 \cdot 2)/6 = 48/6 = 8$
(b) $(24/6) \cdot 2 = 4 \cdot 2 = 8$
(c) $(24/2) + 6 = 12 + 6 = 18$

$$c > a \text{ and } a = b$$
$$18 > 8 \text{ and } 8 = 8 \quad ✔$$

ANSWER: (B)

176.
ANALYSIS
Let $b = -1$ and substitute into the given terms.

WORK
Let $b = -1$: (A) $b^2 = (-1)^2 = +1$
　　　　　　　 (B) $-b = -(-1) = +1$
　　　　　　　 (C) $b^0 = (-1)^0 = +1$
　　　　　　　 (D) $b^3 = (-1)^3 = (-1)(-1)(-1) = -1$

ANSWER: (D)

177.
ANALYSIS
Simplify each expression, and then substitute.

WORK
(a) $5^2 = 5 \cdot 5 = 25$
(b) $2^5 = 2 \cdot 2 \cdot 2 \cdot 2 \cdot 2 = 32$
(c) $2^3 = 2 \cdot 2 \cdot 2 = 8$

$$b < a \text{ or } c < b$$
$$32 < 25 \text{ or } 8 < 3 \quad ✔$$

ANSWER: (D)

178.
ANALYSIS
Divide 3^9 by 3^7, and then simplify.

WORK

$$\frac{\overset{3^2}{\cancel{3^9}}}{4 \times \underset{1}{\cancel{3^7}}} = \frac{9}{4} = 2\frac{1}{4}$$

ANSWER: (C)

179.
ANALYSIS
Simplify all the expressions, and then arrange from the largest to the smallest.

WORK
(a) $4^2 + 5(9 - 3) = 16 + 5 \cdot 6 = 16 + 30 = 46$
(b) $3 \cdot 17 - 4 \cdot 6 = 51 - 24 = 27$
(c) $7 + 9 \cdot 4 - 6(9 - 7)^3 = 7 + 36 - 6(2)^3 =$
    $43 - 6(8) = 43 - 48 = -5$
(d) $6 + 2 + 42/8 - 2(3 - 1)^2 = 8 + 6 - 2(2)^2 =$
    $14 - 8 = 6$

$$46 > 27 > 6 > -5$$
$$a > b > d > c$$

ANSWER: (A)

180.
ANALYSIS
Look at the tens' place. If the tens' digit is five or more, round the hundreds' digit one unit higher. If the tens' place is less than five, let the hundreds' digits stand.

WORK

$$1{,}742{,}143 \qquad \approx 1{,}742{,}100$$
$$\uparrow$$
$$\text{the tens' digit} < 5$$

ANSWER: (D)

181.
ANALYSIS
They'll meet again at the start of the track whenever 3 and 5 share a common multiple.

WORK

Dwayne

Minutes per track	×	Turns around track	=	Total minutes
3	×	1	=	3
3	×	2	=	6
3	×	3	=	9
3	×	4	=	12
3	×	**5**	=	**15**

Malcolm

Minutes per track	×	Turns around track	=	Total minutes
5	×	1	=	5
5	×	2	=	10
5	×	**3**	=	**15**
5	×	4	=	20
5	×	5	=	25

Dwayne and Malcolm will meet in 15 minutes.

ANSWER: (B)

182.
ANALYSIS
Multiply the mixed numbers and then substitute into the inequalities.

WORK
(a) $1\frac{1}{2} \cdot 2\frac{3}{4} = \frac{3}{2} \cdot \frac{11}{4} = \frac{33}{8} = 4\frac{1}{8}$

(b) $\frac{3}{4} \cdot 4\frac{1}{2} = \frac{3}{4} \cdot \frac{9}{2} = \frac{27}{8} = 3\frac{3}{8}$

(c) $3\dfrac{1}{2} \cdot \dfrac{3}{4} = \dfrac{7}{2} \cdot \dfrac{3}{4} = \dfrac{21}{8} = 2\dfrac{5}{8}$

(d) $\dfrac{1}{2} \cdot 3\dfrac{1}{4} = \dfrac{1}{2} \cdot \dfrac{13}{4} = \dfrac{13}{8} = 1\dfrac{5}{8}$

$$c < d \quad \text{or} \quad c < a$$
$$2\dfrac{5}{8} < 1\dfrac{5}{8} \ \text{or} \ 2\dfrac{5}{8} < 4\dfrac{1}{8} \quad \checkmark$$

ANSWER: (A)

183.

ANALYSIS

Divide the distance, 206.5 miles, by the rate of speed, 59 mph, in order to determine the time it takes to drive from Middletown to Rockville. Then add the number of hours to 2:30 P.M., the starting time.

WORK

$$
\begin{array}{r}
3.5 \\
59\overline{)206.5} \\
177\text{x} \\
\hline
29\ 5 \\
29\ 5 \\
\hline
\end{array}
$$

2:30 P.M. + 3.5 hours = 6 P.M.

ANSWER: (D)

184.

ANALYSIS

Divide 236.5 by 12.4 and round off to the nearest tenth.

WORK

$$
\begin{array}{r}
1\,9.07 \approx 19.1 \\
12{\wedge}4\overline{)236{\wedge}5.00} \\
124\ \text{x x x} \\
\hline
112\ 5 \\
111\ 6 \\
\hline
9\ 00 \\
8\ 68 \\
\hline
3\ 2 \\
\end{array}
$$

ANSWER: (D)

185.

ANALYSIS

Add the right- and left-handed numbers of students to obtain the total number. Then divide the total into the number of left-handed students.

WORK

Total number of students: 6 + 24 = 30
Left-handed students/total: 6/30 = 0.20
                                        0.20 = 20%

ANSWER: (C)

186.

ANALYSIS

Change all the numbers to decimals and then compare them.

WORK

.77 = .770
7/8 = .875
2/3 = .666 . . .
3/4 = .750
.82 = .820
.913 = .913

.7700 < .820 < .875

ANSWER: (C)

187.

ANALYSIS

Let x = the unknown number.

WORK

$$x = \dfrac{2}{3} \times 54 - 14$$
$$x = 36 - 14$$
$$x = 22$$

ANSWER: (A)

188.

ANALYSIS

Determine which number, when multiplied by itself three times, is equal to −0.027.

WORK

$$\sqrt[3]{-0.027} = -0.3$$

Check: $(-0.3)(-0.3)(-0.3) = -0.027$

ANSWER: (C)

189.
ANALYSIS
Test out all the possibilities.

WORK
$$-3 \le \ |2x + 1| < 2$$
$x = 0$: $\quad -3 \le \ |2(0) + 1| < 2$
$$-3 \le \ \ \ \ \ \ |1| \ \ \ < 2$$
$$-3 \le \ \ \ \ \ \ \ 1 \ \ \ < 2 \ ✔$$

ANSWER: (B)

190.
ANALYSIS
Simplify a, b, and c, and then substitute
into (A), (B), (C), and (D).

WORK
(a) $4(r + s) = 4r + 4s$
(b) $4rs$
(c) $4r + 4s$

$$c = a \quad\quad \text{and} \quad b \ne a$$
$$4r + 4s = 4r + 4s \ \ \text{and} \ \ 4rs \ne 4r + 4s$$

ANSWER: (C)

191.
ANALYSIS
Develop a chart for all the given informa-
tion, and then add all their weights.

WORK
Mildred's
    weight: $\quad\quad\quad\quad\quad\quad\quad\quad x - 3$
Hector's
    weight: $\quad (x - 3) + 8 = x - 3 + 8 = x + 5$
Stacey's
    weight: $\quad (x + 5) - 12 = x + 5 - 12 = x - 7$
Total
    weights: $\quad\quad\quad\quad\quad\quad\quad\quad 3x - 5$

ANSWER: (D)

192.
ANALYSIS
Remove the absolute value signs and then
divide all the numbers.

WORK
$$\frac{-45|-63|}{5|9|} = \frac{\overset{9}{\cancel{-45}} \times \overset{7}{\cancel{63}}}{\underset{1}{\cancel{5}} \times \underset{1}{\cancel{9}}} = 63$$

ANSWER: (A)

193.
ANALYSIS
Find 1/100 of 90. The answer is in feet.
Then convert feet into inches.

WORK
$$\frac{1}{100} \times 90 = 0.90 \text{ feet} \quad\quad 0.9 \times 12 = 10.8$$

ANSWER: (D)

194.
ANALYSIS
Let x = the first integer, and let $x + 1$ = the
next consecutive integer.

WORK
$$x + (x + 1) = 51$$
$$2x + 1 = 51$$
Subtract 1: $\quad\quad\quad\quad 2x = 50$
Divide by 2: $\quad\quad\quad\quad x = 25$
$$x + 1 = 26$$

ANSWER: (D)

195.

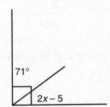

ANALYSIS
The two angles add up to a right angle.

WORK
$$(2x - 5) + 71 = 90$$
$$2x + 66 = 90$$
Subtract 66: $\quad\quad\quad\quad 2x = 24$
Divide by 2: $\quad\quad\quad\quad x = 12$

ANSWER: (A)

196.
ANALYSIS
Two angles are complementary when they
add up to 90°. Let x = the unknown angle.

WORK
$$x + a = 90$$
Subtract a: $\quad\quad\quad\quad x = 90 - a$

ANSWER: (C)

197.

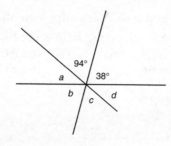

ANALYSIS

Together, m∠a + 94° + 38° = 180°.

WORK

$$m\angle a + 94° + 38° = 180°$$
$$m\angle a + 132° = 180°$$

Subtract 132°:
$$m\angle a = 48°$$

ANSWER: (B)

198.

ANALYSIS

A septagon is a seven-sided figure, so simply draw any seven-sided figure and count the points of intersection.

WORK

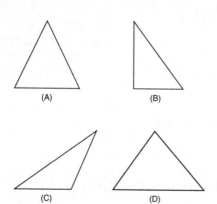

7 points of intersection

ANSWER: (D)

199.

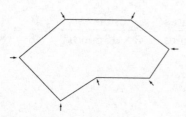

ANALYSIS

An obtuse triangle has one obtuse angle (an angle > 180°).

WORK

(C) is the only triangle with an angle greater than 180°.

ANSWER: (C)

200.

ANALYSIS

Let w = width, and let $2w + 4$ = length.

WORK

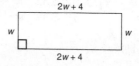

Perimeter = $(2w + 4) + (2w + 4) + w + w$
$$= 2w + 4 + 2w + 4 + w + w$$
$$= 6w + 8$$

ANSWER: (D)

201.

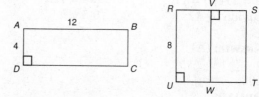

ANALYSIS

Find the perimeters of $ABCD$, $RSTU$, $RVWU$ and $VSTW$. Since $RSTU$ is a square and $RU = 8$, all the sides are equal to 8. The midpoints, V and W, divide RS and TU in half respectively.

WORK

Perimeter of $ABCD = 2 \times 4 + 2 \times 12$
$$P(ABCD) = 8 + 24$$
$$P(ABCD) = 32$$

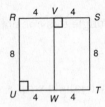

$$P(RSTU) = 32$$
$$P(RVWU) = 24$$
$$P(VSTW) = 24$$

One half the perimeter of *ABCD* is less than the perimeter of *RSTU*.

$$(1/2)\ 32 < 32$$
$$16 < 32\ \checkmark$$

ANSWER: (D)

202.
ANALYSIS
Let h = the height. Use the formula for the area of a parallelogram, $A = bh$.

WORK

$$A = bh$$
$A = 114, b = 12$: $114 = 12h$
Divide by 12: $9.5 = h$

ANSWER: (A)

203.
ANALYSIS
Draw a diagram of an isosceles triangle. Let x = each of the base angles. Then set the sum of the measures of all three angles equal to 180°.

WORK

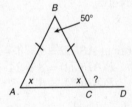

$$(x) + (x) + (50) = 180$$
$$2x + 50 = 180$$
Subtract 50: $2x = 130$
Divide by 2: $x = 65$

∠*BCD* and ∠*BCA* are supplementary:

$$m\angle BCA + m\angle BCD = 180$$
$x = m\angle BCA = 65$: $65 + m\angle BCD = 180$
Subtract 65: $m\angle BCD = 115$

ANSWER: (C)

204.
ANALYSIS
Simplify each expression and then substitute.

WORK
(a) $(r + 4)^2 = (2 + 4)^2 = 6^2 = 36$
(b) $9(s - 3)^2 = 9(5 - 3)^2 = 9(2)^2 = 9(4) = 36$
(c) $2r^2s = 2(2)^2(5) = 2(4)(5) = 40$

$$a < b \text{ and } c > b$$
$$36 < 36 \text{ and } 40 > 36\ \checkmark$$

ANSWER: (A)

205.
ANALYSIS
1 pound = 16 ounces.

WORK

$$\frac{6\,\text{ounces}}{3\,\text{pounds}} = \frac{6\,\text{ounces}}{3 \times 16\,\text{ounces}} = \frac{6}{48} = \frac{1}{8}$$

ANSWER: (C)

206.
ANALYSIS
Multiply the expression inside the parentheses by 2.

WORK

$$62 + 2(8 - x) = 72$$
$$62 + 16 - 2x = 72$$
$$78 - 2x = 72$$
Subtract 78: $-2x = -6$
Divide by –2: $x = 3$

ANSWER: (D)

207.
ANALYSIS
Divide 9 into 45 in order to determine how many $\frac{1}{2}$ inches are needed to display a distance of 45 miles. Then multiply the answer by $\frac{1}{2}$.

WORK

$$\frac{45}{9} = 5$$

$$5 \times \frac{1}{2} = \frac{5}{2} = 2\frac{1}{2}\,''$$

ANSWER: (D)

208.
ANALYSIS
Use the formula $C = 2\pi r$, and substitute 62.8 for C and 3.14 for π.

WORK

$$C = 2\pi r$$
$C = 62.8,\ \pi = 3.14$: $62.8 = 2(3.14)r$
$62.8 = 6.28r$
Divide by 6.28: $10 = r$

ANSWER: (B)

209.

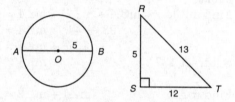

ANALYSIS
Find the areas and perimeters of the circle and the triangle and then substitute into the statements below.

WORK
Circumference of Circle O:
$$C = 2\pi r$$
$\pi = 3.14,\ r = 5$: $= 2(3.14)(5) = 31.4$

Area of Circle O:
$$A_{\mathrm{C}} = \pi r^2$$
$\pi = 3.14,\ r = 5$: $= (3.14)(5)^2 = (3)(25) = 78.5$

Perimeter of Triangle RST:
$$P = 5 + 12 + 13 = 30$$

Area of Triangle RST:
$$A_{\mathrm{T}} = \frac{1}{2} bh$$

$b = 12,\ h = 5$: $= \frac{1}{2}(12)(5) = 30$

The area of triangle $RST < \frac{1}{2}$ area of circle O

$$30 < \frac{1}{2}\,(78.5)$$

$$30 < 39.25 \quad \checkmark$$

ANSWER: (A)

210.
ANALYSIS
Find the volume of the room and then divide by the rate of the flow of oxygen, 3 cubic meters per minute.

WORK
$$V = l \cdot w \cdot h$$
$l = 9,\ w = 6,$
 $h = 4$: $= (9)(6)(4) = 216$ cu. meters
Divide by
 3 cu m: $216/3 = 72$ minutes

ANSWER: (B)

211.
ANALYSIS
Divide whole numbers and radical expressions separately and then simplify the result.

WORK

$$\frac{56\sqrt{b^3 c^4}}{7\sqrt{bc^3}} = \frac{\overset{8}{\cancel{56}}}{\cancel{7}}\sqrt{\frac{\overset{b^2 c}{\cancel{b^3 c^4}}}{\cancel{bc^3}}} = 8\sqrt{b^2 c} = 8b\sqrt{c}$$

$1 \cdot 1 \cdot 1$

ANSWER: (D)

212.

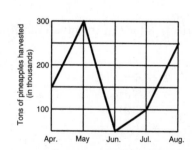

ANALYSIS
Determine the number of tons of pineapples harvested in each month. Then substitute into A, B, C, and D.

WORK

    April = 150,000 tons
    May = 300,000 tons
    June = 50,000 tons
    July = 100,000 tons
    August = 250,000 tons

May harvest – April harvest > July harvest
        300,000 – 150,000 > 100,000
              150,000 > 100,000 ✔

ANSWER: (B)

213.

ANALYSIS

Find the area of the floor (20×32) and then divide the total weight (2,560) by the area.

WORK

        $20 \times 32 = 640$
    $2,560/640 = 4$ lb per sq ft

ANSWER: (A)

214.

ANALYSIS

First change $\dfrac{3}{4}$ to a decimal. Then add the result to 4.

WORK

    $\dfrac{3}{4} = 0.75$

    $4\dfrac{3}{4} = 4.75 = 475\%$

ANSWER: (D)

215.

ANALYSIS

Substitute 3 for t in the given formula.

WORK

            $d = 16t^2$
    $t = 3$: $= 16(3)^2$
               $= 16(9)$
               $= 144$

ANSWER: (A)

216.

ANALYSIS

Determine both wages and then subtract.

WORK

    Shanequa's wages: $12 \times \$15.93 = \$191.16$
     – Julio's wages: $12 \times \$13.54 = \$162.48$
    _____
                                    $\$28.68$

ANSWER: (C)

217.

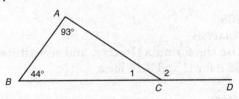

ANALYSIS

The sum of the measures of angles A, B, and C add up to 180°, so first find the measure of angle 1. Then the sum of the measures of angles 1 and 2 add up to a straight angle or 180°.

WORK

Find m∠1: $m\angle A + m\angle B + m\angle 1 = 180°$
                   $93° + 44° + m\angle 1 = 180°$
                         $137° + m\angle 1 = 180°$
Subtract 137°: $m\angle 1 = 43°$

Find m∠2: $m\angle 1 + m\angle 2 = 180°$
                   $43° + m\angle 2 = 180°$
Subtract 43°: $m\angle 2 = 137°$

ANSWER: (D)

218.

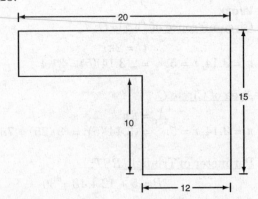

ANALYSIS

Divide the large figure into two rectangles, A and B, and then use the formula $A = bh$, where A = the area of a rectangle, b = the base, and h = the height. Finally, add the areas of the two rectangles together.

WORK

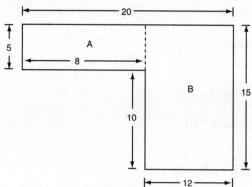

Area A: $A = bh$
$A = 8 \times 5 \quad = 40$
Area B: $A = bh$
$+ A = 12 \times 15 = 180$
_____
Totals: 220

ANSWER: (C)

219.

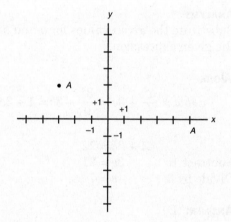

ANALYSIS
The x-coordinates of points to the left of the y-axis are negative. The y-coordinates of points above the x-axis are positive.

WORK
3 units to the left and 2 units up: $(-3,2)$

ANSWER: (B)

220.
ANALYSIS
Change both units to the smallest common unit, seconds.

WORK
$$\frac{15\,\text{seconds} = 15\,\text{seconds}}{3\,\text{minutes} = 3 \times 60\,\text{seconds} = 180\,\text{seconds}} = \frac{1}{12}$$

ANSWER: (A)

221.
ANALYSIS
Substitute the values for x, y, and z into the given algebraic expression.

WORK

$x = 3, y = -2, z = 4$:
$$5x^2 + 2yz$$
$$5(3)^2 + 2(-2)(4)$$
$$5(9) + 2(-8)$$
$$45 - 16$$
$$29$$

ANSWER: (B)

222.
ANALYSIS
Find the greatest and the least common factors of 30 and 70 and multiply.

WORK

$30 = 2 \times 5 \times 3$ ⎫ Greatest common factor = 5
$70 = 2 \times 5 \times 7$ ⎭ Least common factor = 2

The product of 5 and 2 is 10.

ANSWER: (A)

223.
ANALYSIS

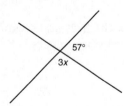

The two angles lie on a straight line, so they are supplementary and add up to 180°.

WORK
$$3x + 57 = 180$$
Subtract 57: $\quad 3x = 123$
Divide by 3: $\quad x = 41$

ANSWER: (B)

224.
ANALYSIS
Change to improper fractions and multiply.

WORK

$$6\frac{2}{3} \times 5\frac{1}{4} = \frac{\overset{5}{\cancel{20}}}{\underset{1}{\cancel{3}}} \times \frac{\overset{7}{\cancel{21}}}{\underset{1}{\cancel{4}}} = 35$$

ANSWER: (D)

225.
ANALYSIS
Let y = the number of runs the team has to score in the last game, and set up an equation to solve for the mean.

WORK
$\bar{x}$ = mean:
$$\bar{x} = \frac{12 + 7 + 10 + 6 + 9 + y}{6}$$

$\bar{x} = 9$:
$$9 = \frac{44 + y}{6}$$
Multiply
by 6: $54 = 44 + y$
Subtract 44: $10 = y$

ANSWER: (B)

226.
ANALYSIS
Let x = the first even integer.
Let $x + 2$ = the second even integer.
Let $x + 4$ = the third even integer.
Let $x + 6$ = the fourth even integer.

WORK
The sum of the first and second of four consecutive even integers is 8 more than the fourth:
$$(x) + (x + 2) = (x + 6) + 8$$
$$2x + 2 = x + 14$$
Subtract 2: $2x = x + 12$
Subtract x: $x = 10$

ANSWER: (D)

227.
ANALYSIS
Let x = the original price before the increase two years ago. $110\%x$ or $1.10x$ = the price after the first increase
$120\%(1.10x)$ or $1.20(1.10x)$ = the price

after the second increase. Set the price after the second increase equal to $6.60.

WORK
$$1.20(1.10x) = \$6.60$$
$$1.32x = \$6.60$$
Divide by 1.32: $x = \$5$

ANSWER: (B)

228.
ANALYSIS
There are 100 centimeters in one meter.

WORK
1 centimeter = 1/100 of a meter
2 centimeters = 2/100 = 1/50 of a meter
1/50 = 0.02 = 2%

ANSWER: (B)

229.
ANALYSIS
Substitute the given values for a and b into the given expression.

WORK
$$a\#b!c = \frac{a^2}{b} + 3c = \frac{3^2}{9} + 3c = 1 + 3c$$

$$1 + 3c = 22$$
Subtract 1: $3c = 21$
Divide by 3: $c = 7$

ANSWER: (D)

230.
ANALYSIS
Let x = the unknown percent, and translate the information into an equation.

WORK
$$x \cdot 120 = 45$$

Divide by 120: $x = \frac{45}{120} = \frac{9}{24} = 0.375$

$$= 37.5\% \approx 38\%$$

ANSWER: (C)

231.
ANALYSIS
Use the formula $P = 2b + 2h$ for the perimeter, P, of a rectangle with base b and height

h. For the area of a rectangle, use the formula $A = bh$, where A = area and b and h represent base and height, respectively.

WORK

Area of rectangle:	$A = bh$
$A = 36$, $b = 9$:	$36 = 9 \cdot h$
Divide by 9:	$4 = h$

Perimeter of rectangle:	$P = 2b + 2h$
$b = 9$, $h = 4$:	$P = 2 \cdot 9 + 2 \cdot 4$
	$= 18 + 8 = 26$

ANSWER: (D)

232.
ANALYSIS
Substitute each of the choices into the given inequality.

WORK

$$-2.4 < x + 2 \leq 3.8$$
$$x = 0: \quad -2.4 < 0 + 2 \leq 3.8$$
$$-2.4 < 2 \leq 3.8 \checkmark$$

ANSWER: (A)

233.
ANALYSIS
Combine similar terms.

WORK

$$3\sqrt{7} + 11\sqrt{7} = 14\sqrt{7}$$
$$-\ 4\sqrt{3} - 6\sqrt{3} = -10\sqrt{3}$$
$$\overline{\qquad\qquad 14\sqrt{7} - 10\sqrt{3}}$$

ANSWER: (C)

234.
ANALYSIS
A prime number has only two factors, itself and 1.

WORK
11, 13

ANSWER: (A)

235.
ANALYSIS
The measures of the three angles of a triangle add up to 180°.

WORK

$$59 + 53 + 68 = 180$$

ANSWER: (D)

236.
ANALYSIS
Add up all the ratios and divide into 124. Find the remainder and then check to see which is the last book in the remainder.

WORK

$$5 + 2 + 3 + 3 = 13$$
$$\frac{124}{13} = 9\frac{7}{13}$$

There is a remainder of 7. In order, we can purchase 5 fiction and 2 historical books. The historical book is the last book we can order.

ANSWER: (B)

237.
ANALYSIS
If we set up two similar triangles, their corresponding sides are in proportion.

WORK

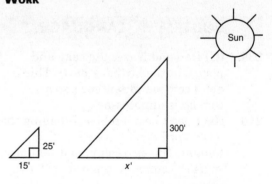

$$\frac{25}{15} = \frac{300}{x}$$

Multiply by x:	$15x < \dfrac{25}{15} = \dfrac{300}{x} >$
	$25x = 4500$
Divide by 25:	$x = 180$ ft

ANSWER: (A)

238.

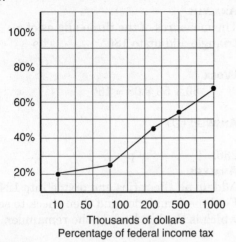

Thousands of dollars
Percentage of federal income tax

ANALYSIS

The horizontal axis represents income in thousands of dollars, while the vertical axis represents the percent income tax. Find the percent income tax on $100,000, change the percent to a decimal, and multiply times $100,000.

WORK

According to the graph, it looks like the percent income tax on $90,000 is about 25%.

$$25\% = 0.25$$
$$0.25 \times \$90,000 = \$22,500 \approx \$23,000$$

ANSWER: (B)

SUBTEST 5   LANGUAGE

239. **(C)** Dan and Nazee <u>ate</u> cake and <u>played</u> at the birthday party. This is not a compound sentence, so a comma is unnecessary.

240. **(B)** I don't have problems reading the book, but I don't have a lot of time tonight. This is a compound sentence, so use a comma to separate the two parts.

241. **(C)** She and <u>I</u> are best friends, and we chat on the Internet often. Capitalize the pronoun I.

242. **(C)** Because the last volume is checked out of the library. This is a fragment.

243. **(A)** I could <u>have</u> listened to them sing all day. Be careful not to confuse the

preposition *of* with the helping verb *have*.

244. **(B)** I didn't fall asleep until after he <u>had begun</u> speaking. The past participle is *had begun*, not *had began*.

245. **(A)** With an outline, <u>authors</u> know what <u>they</u> are going to write next. Check pronoun-antecedent agreement. *Authors* and *they* should both be plural.

246. **(A)** To <u>whom</u> shall I address this letter? *Whom* is the object form.

247. **(B)** Oh my goodness, I almost forgot the cake. Use a comma or exclamation point after an interjection.

248. **(A)** Which of the twins can swim <u>faster</u>? The suffix *-er* is used when comparing two people or items.

249. **(B)** Nick is always <u>drumming</u> the desk, <u>tapping</u> his feet, or <u>bobbing</u> his head. Keep words in parallel form in a series.

250. **(C)** <u>It's</u> the humidity that really makes us feel the heat. *It's* is the contraction for *It is*.

251. **(D)** No mistakes.

252. **(B)** Daphne doesn't like <u>a lot</u> of fuss. *A lot* is two words.

253. **(C)** The groundhog didn't see <u>its</u> shadow this year. The possessive form of *it* is *its*.

254. **(C)** The **stories** [of sea adventure] always <u>give</u> me a thrill. Check subject-verb agreement, disregarding any words in between.

255. **(B)** Neither she <u>nor</u> I have missed a day of school this year. Use *neither* and *nor* together.

256. **(D)** No mistakes.

257. **(A)** I want to see you <u>rested and relaxed,</u> tomorrow. Keep the words in a series parallel.

258. **(C)** Sam said, "I know I have something to do." When you open a quote, be sure to close it.

259. **(B)** Will you call the restaurant for me? This is a question.

260. **(A)** The clock in the old, <u>red tower</u> chimes at noon. Remove the comma between *red* and *tower*. You do not use a comma between the last adjective and the modified noun; you would not call it *the old and red and tower*.

261. (**B**) Include the following in your paragraph: a topic sentence, supporting details, and a closing statement. Use a colon before a list.

262. (**A**) I was <u>amazed and</u> delighted by the music. Do not use a comma to separate a compound verb.

263. (**B**) Joe and Joan are happy with <u>their</u> new business. Check the use of *there*, *their*, and *they're*.

264. (**A**) Jorge thought about it and said, "I don't recall sugar as one of the ingredients<u>."</u> A period goes inside quotation marks.

265. (**A**) Coach Thacker, my social studies teacher, is a big movie fan. Use commas to set off nonessential information. We don't need to be told that the coach teaches social studies.

266. (**B**) On the <u>fourth</u> day, he sent me some birds. The correct spelling is *fourth*.

267. (**C**) I still enjoy reading <u>children's</u> books. The word *children* is already plural and does not need an *s* to make it so.

268. (**A**) Mary Shelley was a teenager when she wrote her novel *Frankenstein*. Novels are italicized or underlined.

269. (**D**) No mistakes.

270. (**B**) Which doctor did you see? The word *doctor* is not capitalized unless you refer to a specific doctor.

271. (**A**) I was <u>accepted</u> into the club last year. Be careful not to confuse the words *accept* and *except*.

272. (**C**) If Mr. Cerulean would assign less homework, he would have <u>fewer</u> papers to grade. Use the word *less* with noncountable items; use *fewer* with countable items.

273. (**D**) No mistakes.

274. (**C**) The special <u>effects</u> in the movie were amazing. Be careful not to confuse the words *effect* and *affect*.

275. (**B**) Josh, Sean, and <u>I</u> formed a jazz band. The word *I* is a subject; the word *me* is an object.

276. (**B**) She felt sick, so she went to <u>lie</u> down. You *lie yourself* down. You *lay* down something else.

277. (**C**) <u>Lay</u> your head on the pillow and sleep. You *lie yourself* down. You *lay* down something else—even if it's your head.

278. (**D**) No mistakes.

279. (**B**) He was <u>too</u> popular to be defeated in the election. Always double-check *to*, *two*, and *too*.

280. (**A**) I declined the <u>role</u> of Hamlet, considering it too demanding on my memory.

281. (**D**) No mistakes, but it would be nice if educated people could pronounce *nuclear*.

282. (**C**) I get weary of the cold weather during <u>February</u>, March, and April.

283. (**B**) Due to the sheriff's <u>courageous</u> efforts, no one was hurt.

284. (**B**) Pam said she'd meet me at the <u>library</u>, but she must have been detained elsewhere.

285. (**B**) We have a lot of <u>athletes</u> attending our school.

286. (**D**) No mistakes.

287. (**A**) I assumed a long speech was <u>unnecessary</u> for this occasion.

288. (**A**) Oh, she can be <u>mischievous</u> when she's in a spunky mood. *Mischievous* is another word most people misspell and mispronounce.

289. (**B**) The conjunction *yet* is the only one that logically connects these contrasting sentences. The word *however* cannot be a conjunction.

290. (**B**) The conjunction *but* indicates a contrast.

291. (**D**) This sentence is most concise. The other choices are neither brief, witty, nor stylish.

292. (**C**) This sentence includes all of the information in the most efficient way.

293. (**B**) This is the clearest choice. Choice A is passive, choice C is wordy, and choice D is awkward.

294. (**B**) This is the only sentence that deals with legend or mythology.

295. (**D**) None of these topics focuses on a single, brief idea.

296. (**D**) This sentence is not about how rainwater affects worms.

297. (**C**) This sentence concludes the paragraph.

298. (**A**) The sentence fits logically between the first and second sentences. The words "This spin" in the second sentence must refer to the "twist" in the added sentence.

Index

NOTES

NOTES

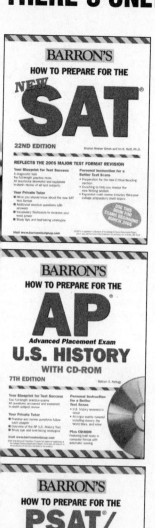
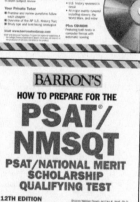

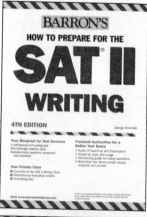
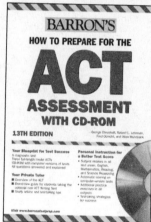

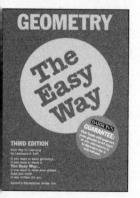

Really. This isn't going to hurt at all . . .

Barron's *Painless* titles are perfect ways to show kids in middle school that learning really doesn't hurt. They'll even discover that grammar, algebra, and other subjects that many of them consider boring can become fascinating— and yes, even fun! The trick is in the presenta-tion: clear instruction, taking details one step at a time, adding a light and humorous touch, and sprinkling in some brain-tickler puzzles that are both challenging and entertaining to solve.

Each book: Paperback, approx. 224 pp., $8.95–$10.95 Canada $11.95–$15.50

Painless Algebra
Lynette Long, Ph.D.
ISBN 0-7641-0676-7

Painless American Government
Jeffrey Strausser
ISBN 0-7641-2601-6

Painless American History
Curt Lader
ISBN 0-7641-0620-1

Painless Fractions
Alyece Cummings
ISBN 0-7641-0445-4

Painless Geometry
Lynette Long, Ph.D.
ISBN 0-7641-1773-4

Painless Grammar
Rebecca S. Elliott, Ph.D.
ISBN 0-8120-9781-5

Painless Math Word Problems
Marcie Abramson, B.S., Ed.M.
ISBN 0-7641-1533-2

Painless Poetry
Mary Elizabeth
ISBN 0-7641-1814-2

Painless Reading Comprehension
Darolyn E. Jones
ISBN 0-7641-2766-7

Painless Research Projects
Rebecca S. Elliott, Ph.D.,
and James Elliott, M.A.
ISBN 0-7641-0297-4

Painless Science Projects
Faith Hickman Brynie, Ph.D.
ISBN 0-7641-0595-7

Painless Speaking
Mary Elizabeth
ISBN 0-7642-2147-2

Painless Spelling
Mary Elizabeth
ISBN 0-7641-0567-1

Painless Writing
Jeffrey Strausser
ISBN 0-7641-1810-2

Barron's Educational Series, Inc.
250 Wireless Boulevard, Hauppauge, NY 11788
In Canada: Georgetown Book Warehouse
34 Armstrong Avenue, Georgetown, Ont. L7G 4R9
Visit our website @ www.barronseduc.com

Prices subject to change without notice. Books may be purchased at your local bookstore, or by mail from Barron's. Enclose check or money order for total amount plus sales tax where applicable and 18% for shipping and handling ($5.95 minimum). NY State, New Jersey, Michigan, and California residents add sales tax.

(#79) R11/04